THOMAS LINCOLN
ABRAHAM'S FATHER

DANIEL CRAVENS TAYLOR

Beacon Publishing Group
ISBN (Paperback): 978-1-961504-20-2
ISBN (Hardcover): 978-1-961504-21-9

Thomas Lincoln: Abraham's Father *2nd Edition*
© 2026 Daniel Cravens Taylor

Cover Design by Jerry Parsons
Cover Layout by Lori Pace
Edited by Gerard Hernandez

Beacon Publishing Group, New York, NY 10001
www.beaconpublishinggroup.com

Manufactured in the United States of America

"If you make a bad bargain,
hug it the tighter."

Thomas Lincoln

Abraham Lincoln

Thomas Lincoln

<h1 align="center">Preface</h1>

History is wrong.

Well, history itself isn't wrong, but there are times when the stories told of history are misinterpretations of the history that actually occurred. Thomas Lincoln's life is one of those times.

In trying to understand Abraham Lincoln's life and persona, much has been written about his mother and stepmother. Nancy Hanks Lincoln has been exalted and debased. Her life and history have been covered in a number of biographies. She was Lincoln's mother. As such, the nation looked into every nook and cranny to find out what kind of mother she was because she molded the early life of our greatest president.

No less scrutiny has been applied to Sarah Bush Johnston Lincoln, the stepmother. She took a new husband and two children into her heart and life. As with Nancy, the nation has endeavored to discover her influence on Abraham. For Sarah and Nancy, books are in print to lay what we know of their lives and influence before the public.

But for Thomas Lincoln there is a gap. Comparatively little has been compiled on Thomas compared to other areas of Lincoln study and research. He is touched on in a chapter or two of books dedicated to his son's life. He is noted in passing in books about Nancy and Sarah. Some lengthy pamphlets have been put together to portray his life along with a short book or two that mainly deal with dry facts in public records. Thomas' final home and farm are now a part of the Abraham Lincoln National Heritage Area and maintained to provide a Lincoln educational and history opportunity.[1]

The early stories of Thomas' failure as a father have precluded the same interest being paid to him as are paid to Nancy and Sarah. Thomas has been known as the uneducated, slothful father mired in poverty by laziness, the father who was unsupportive of Abraham's desire to learn. Thomas has been used as the obstacle Abraham overcame to be a success. Thus, it became an approved

---

[1] Thomas' Illinois home and farm are an Illinois State Historic Site. The Lincoln Log Cabin Foundation is a key resource providing support and historical expertise at the site.

approach to mainly ignore Thomas, to treat him as an historical footnote, and move on to those who were positive influences on Abraham.

That story, that approach, is wrong history. Research shows a different side, a different story. Thomas Lincoln was not an obstacle. He and his son were different in many ways and alike in many ways just as other fathers and sons. Thomas' influence on Abraham was not something that had to be overcome for Abraham to move on to success.

This book will not endeavor to repeat in detail the excellent research into Abraham Lincoln's early years done by such giants in Lincoln history as William E. Barton, Ida M. Tarbell, R. Gerald McMurtry, Charles H. Coleman, Louis A. Warren and others. Their persistent and even stubborn digging for truth in dusty record files across multiple states has provided invaluable reference material, material this work will build from but not reproduce in its entirety.

In the following pages Thomas' story will be built from known facts, based on the times in which he lived.

Thomas Lincoln Timeline

1778: Jan 6	Thomas Lincoln born in Rockingham County, Virginia.
1782	Lincoln family moves to Kentucky.
1784: Feb 5	Nancy Hanks born in Hampshire County, Virginia. (Her birthplace is now part of Mineral County, West Virginia.)
1786: May	Thomas' father, Abraham Lincoln, killed.
1786	Approximate date for the Hanks family to Kentucky.
1788: Dec 13	Sarah Bush born in Hardin County, Kentucky.
1793	Joseph Hanks (Nancy's father) dies. Wife, Ann, returns to Virginia.
1795: Jun 8	Serves in the Kentucky state militia.
1799: Jan 6	Turns 21, his year of majority under the law.
1802: Fall	Moves to Elizabethtown, Hardin County, Kentucky.
1803: Sept 2	Purchases 238-acre farm on Mill Creek.
1803	Serves as constable in Cumberland County, Kentucky.
1803	Bathsheba Herring Lincoln, Thomas' mother, moves to Thomas' farm along with sister Nancy Lincoln Brumfield and brother-in-law William Brumfield.
1803: Nov	Serves as prison guard.
1805	Nominated to become an Ensign in the Kentucky Militia.
1805: Aug	Appointed Cumberland County Marshall.
1806: Mar	Appointed a patroller in Hardin County.

1806	Ferries flatboat to New Orleans.
1806: Jun 12	Marries Nancy Hanks.
1807: Feb 10	Sarah Lincoln born in Elizabethtown, Kentucky.
1808: Dec 12	Purchases 300 acre Sinking Spring Farm on the South Fork of the Nolin River.
1809: Feb 9	Abraham Lincoln born at the Sinking Spring Farm.
1811	Leases 30 acres of Knob Creek Farm and moves family there.
1812: June	Son Thomas born. Only lives three days.
1814: April	Daniel Johnston, husband of Sarah Bush Johnston, dies.
1816: Fall	Goes to Indiana and stakes out a claim in the Little Pigeon Creek community.
1816: Dec	Moves family to Indiana.
1818: Early Fall	Tom and Betsy Sparrow die. Dennis Hanks and Sophie Hanks are taken in by the Lincolns.
1818: Oct 5	Nancy Hanks Lincoln dies.
1819: Dec 2	Marries Sarah Bush Johnston in Elizabethtown, Kentucky.
1821: Jun 9	Dennis Friend Hanks marries Sarah Elizabeth "Betsy" Johnston.
1822: Jun 14	Granddaughter Sarah Jane Hanks born.
1823: May 5	Grandson John Talbot Hanks born.
1824: Oct 23	Granddaughter Nancy Melvina Hanks born.
1826	Squire Hall marries Matilda Johnston.
1826	Granddaughter Harriet Hanks (Chapman) born.

1826: Aug 2	Sarah Lincoln marries Aaron Grigsby.
1827: Jun 13	Sophie Hanks marries Dillings Lynch.
1828: Jan 20	Sarah Lincoln Grigsby dies in childbirth. The child also dies.
1829: Apr 12	Grandson John Johnston Hall born.
1830: Mar 1	Moves family to Macon County, Illinois.
1831: April	Abraham Lincoln takes a flatboat to New Orleans.
1831: July	Abraham Lincoln moves to New Salem.
1831	Moves family to the Buck Grove farm in Coles County, Illinois.
1832	Granddaughter Nancy Ann Hall born.
1833: May 7	Abraham Lincoln appointed New Salem postmaster.
1833	Granddaughter Amanda Hanks born.
1834: Aug 4	Abraham Lincoln wins election to the Illinois House of Representatives as a Whig**Error! Bookmark not defined.**.
1834	Moves family to the Muddy Point farm in Coles County, Illinois.
1834: Oct 13	John D. Johnston marries Mary Barker.
1836	Bathsheba Lincoln, Thomas' mother, dies in Washington County, Kentucky. Buried in Hardin County, Kentucky in the Lincoln Memorial Cemetery (now on the grounds of Fort Knox).
1835	Granddaughter Mary Hanks born. Year is uncertain.
1837	Granddaughter Elizabeth Jane Hall born.
1837: Jan 10	Grandson Thomas Lincoln Davis Johnston is born.

1837: Apr 15	Abraham Lincoln moves to Springfield, Illinois.
1837: May	Purchases the Plummer Place.
1837: Aug	Moves family to what will be known as the Abraham Forty, land that will become part of the Goosenest Prairie farm.
1838: Mar 27	Grandson Abraham Lincoln Barker Johnston is born.
1839	Grandson Alfred L. Hall born.
1839	Granddaughter Sarah Jane Hanks marries Thomas Scott Dowling.
1840: Jan 21	Granddaughter Marietta Sarah Jane Johnston is born.
1840	Purchases the Goosenest Prairie farm.
1841	Grandson Charles Friend M. Hanks born.
1841	Granddaughter Sarah Louisa Hall born.
1841: Dec 15	Grandson Squire H. Johnston born.
1842: Nov 4	Abraham Lincoln marries Mary Todd in Springfield, Illinois.
1843	Grandson Joseph A. Hall born.
1843: Aug 1	Grandson Robert Todd Lincoln born.
1843: Oct 26	Grandson Richard M. Johnston born.
1843: Dec	Granddaughter Nancy Melvina Hanks marries James Shoaff.
1844: Dec	Abraham Lincoln forms law firm with William H. Herndon as his partner.
1845: Nov 18	Grandson Dennis Friend Johnston born.
1845	Granddaughter Amanda Hall born.

1845	Great-grandchild Missouri M. Shoaff born.
1846: Mar 10	Grandson Edward Baker Lincoln born.
1846	Great-granddaughter Elizabeth Jane Dowling born.
1846: Aug 3	Abraham Lincoln elected to the United States House of Representatives.
1847	Granddaughter Harriet Hall born.
1847: Sep 8	Granddaughter Harriet Ann Hanks marries Col. Augustus H. Chapman.
1847: Dec 13	Grandson Daniel W. Johnston born.
1848	Great-grandson Zachariah T. Dowling born.
1849	Great-grandson Robert Newton Chapman born.
1849	Grandson Theophilus Hanks born.
1849	Great-granddaughter Alice Shoaff born.
1849: Jul 5	Grandson Daniel W. Johnston dies.
1850: Feb 1	Grandson Edward Baker Lincoln dies.
1850: Sep 21	Mary Barker Johnston dies.
1850: Dec 21	Grandson William Wallace Lincoln born.
1851: Jan 17	Dies at the Goosenest Prairie farm. He is buried in the Shiloh Cemetery.
1853: Apr 4	Grandson Thomas "Tad" Lincoln born. Named after his deceased grandfather.
1869: Apr 12	Sarah Bush Lincoln dies.

Table of Contents

Thomas Lincoln Family: Quick Facts

Hanks, Dennis

B: May 5, 1799 M: June 9, 1821 D: October 21, 1892 Age: 93	Farmer and shoemaker. Cousin of Nancy. Married Sarah Elizabeth "Betsy" Johnston.

(Hanks) Legrand, Sophie

B: March 14, 1809 M: June 13, 1827 M: October 1842 D: November 12, 1893 Age: 84	Homemaker. Cousin of Nancy. Widowed in first marriage to Dillings Lynch. Second marriage to John Legrand.

Johnston, John Daniel

B: May 10, 1810 M: October 13, 1834 M: March 5, 1851 D: September 20, 1860 Age: 50	Farmer. Stepson of Thomas. First marriage to Mary Barker. Second marriage to Nancy Jane Williams.

(Johnston) Hall, Matilda Anne

B: 1811 M: 1826 D: February 20, 1878 Age: 67	Homemaker. Stepdaughter to Thomas. Married Squire (Levi) Hall.

(Johnston) Hanks, Sarah Elizabeth "Betsy"

B: January 9, 1807 M: June 9, 1821 D: December 18, 1864 Age: 57	Homemaker. Stepdaughter of Thomas. Married Dennis Hanks.

Lincoln, Abraham

B: February 12, 1809 M: November 4, 1842 D: April 15, 1865 Age: 56	Lawyer, Politician, President. Son to Thomas. Married Mary Todd.

Lincoln, Nancy Hanks

B: February 5, 1784 M: June 12, 1806 D: October 5, 1818 Age: 34	Homemaker. Pioneer. Thomas' first wife. Abraham Lincoln's mother.

(Lincoln) Grigsby, Sarah

B: February 10, 1807 M: August 2, 1826 D: January 20, 1828 Age: 20	Homemaker. Daughter of Thomas and Nancy. Married Aaron Grigsby.

Lincoln, Sarah "Sally" Bush

B: December 13, 1788 M: March 13, 1806 M: December 2, 1819 D: April 12, 1869 Age: 80	Homemaker. Pioneer. Thomas' second wife. First marriage to Daniel Johnston.

Lincoln, Thomas "Tom"

B: January 6, 1778
M: June 12, 1806
M: December 2, 1819
D: January 17, 1851
Age: 73
	Pioneer, Carpenter, Furniture Maker,
	   Wheelwright, Cabinetmaker, Cooper,
	   Millwright, Blacksmith.
	First marriage to Nancy Hanks.
	Second marriage to Sarah Bush Johnston.

Virginia

Rockingham County sits in Virginia's beautiful Shenandoah Valley. The Valley would later be known as the breadbasket of the Confederacy. It is fertile and productive farmland nestled between the Blue Ridge Mountains to the east and the Allegheny Mountains to the west. It was there that Thomas Lincoln was born to Abraham and Bathsheba Lincoln. It was there that Nancy Hanks was born to Lucy Hanks and an unknown father.

President Abraham Lincoln would later say of his family that his "parents were both born in Virginia, of undistinguished families – second families, perhaps I should say."[1] When Mr. Lincoln made that comment, he was unfamiliar with his family history. He later wrote that "owing to my father being left an orphan at the age of six years, in poverty, and in a new country, he became a wholly uneducated man; which I suppose is the reason why I know so little of our family history."[2] What the president did not know was that his family was not so undistinguished as he believed.

The Lincoln Family Tree

Samuel Lincoln

The Lincoln family came to America in the person of Samuel Lincoln, Thomas' great-great-great grandfather. Samuel was an apprentice to weaver Francis Lawes in Norfolk County, England when Lawes decided to move to America. Lawes brought Samuel with him to the Puritan Colony of Boston Bay in 1637. Samuel was seventeen or eighteen years of age.

Two of Samuel's brothers, Thomas and Daniel, moved to America four years earlier and established themselves as landowners in Hingham, Massachusetts. It was not long before Samuel left Lawes to join his brothers.

---

[1] Roy P. Basler. *The Collected Works of Abraham Lincoln*, volume 3, page 511. Taken from a letter from Abraham Lincoln to Jesse W. Fell enclosing an autobiography for use in campaigning.

[2] Roy P. Basler. *The Collected Works of Abraham Lincoln*, volume 1, page 456. Taken from a letter from Abraham Lincoln to Solomon Lincoln dated March 6, 1848.

Once in Hingham, Samuel settled down to his trade and building a life. He began to obtain land and establish himself firmly in the community. He married Martha and they had eleven children, eight of whom lived to raise their own families. By the time Samuel died in May of 1690, he was a prosperous, respected landowner and businessman. His descendants would continue that tradition, gaining wealth and prestige. Samuel's home still stands in Hingham, Massachusetts.[3]

Mordecai Lincoln

In 1657, Mordecai Lincoln, Thomas' great-great grandfather, was born to Samuel and Martha. Samuel provided Mordecai a good education and raised him in the church. Mordecai was an entrepreneur. He bought land and opened a sawmill, a grist mill, and a forge. His forge was one of the first in America to work in iron. He was a businessman, landowner, and blacksmith.

Mordecai married Sarah Jones. Mordecai's first son was named Mordecai, after his father. His second son was named Abraham, after Sarah's father. This is the first known Abraham in the Lincoln family and the name would become a family tradition.

Mordecai lived in Massachusetts during the time of the Salem witch trials. It was a turbulent time. Mordecai and his brother Daniel, though Puritans, did not accept the reasoning behind the trials or the painful executions of "witches" on scanty testimony. They did not break with the Puritan church but through their business contacts they pressed the interests of change and independence from the hardline teaching of the Puritans who ruled Massachusetts.

Mordecai's family grew large and prosperous in Massachusetts. The early records of Hingham and Cohasset, Massachusetts mention the Lincoln name over and over, more than any other. At his death in 1727, Mordecai left an estate valued at over £3,000, a considerable sum for the time.[4]

---

[3] Ida Tarbell. *In the Footsteps of the Lincolns*, Chapter One. / Ralph Gary. *Following Lincoln's Footsteps*, page 251.

[4] Ida Tarbell. *In the Footsteps of the Lincolns*, Chapter Two.

Mordecai Lincoln

Mordecai, Thomas' great grandfather, moved to Monmouth County, New Jersey after his mother died and his father remarried. His brother Abraham moved with him. Mordecai was 21 years of age at the time. New Jersey was advertising itself as a land of freedom with fertile soil and lots of opportunity. For young men who lived under the strict laws of the Puritans and longed to find their own way, New Jersey sounded like a good dream.

The Lincolns settled near Middletown, New Jersey where there was need for a forge. Mordecai and Abraham had trained in their father's forge and took this opportunity. Their forge was located on land owned by Richard Saltar, a very well-off businessman and landowner. Through the association of operating Saltar's forge, Mordecai met and courted Hannah Saltar, the only daughter of Richard. Mordecai married Hannah and his in-laws connected him to New Jersey's wealthy and influential.

Mordecai and Hannah had six children and made a good home, prospering and happy. But for the Lincoln brothers, the means of transporting their forge's products was not as effective as they had in Massachusetts. In their travels they went to Philadelphia. Philadelphia was growing, had good transport for products, and needed ironmasters.

Mordecai moved to Philadelphia in 1722 to join a partnership with two other ironmasters. The partnership lasted three years before Mordecai struck out on his own, buying land and setting up a new forge in Berks County, Pennsylvania. There, Mordecai settled his large family with his second wife Mary. (Hannah died around 1727.) The family consisted of the oldest son John and four daughters.

It was in Berks County that the Lincolns met the Boones. Mordecai lived close to Squire Boone and his family which included son Daniel. The Lincoln and Boone children grew up together and intermarried, joining the families. This was the time when the Lincolns changed from their Puritan faith to the Quaker faith of the Boones.

Many have credited these Quaker roots as a possible starting point for the anti-slavery position of Thomas but that may not be the case. The Quaker faith was changing. At the start, in

Pennsylvania, William Penn had Quaker connections in Barbados to purchase and trade in slaves. The majority of Quakers were not anti-slavery. However, over time, that position changed. By the Civil War, a majority of Quakers were anti-slavery.[5] The gradual movement and change in Quaker theology may have had some influence down the family with Thomas but to assume it was a major influence is likely a stretch.

Mordecai and Mary had additional children, growing the family by three sons but the line leading to Thomas runs through Mordecai and Hannah's eldest son, John.

Mordecai was prosperous and successful. He was a blacksmith, an ironmaster, Justice of the Peace, and inspector of highways. Mordecai died in 1735, leaving 1,000 acres of land plus other gathered wealth to his children and wife. His house can be seen in Amity, Pennsylvania. He is buried in Exeter, Pennsylvania in Exeter Friends Meetinghouse cemetery.[6]

John Lincoln[7]

John Lincoln, Thomas' grandfather, was born in 1716. John returned to an earlier family occupation and became a weaver. Details of John's life are sketchy. He lived in Lancaster County, Pennsylvania for much of his life where he plied his trade with success and was something of a land speculator. Amongst other records, there is record of a two-year period when John made a profit of £534 buying and selling land in Berks County. Land speculating was a common way in an agricultural barter economy of building wealth.

In 1743, John married Rebecca (Flowers) Morris, a widow with one son. John and Rebecca had ten children of their own.

John was settled and prosperous in Lancaster County. His family was large and growing, but the Boone family was traveling and exploring. The Shenandoah Valley of Virginia got a lot of attention from Pennsylvanians and many were migrating south.

---

[5] Katharine Gerbner. *Slavery in the Quaker World.*
[6] Ida Tarbell. *In the Footsteps of the Lincolns*, Chapter Three.
Ralph Gary. *Following Lincoln's Footsteps*, page 280.
[7] See *Abraham Lincoln's Ancestry Letters* in the Appendices. Lincoln knew little of his family history earlier than Thomas' father Abraham and Thomas' grandfather John.

From those who moved, word went back to Lancaster of the good land and beauty of the Shenandoah. John listened.

In 1768, John bought 600 acres on Linville Creek north of where Harrisonburg now stands in Rockingham County, Virginia (the land was part of Augusta County in 1768). When John moved his family to Augusta County, the area was being heavily settled and developed. It was growing quickly. Businesses, churches, and schools were established, many of them by people John knew from Lancaster.

When the Revolutionary War came, John and his sons embraced the cause. There is no record of whether John knew George Washington – whose vast holdings were some 125 miles to the northeast of John's – and no record of whether any of the Lincolns served directly in Washington's forces. It is known the Lincolns served the revolution in Virginia and helped bring the United States into existence.

John, and most landowners in the Shenandoah Valley, raised tobacco. Tobacco was used as means of payment in bartering. Colonel Augustus H. Chapman (one of Thomas' grandsons-in-law) told a picturesque story of handling tobacco in the Shenandoah Valley. A common means for transporting tobacco was to pack it in a hogshead with a pole run through it. Men, women, and children would guide with the pole while using hand spikes to roll the tobacco to market. Some of John's tobacco was rolled all the way to Richmond.[8]

John died in 1788, leaving a large estate and having helped his children (many of whose descendants still reside in the Shenandoah Valley) establish their homes and businesses.[9]

Captain Abraham Lincoln

Abraham Lincoln, Thomas' father, was born on May 13, 1744 at John and Rebecca's Pennsylvania home. Abraham was educated in Pennsylvania and he learned the family occupations: weaving, blacksmithing, and working the forge.

---

[8] Douglas L. Wilson and Rodney O. Davis. *Herndon's Informants*, page 439.

[9] Ida Tarbell. *In the Footsteps of the Lincolns*, Chapter Four.

Ralph Gary. *Following Lincoln's Footsteps*, pages 317-319.

The French and Indian war began in 1756 when Abraham was 12 years old. Pennsylvania was subjected to repeated raids from various tribes allied with the French. Families worked and traveled with care. Weapons were always kept close by. Abraham learned to shoot and to stand watch while others worked.

The war ended in 1763 but raids continued on a less frequent basis for several years. When John Lincoln packed up his family to go to Virginia, there is little doubt that the journey was made with caution.

In Virginia, Abraham met Bathsheba Herring (called and spelled Bersheba in local dialect). The Herrings were one of the first families to settle Augusta County. Tradition has the Herrings as an aristocratic family and that Bathsheba's father, Alexander Herring, objected to Abraham courting Bathsheba. They considered Abraham to be poor and plain.[10] Bathsheba, however, was her own woman.

Bathsheba was a "woman of imperturbable gentleness of spirit, and an ineffable winsomeness of manner that won and bound all hearts in her circle to her."[11] She had her choice of suiters desiring her hand in marriage, but Bathsheba chose Abraham Lincoln, a man reputed to be somewhat wild and adventuresome. Their daring natures were a good match.

Bathsheba loved Abraham and readily agreed to marry him. A marriage bond) was issued in Augusta County on June 9, 1770.[12] They were wed later that month.[13] The marriage yielded five children: Mordecai (1771), Josiah (1773), Mary (1775), Thomas (1778), and Nancy (1780).

Not long after the marriage, John Lincoln deeded 210 acres of his 600 to Abraham who built a home on the land across Linville Creek from his parents' home. He built the house on a

---

[10] Many of the Virginia Lincoln's have been described as plain. While President Lincoln did not have a strong resemblance to his father, he did have a strong resemblance to others in the Lincoln family. It was this family resemblance, this plainness in appearance, that was told of the Lincoln men.

[11] Herring Chrisman. *Memoirs of Lincoln*, page 5.

[12] John W. Wayland. *The Lincolns in Virginia*, page 41.

[13] There are some records that indicate Bathsheba was Abraham's second wife, his first being Mary Shipley. Most Lincoln historians believe Abraham had only one wife, Bathsheba. Regardless, there is little question that Bathsheba Herring Lincoln was Thomas' mother.

gentle slope, the back of the house overlooking a bluff, the front looking downhill to the creek.[14] The house was yellow pine and was near enough to the Linville Creek water mill for the sound of the waterwheel to be a constant and peaceful background.[15]

Abraham watched his father and grandfather buy and sell land. He learned. Abraham worked his trades, farmed, speculated on land, and accumulated wealth.

Lincoln Ancestry

President Lincoln saw his family in comparison to the Todds and considered his own family as poor relations but had he known his family history he would have known he had cousins who became governors. He had uncles and aunts and grandparents who were educated, ran successful businesses, owned large tracts of land, were leading citizens in their communities, and were influential in local, state, and even federal government. Thomas' family had every reason to be proud of the family history. The Lincolns were neither undistinguished nor a second family.

Birth and Early Life

In January of 1778, the French were preparing to declare war on England and ally with the Americans in the Revolutionary War. George Washington was encamped at Valley Forge. Captain Abraham Lincoln was serving as Judge Advocate for the military court in Virginia and supporting the revolution. Into this historical moment, Thomas Lincoln was born on Tuesday, January 6, 1778.

Thomas was born at the family home in Augusta County (soon to be Rockingham County), Virginia, alongside Linville Creek in the Shenandoah Valley. He was the fourth child of Abraham and Bathsheba Lincoln. In 1880 he got a little sister and the family of seven was complete. To this point in time, all of President Abraham Lincoln's ancestors had been born in the northern states. His father Thomas was the first to be born in the south. Thomas spent less than five years in the Shenandoah Valley. As with the memories of most four-year-olds, he probably retained little of the time in his memory.

---

[14] Herring Chrisman. *Memoirs of Lincoln*, page 5.
[15] Herring Chrisman. *Memoirs of Lincoln*, page 19.

Surrounded by War

While Thomas was a baby in 1778, his father Abraham was a very busy and important man. Abraham was 34 years of age and owned 415 acres of very fertile and productive Shenandoah Valley farmland.[16] In addition to farming and being involved in community affairs and governance, Abraham was a leader in the militia fighting the Revolutionary War. Unlike today's wars, enlistments were shorter and conditional, dependent on the circumstances and urgency at the time of enlistment. Abraham was not a member of the regular army. The militias were generally stationed near the homes of their men with the members living at home unless called to engage in an expedition.

While in the Augusta County militia, Abraham served as a company commander in one of the four battalions defending the county. When Rockingham County was formed out of Augusta County in 1778, seven companies of militia were formed, and Abraham was appointed captain over one. Each company was formed by sixty enlisted men of varying rank. The militia were the armed forces of the County and of Virginia.[17] Captain Lincoln was honored with being one of the seven men in Rockingham County to receive the rank of captain.

Abraham was also honored with the office of Judge Advocate for the Augusta and Rockingham County militia. A Judge Advocate is a military lawyer. The Continental Congress established the office and rank of the Judge Advocate General in 1775. Judge Advocates were appointed throughout the military departments of the colonies.[18] Captain Lincoln was given appointment as Judge Advocate for both county militias in which he served.

Records are lacking in detail about how much action Captain Lincoln and his company of men saw in the Revolutionary War. Virginia was the largest and most prosperous of the colonies. As such it was extremely important to the British to hold Virginia.

---

[16] D. M. Coleman. *Thomas Lincoln, The Father of Abraham Lincoln*, page 6.

[17] Louis A. Warren. *The Filson Club History Quarterly.* "Abraham Lincoln, Senior, Grandfather of the President", page 139.

[18] Major William F. Fratcher. *The Judge Advocate Journal.* "Notes on the History of the Judge Advocate General's Department, 1775-1941." Page 5.

There were many battles and skirmishes within the state. The Revolutionary War had several encounters in Augusta County and the surrounding area.

In 1776, Captain Lincoln led his company in an expedition under Colonel William Christian against the Overhill Cherokee. The British had made treaty with numerous Native American tribes and sent them against the rebelling colonists. The expedition did not see a lot of action, but it did result in several peace treaties reducing Cherokee involvement with the British in Virginia during the Revolutionary War.[19] Beyond this expedition, no record is found to document Abraham Lincoln's battle engagements in the war.

In 1778, the year of Thomas' birth, his father traveled Augusta and Rockingham Counties conducting investigations and trials as Judge Advocate. It is doubtful Abraham served in the militia or directly in the war after 1778.

Thomas' early life, from newborn to four-year-old was surrounded by the workings of a large farm, cautions to safeguard against the threats and dangers of the Revolutionary War, and the family preparation to move. The preparations for moving to Kentucky began before Thomas was born.

A Long Period of Preparation

When Abraham decided to move his family to Kentucky, it was not a quick and easy process. The family was well connected in important social and political positions. Abraham and Bathsheba did not just sell their lands, pack up, and move. There were preparations to be made and times were complicated, making the preparation time consuming.

In February of 1775, Colonel Richard Henderson, representing the Transylvania Land Company, arrived at Sycamore Shoals (the ancient treaty grounds of the Cherokee) and in March 1775 he signed a treaty with the Cherokee purchasing 20 million acres for 10,000 pounds of trade goods.[20] The purchase included most of eastern Kentucky and a part of middle

---

[19] Charles E. Kemper. *The Virginia Magazine of History and Biography*. "Valley of Virginia Notes", page 400.
[20] Daniel Boone Wilderness Trail Association. *danielboonetrail.com*.

Tennessee.[21] The Shawnee, who also used the land as hunting grounds, were not consulted about their claim on the land and did not recognize the treaty. The Transylvania Land Company ignored the Shawnee and worked to start new settlements in Kentucky. The company hired a well-known scout and pioneer to make the Native American trails through the Cumberland Gap into a road to accommodate settlers. They hired Lincoln family friend and relative Daniel Boone.

Well before European settlers came to America, Native Americans followed the buffalo and discovered routes across the mountains. They developed a system of trails, called traces, connecting their settlements and traversing their hunting lands. One of these trails led from the Ohio Valley into Kentucky, then across the Cumberland Gap to points east. Native Americans called the trail Athawominee, the Great Warrior's Path. It was this trail that became the main route used by Boone to blaze and cut the Wilderness Trail.[22]

Boone was waiting in anticipation of the treaty. He hired thirty axmen and he knew the route he wanted to follow. He and his men set out from the Anderson Blockhouse near Holston Settlement (on the North Fork of the Holston River) to blaze the trail and make it a road fit for wagons to travel.[23] The Blockhouse became the gathering place, the starting point, for the thousands who followed the call of the wilderness to pioneer settling Kentucky.

Boone did not just blaze the Wilderness Trail. As a representative of the Transylvania Land Company, he founded a settlement, Boonesborough, and registered land sales in Kentucky. Boone shared stories of the land and its potential with Captain Lincoln. Abraham was a man of his times. Pioneers gained wealth and prosperity by owning land and building income from it. Abraham saw the opportunity to use his current wealth and land in the populated areas of the Shenandoah Valley to purchase a bigger portion of land in Kentucky.

---

[21] Louis A. Warren. *The Filson Club History Quarterly.* "Abraham Lincoln, Senior, Grandfather of the President", page 138.

[22] Daniel Boone Wilderness Trail Association. *danielboonetrail.com.*

[23] Daniel Boone Wilderness Trail Association. *danielboonetrail.com.*

When Boone returned to Kentucky in 1776, his Survey Book records a July entry of 1,000 acres to Captain Lincoln.[24] This was Abraham's first purchase in Kentucky and shows he was planning for his family's move well in advance. Captain Lincoln went to Kentucky with Daniel Boone in 1779 to see his land.[25] He liked what he saw.

In March of 1780, when Thomas was two, Captain Lincoln began selling parts of his Virginia holdings. Shortly after this he went to Kentucky again with Boone. This was a long trip, one in which he was away from his family for over a year as he prepared a new home. It is unknown who accompanied Abraham on this journey and in his preparation. We do know he added to his holdings very soon after arriving in Kentucky and those purchases were likely the result of his trip and exploration.

In May 1780, Abraham entered record for 400 acres on Floyd's Fork in what is now Jefferson County, Kentucky. On this land he constructed a cabin and began clearing ground for crops. In June he added another 800 acres, claiming ground along the Green River in Lincoln County.[26] He was quickly becoming a major Kentucky landholder.

To ensure his land claims held, Abraham maintained residence in the area until Spring 1781. He built a cabin, cleared land, planted crops, and harvested those crops before wintering in his new home. There is a legend that Captain Lincoln was captured by Native Americans in 1780 while in Kentucky and made to run the gauntlet, and survive it, as a condition of his release.[27]

With preparations made on his new land, Abraham returned to Virginia in 1781 to complete the sale of his remaining holdings and make final preparations for the move. As the Lincolns harvested their crops in 1781, part of their final preparations, October witnessed a defining victory for America. Cornwallis surrendered to Washington. The war would drag on with smaller skirmishes and battles until the peace treaty was ratified in early 1783 but for all practical purposes, independence was won.

---

[24] J. Henry Lea & J. R. Hutchinson. *The Ancestry of Abraham Lincoln*, page 81.
[25] Robert Morgan. *Boone*, page 30.
[26] Louis A. Warren. *The Filson Club History Quarterly*. "Abraham Lincoln, Senior, Grandfather of the President", page 144.
[27] Ralph Gary. *Following in Lincoln's* Footsteps, page 206.

The Revolutionary War was winding down but not over. The British in the west were allied with several Native American tribes. British troops in Fort Detroit reinforced and supported Native American raids into Kentucky and Western Virginia. Despite the purchase of Kentucky from the Cherokee by the Transylvania Land Company, other Native American tribes and the Chickamauga Cherokee group did not recognize the settlers' claims. They saw the land as theirs, their ancestral hunting ground. They were happy to team up with the British to push the settlers off the land. This was the time period in which the Lincolns embarked on a great adventure to start their life in the wilderness of Kentucky.

Moving to Kentucky

The journey to Kentucky was an arduous adventure for a four-year-old boy. It offered excitement and boredom, walking and riding a horse day after day along a trail that presented constant danger and distraction. There is nothing telling us what Thomas remembered of the journey, but it is likely it planted a lasting memory and stories told by the family years later made it real for him regardless of how vague the actual memory was.

The land to which Abraham Lincoln took his family began as Kentucky County, the very large western county of Virginia. As the population grew, Virginia divided Kentucky County into three counties – Lincoln, Fayette, and Jefferson – knowing it would soon separate and become the state of Kentucky.[28] Revolutionary War history is strongly seen in the names of these three counties. Lincoln County was named for General Benjamin Lincoln, a key member of Washington's staff and army. General Lincoln's relation to Thomas has been debated. He is a relative but how close a relative is in question. Fayette County was named for Gilbert du Motier, the French Marquis de Lafayette, another close friend of Washington and leader in the Continental Army. Jefferson County was named for Virginian Thomas Jefferson.

---

[28] Kentucky became the 15th state of the United States in 1792. As with the Commonwealth of Virginia, Kentucky wrote its Constitution naming itself the Commonwealth of Kentucky.

The Lincolns packed their possessions into a wagon. Once loaded, Captain Lincoln and his family left Rockingham County Virginia and their Linville Creek farm for Kentucky. Abraham (38 years of age), Bathsheba (34)[29], Mordecai (11), Josiah (9), Mary (7), Thomas (4), and Nancy (2) were ready to start a new adventure. Knowing all the possible dangers, Abraham and Bathsheba Lincoln braved the coming hardship and took their wagon and horses and children south, a journey of over 250 miles, to the Anderson Blockhouse, the start of the Wilderness Trail.

Following the Wilderness Trail

After days of traveling in the wagon and on horseback, experiencing pioneer hospitality at homes along the way and camping when needed, the Lincolns reached Anderson's Blockhouse. Built by John Anderson, the blockhouse sat at the start of the Wilderness Trail. A blockhouse was a defensive, fortified location. It was much smaller than a fort, but it was well designed to defend those inside.

The typical Revolutionary War blockhouse was a square building built of sturdy logs. Sometimes the logs were cut to form a flat side, sometimes left rounded. The second story was larger, wider than the ground floor, creating an overhang around the building. The door was sturdy and able to be barred and secured. There were no windows. Each wall had gun portals cut into it providing a means of seeing and firing at enemies approaching the blockhouse. The gun portals were usually small rectangular openings on the outside, angle cut getting wider toward the inside. This provided the defender the ability to see a broad angle and fire over that broad angle with only a small opening available to the attacker through which to try to injure or kill the defender. In the overhang floor of the second story there were also gun portals allowing defenders to fire down at anyone getting close to the blockhouse.[30]

The Anderson Blockhouse was a gathering point for settlers heading to Kentucky. Pioneers stopped at the blockhouse and

---

[29] There is some debate on Bathsheba Lincoln's age. Various sources record her birth date as 1742, 1744, 1746, and 1748. There are neither birth year or death year on her grave marker.

[30] Daniel Boone Wilderness Trail Association. *danielboonetrail.com.*

waited until a sizeable enough group of people with rifles and weapons formed to venture safely over the Wilderness Trail.

Moving with his family was Captain Lincoln's third known trip into Kentucky. When Lincoln first followed the trail with Boone in 1779, it was little more than the wildlife and Native American trace through forests and mountains. Boone and his men had since worked it. Settlements and fortifications were built to protect travelers and the trail was marked and improved, but in 1782 the Lincoln family still found a way through the woods and mountains that could only handle a single file of travelers and horses. Wagons could not pass. It would be another thirteen years before the Trail would be widened and made fit for wagons.[31]

As the Lincolns waited at the often-festive blockhouse for fellow travelers, they made the change from their wagon to packhorses. It is likely that the captain had a pack train to carry household goods, tools, and farm implements that could not be purchased in Kentucky. It was not unusual for travelers coming from Kentucky to trade harness and horses for wagons. Whether Abraham did this is unknown, but he would have sold or traded his wagon and, if he did not already have them, he purchased or bartered for pack saddles.

Pack saddles were made from forked tree branches or wooden blocks designed to spread the weight of a load over the horse's back. Items were tied to the pack saddle and often hung down the sides using rope or leather harness.[32] It was on horses with pack saddles that the Lincolns packed their worldly goods to go to their new home.

Captain Lincoln may not have needed to wait too long at the Anderson Blockhouse. He grew up knowing Daniel Boone and had arranged to meet Boone just up the Wilderness Trail at Moccasin Gap.[33] Boone still worked for the Transylvania Land Company and he was needed back in Kentucky. British and Native American raids were happening in the territory the company had purchased. Britain hoped in some way from these raids to maintain its western territory in the Americas even if the eastern

---

[31] Thomas Speed. *The Wilderness Road*, pages 29-30. The Kentucky Legislature would pass "An Act Opening a Wagon Road to Cumberland Gap" in 1795.
[32] Thomas Speed. *The Wilderness Road*, pages 72-73.
[33] John Mack Faragher. *Daniel Boone*, pages 203-204.

colonies gained their freedom. The Native American tribes wanted to keep Kentucky as their hunting grounds regardless of any treaties with the Cherokee selling the land. There was much unrest and Boone was needed. Captain Abraham Lincoln was finished with the Revolutionary War but Daniel Boone was still fighting.

The exact dates for the Lincolns entering Kentucky are unknown. It is known that Daniel Boone and his men guided and protected the Lincolns as they migrated to Kentucky. The timing must have been early in the Spring of 1782 because in August of 1782 Boone had been through his home, gathered his troops, and was fighting in the Battle of Blue Licks against the British and Shawnee.[34]

The group traveling with the Lincolns under Boone's guidance had a lot of variety and was sizable. The Lincolns had several packhorses carrying their possessions. Boone had several packhorses carrying supplies to his home as did his men. People moved to Kentucky with much and with little. Contrasting to the better off with many packhorses and riding horseback were those who walked and carried what little they had. Some went the whole way barefoot.[35]

It was routine for the Transylvania Land Company to have scouts and guides leading people across the mountains to Kentucky. The scouts rode ahead to look for danger. There were many points in the valleys and gaps that provided perfect locations for ambush. Peter Cartwright, the preacher who would face off against future President Abraham Lincoln for a seat in the House of Representatives, told of his parents traveling the Wilderness Trail in 1783. He said it was a rare day when they did not see the remains of those killed in skirmishes with Native Americans.[36] The Lincolns were fortunate to be longtime family friends of the Boones and to be able to travel with Daniel and his men.

The Transylvania Company scouts hunted as they scouted. The Trail had plenty of game and the scouts killed game and left it along the trail for the convoys of settlers to find.[37] Travelers reported seeing bear, buffalo, wolves, wildcats, and herds of deer

---

[34] Daniel Boone Wilderness Trail Association. *danielboonetrail.com.*
[35] Robert Morgan. *Boone*, page 28.
[36] Thomas Speed. *The Wilderness Road*, page 40.
[37] Thomas Speed. *The Wilderness Road*, page 45.

amongst other game. There was no shortage of food for the hunter. It was also this abundant game that brought danger both from the wild animals and from the Native Americans who wanted to keep the land for their own hunting. At night, owls could be heard screeching and hooting, wolves howled, panthers and wildcats cried out. Venomous snakes slithered beneath the leaves and undergrowth.

William Brown traveled the Wilderness Trail in July of 1782, not long after the Lincolns made their journey. He recorded his experience.

This is generally a good-watered road as far as the Blockhouse. We waited hereabouts near two weeks for company and then set out for the wilderness with twelve men and ten guns, this being Thursday, 18th July. The road from this until you get over Wallen's Ridge generally is bad, some parts very much so, particularly about Stock Creek and Stock Creek Ridge. It is a very mountainous country hereabout, but there is some fine land in the bottoms, near the water courses, in narrow slips. It will be but a thin-settled country whenever it is settled. The fords of Holstein and Clinch are both good in dry weather, but in a rainy season you are often obliged to raft over. From them along down Powell's Valley until you get to Cumberland Gap is pretty good; this valley is formed by Cumberland Mountain on the northwest, and Powell Mountain on the southeast, and appears to bear from northeast southwestwardly, and is, I suppose, about one hundred miles in length, and from ten to twelve miles in breadth. The land generally is good, and is an exceeding well-watered country, as well as the country on Holstein River, abounding with fine springs and little brooks. For about fifty miles, as you travel along the valley, Cumberland Mountain appears to be a very high ridge of white rocks, inaccessible in most places to either man or beast, and affords a wild, romantic prospect. The way through the gap is not very difficult, but from its situation travelers may be attacked in some places, crossing the mountain, by the enemy to a very great disadvantage. From thence until you pass Rockcastle River there is very little. Good road; this tract of country is very mountainous, and badly watered along the trace, especially for springs. There is some good land on the water-courses, and just on this side Cumberland River appears to be a good tract, and within a few years I expect to have a settlement on it. Some parts of the road is very miry in rainy weather. The fords of Cumberland and Rockcastle are both good unless the waters be too high; after you cross Rockcastle there are a few high hills, and the rest of the way tolerable good; the land appears to be rather weak, chiefly timbered with oak, etc. The first of the Kentucky waters you touch upon is the head of Dick's River, just eight miles from English's. Here we arrived Thursday, 25th inst., which is just seven days since we started from the Blockhouse. Monday, 29th inst., I got to Harrodsburg, and saw brother James.[38]

Four-year-old Thomas saw all these things as the Lincolns followed the same route in the tracks of Daniel Boone.

---

[38] Thomas Speed. *The Wilderness Road*, pages 19-20.

Kentucky

In 1782, Kentucky was sparsely populated. It was a wilderness area with picturesque streams and rivers winding through forests and rolling hills. It was a land of rich soil and bountiful game. Ernest Duvergier de Hauranne, a French aristocrat who traveled across America in the mid-1800s, described Kentucky with high praise.

> *Those who praised the beauty of Kentucky did not deceive me. All along the way I admired the gentle, pastoral aspect of this rich countryside. Valleys partly under cultivation, surrounded by low wooded mountains covered with greenery, pastures dotted with trees like the lawns of a park, an infinite variety of curing shapes in the hills, and yet a certain monotony due to the repetition of the same scenes — such is the Kentucky landscape. The forest is so beautiful that the hills lose their contours amidst the waving tufts of foliage which cover their steep slopes like a curly fleece. Some hills are conical and pointed, others gently rounded. Soon they fall back and make way for a river which flows between two leaning rows of tall trees; later the mountains come closer again and take on a wilder look; the narrow valleys become twisting ravines. The meadows and cornfields still border the twisting riverbank with bright bands of green at the bottom of the gorge. Farther on there is no room for them; the ravine becomes a narrow defile and nothing more is visible but the jumble of the forest.*[1]

Multiple Native American tribes hunted Kentucky from north of the Ohio River to south in Tennessee. Some of these tribes were friendly. The Cherokee sold land to the Transylvania Land Company and were peaceful toward settlers coming in. Other tribes were hostile, allied and armed by the British as part of their Revolutionary War strategy to drive the settlers out of Kentucky.

---

[1] Ernest Duvergier de Hauranne. *A Frenchman in Lincoln's America*, volume 1, page 348.

The Chickamauga, Shawnee, and Wabash hunted in Kentucky for game and raided Kentucky settlements to kill pioneers they saw as intruders.

It was into this beautiful but dangerous Kentucky that Captain Abraham Lincoln bought land and brought his family to live. It was here that 4-year-old Thomas grew up.

Early Years in Jefferson County

The Lincolns followed the branch of the Wilderness Trail that led toward the Falls of the Ohio (Louisville) into Jefferson County, Kentucky. There they settled in the area of Hughes Station.[2] The station was a small fort with eight cabins inside a wooden blockade with four blockhouses, one at each corner.[3] It was not a strong fortification, but it protected the families living there from small raiding parties.

At the time the family arrived at Hughes Station, Captain Lincoln owned 1200 acres of fertile Kentucky land. He had 800 acres on the Green River in Lincoln County and 400 acres on Long Run in Jefferson County.[4] On December 11, 1782, Abraham added another 500 acres and continued to add land on the Green River and Licking River, ending up with 3200 acres of good farming land by the time of his death.[5]

In Thomas' fifth year he experienced an event that would be duplicated again later in his life. He lived through the climate aftermath of a volcanic eruption. Though Thomas may have remembered little or none of the winter of 1783-4 due to his young age, he most likely was told the story of the strange and cold winter.

On June 8, 1783, the Laki eruption began in Iceland. The eruption would continue for eight months until February of 1784. It would rip open nearly 17 miles of volcanic fissures in Iceland and spew a volcanic haze into the atmosphere that dropped the winter temperature of the eastern United States eight degrees

---

[2] The area of Hughes Station is now a part of greater Louisville.

[3] Louis A. Warren. *Lincoln's Parentage and Childhood*, page 5.

[4] D. M. Coleman. *Thomas Lincoln, The Father of Abraham Lincoln*, page 8.

[5] J. Henry Lea & J. R. Hutchinson. *The Ancestry of Abraham Lincoln*, page 81.

below the normal average. The winter temperature of the northern hemisphere dropped by two degrees.[6]

The winter during the ongoing eruption was extremely cold and very long. Charleston Harbor in North Carolina froze completely over, allowing ice skaters to skate completely across it. Ice went down the Mississippi past New Orleans into the Gulf of Mexico where it stayed without melting. George Washington complained that his household was trapped in Mount Vernon by snow from Christmas until March.[7]

The results of the atmospheric damage from the Laki eruption was crop loss and famine. Thousands starved to death around the world. The Laki eruption famine was one of the factors leading to the rebellion of the starving masses in France that became the French Revolution.

Captain Lincoln and his family were no doubt impacted but they persevered and came through the disaster intact, the Captain keeping his family clothed and fed and prospering. From 1782 to 1786, Captain Lincoln was prospering. He was increasing his wealth and holdings through land acquisition, farming, and raising livestock and horses. From age four to age eight Thomas was part of caring for the family's fields and animals as well as helping in the stockade at Hughes Station. These happy and prosperous times changed in May of 1786.

Captain Abraham Lincoln's Death

In May 1786, at the Lincoln cabin, roughly a half mile distant from Hughes Station, Abraham and his three sons were working to plant a cornfield when they were ambushed by a small Native American raid. Shots were fired from the nearby woods. Captain Lincoln was hit and killed. The eldest son, Mordecai, 15-years-old, sent his younger brother Josiah, 13, to Hughes Station for help. Mordecai went to the cabin where he aimed a rifle through a gun portal in the wall. Thomas, 8, was sitting in the field beside his father's body. He was a tempting prize to be taken as a slave for the tribe. One of the Native Americans came out of the woods to snatch Thomas, but Mordecai saw him coming. The Native was

---

[6] Oregon State University. volcano.oregonstate.edu/laki-iceland-1783.
[7] Ultimate History Project. ultimatehistoryproject.com/the-eruption-of-laki.html.

wearing a silver pendent around his neck. It reflected the sunlight. Mordecai aimed for the pendant and dropped the Native before he could take Thomas.[8]

The half mile to the station was quickly covered by a young, strong pioneer boy used to running. Josiah reached the station in minutes. Help reached the Lincoln cabin in no more than ten or fifteen minutes. By the time they arrived, Thomas had been taken into the cabin with his mother and sisters while one tradition says Mordecai climbed into a tree to keep better watch for any lingering or returning Native Americans fearing that the Natives who killed his father could be scouts for a larger group. With the arrival of help, the danger was averted. There were no further attacks.

A lesser known version of this family legend has come down through historian Wayne C. Temple. After the Captain was shot,

Mordecai, about fifteen years of age, fled immediately to the tiny log cabin close at hand, taking with him little Thomas, eight years of age. But Josiah, about thirteen, headed out for Hughes' Station to warn the other pioneer settlers of an impending Indian attack. Inside the cabin, Mordecai took up his rifle while Bathsheba took the Captain's rifle in hand.[9] One of the Indians left the cover of the forest to scalp the Captain. It was during that moment, as the Indian began to take the scalp, that both Mordecai and Bathsheba shot the Indian."[10]

Abraham Lincoln told the version with Thomas sitting in the field. Most historians have followed that version in some form. This story became legend in the Lincoln family. Thomas told it over and over across the years. It was a story he told to his son Abraham[11], named for Thomas' father, and he implanted the story in his memory, repeating it over and over as the background to how he came by his name.

---

[8] David Donald. *Lincoln*, page 21.

[9] There is a question of why the Captain would not have had his rifle near him in the field as most pioneers kept their weapons near at hand. It could be Mordecai had carried the rifle with him from the field.

[10] Wayne C. Temple. *Thomas and Abraham Lincoln As Farmers*, pages 12-13.

[11] William H. Herndon & Jesse W. Weik. *Herndon's Life of Lincoln*, page 10.

The story grew over time. Augustus Chapman, a later neighbor and friend of the Lincolns who married one of Thomas' granddaughters, told that Mordecai killed three Native Americans after his father was shot.[12]

Captain Lincoln was buried in deerskins[13] near Hughes Station.[14]

Bathsheba and her children stayed on the farm through harvest, but she was planning to move her family to Washington County where there were relatives and friends to help her. In September 1786, an expedition was sent out against the Wabash.[15] The expedition was in response to raids by the Wabash, the Wabash very possibly being the tribe responsible for the death of Captain Lincoln. Records from the expedition indicate that Bathsheba strongly supported it by donating the best rifle the family owned.[16]

Captain Lincoln left no will. It was normal law for a widow to be able to claim either her dower rights or one-third of the estate.[17] Kentucky was still a part of Virginia in 1786 so Kentucky followed Virginia law. In Virginia, Thomas Jefferson pressed for the ancient law of primogeniture to be replaced and Virginia did so in 1785, the year before Captain Lincoln's death. The new law, implemented over the next seven years, provided the widow with one-third of the estate and each child with an equal portion.[18] Unfortunately for Thomas, the law was not fully implemented at the time of his father's death.

In October 1786, John Caldwell was appointed administrator of Captain Lincoln's estate.[19] Caldwell was a wealthy and important citizen in Washington and Nelson Counties and in the

---

[12] Douglas L. Wilson and Rodney O. Davis. *Herndon's Informants*, page 439.

[13] 13 Ronald C. White Jr. *A. Lincoln*, page 12.

[14] Captain Lincoln's name is spelled *Linkhorn* on the gravestone. The person who did the engraving spelled the name reflecting the way most said the name rather than the correct spelling.

[15] Louis A. Warren. *Lincoln's Parentage and Childhood*, page 6.

[16] Louis A. Warren. *Lincoln's Parentage and Childhood*, page 7.

[17] Carole Shammas, Marylynn Salmon, and Michel Dahlin. *Inheritance in America: from Colonial Times to the Present*, pages 64 and 66.

[18] Carole Shammas, Marylynn Salmon, and Michel Dahlin. *Inheritance in America: from Colonial Times to the Present*, pages 64, 66, and 72.

[19] Charles H. Coleman and Mary Coleman. *Thomas Lincoln*, page 13.

growing movement to make Kentucky a state. By 1792, General Caldwell would serve under General Anthony Wayne before moving up the political ranks to become Kentucky's second Lt. Governor, the first to be elected by the popular vote.[20]

Details of how Caldwell settled the Lincoln estate are unclear. The estate was not completely settled until 1790, following a suit by Caldwell against Hananiah Lincoln to regain monies loaned to Hananiah by Captain Lincoln. The suit was settled in the family's favor through arbitration.[21]

Mordecai received the bulk of the estate, probably two thirds (it is known he received all of the land), with the remainder of the estate going to Bathsheba, some possibly being divided out to the other children, including Thomas. With this settlement, the family was not impoverished. Evidence that the Lincoln family was not impoverished comes from the tax records of the period. In one tax census, 1792, six years after Captain Lincoln was killed, Bathsheba lists one horse and ten head of cattle.[22] Such holdings were well above being in poverty.

The Impact of Captain Lincoln's Untimely Death

The story of Captain Lincoln's death has more in it than is often seen. Mordecai became a leading citizen in Washington County, using the land and income from his inheritance to become a man of significant wealth. He was witty and talented. His nephew would come to know and respect him, his lifestyle, his manners, his wealth. President Lincoln said "Uncle Mord had run off with all the talents in the family."[23] This influence, the success of Mordecai, was without doubt an inspiration for the future president's ambition. When Abraham compared Thomas' cabins and limited resources to Uncle Mordecai, Thomas was left in a poor light. He was not the man Abraham wanted to be like when he grew up. The seed was planted on which Abraham Lincoln would build a career that would make him a success, someone memorable, someone unlike how he saw Thomas.

---

[20] Sandy Caldwell. "The Life and Family of Lt. Gov. John Caldwell." *Kentucky Ancestors*, page 118.

[21] Charles H. Coleman and Mary Coleman. *Thomas Lincoln*, page 13.

[22] William E. Barton. *The Lineage of Lincoln*, page 280.

[23] David Donald. *Lincoln*, page 22.

Thomas, at eight years of age, was left to find his own way. Bathsheba did all she could but she was limited. She was without power over much of the Captain's estate. She did not have much to pass on to the four children left with a meager inheritance. Where Mordecai had resources, Thomas had his hands and his mind. Thomas was put out into the world to learn how to make a living. Thomas, starting later and with less, would never accumulate material wealth to match his brother.

The other and usually overlooked impact of Captain Abraham's death was the trauma it caused Thomas. One minute the family was whole; mother and daughters working in and around the family home; father and sons in the fields planting. Life was good. And then, tragedy. A gunshot rang out from the woods and the father fell to the ground mortally wounded.

An eight-year-old boy was left sitting in a field beside the bloodied body of his father. Shock, terror, and heart-sickening sorrow all blended together as that boy stared at his father, the strong hands still and unmoving, the eyes that had lit his life with joy now staring unseeing. Into this comes the sound of someone running toward him. He looks up to see a Native American rushing at him. Another gunshot, this time from the cabin, and the Native stumbles and falls, dead.

This kind of trauma would touch anyone to the core. Thomas went through it as an eight-year-old boy. The images were seared into his mind. In one swift instant Thomas went from being the happy son of a well-respected and well-off soldier and citizen to being one of the widow's sons with little to his name and no apparent path into life. Everything had changed. Eight-year-old Thomas was thrust into a new life, a life that was nothing like he had expected.

Washington County

Bathsheba, with help from her children, friends, and neighbors, stayed in Jefferson County near Hughes Station for the summer and harvest of 1786. There is nothing to tell of her emotions and loss, of her hard work and struggles as she kept her family together and comforted them in their time of loss and grief. It is known that toward the end of the year she moved her family some forty miles south into Washington County near Springfield, Kentucky.

The community where she settled was known as Beechland. Beech Fork, a Salt River tributary, made a very large horseshoe-shaped run and it was the land surrounded by the horseshoe where Bathsheba settled her family.[24] Instead of living well away from her nearest neighbors, she would live in a small gathering of friends. Captain Lincoln's cousin Hananiah[25] had a cabin and holdings not far from Bathsheba.[26]

Beechland increased the historical impression that the place of Thomas' childhood was impoverished because Beechland was sometimes called Poortown[27] and that name conveyed a negative image. Why Beechland was called Poortown is unknown. Perhaps it was because of the smaller cabins where the hired help for the better-off farmers lived. Regardless, Beechland was not poor. The area had a good number of well-to-do farmers and those living in the area were no poorer than other early communities.

Captain Lincoln's cousin, Hananiah Lincoln, served in the Revolutionary War as a Captain. Unlike his cousin Abraham who served in the militia, Hananiah served for a longer period in the Continental Army. Hananiah ended his service in the Continental Army in 1777. It was sometime after this that he moved to Kentucky.[28] He migrated to Kentucky from his home in Pennsylvania. Hananiah followed the river route along the Ohio to get to Kentucky and began buying land. His home, while close to the cabin he helped build for Bathsheba, was a short distance away and, eventually, in a different county – Nelson County – as

---

[24] Louis A. Warren. *Indiana Magazine of History*. "The Romance of Thomas Lincoln and Nancy Hanks", page 213.

[25] At the time in his life when President Lincoln was writing letters to friends and possible relatives to explore his family history, he wrote to Richard V. B. Lincoln on April 6, 1860. Richard was proposing that he was a cousin of Lincoln through Hananiah. Though the President's knowledge of his family was scant, he did remember something about Hananiah. "I remember, long ago, seeing Austin Lincoln, & Davis Lincoln, said to be sons of Hannaniah, or Annaniah Lincoln, who was said to have been a cousin of my grand-father." [Abraham Lincoln. *The Collected Works of Abraham Lincoln*, volume 4, page 39]

[26] Ronald C. White Jr. *A. Lincoln*, page 13.

[27] Raymond Warren. *The Prairie President*, page 6.

[28] Louis A. Warren. *Indiana Magazine of History*. "Hananiah Lincoln in Revolutionary and Pioneer History", page 29.

population grew and larger counties were divided into smaller areas.

It was at this new Beechland home[29] that Thomas would grow into a man. It was here he lived near some of his father's family and that the Lincoln family came to know the Berrys and the Hanks.

The Traditional Thomas

It is at this point in Thomas' life that traditional biography of him commences to disparage his life. In the late 1800's and early 1900's it was common to write stories of men who built themselves up from nothing, who overcame great hardship to become successful. Heroes were frequently portrayed as self-made men who were morally and culturally superior to those around them. These self-made men were the role models for how to achieve success in the modern era into which America was moving, the era into which America was leading the world. It is no surprise that much early Lincoln biography followed this pattern, portraying Abraham as pulling himself up in the world against extreme odds and with little help. This biographical writing style and bias did great harm to Thomas' image in history.

Even what President Lincoln would later write about his father was less than flattering. In his brief autobiography for Scripps, Lincoln wrote: "Thomas, the youngest son, and father of the present subject, by the early death of his father, and very narrow circumstances of his mother, even in childhood was a wandering laboring boy, and grew up literally without education."[30] Compared to the educated men and women Abraham would meet in his travels and career, the past education of Thomas was greatly wanting.

Robert Todd Lincoln, Abraham Lincoln's oldest son and his only child to live into adulthood, responded to a lot of magazines and newspapers to confirm or deny information about his father and his family. To one he wrote a reminder that not everything

---

[29] The Springfield home is preserved and commemorated by the Lincoln Homestead Park in Springfield, Kentucky.
[30] Roy P. Basler. *The Collected Works of Abraham Lincoln*, volume 4, page 60.

they heard, or saw was accurate because Abraham Lincoln had become "a peg on which to hang many things."[31]

As was done with Abraham, so it was done with Thomas. Thomas Lincoln's history was written and embellished to support a multitude of purposes and he did not fare well in the early stories.

William Herndon, the president's law partner and the man whose notes and history set the stage for the world's early view of Thomas Lincoln, followed this method and pattern. "It is said that the most of our great statesmen were self-made men, and this is as a general rule true, rising from the bottom round of the ladder and climbing to the topmost round, gradually through struggle; Lincoln rose from a lower depth, from a stagnant, filthy, putrid pool, like the gases of it set on fire by its own energy and self-combustible power in jets rising, blue, on fire, bright, blazing, pure, up toward the sky far, far above the topmost round."[32]

As Herndon worked with Jesse Weik, the man Herndon chose to ghost write his biography of Lincoln, Herndon encouraged Weik to make Thomas as low, as worthless as possible. "So far as I am concerned, I don't care how Lincoln came into the world; the lower he was created, the higher and grander – looking at all things – to me he is."[33] This approach to Lincoln's history is skewed. John Zane, the son of Charles Zane, Herndon's law partner following Abraham Lincoln's death, has put it succinctly. "After reading all that Herndon has written, including the suppressed book [Herndon's Lincoln biography], I am persuaded that the Lincoln he pictures is mainly Herndon, but almost all the writers borrow heavily from him."[34]

This skewing of history to fit Herndon is admitted by Herndon. "When I was around taking Evidence soon after and

---

[31] William Hanchett. *The Lincoln Murder Conspiracies*, page 241. The quote originally came from Thomas F. Meehan, "Lincoln's Opinion of Catholics," *United States Catholic Historical Society, Historical Records and Studies*, 16 (1924), page 88.

[32] Emanuel Hertz. *The Hidden Lincoln, From the Letters and Papers of William H. Herndon*, page 442.

[33] Emanuel Hertz. *The Hidden Lincoln, From the Letters and Papers of William H. Herndon.* Garden City, page 53.

[34] John Maxcy Zane. *Abraham Lincoln Association Papers.* "Lincoln, the Constitutional Lawyer", page 30.

long after Mr. Lincoln's death much – much was told me which I did not reduce to writing, but which, much of which, floats about in my memory. Time may have modified – altered or changed what was told me. I rejected much which was told me, because what was told me was contrary to what I knew."[35] If something was told him that did not agree with his bias, he rejected it and left it out of the record. He included only what fit his view of what he wanted to be the truth.

This approach, a subtle use of subterfuge to gain the conclusion Herndon desired, shows in Herndon once trying to persuade Abraham to make use of such in court.

> *The plea was as skilfully drawn as I knew how, and was framed as if we had the evidence to sustain it. The whole thing was a sham, but so constructed as to work the desired continuance,...At length, before further steps were taken, Lincoln came into court. He looked carefully over all the papers in the case, as was his custom, and seeing my ingenious subterfuge asked, "Is this seventh plea a good one?" Proud of the exhibition of my skill I answered that it was. "But," he inquired, incredulously, "is it founded on fact?" I was obliged to respond in the negative,...[36]*

Before Herndon published his views of Lincoln's early life, little had been known about Thomas or Nancy or Sally or how Abraham Lincoln was raised and lived. Herndon set the standard – and it was a low standard – for how Thomas would be seen by the world. For Herndon, Thomas was shiftless and lazy, lacking in intelligence and ambition, willfully uneducated, harsh with his son, and not even Abraham's biological father. This was the Thomas early biography portrayed, the man Herndon wanted the world to see.

Popular author Horatio Alger Jr. made this Thomas well known. "Thomas Lincoln, born in 1778, was the third child, and the future President was his son. He was a good-natured, popular

---

35 William H. Herndon. *Herndon on Lincoln: Letters*, page 97. From a Herndon letter to Ward Hill Lamon dated from Springfield, Illinois on March 6, 1870.
36 William H. Herndon. *Herndon's Life of Lincoln*, page 263.

man, but inefficient and unsuccessful, and whatever there was great in his eminent son did not come from him."[37] Alger would go on to describe Thomas as a failed and incompetent carpenter who was held in low regard for his lack of skill, a shiftless and unambitious man. This lack of skill and ambition left the Lincoln family with possessions that "were altogether beneath the notice of even the poorest tramp."[38]

Ward Hill Lamon, a friend of Abraham Lincoln who would become closely allied with Herndon when he put together his own biography of Lincoln, followed Herndon's material for Abraham's early life and adopted Herndon's view of Thomas. Lamon's biography referred to Thomas as the "only member of the [Lincoln] family whose character was not entirely respectable. He was idle, thriftless, poor, a hunter, and a rover."[39]

These early writings from Herndon and Lamon based on Herndon drove the view of Thomas for decades and, unfortunately, it is even found in more recent books on Abraham Lincoln. But making Thomas lowly in order to let Abraham appear that much grander is not a fair look at Thomas Lincoln. The traditional view of Thomas Lincoln is not the real Thomas Lincoln.

David Reynolds sums it up well. "History has not treated Thomas Lincoln fairly. He is normally presented as a lowly, ignorant rube who was lazy, unambitious, and resistant to the young Abe's penchant for reading. Several biographies of Lincoln use his father as the bogeyman against whom Lincoln vigorously rebelled. The facts, however, say otherwise. Tom Lincoln was known as a solid, upstanding, honest man who provided for his family even in hard times…"[40]

Thomas Grows Up

The home where Thomas lived most of the time from age eight until he moved to Elizabethtown is preserved in Kentucky's

---

37 Horatio Alger Jr. *Abraham Lincoln, The Backwoods Boy; or , How a Young Rail-Splitter Became President*, pages 26-27.
38 Horatio Alger Jr. *Abraham Lincoln, The Backwoods Boy; or , How a Young Rail-Splitter Became President*, page 12.
39 Ward Hill Lamon. *The Life of Abraham Lincoln*, page 8.
40 Sara Gabbard. "Interview with David S. Reynolds", page 5.

Lincoln Homestead State Park just north of Springfield, Kentucky. The park has both historic buildings and reconstructions.

The Francis Berry home is where Nancy Hanks lived and worked as a seamstress. There is the workshop where Thomas learned carpentry and blacksmithing. And, of course, there is Bathsheba Lincoln's cabin where Thomas lived with his mother and four siblings. The Lincoln cabin was sixteen feet by eighteen feet, a standard size cabin for the pioneers in Kentucky. Thomas would live most of his life in cabins of similar size.

Though the cabins are now set closely together in the park, Bathsheba's home was actually about a mile from the Berry's, a distance that was considered close for neighbors in pioneer days.

During the next several years, Thomas is said to have become a wandering labor boy, bouncing from farm to farm to do whatever labor they might hire him for to provide income and food for the family, missing educational opportunities to work. This view cannot be completely accurate. Granted, Thomas did not become a highly educated man, but neither was he completely without education.

Thomas' father was educated. Captain Lincoln was a Judge Advocate. It is only logical that he educated his youngest son. It is known that Thomas learned to read and write at a very basic level. One tradition claims his wife (Nancy) taught him what little he knew but records indicate Thomas signed his name and kept records before marrying Nancy.[41] It is likely Thomas began learning under his father's watchful eye, an education disrupted by the Captain's untimely death. Bathsheba may also have played a role in Thomas' education before and after Captain Lincoln's death. She could read and write[42], a novelty for a pioneer woman but Bathsheba was raised in a well-to-do Virginia family and an education was provided her.

Contrasting with tales of Thomas being an unskilled, wandering labor boy is the fact that during his formative years Thomas learned to be a skilled carpenter, cabinet maker, furniture maker, house-joiner, and cooper.[43] These are not the skills of a

---

[41] William E. Barton. *The Parents of Abraham Lincoln*, page 5.
[42] Richard E. Hart. *Thomas Lincoln Reconsidered*, manuscript page 30.
[43] Wayne C. Tample. *Thomas and Abraham Lincoln As Farmers*, page 15.

simple, wandering, day laborer. Thomas also learned rudimentary math along with his limited reading skills and being able to sign his name in cursive script. It was while growing up in Beechland that Thomas learned these things.

A thorough education was out of reach in Beechland but there were resources available for Bathsheba to provide Thomas with a path into life. This began with their neighbor, Richard Berry Sr. A long held tradition has Thomas learning carpentry and some blacksmithing from Berry who had both a carpenter's shop and a smithy. As there were close ties between the Lincolns and the Berrys, Thomas worked on the Berry farm and it is very likely that Thomas began his carpentry training under Berry during these early years.[44]

The detail of Thomas' life from late 1786 (when the family moved to Beechland) through the early 1790's is sparse. From age 8 to age 14 or 15, Thomas did what all the other pioneer boys did in Beechland. He hunted, fished, worked on the family land, and worked on other farms. He learned carpentry and blacksmithing. In reality, these years that have come to be known as the time when Thomas was little more than a wandering labor boy were little different from the way Thomas' son Abraham was later raised in Indiana, little different from the way most pioneer children were raised.

We get more information in 1792 when Thomas' brother Mordecai turned 21 and came of age to claim his share of Captain Lincoln's estate. This event heavily impacted the family. Whatever income there had been from the estate became Mordecai's to do with as he chose. There is some evidence that Mordecai divided some of his portion of the estate among his family[45] but that division was far from equal. It would take Mordecai four years to settle the estate and enter the land under his own name. When he did so he held title to 100 acres on Beech Fork (possibly the location of Bathsheba's family home), 400 acres on Floyd Ford, 1134 acres on Green River, 1000 acres on Kentucky River, 800 acres on Green River, and 1000 acres on Kentucky River. 4434

---

[44] D. M. Coleman. *Thomas Lincoln, The Father of Abraham Lincoln*, page 9.

[45] R. Gerald McMurtry. *A Series of Monographs Concerning the Lincolns and Hardin County, Kentucky*, page 1.

acres became Mordecai's legal possession. He kept most of the land but in 1797 he did sell the land where his father was killed.[46]

Also, in 1792, Mordecai wed Mary Mudd. In a strange twist of history, Mary's Uncle Henry (Henry Thomas Mudd) became the great, great, great grandfather of Dr. Samuel A. Mudd who tended John Wilkes Booth and was tried as a conspirator in the assassination of President Lincoln.

In 1795, at age 17, Thomas is listed on the tax records of Washington County as a minor above age 16.[47] He served in the Kentucky militia in an excursion fighting Native Americans. Thomas was a member of the Guard of the Fourth Regiment and served under Lieutenant George Ewing and Lieutenant Philip Washburn. He served from June 8 to August 5, 1795.[48] Thomas' 1795 militia excursion was part of the Northwest Indian War against the Shawnee.

After his militia service was completed, descendants of the Herring family, Thomas' mother's family, say that Thomas visited them in Virginia. The purpose of the visit is unknown, and it is not known if others traveled with him, but the family tells that Thomas spent some time with them when he was just grown into manhood. Family tradition reports the young Thomas was a joyous personality, a good man who was handy and helped in the house and outdoors during his visit.[49]

It is at this point that one tradition has Thomas apprenticing with Jesse Head (the preacher who would later conduct Thomas' marriage to Nancy) to learn cabinet making. Head migrated to Kentucky from Baltimore to find a new home where competition was not as tough as his business faced Maryland. Head settled in Springfield, Kentucky and advertised in the Lexington newspaper for apprentices. Apprenticeship lasted from four to seven years and an apprentice was required to know or learn how to read, write, and cipher to the rule of three.[50] This training fits with

---

[46] Louis A. Warren. "Uncle Mordecai Lincoln." *The Lincoln Kinsman*, pages 3-4.
[47] W. E. Barton, *Life of Abraham Lincoln Volume I*, page 10.
[48] Louis A. Warren. "Abraham Lincoln's Father." *The Lincoln Kinsman*, page 1.
[49] Herring Chrisman. *Memoirs of Lincoln*, pages 13-14.
[50] Tretter, Kathy. "Lincoln Family Corner Cabinet Hidden for Years in Southern Indiana."

Thomas knowing how to read and write and with the fact that Thomas kept business ledgers.

The timing for this apprenticeship is questionable. There is an historic marker in Springfield, Kentucky at the location where the Head homestead stood. This marker (historical marker #1038) notes that Head migrated to Springfield in 1798 but some genealogical resources note Head as moving to Kentucky earlier, in 1795.[51] Whatever apprenticeship Thomas had with Head would have been short as Thomas was working in Elizabethtown in 1797.

1796 finds Thomas at age 18 listed in the Washington County tax record but he is beginning to move away from his Beechland home. His carpentry skills got him work with Samuel Haycraft in Elizabethtown, work that was well paid. His work in 1796 proved to be of good service to Haycraft who hired Thomas for several months in 1797 to work on building Haycraft's mill and mill race on Severn's Valley Creek near Elizabethtown.[52] The 1797 Hardin County tax list on August 27, 1797 listed Thomas working for Haycraft and being 21 or over. This is a discrepancy with his birth date in 1778 and may have been because he was still an underage male and away from home. It could also have been because Thomas was tall and strong and appeared to be over 21. Tax lists were notoriously slack in accuracy due to lack of records and verification.[53] This work with Haycraft led to Thomas moving to Elizabethtown.

While not legally an adult, the 18-year-old Thomas had reached manhood. He stood 5 feet 10 inches tall (some say 6 foot), weighed around 190 pounds, had coarse dark hair, grey eyes (the color eyes Abraham would inherit), high cheek bones, and a rather large nose. His face was well rounded though some called him long of face. He was not considered a handsome man. He was very strong and muscular, walked slowly, and never seemed to be in a hurry. He had become a man of good morals, good habits, and good humor. Thomas signed his name as "Thomas Lincoln"

---

[51] Warren Greer. "Jesse Head Homesite."

[52] Louis A. Warren. "The Romance of Thomas Lincoln and Nancy Hanks." *Indiana Magazine of History*, page 216.

[53] R. Gerald McMurtry. *The Lincolns in Elizabethtown, Kentucky*, page 2.

but everyone, probably including Thomas, pronounced it "Linkhorn".[54]

A Frenchman traveling America gives a poignant description of Kentuckians that fits Thomas well. "The population of 'Old Kentucky' differs visibly from that of the Northern states. The Kentuckians are tall, strong, bold, full of life and movement: they joke, they laugh, their voices are loud, and they sing at the top of their lungs. They do not have the dry, stiff seriousness of their Yankee cousins."[55]

In late 1797, Thomas was staying with Hananiah Lincoln on land Hananiah owned in Hardin County near Elizabethtown. In 1798, Hananiah bought land in Cumberland County and Thomas went with him to work that land.[56] Later in 1798, Thomas went south into Tennessee and worked for his Uncle Isaac at his farm on the Watauga River.[57]

It was during these developmental years when Thomas was learning carpentry and cabinet making and beginning to move out into life on his own that he became active in the Primitive Baptist church (also known as Predestinarian or Separate Baptists). Thomas was baptized in the Rolling Fork River[58] and his Christian beliefs and morals became the guiding principle in his life.

---

[54] The description of Thomas is brought together from several sources.
*Douglas L. Wilson and Rodney O. Davis. *Herndon's Informants*, page 142. From a David Turnham letter to Herndon dated December 6, 1865.
*Douglas L. Wilson and Rodney O. Davis. *Herndon's Informants*, page 145. From Harriet A. Chapman letter to Herndon dated December 17, 1865. Chapman was one of Thomas' granddaughters.
*rogernorton.com.
*Emanuel Hertz. *The Hidden Lincoln, From the Letters and Papers of William H. Herndon*, page 353.From Nat Grigsby's statement to Herndon.
[55] Ernest Duvergier de Hauranne. *A Frenchman in Lincoln's America*, volume 1, page 340.
[56] Louis A. Warren. "Hananiah Lincoln in Revolutionary and Pioneer History". *Indiana Magazine of History*, page 30.
[57] Wayne C. Temple *Thomas and Abraham Lincoln As Farmers*, page 15.
[58] Douglas L. Wilson and Rodney O. Davis. *Herndon's Informants*, page 234. From a Charles Friend letter to Herndon dated from Hodgenville, Kentucky on March 19, 1866.

Legally an Adult

On January 6, 1799, Thomas turned 21 and became an adult under the law. He had been on his own for at least three years but did not have legal standing until his 21st birthday. This also put Thomas on the tax census records under his own name. On June 29, 1799 in the Washington County tax list, Thomas listed two horses for taxation.[59] Thomas was known to have owned at least one horse before he came of age. Owning horses was something that would be consistent throughout his life. There is some evidence that Thomas bred horses, owning a stallion and several mares.[60] This could have been from the influence and encouragement of his brother Mordecai who was well known for the horses he kept, bred, and sold. Regardless, for a young man just turning 21, having two horses showed that Thomas was doing well for himself as he entered legal adulthood.

The year 1800 found Thomas continuing in his carpentry work and learning new techniques and methods from apprenticing and working with other carpenters.

In 1801, age 23, Thomas began to follow the family tradition of buying land. In May, he entered 200 acres of land in Cumberland County, possibly guided in his purchase by cousin Hananiah who owned land in the County, land Thomas had helped him open. What Thomas did on the land, if anything, is unknown. He did not live here as he was still listed on the Washington County tax lists.

The records indicate Thomas was an active part of his community and becoming a very respected man. August of 1801 saw him act as a witness of a friend's marriage. In October, he signed as witness and surety to a note for the Mudd family – Joseph, Thomas, and Luke. Luke was Mordecai's father-in-law.[61]

1801 was a momentous year for the Lincoln family. February was the wedding of Thomas' sister Nancy to William Brumfield (February 12, 1801) and his brother Josiah to Catey Barlow (February 28, 1801). Later in the year his sister Mary married

---

[59] Louis A. Warren. "Abraham Lincoln's Father." *The Lincoln Kinsman*, page 2.
[60] William E. Barton. *The Parents of Abraham Lincoln*, pate 7.
[61] Louis A. Warren. "Abraham Lincoln's Father." *The Lincoln Kinsman*, page 2.

Ralph Crume (August 5, 1801). All of Bathsheba's children were married except Thomas.

Thomas was well known and respected enough as he came to his 24th year that he was given bond and appointed a Cumberland County constable in January 1802.[62] There is nothing in the records of his early life to indicate that Thomas was anything except a hard-working young man making a successful start to his life.

Those who remembered him from this time gave good reports. William Greene talks of Thomas' manners being backwoodish "yet they were easy so much so that I almost would say they were polished." Greene would go on to say Thomas was passionately fond of funny jokes and stories and no one beat him in storytelling.[63] From his early days Thomas was a good-humored man with a keen wit and great skill in telling jokes and stories. It was from Thomas that Abraham inherited and learned the art of storytelling that would serve him so well in his legal and political careers. Many of Abraham's stories were from his father. Thomas was said, much like the future reputation of his son, to have had an inexhaustible supply of anecdotes and stories.[64]

As Thomas prepared to move to Elizabethtown, he had a reputation of fairness and was a trusted member of his communities and family. He was establishing himself in a career of carpentry and cabinetmaking.[65] He was known as a good carpenter and a local physician, Dr. Christopher Columbus Graham, remembers Thomas as having the best set of tools in Washington County. Thomas' life was off to a very good start, overcoming early hardship.[66]

In the Fall of 1802, Thomas moved to Elizabethtown. The Washington County tax list for 1803 would note Thomas' name with "gone to Hardin County."[67]

---

[62] Louis A. Warren. "Abraham Lincoln's Father." *The Lincoln Kinsman*, page 2.

[63] Douglas L. Wilson and Rodney O. Davis. *Herndon's Informants*, page 145. From a William G. Greene letter to Herndon dated December 20, 1865.

[64] David Donald. *Lincoln*, page 39.

[65] Douglas L. Wilson and Rodney O. Davis. *Herndon's Informants*, page 646. From an interview of Jesse W Weik with Chapman in 1886 or 1887.

[66] Ida M. Tarbell. *The Early Life of Abraham Lincoln*, page 233.

[67] Louis A. Warren. "Abraham Lincoln's Father." *The Lincoln Kinsman*, page 2.

Elizabethtown

Thomas was familiar with Elizabethtown and had spent time there. He had worked for Samuel Haycraft and done other carpentry work in the town as well as doing business in Elizabethtown. There is no record of where Thomas lived when he first moved to Elizabethtown. It is very probable he stayed in a boarding house or with friends. The record of his life begins to show a variety of work and community participation in early 1803.

As Thomas turned 25 in January 1803, he was called to serve as a prison guard under Deputy Sherriff Charles Helm.[68] Later, in June, Thomas signed as witness to a promissory note for Jacob Vanmater. During this time, Thomas plied his trade as carpenter and cabinetmaker.

Somewhere during the Elizabethtown years, there is a tradition that Thomas worked in a kind of apprenticeship to Joseph Hanks, Nancy Hanks' uncle. The timing around this tradition is somewhat sketchy but it would make sense that Thomas knew Joseph and learned from him. This would also have been a way to court Nancy who spent some time at her uncle's home when she was not in Beechland.

As the year progressed, Thomas accumulated cash from his trade work as well as from guarding prisoners. He worked in multiple fields and was successful at it. That success shows clearly in his September land purchase.

On September 2, 1803 he bought the Mill Creek Farm from Dr. John Slater for 118 Pounds ($574.07). Thomas paid cash.[69] The farm had a house and buildings in place with land cleared for cultivation.

There is a question as to whether Thomas ever lived at Mill Creek Farm. Some records indicate he continued to reside in Elizabethtown and worked the farm without being resident on it but both McMurtry and Warren say that Thomas lived on the farm from its purchase until his marriage to Nancy.[70] It is also possible

---

[68] Louis A. Warren. "Abraham Lincoln's Father." *The Lincoln Kinsman*, page 2..
[69] Louis A. Warren. "The Romance of Thomas Lincoln and Nancy Hanks." *Indiana Magazine of History*, page 216.
[70] R. Gerald McMurtry. *The Thomas Lincoln Mill Creek Farm*, page 2.

that he and Nancy lived on the farm for a brief period while Thomas was building their home in Elizabethtown.

After Thomas purchased Mill Creek Farm, he brought his mother, Bathsheba, to Hardin County and settled her on the farm. His sister Nancy Lincoln Brumfield also moved to Mill Creek with her husband William. Thomas was doing well enough that he could provide for his extended family.

With October of 1803, Thomas was found on jury duty, a civic responsibility he took seriously and would perform many times. He served on the case of Isaac Bush versus Bennon and Sarah Shaw.[71] Isaac was the brother of Sarah Bush Johnston who would later become the second Mrs. Thomas Lincoln.

In November Thomas again served as prison guard.[72] His deed to the Mill Creek farm was recorded in November and he paid taxes on the property as listed in the Commissioner's book. What is seen of Thomas in these records is the pattern of his life in Elizabethtown. He works as a carpenter, cabinetmaker, farmer, prison guard, patrolman, and civic-minded citizen, paying his taxes, buying land, and making a successful living.

1804 is more of the same.[73]

- April 19 – served on an Elizabethtown jury with two different lawsuits.
- April 20 – served on an Elizabethtown jury for a lawsuit.
- August 8 – bought a new saw for $4.38.
- August 13 – appointed as a Cumberland County Marshall.
- October 16 – sold beef to Bleakley & Montgomery (merchants) in Elizabethtown. Merchant store records at Elizabethtown show Thomas had credit accounts with various businesses and that he paid his debts, keeping the accounts current.

Throughout 1804 there is record of Thomas making purchases for new tools and supplies and general merchandise for the home. In addition to taxes on his land, Thomas listed one horse on the Hardin County tax list. He also signed his name to a

---

[71] Louis A. Warren. "Abraham Lincoln's Father." *The Lincoln Kinsman*, page 2.
[72] Louis A. Warren. "Abraham Lincoln's Father." *The Lincoln Kinsman*, page 2.
[73] Louis A. Warren. "Abraham Lincoln's Father." *The Lincoln Kinsman*, page 3.

road petition along with his brothers Mordecai and Josiah, Francis Berry, and other neighbors and friends.

Somewhere in the early 1800's, Thomas was employed to construct a sawmill for Denton Geoghegan in Elizabethtown. Court records show that Geoghegan disputed Thomas' wages on the mill and that Thomas sued Geoghegan for payment. Thomas won the suit on March 25, 1807 and the judgment in Thomas' favor was upheld on appeal, but more time would drag on with more appeals before Thomas was paid.[74]

In 1805, Thomas was nominated to serve as an Ensign in the Kentucky Militia. He had served in active duty with the militia in 1795 and then continued in the militia until leaving Kentucky for Indiana. An Ensign was a step above the enlisted men, something equivalent to a Corporal or Sargent in today's terms but considered an officer in the militia. As an Ensign he mustered a company of Hardin County men four times a year, drilled them, and was prepared to lead them in battle if they were called to serve.[75] Thomas later purchased a sword (in 1807) to use as an appropriate weapon for a militia officer. Full records for Thomas' service were lost when the Commonwealth of Kentucky cleared out and destroyed older records to make room for Civil War records. The knowledge of Thomas' promotion to serve as Ensign was fortunately preserved in records in the governor's office.

During his years of living in Elizabethtown and at Mill Creek Farm, Thomas took the time to ride back to Beechland to visit with his brothers, friends, former neighbors, and Nancy Hanks. He had become a young man of good standing. He had a prospering trade in carpentry and cabinetmaking. He served in the militia. He owned a good farm where he was caring for his mother along with providing a place for his sister and her family. He was respected and looked to as prison guard and marshall. Thomas had taken the hard circumstances of his childhood and turned them with integrity into a life that made him a very eligible bachelor.

---

[74] R. Gerald McMurtry. *The Lincolns in Elizabethtown, Kentucky*, pages 2-3.
[75] James Cornelius. "Episode 22, Abraham Lincoln's Relationship with His Father, Thomas."

Mill Creek Farm, which Thomas worked alongside his family, was productive. Bleakley & Montgomery records show the merchants were purchasing produce and product from Thomas. Thomas sold beef and farm produce along with cupboards and cabinets. Thomas had expanded his craftsmanship to include being a cooper, making barrels. Thomas' account with Bleakley & Montgomery was often in Thomas' favor with more being credited for the merchants buying from Thomas than Thomas bought from them.[76]

The merchant records show that Thomas occasionally purchased tobacco. Thomas did not smoke but as with many in pioneer times, Thomas did on occasion chew. He also made occasional purchases of liquor but those were very occasional as Thomas rarely drank alcohol.

From the purchases Thomas made from Bleakley & Montgomery, Thomas must have dressed rather well for his day. Thomas did not buy the cheap stuff and did not solely rely on homespun and homemade. In 1805, Thomas purchased a hat costing $8.75 and suspenders priced at $2.19. Other items of clothing purchased showed the same flare toward being fashionably dressed. He was a successful young man courting the woman he hoped to marry and he dressed the part.[77]

As 1806 dawned, Thomas began preparations to marry Nancy Hanks. He had a wedding and infare to pay for and it was not going to be a simple affair. Fortunately, Mill Creek Farm was doing very well. In February, Thomas sold Bleakley & Montgomery 2400 pounds of pork and 494 pounds of beef.[78]

In March 1806, Thomas was appointed a patroller for the "northwardly" Hardin County district serving under Captain Christopher Bush. He was also employed in March by Bleakley & Montgomery to take a load of merchandise to New Orleans by flatboat. Thomas made a good profit selling product to the merchants and then made a good profit transporting it for them.

---

[76] Louis A. Warren. "The Romance of Thomas Lincoln and Nancy Hanks." *Indiana Magazine of History*, pages 216-217.

[77] Louis A. Warren. "The Romance of Thomas Lincoln and Nancy Hanks." *Indiana Magazine of History*, pages 216-217.

[78] R. Gerald McMurtry. *The Thomas Lincoln Mill Creek Farm*, page 4.

For the trip, which lasted from March through April and into May, Thomas made $150.[79]

Isaac Bush was Thomas' partner on the trip to New Orleans. They were on the flatboat when Sarah Bush married Daniel Johnston on March 13, 1806.[80] Isaac missed his sister's wedding. It is unknown if it was simply the timing of the business which caused him to miss the wedding or if the wedding was hastily arranged in his absence. After their business was completed in New Orleans, Thomas and Isaac returned to Kentucky by walking the entire distance.[81]

On the second of June 1806, Thomas signed his wedding bond to marry Nancy Hanks. Richard Berry Jr. signed as witness, representing Nancy.[82] It was time for a wedding.

Nancy Hanks

The family history of Nancy Hanks Lincoln is a maze that modern record searches and discoveries have not resolved. Albert Beveridge put it simply and poignantly. Nancy's ancestral history is as "dim as a dream of a shifting mirage, her face and figure waver through the mists of time and rumor."[83] It is hard to fit Nancy into a firm place in her family tree. The facts, such as they are, have been possibly forever clouded by the exaggerations and misstatements of her cousins Dennis Hanks and John Hanks who wanted to portray her a legitimate child, not a child born out of wedlock.

This lack of certainty fed the low place Nancy was given as William Herndon told the world she was a woman of low moral standards and that not only was Nancy born out of wedlock but she bore her children, including the future president, out of wedlock. History may not be clear on Nancy's ancestry and early years, but Herndon was wrong to malign her character. Herndon's

---

[79] Louis A. Warren. "The Romance of Thomas Lincoln and Nancy Hanks." *Indiana Magazine of History*, page 217.

[80] Louis A. Warren. *Lincoln's Youth Indiana Years Seven to Twenty-one 1816-1830*, pages 60-61.

[81] Douglas L. Wilson and Rodney O. Davis. *Herndon's Informants*, page 102. From a statement to Herndon by A. H. Chapman dated September 8, 1865.

[82] Louis A. Warren. "Abraham Lincoln's Father." *The Lincoln Kinsman*, page 4.

[83] Albert J. Beveridge. *Abraham Lincoln, Volume 1*, page 15.

Nancy, like Herndon's Thomas, provided early biography with a completely warped and inaccurate picture of Nancy Hanks Lincoln. Had the president lived, Herndon would never have dared paint Nancy as immoral, poor white trash.

President Linocln himself gives us the best starting place to understand Nancy's character. He said, "All that I am, or hope to be, I owe to my angel mother."[84] President Lincoln's love for his mother never waned. To the small boy in the grown man, she had stepped from this life to the next and it was to the inherited traits and teaching of this angel mother[85] that he owed who he had become.

Early Life

Nancy Hanks was born on February 5, 1784. Several locales have claimed to be her birthplace. Virginia, West Virginia, North Carolina, and Kentucky have all staked claims as her birth state.

- Kentucky: Mercer County, near the site of the Perryville Civil War battlefield.[86]
- North Carolina: Gaston County, near Belmont.[87]
- West Virginia: Mineral County, near Romney at a point known as Mile's Run on Patterson Creek. At the time of Nancy's birth, the site was part of Hampshire County, Virginia.[88]
- Virginia: Richmond County, near Tidewater.[89]

---

[84] J. G. Holland. *Holland's Life of Abraham Lincoln*, page 23.

[85] Referring to the dead as an angel was common in the 19th century. The dead became angels on the other side of death.

[86] One handwritten document in a Lincoln Financial Collection folder supports the Kentucky tradition. There is little support for Nancy having been born in Kentucky.

[87] The Carolina tradition is based on the future President's father not being Thomas but rather a man by name of Abraham Enloe. Enloe being the President's father has long since been disproven and even denied by Enloe.

[88] The West Virginia location was first documented by Lincoln scholar William Barton and supported by Ida Tarbell.

[89] The Tidewater tradition was proposed by Paul Verduin after researching additional archived records in Virginia. Most official Lincoln sites as well as most Lincoln scholars do not accept this location. There are also Virginia claims made for Amelia County where a large numbers of Hanks lived, and Nottoway County along Barebone Creek.

While there is still some controversy and disagreement over which of these is Nancy's birthplace, official Lincoln sites and most Lincoln scholars have settled on Nancy being born in Hampshire County, Virginia which, courtesy of the Civil War, became Mineral County, West Virginia. [90]

Lucy Hanks, Nancy's mother lived with her parents, Joseph and Ann Hanks, at the time Nancy was born. The Hanks' home was property Joseph owned in Hampshire County. Lucy was unwed when Nancy was born. Nancy's father has long been a matter of speculation and there remains no proof for who the father was. Speculation has made Nancy the daughter of Judge John Marshall, who lived in the area, or even George Washington who was known to have passed through the area in the general time period when Nancy would have been conceived.

The only indication we have of who Nancy's father was comes through an unsubstantiated statement William Herndon claimed President Lincoln told him. Herndon told of a buggy-ride with the President in 1850 in Mercer County, Illinois. He reports that Mr. Lincoln told him Nancy was the illegitimate daughter of a well-bred Virginia farmer.[91] Herndon did not tell this story until after Lincoln was dead and Herndon had begun gathering his records from friends and family.[92] It is odd that Lincoln, who did not share his inner thoughts except with the very closest of friends, would share this information with Herndon. Herndon was his law partner but they were not close personal friends and Herndon was never a confidante of Lincoln.

The story of Nancy being an illegitimate child proved true though some have tried to find a way around it. One theory was that her mother Lucy was not a Hanks by birth but rather Lucy Shipley. Lucy Shipley married James Hanks and it was stated Nancy was their legitimate daughter. This story explained why Nancy would have later gone to live with the Berry's as Lucy

---

[90] The West Virginia location was first documented by Lincoln scholar William Barton and supported by Ida Tarbell.

[91] David Herbert Donald. *Lincoln*, page 20.

[92] Following Lincoln's death, Herndon made no secret of the President's mother being illegitimate. In Emanuel Hertz' published collection of Herndon's letters (Emanuel Hertz; *The Hidden Lincoln, From the Letters and Papers of William H. Herndon*), Herndon repeats the information over and over to several people.

Shipley's sister Rachel married Richard Berry Sr. This version of Nancy's birth was widely accepted until DNA technology came into existence.

Mitochondrial DNA tests, reported in 2015, confirmed that Nancy was the descendent of Lucy Hanks but not Lucy Shipley Hanks. Lucy Hanks, the mother of Nancy Hanks, is a maternal match to the Hanks family through Annie Lee Hanks, wife of Joseph Hanks, who was sometimes called Nancy. The Nancy Hanks who would become Nancy Hanks Lincoln was named after her grandmother. There was no mitochondrial DNA match with the Shipley's. Lucy Hanks was the mother of Nancy Hanks and Lucy was the unwed daughter of Joseph and Ann Hanks.[93] These tests have fairly settled the question of Nancy's mother being Lucy Hanks and not Lucy Shipley.

Much of the confusion in Nancy's early life is caused by there being several women named Nancy Hanks, a few of them quite disreputable. The confusion around which Nancy Hanks was being spoken of and which history belonged to which Nancy was used to portray Lincoln's mother with an ugly past that we now know is not accurate.

Following Nancy's birth, Joseph Hanks moved his family from Virginia to Kentucky. Some tell that he came early, at about the same time or even the very same time as Captain Lincoln moved his family to Kentucky. Some say he came later. While there is a remote possibility that Joseph Hanks came to Kentucky at the same time as the Lincolns and Berrys,[94] it is most likely that the Hanks family moved to Kentucky somewhere in the mid 1780's, traveling the Wilderness Trail as had the Lincolns.

Joseph Hanks settled his family in Beechland with the Berrys and not far from the Lincolns. Soon after arriving in Kentucky, Nancy's mother Lucy left the family cabin and went out on her own. Lucy's reputation was not a good one. She was considered an immoral woman who left her illegitimate daughter with the grandparents so she could pursue her licentious ways. In 1790, Lucy was charged with fornication as a result of her lifestyle.

---

[93] Suzanne Hallstrom. "Nancy Hanks Lincoln mtDNA Study." *Family Tree DNA.*
[94] Star-Times. "Rumors Regarding Lincoln Family's Origin Disproved." *St. Louis Star-Times.*

Henry Sparrow stepped in to keep her from facing further shame and married her. It was then that Lucy changed her ways and became a fine Christian woman.[95] Two of her sons with Henry Sparrow became ministers. During this time, Nancy lived with and was raised by her grandparents.

In 1793, when Nancy was nine, Joseph Hanks died. Ann returned to Virginia. It is here that the confusing story of Nancy Hanks Lincoln diverges into two possible paths with history undecided on which is correct.

Nancy's Early Life – Version 1

In one version, Nancy goes to live with her mother and is raised by the Sparrows. This story has some support. It would have been the logical thing for Nancy to move from the Hanks' cabin to live with her mother. That Nancy lived with her mother and stepfather for any length of time, however, is doubtful. Henry and Lucy Sparrow visited Nancy after she and Thomas were married. Young Abraham knew them as Uncle Henry and Aunt Lucy because that was what Nancy called them.[96] That is not the form of address Nancy would have used had she been raised by her mother. It was Thomas and Betsy Sparrow, her mother's sister and husband, that she called mother and father.[97]

The issue of why Nancy called her mother "aunt" is resolved by the second part of this version of Nancy's history. Nancy left her mother's home after only a short stay and went to live with her aunt Elizabeth (Betsy), Lucy's sister, who had married Henry's brother Thomas. Betsy was childless and took Nancy in as her own to raise her. She became Nancy's mother and Lucy was called Aunt Lucy. Later, when Lucy and Betsy's sister Nancy had a child out of wedlock in 1799, Tom and Betsy took him in and raised him. That child was Dennis Hanks.

Nancy was 15 years old when Dennis was born. If she was still living with Tom and Betsy at this time, she would not have lived there for long. Dennis Hanks provided lots of information about Abraham Lincoln's life and the lives of his family but he

---

95 William E. Barton. *The Women Lincoln Loved*, page 41.
96 Ralph Gary. *Following In Lincoln's Footsteps*, page 208.
97 William E. Barton. *The Women Lincoln Loved*, page 66.

says little to indicate he was raised as a brother to Nancy. With Dennis' propensity to exaggeration and self-importance as an expert on Lincoln history, he would have made that point to prove he knew more than others. He did not.

The version of Nancy's early life being lived with the Hanks and then the Sparrows has Betsy Sparrow teaching Nancy to weave and sew, becoming a skilled seamstress who would then do some occasional work for the Berrys where she and Thomas would become acquainted and fall in love.

Nancy's Early Life – Version 2

The second version of Nancy's history has her going to live with the Berrys following her grandfather's death. Joseph lived in Beechland with his family and Nancy was a playmate of Richard Berry's children. She was frequently in his home. It is possible that the James Hanks who married Lucy Shipley brought the Hanks and Berry families together as relatives. This could be the reason Nancy's story so often mentioned Richard Berry Sr. as an uncle to Nancy and a part of the extended family structure she grew up in when she lived with her grandparents. When Joseph died, it was a simple step for Nancy to move in with the Berrys. This version of Nancy's life lines up with and makes sense of later events.

At age nine, when Nancy went to live with the Berrys, there were two Berry children still in the home: Francis and Edward. Richard Jr. and John had married and lived close by in homes of their own. The Berry family was well off. The Berry home, one of the largest in Washington County, was a double cabin made with hewn logs.[98] In an odd twist of fate, Richard Berry Sr. had two Black servants, Nan and her daughter Hannah. In 1792, the year before Nancy went to live with the Berrys, Richard listed two

---

[98] Raymond Warren. *The Prairie President*, page 6. It is known that the Berrys were among the richest in Beechland. Richard and Rachel's son Francis' home can be seen at the Lincoln Homestead Park near Springfield, Kentucky. Francis' home speaks of wealth and prestige. A different story is told by the cabin maintained and honored at Old Fort Harrod State Park in Harrodsburg, Kentucky. This cabin, supposedly the home of Richard and Rachel Berry where Nancy was married, is a small on room cabin, a cabin smaller than the cabin of Bathsheba Lincoln, Thomas' mother. The cabin at Fort Harrod, while vouchsafed as being the actual Richard Berry Sr. cabin, does not look like the cabin of a man of wealth, a slaveowner, with a large family.

slaves, ten horses, and thirty-four cattle for taxation purposes.[99] Since the two slaves were still with the Berry's at the time of Richard's death in 1797 but are not listed in Richard's will, it is likely they were freed prior to his death. Still, this puts both Nancy's and Thomas' childhoods in very close proximity to slavery.

Growing up with the Berrys would have given Nancy advantages. She was not reared in poverty. She learned the skills and crafts she needed to live in pioneer Kentucky. In the Berry home, she learned to read, a skill she would later teach to her famous son, a skill that was not likely in either the home of her mother or that of Tom and Betsy Sparrow. Though she could read, there are no existing records showing Nancy knew how to write. The known documents show her only making her mark.

Also, in the Berry home, Nancy learned to be a seamstress of some skill along with doing needlework. Nancy sewed for the Berrys and she hired out to make clothing.[100] She was known as being cheerful, intelligent, neat, and having a strong work ethic.

In 1797, Richard Berry died. His estate was divided among his children. Mordecai Lincoln, Thomas' brother, served as an appraiser[101] for the estate. Nancy continued to live in the family home with her Aunt Rachel, but as she was still a minor, Richard Berry Jr. became her legal guardian.[102] With Richard Berry Jr., Nancy would still be around slavery. At the time of his death, Richard Jr. owned nine slaves.[103]

Rachel died in 1804 when Nancy was twenty years old. There is no strong record for where she lived from that date until her marriage to Thomas. It is likely she stayed with either Richard Berry Jr. or, more likely, Francis Berry. Francis had built his home on a portion of his father's 800 acres that was deeded over to him when he married.

From the records of Washington County, Kentucky there is little doubt that Nancy, if brought up in the Berry family, was not

---

[99] Louis A. Warren. "The Richard Berry Family." *The Lincoln Kinsman*, page 2.
[100] Roger Norton. rogernorton.com.
[101] Louis A. Warren. "The Romance of Thomas Lincoln and Nancy Hanks." *Indiana Magazine of History*, page 213.
[102] Louis A. Warren. "The Richard Berry Family." *The Lincoln Kinsman*, page 8.
[103] Louis A. Warren. "The Richard Berry Family." *The Lincoln Kinsman*, page 8.

impoverished. With the Berrys, she would have been raised as a daughter, not a servant. She was provided a fair education for the time and place. She was popular amongst the people and was sought after by the men as a bride of worth.[104]

Nancy's Early Life – Summary Version

While both versions have their early and current proponents, something blended is likely closer to accurate. It is generally agreed that Nancy lived with her grandparents, Joseph and Ann Hanks, until 1793. At that point, she went to live with her mother and stepfather, Lucy and Henry Sparrow, but only briefly, probably for around a year or even less. From there Nancy lived with Betsy and Tom Sparrow, a couple near whom Nancy would live most of her life. The big question remains on when she moved out of the Sparrow home and in with the Berrys. Nancy would have gone to live with and work for the Berrys no later than 1800, probably earlier, prior to Dennis Hanks' birth in 1799. The date remains uncertain. Nancy lived with Richard and Rachel Berry until 1804 and then most likely with Francis Berry until her marriage to Thomas.

Regardless of preferred version, it was in the Beechland area that Nancy grew up and became the woman Thomas would court and marry. She had dark hair, dark complexion, hazel eyes, and a lean, tall frame. She is said to have stood almost as tall as Thomas (who was just under 6'). Nancy was somewhere from 5'7' to 5'10' tall. She weighed approximately 120 pounds. She was virtuous, respectable, shrewd, somewhat on the quiet side, good of memory, a woman with good judgment, and deeply religious.[105]

Marrying Thomas Lincoln

An old story is told about a revival in the early 1800's. This was the period of the Second Great Awakening and revivals were large events that often drew thousands to attend. As the story goes, Peter Cartwright was conducting such a revival. The

---

[104] Star-Times. "Rumors Regarding Lincoln Family's Origin Disproved." *St. Louis Star-Times.*

[105] Douglas L. Wilson and Rodney O. Davis. *Herndon's Informants*, page 615. From a letter of John Hanks to Jesse W. Weik dated June 12, 1887 from Linkville, Klamath County, Oregon.

meeting, as they often did, became active and emotional. A young man rose to his feet in fervor and began dancing and singing. In a few moments a young woman rose and joined the young man in dancing and singing and shouting praise. The two were Thomas Lincoln and Nancy Hanks. Later, Thomas and Nancy were introduced to each other and Thomas began courting this religious young woman who followed religion with the same gusto he did.[106]

Another romanticized story of Thomas meeting Nancy is told by noted Lincoln historian Carl Sandburg. Sandburg tells of how Thomas had first courted Sarah Bush, but she had turned him down. Then Thomas, beginning to wonder if he would ever find the woman God had destined to be his wife, fell asleep.

> *There came a strange dream of a path that led to a house he'd never seen before. Inside that house the chairs, the table, the fireplace was as real as though he were awake. At the fireside sat a young woman. As he came closer, he could see clear as crystal her face, eyes, and lips. She was paring an apple. The next morning, he valiantly tried to figure out what the dream meant. Was God trying to tell him something? It so haunted him that he left his brother Mordecai's cabin and took a walk. It wasn't long until the path ahead of him began to look familiar. So did the house at the end of it. The door was open, just as was true in the dream. As he peered in, chills went up his spine: there, by the very same fireplace, the exact woman in the dream sat – her face, eyes, and lips the same. And she was paring an apple! Years later, Thomas told this experience to his son. His son would never forget it.[107]*

These stories are quaint and fun, but they are fancier than history. When history does not provide all the details that are

---

[106] D. James Kennedy. *What They Believed: The Faith of Washington, Jefferson, and Lincoln*, page 2. Dr. Kennedy put the date of this revival as being 1809. If the Cartwright revival was in 1809, then the couple was not Thomas and Nancy. However, this revival and the response of the young couple represents the religious environment Thomas and Nancy would have participated in.

[107] Carl Sandburg. *The Prairie Years*, volume 1, pages 65-66.

wanted, legends and stories are often made to fill in the blanks. The story of the revival represents the religious tradition both Thomas and Nancy were raised in and lived in, but it is very unlikely that Thomas met Nancy at such an event. It is also unlikely that he dreamed of her in a vision. Reality was that the Hanks family lived in the Beechland area and were closely connected to the Berrys. The Berrys were close friends to Thomas and Bathsheba and Thomas' siblings. Thomas would have met the Hanks – and Nancy –after they came to Kentucky.

How and when Thomas began courting Nancy is a lost story. The tradition reflected in Sandburg's story that Nancy was Thomas' second choice comes mainly from William Herndon who held a certain bias against both Thomas and Nancy in his research. Herndon held Sarah Bush Lincoln in respect and gave her much credit for making Abraham the man he became. For Herndon, it made a better story if Thomas could not get a good woman on his first try, rather having to settle for a victim of poverty. It is possible that Thomas did court Sarah in Elizabethtown but the mists of time block that from sight. The historical coloring done by Herndon could reflect a truth that Thomas had early asked Sarah to be his wife and she turned him down in favor of Daniel Johnston but that does not in any way mean Nancy was less of a person or that Thomas had to settle for what he could get.

As Thomas grew into manhood and Nancy grew into womanhood, their families and friends drew them together. Thomas left the Beechland area to pursue his work as carpenter and cabinetmaker. He purchased land and established a farm. He worked as a prison guard, constable, and patroller. He became a respected part of his community. Nancy learned to be a skilled seamstress and weaver with all the skills necessary to run a pioneer household. They were not rich, but they were far from being impoverished.

It was in this reality that Thomas rode back and forth between his Elizabethtown home and Beechland to court Nancy and win her love. Somewhere in late 1805 or early 1806, Thomas rode again to Beechland, going to the home of Francis Berry where

Nancy was living. While he and Nancy were by the fireplace in the front room, Thomas proposed to Nancy and she accepted.[108]

There are no records to document the preparations Nancy made for her wedding. There are records of Thomas' preparations. The records are incomplete but what is extant is impressive. On May 3, 1806, Thomas went to Bleakley & Montgomery where he purchased a one-half cow skin for three shillings. This purchase is thought to have been turned into a new pair of boots made special for his wedding attire.[109]

A little later in May he made additional purchases to make a wedding outfit to be proud of.[110]

May 16, 1806	Pounds	Shillings	Pence
2 yards of cloth	3	12	0
1.75 yards of Jeans		11	10
1.5 yards Brown Holland		4	6
.25 yards Scarlet Cloth		15	0
3 Sticks of Twist		2	2
3 Skeins of Twist		2	3
3 Dozen Buttons		13	3
3.5 Yards Cassimere	2	12	3
2 Yards Tape			9
12 Buttons		1	6
108 Buttons		16	2
2 Yards B. H.		1	4
6 Skeins Thread			6
May 22, 1806			
3 Yards Coating	3	4	3

[108] There is also a tradition that Thomas proposed to Nancy at his mother's cabin in Beechland. It is impossible to know for certain but it seems more likely that Thomas would have met Nancy and proposed in the home where she was living.
[109] Louis A. Warren. "Kentucky's Most Important Wedding." *Lincoln Lore*, page 1.
[110] R. Gerald McMurtry. *A Series of Monographs Concerning the Lincolns and Hardin County, Kentucky*, page 2.

1 ½ Yards Br. Holland		4	9
1 ½ Yards Red Flannel		7	6
1 2/3 Dozen Buttons		6	3
2 Skeins Silk		1	6
1 Stick of Twist			9
2 Skeins of Thread			6
Paid May 22 in Cash	33	16	2

When Thomas made his purchases, he had a store credit with Bleakley & Montgomery of 49 pounds or around $200.[111] This was a substantial sum in 1806. It shows both that Thomas intended his wedding to be a well-dressed affair and that he had the means to make it so. His purchases used about three-fourths of his credit, leaving him additional funds for expenses to settle Nancy into their Elizabethtown home. In late 1805, Thomas had purchased a new hat for $8.75 and a pair of suspenders for $2.19. These were likely part of his wedding attire.[112] The record shows Thomas could afford good quality and he spent what he needed to get it.

For use after the wedding, Thomas purchased a tipt bridle for his horse. It cost him over $3.[113] The tipt bridle allowed for the bride to be comfortably seated behind the groom on his horse.

On June 10, 1806, Thomas was in Washington County making final preparations for the wedding. The law required that a bond be sworn out declaring there were no obstacles, legal or moral, to the couple being wed. Richard Berry Jr. went with Thomas to sign for Nancy, as tradition had the bride's attestation made by her father or legal guardian. Nancy was of legal age and did not technically require the signature of a guardian, but she honored Richard Jr., who was also a close friend of Thomas, with signing the bond as her representative.

---

[111] R. Gerald McMurtry. *A Series of Monographs Concerning the Lincolns and Hardin County, Kentucky*, page 3.

[112] R. Gerald McMurtry. *A Series of Monographs Concerning the Lincolns and Hardin County, Kentucky*, page 3.

[113] Louis A. Warren. "Kentucky's Most Important Wedding." *Lincoln Lore*, page 1.

Thomas' signature on the bond shows a legible, even somewhat fancy signature. Thomas may not have been a highly educated man, but his signature shows he was not illiterate.

A pioneer wedding in the early 1800's was a big happening. It provided a major social outlet to come together and celebrate community. Thomas and Nancy's wedding was a major event. The Hanks family came. The Berrys came. Friends and family travelled in from Elizabethtown and other communities. Four of Thomas' siblings were married with families of their own. They came. Homes were crowded with guests and others were camping where space was available.

Richard Berry Jr., with other relatives, was due in court on June 12, the day of the wedding. Thomas' brother, Mordecai, was a defendant in two lawsuits scheduled on that date. Jesse Head, the Methodist preacher who was to perform the ceremony was also a magistrate of the court and he also had business on the June 12 court docket. Court records show no business was conducted on that Thursday. Court was canceled to give the wedding priority.[114]

The family doctor, the man who would later give young Abraham his first book, Dr. Christopher C. Graham, was on hand for the festivities.[115] A childhood friend and possibly a distant cousin, Sarah Shipley Mitchell, served as Nancy's bridesmaid.[116]

There are two traditions for the location of the wedding. One tradition says the marriage was conducted in the home Richard and Rachel Berry. A building claimed to be that home is on the grounds of the Old Fort Harrod State Park in Harrodsburg, Kentucky. That cabin is too small to have been the actual home of the Berrys, one of the richest families in Beechland. It may have been a cabin on the Berry's land, and it could have been used for some purpose during the wedding festivities, but it was not the site of the ceremony.

---

[114] Louis A. Warren. "The Romance of Thomas Lincoln and Nancy Hanks." *Indiana Magazine of History*, page 221.

[115] Lincoln Financial Collection. Nancy Hanks wedding folder. Letter from John W. Muir to Mrs. Mary Jane Hubler of the Lincoln Library and Museum in Fort Wayne, dated July 20, 1981.

[116] Louis A. Warren. "Kentucky's Most Important Wedding." *Lincoln Lore*, page 1.

The other, and more likely, tradition is that Thomas and Nancy were married at the Francis Berry home. With the number of people attending, the ceremony would have been held on the grounds, not actually in the house. The area has been described as near the meandering Beech Fork, a small river flowing in a horseshoe around Beechland, surrounded by an amphitheater of rolling hills.[117] The grounds of Francis Berry's home made a beautiful site for the wedding which was held at sunset.

As mentioned previously, the Berrys owned slaves. Thomas' Uncle Isaac, the uncle he worked for in Tennessee, owned six slaves.[118] It is very probable these slaves were in attendance and working as servants catering the needs of the wedding. Thomas and Nancy's wedding was a fancy affair, a community gathering and celebration that would have been the talk of the area for a long time.

The wedding was consecrated by the Rev. Jesse Head on June 12, 1806. Jesse was a well-known local minister and someting of a character. A jingle has survived time and tells us about his appearance. "His nose is long, and his hair is red, and he goes by the name of Jesse Head."[119]

The wedding was just the start of the festivities. June 13 continued the festivities with the infare. The infare was a reception held the next day to provide a feast and continue the celebration of the newlywed couple. The Lincoln's infare was at the home of Richard Berry. This could be where the confusion comes in with some believing that the wedding was at Richard Berry's rather than Francis Berry's. The infare was major feast. Richard Berry Jr. hosted the infare and it featured the best of all that was available: roast venison, bear steak, barbecued sheep, roasted wild turkeys and ducks, fruit and maple syrups, peaches and honey, and a wide range of side dishes. There was singing and music and dancing. It

---

[117] Douglas L. Wilson and Rodney O. Davis. *Herndon's Informants*, page 585. The scene and story of the wedding is taken from a story in the Indianapolis Journal. The clipping was sent to Herndon in 1874. It was then carried in the Louisville Courier-Journal on February 20, 1874. The story's origin appears to be Charlotte S. Hobart Vawter who claimed that her grandmother, Sarah Mitchell, was first cousin to Nancy.

[118] Ronald C. White Jr. *A. Lincoln*, page 16.

[119] William E. Barton. *The Women Lincoln Loved*, page 76.

was a luxurious affair to honor the joining of Thomas and Nancy in matrimony.[120]

Following the wedding and celebration, Thomas and Nancy took up residence in Elizabethtown. Thomas was 28. Nancy was 23.

Elizabethtown Continued

Following the wedding and infare, Thomas took his bride to their new home in Elizabethtown, often called E-Town as it still is today. Elizabethtown, the county seat of Hardin County, was a prosperous and growing community comprised mainly of families which had come from Pennsylvania and Virginia.[121] It was a pioneer town in what was then the far west of American settlement.

Thomas had purchased two lots in Elizabethtown and built a log cabin on one. The location of the lots has never been determined but it is known that he bought his lots from the sections laid out in 1793 by Andrew Hynes. Each lot was a half-acre in size except for a few lots around the town square which were a quarter acre each.[122] By the assessed value of $40, Thomas' lots were not the smaller ones. He had a town cabin on an acre of ground. This property was in addition to his Mill Creek farm.

The cabin was like other cabins built in Elizabethtown with hewed logs, shingled roof, plank flooring, and windows either of glass or greased paper. It was a comfortable home for Thomas and Nancy. Thomas was known to have built several of the homes in Elizabethtown as well as his own. This fact has added to the confusion in identifying where Thomas' home stood. Further confusion was added by Samuel Haycraft later identifying Sarah Bush Johnston's home as that of Thomas and Nancy. Haycraft wrote to Herndon letting him know that Thomas and Nancy's home was still standing in 1865 but had been moved three times, twice used as a slaughterhouse, and was — at the time of the letter — a stable standing approximately fifty yards from its original

---

[120] Ida Tarbell. *Boy Scouts Life of Lincoln*, page 2.

[121] R. Gerald McMurtry. *The Lincolns in Elizabethtown, Kentucky*, pages 1-2.

[122] R. Gerald McMurtry. *The Lincolns in Elizabethtown, Kentucky*, page 5.

location.[123] Haycraft was in error and had described the history of the Johnston home.

As Thomas and Nancy began their married life, Thomas is described as a man of great physical strength, though slightly stoop shouldered (which made him appear shorter than his full height) and with a prominent nose. Those who knew him said he was peaceable but could be a fierce antagonist when the need arose. He was very fond of jokes and stories and was a master at telling them.[124] He had a scant education though enough to read some and write enough to sign his name and keep records. He knew enough math to handle the needs of his personal accounting and business requirements. Nancy, though we have no evidence she could write, could read and was noted for a keen intellect and a fine memory. It was a common thing for the times that someone would learn to read but not learn how to write.[125]

Thomas and Nancy settled into their new home. Thomas no doubt made some of their furniture and he purchased items he could not make. On June 14, he purchased household items, knives, and forks from Bleakley & Montgomery.[126] At the same time, he purchased three skeins of silk for Nancy.[127] On August 4, he bought a set of spoons.[128] Throughout 1806 Thomas made various household purchases as Nancy settled into the cabin and let him know what was needed to make the cabin a proper home. One such purchase was from the auction of Thomas McIntire's estate. Thomas purchased a "Bason and Spoons" for $3.34 along with a "Dish and Plates" for $2.68.[129] The money doesn't sound like much to today's ears but those were substantial purchases at the time.

---

[123] Douglas L. Wilson and Rodney O. Davis. *Herndon's Informants*, page 67. From a letter of Samuel Haycraft to Herndon from Elizabethtown, Kentucky dated June 1865.

[124] William H. Herndon & Jesse W. Weik. *Herndon's Life of Lincoln*, page 12.

[125] Charles B. Strozier. "Lincoln's 'Angel Mother' and His Surrogate Fathers" page 2.

[126] Louis A. Warren. "Abraham Lincoln's Father." *The Lincoln Kinsman*, pages 5-6.

[127] Louis A. Warren. "Kentucky's Most Important Wedding." *Lincoln Lore*, page 1.

[128] Louis A. Warren. "Abraham Lincoln's Father." *The Lincoln Kinsman*, pages 5-6.

[129] W. E. Barton. *Life of Lincoln Volume I*, page 73.

What kind of man was it Nancy Hanks had married? Dennis Hanks' son-in-law, Colonel A. H. Chapman, spoke of Thomas as being very industrious, remarkably good-natured, fond of hearing a good joke and telling one, fond of hunting and a good hunter who always kept a fine rifle but who never neglected work on the farm to go hunting. Thomas never cared for fishing. He was temperate in his habits, never intoxicated in his life. He was a very hearty eater but did not much care what kind of food he had. (This is another characteristic he would share with Abraham.) He was happy with plenty of cornbread and milk. Thomas was a strictly moral man who did not use profane and vulgar language. He could read and write some but was not highly educated. He took the world easy, generally happy with his lot in life even though he found himself unlucky in business in his later life.[130]

Thomas' strength and ability are illustrated by an incident that occurred in Hardinsburg, Kentucky. A man named William Breckenridge was declared the best man in Breckenridge County, able to defeat any comer. Thomas' friends took exception to the claim and made counterclaim that Thomas could defeat Breckenridge. The challenge was brought to the two men and they accepted. Such sport was common on the frontier. One version of the story has Thomas defeating his opponent in less than two minutes without getting a scratch for his trouble.[131] Another version has the contest being long and tedious but with the same result. This version reported the man's name as Hardin rather than Breckenridge.[132]

Thomas was a man who did not fatigue easily, who had uncommon endurance. He was known for courage and honesty.

With the dawn of 1807, Bleakley & Montgomery records show Thomas continued to keep his account in good standing and to purchase various household items and carpentry supplies. In

---

[130] Douglas L. Wilson and Rodney O. Davis. *Herndon's Informants*, pages 96-97. From the statement of A. H. Chapman to Herndon on September 8, 1865.
[131] Douglas L. Wilson and Rodney O. Davis. *Herndon's Informants*, page 28. From an Erastus Wright interview of Dennis Hanks sent by letter to Herndon from Chicago, Illinois on June 8, 1865.
[132] Douglas L. Wilson and Rodney O. Davis. *Herndon's Informants*, page 37. From interview of Dennis Hanks at Chicago, Illinois on June 13, 1865. Dennis Hanks was not the most consistent source of information as evidenced by both versions of the story having their source in him.

January, at a sale, he purchased more dishes and plates for the home.[133]

On February 10, 1807, Nancy gave birth to their firstborn child, Sarah, at the home in Elizabethtown. No stories record the couple's reaction, but Thomas is noted by family and friends as a man who loved his wife and children. There can be little doubt that he was a proud father. The February birth date raises a question that cannot be answered. Sarah was born eight months after the wedding. Was she a month premature or did the engaged couple consummate their union a month before the wedding? History has no answer for that question.

Early 1807 saw the start of a long, drawn-out lawsuit with Denton Geoghegan to obtain wages owed to Thomas. Lawsuits in the 1800s were common. As Thomas pursued his lawsuit, in April 1807 he was once again called to serve on a jury.[134]

At this point in his life Thomas had an established reputation as a skilled furniture maker, cabinetmaker, and carpenter. He helped in or managed the construction of several homes and businesses in the town and area. He built a mill dam. He built furniture and cabinets of all kinds. He was skilled in making mantels, stairways, door sills, and window facings. The farm where Bathsheba Lincoln lived was a land investment and sideline to his carpentry business but, in later life as his sight failed, farming would become a means of earning a living and putting food on the table.

In Elizabethtown and the surrounding area, Thomas' reputation as an expert woodworker kept him busy. In addition to his carpentry skills, he was a wheelwright and a cooper. He was very skilled in woodworking of all types. Thomas' work as a cabinetmaker and furniture maker displays his skill. His work was not rough frontier pioneer furniture featuring sawed logs roughly put together to be functional but little more. Thomas' pieces were finely finished, pieces that became treasured heirlooms in many homes. His furniture is now proudly displayed in homes and museums.

---

[133] Louis A. Warren. "Abraham Lincoln's Father." *The Lincoln Kinsman*, pages 5-6.
[134] Louis A. Warren. "Abraham Lincoln's Father." *The Lincoln Kinsman*, pages 5-6..

The furniture now gracing the Bathsheba Lincoln Cabin at Lincoln Homestead Park is of basic design, sturdy and well built. Thomas built many pieces in that simple style, but others paid him for more ornate work, and he had the skill to do the work.

The Indiana State Museum has a corner cabinet made from cherry wood with a delicate scroll inlay, possibly from beechwood. The Lincoln Presidential Library in Springfield, Illinois is in possession of a "fall front" desk, also made from cherry wood. The desk has glass doored shelves as a second piece setting on the desk. The desk was made for Spencer County, Indiana's first physician, Dr. Crook, and was used as a writing table in his office for many years. It is a beautiful piece of furniture.[135]

Thomas' home was furnished with furniture of his making and the furnishings were not primitive or "make do". An example is a corner cupboard that graced the Lincoln home at Knob Creek. Made from cherry wood, the cupboard has a carved and inlaid dentil running under the cornice along with decorative strips on the front with a four-pointed star and vine inlay.[136] Thomas' skill in woodworking allowed him to make many kinds of pieces in many different styles. It is little wonder that his skill was respected highly in Elizabethtown as he and Nancy settled in.

After marriage, Thomas worked the Mill Creek farm during crop time with his mother, sister, and brother-in-law while maintaining a thriving carpentry/cabinetmaking business in Elizabethtown and the surrounding area. Dennis Hanks told that Thomas split his time between farming and woodworking according to which provided the most profit. Hanks also recorded that Thomas worked as a mechanic.[137] Thomas being a mechanic shows up again later when he works in and runs a mill. It also shows with Abraham who dabbled at inventing and mechanics. Thomas passed some of that skill and interest on to his son.

---

[135] Abraham Lincoln Association. *Thomas Lincoln: Carpenter and Cabinet Maker 2016 Calendar*, cover picture and February.

[136] Abraham Lincoln Association. *Thomas Lincoln: Carpenter and Cabinet Maker 2016 Calendar*, July.

[137] Douglas L. Wilson and Rodney O. Davis. *Herndon's Informants*, page 28. From an Erastus Wright interview of Dennis Hanks and sent by letter to Herndon from Chicago, Illinois on June 8, 1865.

Samuel Haycraft Jr. wrote to Herndon describing the work Thomas had done for his father, Samuel Haycraft Sr. He talked of Thomas as being called *Linkhorn* (the Midwest accent most likely made the name sound more like *Linkern*) even though the name was always spelled Lincoln. Thomas had done the joiners work on the family home when Samuel Jr. was a lad. At the time of his letter, Haycraft said the work was still in place and sturdy.[138] The fact that Thomas' work was still in good condition in 1865 speaks to quality labor and workmanship.

Being a house-joiner was a skill Thomas learned as a youth along with his carpentry and cabinetmaker skills.[139] It was on these skills that Thomas relied for income working in and around Elizabethtown. Farming was a supplement.[140]

Thomas' life in Elizabethtown with Nancy and baby Sarah continued along the same pattern during the remainder of 1807 and 1808 as it had leading up to his marriage. He worked his farm during crop growing season and worked his carpentry and cabinetmaking business at other times. The records of Bleakley & Montgomery show he continued to purchase business supplies and household items. He served on a jury three times in 1808 (April 25, June 17, November 15). The April jury Thomas served on was a Grand Jury which delivered an indictment. He served again as prison guard in 1808.[141]

One thing that should be noted regarded the many times Thomas served on juries is that jurors were not randomly selected in the 1800s. Jurors were chosen to appear for duty by the sheriff. If the sheriff did not want someone, that person was not called to serve.[142] Thomas' reputation in his communities was such that the sheriff trusted him to serve as a juror.

In the Fall of 1808, Thomas moved his family to the Sinking Spring farm, also called the South Fork farm. It was here that his life moved from obscurity into the annals of history with the birth of his son, Abraham.

---

[138] Douglas L. Wilson and Rodney O. Davis. *Herndon's Informants*, page 67. Letter of Samuel Haycraft to Herndon from Elizabethtown, Kentucky dated June 1865.

[139] Wayne C. Temple. *Thomas and Abraham Lincoln As Farmers*, page 15.

[140] Wayne C. Temple. *Thomas and Abraham Lincoln As Farmers*, page 17.

[141] Louis A. Warren. "Abraham Lincoln's Father." *The Lincoln Kinsman*, pages 5-6.

[142] Walter B. Stevens, *A Reporter's Lincoln*, page 33.

Sinking Spring Farm

Thomas owned two lots with a house in Elizabethtown. He owned the Mill Creek Farm where his mother lived with Thomas' sister and her husband. As the Brumfield family took over more of the work at Mill Creek and needed the farm to support them, Thomas looked for another spot to meet the needs of his family. His friend, Isaac Bush, had obtained the Sinking Spring farm and was interested in selling it. In the purchase, Thomas placed his trust in circumstances that would later prove untrustworthy.

Thomas paid Bush $200 in cash for the 300 acre Sinking Spring farm, but the money never made its way to the actual deed owner of the land. Land dealings in pioneer Kentucky could be complicated. Land quickly changed hands and surveys were not consistent. Recording and clearing deeds by the state government was lax.

The Sinking Spring farm was originally part of a 30,000-acre land grant to William Greene in 1783. The land became part of Hardin County in 1792. Joseph James purchased 15,000 acres from Greene, acreage including Sinking Spring farm. He sold out to a New York land speculator, Richard Mather. In 1805, David Vance bought Sinking Spring farm from Mather. Vance turned out to be a problem. Vance did not complete payment to Mather for the land before assigning the land to Isaac Bush. Monies Vance received from Bush did not get paid in turn to Mather. Vance then disappeared.

After Bush sold the land to Thomas, the Mather family began legal action to reclaim the land. Thomas offered to pay but payment was refused for reasons unknown.[143] Thomas, through no fault of his own, would lose the farm.

When Thomas moved to the Sinking Spring farm in the Fall of 1808, he continued to do business in Elizabethtown. Elizabethtown was the county seat and Thomas, farming on the side, worked a busy carpentry and cabinetmaking trade in Elizabethtown. Thomas' main income came from his woodworking trades with farming was a supplement.[144] He also

---

[143] National Park Service. www.nps.gov/abli/planyourvisit/ sinkingspringfarm.htm.
[144] Wayne C. Temple. *Thomas and Abraham Lincoln As Farmers*, page 17.

continued with other work he had previously done, serving as a prison guard in January 1809.[145]

When the family moved to Sinking Spring, Nancy was pregnant with Abraham. If Thomas had remained in Elizabethtown a few more months, Elizabethtown would have had the honor of being the birthplace of America's greatest president, but the honor moved with the family to the Sinking Spring farm outside Hodgenville.

Sinking Spring farm was within an area known as the Barrens. The Barrens was a 400 square mile region that had been repeatedly burned off by Native Americans to create grazing land for game. The area had trees and undergrowth along streams but was largely tall grass.[146] This Native American use of the area made it a prime hunting ground, providing Thomas and other settlers plenty of game for their tables. Thomas loved to hunt and was an excellent hunter. His family was well provided with a variety of meat.

Sinking Spring farm had a large spring that bubbled up from a cave, flowed through a limestone channel, then returned underground via a sinkhole. The spring was sometimes referred to as Rock Creek and Sinking Spring farm was located on the south fork of Nolin Creek. This has led some to call this farm the South Fork farm and some have called it the Rock Creek farm.[147] The proximity of water was a big asset for the farm and cabin.

Thomas built a cabin on the high ground not far from the spring. The cabin was of the same type and size most pioneers built. Roughly 18 feet by 16 feet, it was built from hewn logs with walls about seven or eight feet in height. The space between the logs was chinked with a mixture of clay and stone, insulating the cabin and closing any gaps. Wood shake shingles formed the roof. There was one window in the front wall and one door in the middle of the front wall. Thomas' skills as a carpenter made these sturdy and secure against the weather. The window was likely covered with animal skins or oiled paper when not open or with the shutter closed in cold weather. A fireplace large enough to heat

---

[145] Louis A. Warren. "Abraham Lincoln's Father." *The Lincoln Kinsman*, pages 5.
[146] Robert W. Blythe, Maureen Carroll, and Steven Moffson. Revised and updated by Brian F. Coffey. *Abraham Lincoln Birthplace National Historic Site, Historic Resource Study.*
[147] J. T. Hobson. *Footprints of Abraham Lincoln*, page 16.

the cabin and give plenty of space for cooking and heating water was built on one end of the cabin with the chimney on the outside of the wall. Thomas built a mantel for the fireplace. The floor could have been planked or been left hard packed earth. Tradition says it was hard packed earth.

During the week prior to Abraham's birth, Thomas was in Elizabethtown in court but returned prior to the Sunday when Abraham was born.[148]

Abraham Born

It was into this standard pioneer cabin that Abraham Lincoln was born on February 12, 1809, Thomas and Nancy's second child and first son. Thomas was 31. Nancy had just turned 25.

On the Sunday morning when Abraham was born, Nancy was lying on a pole bed. A young neighbor, Peggy Walters, assisted in the birth. She reported that Nancy's labor was harder than some, easier than others, somewhat slow, but with no problems. Abraham was born near sunrise.[149] Betsy Sparrow, Nancy's aunt by blood but whom she called mother and Abraham would call granny, held little Abraham as he came from the womb. She washed him and dressed him in a small yellow shirt.[150] Peggy Walters remembered Abraham's birth and spoke of it to friends and neighbors after Abraham became president. Her story gives insight into the Lincoln home.

> *It was Saturday afternoon, I remember, when Tom Lincoln sent over and asked me to come, and I got up behind the boy that rode across to fetch me, and I rode across to the cabin that then stood here. It was a short ride, less than a mile. It was winter, but it was mild weather, and I don't think there was any snow. If there was any then, it wasn't much, and no snow fell that night. It was a clear night. I was here all night. They sent for me quite as soon as there was any need, for when I got here nothing much was happening. They sent for the two aunts, Mis' Betsy Sparrow and Mis' Polly Friend, and these both came, but*

---

[148] W. E. Barton, *Life of Abraham Lincoln, Volume I, page 5.*
[149] Roger Norton. www.rogernorton.com.
[150] William E. Barton. *The Women Lincoln Loved*, page 48.

they lived about two miles away, so I was there before them, and we all had quite a spell to wait, and we got everything ready that we could.

They were poor folks, but so were most of their neighbors, and they didn't lack anything they needed. Nancy had a good feather-bed under her; it wasn't a goose-feather bed, hardly anyone had that kind then, but good hen feathers. And she had blankets enough. There was a little girl there, two years old. Her name was Sarah. She went to sleep before much of anything happened.

Well, there isn't much that a body can tell about things of that kind. Nancy had about as hard a time as most women, I reckon, easier than some and maybe harder than a few. It all came along kind of slow, but everything was regular and all right. The baby was born just about sunup, on Sunday morning. Nancy's two aunts took the baby and washed him and dressed him, and I looked after Nancy. That's about all there is to tell. I remember it better than I do some cases that came later, because I was young, and hadn't had so much experience as I had afterward. But I remember it all right well.

Oh, yes, and I remember one other thing. After the baby was born, Tom came and stood beside the bed and looked down at Nancy, lying there, so pale and so tired, and he stood there with that sort of a hang-dog look that a man has, sort of guilty like, but mighty proud, and he says to me "Are you sure she's all right, Mis' Walters?" And Nancy kind of stuck out her hand and reached for his, and said, "Yes, Tom, I'm all right."[151]

Word of the birth spread quickly, and neighbors came to help around the house and to celebrate the newborn. Dennis Hanks tells of following an old pioneer tradition of running to greet the

---

[151] William E. Barton. *The Women Lincoln Loved*, pages 82-83.

newborn and claimed to be the second man, Thomas being the first, to touch the infant boy.[152]

As Thomas held his newborn son, the memories of the little boy who had sat on the ground next his dying father were very present. Those memories, showing the love and respect Thomas held for his own father, placed the name Abraham on the infant boy, naming his first son after Captain Lincoln. For Thomas and Nancy, there was no better name for their son than the name of the father Thomas loved and lost so early in life.

When Abraham was born, Thomas owned both Mill Creek farm and Sinking Spring farm. He also owned two lots, with house, in Elizabethtown. He had yet to try out farming at Sinking Spring, but he had proven successful and competent on the Mill Creek land. He had a thriving and prosperous carpentry and cabinetmaking business. He was respected by his family, friends, and neighbors. Life was simple in pioneer Kentucky, but it was good for Thomas and his small family.

The Paternity Issue

Few rumors and falsehoods have been as damaging to Thomas and Nancy Lincoln as that perpetuated by Abraham Lincoln's law partner, William Herndon. President Lincoln, while not close to his father in later life, would have been appalled and angered at Herndon for the dishonor he heaped on the woman Lincoln credited with making him the man he became, his angel mother, Nancy. In declaring that Thomas was not Abraham's biological father, Herndon put Nancy in the position of being considered a disreputable and immoral woman.

Most historians now recognize that the stories of Thomas not being Abraham's father are baseless. As the stories declaring Thomas impotent have receded from public sight and acceptance, the internet continues to provide a forum for those detractors of President Lincoln who want to find some way to defame him regardless of the lack of substance and fact in their portrayals of Thomas and Nancy. These detractors still somehow believe that making Abraham Lincoln the son of a promiscuous woman and

---

[152] Douglas L. Wilson and Rodney O. Davis. *Herndon's Informants*, page 38. From Herndon's interview of Dennis Hanks on June 13, 1865 in Chicago.

her less than admirable husband somehow places a stain on the noble achievements of the President. That kind of judgmental bias is outdated and foolish, especially when the fact that it is based on falsehoods is brought to light. Still, despite the truth being so readily available, the stories of Thomas not being Abraham's father continue to thrive in a small subculture of America.

The stories of Abraham Lincoln being a bastard child or, as politer nineteenth century people said, low-flung, began circulating closely following his nomination to run for President on the Republican ticket. The game of politics in the nineteenth century was down and dirty, much like it is in twenty-first century America. It was a time when lies and accusations were easily published. Media picked sides and withheld stories about the good of a person while brandishing any story that maligned his character. In the nineteenth century, the sin of the mother carried over to the children. Being an illegitimate child was of great consequence. A bastard child was considered a lesser human, shamed from birth, covered by and guilty of the sin of the parents. The low-flung child was considered to have inherited the low morals of his or her parents. It was the proverbial "the apple does not fall far from the tree" kind of thinking.

Over time, many were claimed as the father of Abraham Lincoln by fornication with Nancy Hanks. Thomas was known as Abraham's father to his friends and neighbors and was the man Abraham claimed as father. Three men of similar name were said to be Abraham's father: Abraham Enloe of Swain County, North Carolina; Abraham Enlow of Hardin County, Kentucky; and Abraham Inlow of Bourbon County, Kentucky. In addition, some claimed others: Martin D. Hardin of Kentucky, Adam Springs of North Carolina, John C. Calhoun of South Carolina, Henry Clay of Kentucky, George Brownfield of Kentucky, and several others.[153] There was a plethora of men who were blamed with fathering Abraham Lincoln.

Herndon latched on to the stories told by the President's political enemies and used his position as Lincoln's law partner to do more harm than any of Abraham Lincoln's enemies could have

---

[153] J. G. De Roulhac Hamilton. "The Many-Sired Lincoln." *The American Mercury*, page 130.

done. Herndon accepted that Abraham Enloe was Abraham Lincoln's father through an affair with Nancy Hanks. His belief and the way he twisted it around is clearly told in his letters. As Herndon researched the early life of the President, he built his theory and searched for facts to support it. In 1866, Herndon wrote to Charles Hart.

> *In the first place his grandmother was a halfway prostitute – not a common one, as I understand the facts. I say this is truth, for Mr. Lincoln told me so. Mr. Lincoln's mother was an illegitimate. This is truth, for Mr. L. told me so. As a matter of course Mr. L. knew this. It saddened his own mother, and it saddened Lincoln – sadness more or less has been stamped on him. Again – and what is worse – Mrs. Lincoln, A. Lincoln's mother, fell – fell in Kentucky about 1805 – fell when unmarried – fell afterward. Thomas Lincoln left Kentucky on that account; and for no other as I understand the story. There can be not much doubt of this as I now think, and yet there is room for mistake. I am going to Kentucky to search this whole matter to the bottom, and if false I shall scare some wicked men, I assure you. I must get absolutely right myself before I dare open. Mr. Lincoln was informed of all this; probably it was thrown up to him in Indiana and – don't know it – have heard so. As a matter of course in so sensitive a soul as Lincoln's it burned its way and left him a withered melancholy man.[154]*

Herndon said he would search out and find the truth, but he was already leaning to the answer that would work best for how he wanted to portray Lincoln for history so Lincoln could rise from the lowest place to the highest honor. In 1870, he wrote to Ward Lamon.

> *In the matter of Lincoln's legitimacy, at one time I thought the world lied in him when it stated that he was a bastard.*

---

[154] Emanuel Hertz. *The Hidden Lincoln, From the Letters and Papers of William H. Herndon,* page 52. From Herndon letter to Charles H. Hart dated December 28, 1866.

On further investigation, I now and have for years believed him the son of Enloe. My opinions are formed from the evidence before you, and in a thousand other things, some of which I heard from Lincoln, others are inferences springing from his acts, from what he said, and from what he didn't say. In the first place, Lincoln himself told me that his mother was a bastard, that she was an intellectual woman, a heroic woman, that his mind he got from his mother, etc. This was told me about 1852, three miles west of this city on our way to court in Petersburg, Menard County, and State of Illinois; he told me about Dennis Hanks' bastardy. He told me that his relations were lascivious, lecherous, not to be trusted. Again, it is a fact that Thomas Lincoln had children when in Kentucky, and when he went to Indiana he had none, ceased to have any. If you remember, Mr. Thomas Lincoln courted his second wife when a girl, that she rejected him, that she subsequently married another man, that Thomas Lincoln married – both Lincoln's mother and Lincoln's step mother by their husbands had children – that Lincoln's second wife was prolific when her husband lived, that in the prime of life she married Thomas Lincoln and ceased suddenly to be prolific when she was so with her first husband. It is true that Thomas Lincoln had a fight with Enloe, as said, because he caught Enloe with his wife. It is true that Lincoln left Kentucky and why, I was informed, to take her away from Enloe and general surrounding bad influences. I may not have recorded this, but I have been told so and it looks to me to be proven forever true. It is true that Lincoln was incapable of getting a child; because he had the mumps, etc. Lincoln was in Indiana in 1844, I think – your records will tell you when – and that he put up no tombstone to his mother's grave; and I forget whether he ever went to see her grave. Your records will state the truth exactly. For these reasons and for others floating in my mind I am convinced that the weight of evidence is that Mr. Lincoln was an illegitimate. The evidence is not conclusive, but men have been hung on less evidence. From what Lincoln has casually and indirectly said, I was convinced that his illegitimacy was thrown up to him when a boy. I think he was told of the fight between his father and Enloe, and the cause of it. I got this as I remember it in casual conversations in Indiana. I did not reduce everything to writing, not at that time deeming it of importance. Now I know better. I left out nothing important to the understanding of Lincoln, standing by himself.[155]

Herndon fully accepted that Nancy had low morals and that Thomas was not Abraham's father. Unfortunately for Herndon, there was no evidence of a fight between Thomas and Enloe. There was no evidence to support the claim that Enloe ever had any relations with Nancy. As Herndon began to spread his ill-founded belief through his lectures and in selling the story to Ward Lamon for use in Lamon's biography of Lincoln, Herndon was called to account. One who derided Herndon for his falsities regarding Lincoln's parents was Major J. W. Gordon. Gordon had written a letter to the Saturday Herald in 1883 publishing the proof that Thomas and Nancy were married before Abraham was born and refuting Herndon's main point in support of Lincoln being illegitimate. Herndon, caught and unable to refute what were solid facts, prevaricated and tried to excuse himself by backing away from what he had been saying and writing. Herndon wrote to the Indianapolis Herald in 1883.

Mr. Gordon says in the published letter, this: 'Mr. Herndon too has seemed equally willing to cast reproach upon the memory of the great martyr's parents.' This I deny. No man cast reproach upon the parents of Mr. Lincoln. Mrs. Lincoln was a good woman – a noble woman and an intellectual one. Thomas Lincoln was a good man and an honest one. In my lecture spoken of here, and by Mr. Gordon, I said on looking over the whole evidence then

---

[155] Emanuel Hertz. *The Hidden Lincoln, From the Letters and Papers of William H. Herndon*, pages 63-64. From Herndon letter to Ward Lamon dated February 20, 1870.

known and before us of the marriage that I knew that Thomas Lincoln and Nancy Hanks were lawfully and honestly married. I simply asked the question, did they jump a broomstick as ceremony of marriage, etc? The question was simply a question and not a charge of any kind. I was debating the question on the proofs. Now the proofs of the marriage in proper form have been put in evidence, and they settle the question of the marriage and that is all they do settle. There is much behind them that is not necessary now and here to mention. I would advise Mr. Gordon not to jump into print, nor enter into this controversy till he understands all the facts. I am glad the records are all produced; they were produced before Mr. Gordon produced them as I am informed. I am satisfied of the lawful marriage of Nancy Hanks and Thomas Lincoln, and now bless their memories forever.[156]

The falsity of Herndon's letter to the Indianapolis Herald was quickly revealed as he continued to pursue any kind of proof that Thomas was not Abraham's father. In 1885, Herndon wrote to Jesse Weik, the man he had hired to ghost write his biography of Lincoln.

Do not say anything about my supposed theory of Lincoln's paternity, as it will be liable to misconstruction. I have the facts of Lincoln's paternity, etc., but have never given them to the world; will sometime, it may be. Some things are not clear to me, only have a kind of "theory" of the thing.[157]

Herndon's theory was that Thomas, when a young man, had the mumps and that the mumps had "castrated" Thomas. He asked Jesse Weik to try and confirm that.

---

[156] Emanuel Hertz. *The Hidden Lincoln, From the Letters and Papers of William H. Herndon*, page 93. Herndon letter to the Editor of the Indianapolis Herald regarding a letter by J. W. Gordan. Herndon's letter to the editor is dated September 15, 1883.

[157] Emanuel Hertz. *The Hidden Lincoln, From the Letters and Papers of William H. Herndon*, page 94. Herndon letter to Jesse Weik dated April 14, 1885.

One word about Dennis Hanks. When you see him, ask him, in a roundabout way, if Thomas Lincoln was not castrated because of the mumps when young. Dennis told me this often and repeated it. Please ask the question, won't you, and note it down.[158]

Herndon believed in a common misconception of the 1800s that mumps in young men caused sterility or what Herndon referred to as being castrated. Dennis Hanks told Herndon often, most likely because Herndon repeated the question often, that Thomas had mumps. When Thomas had mumps is unknown but if Hanks knew about it, it is likely it was while Thomas was a young man, possibly prior to marriage. Herndon most wanted to prove, for the sake of his theory that Abraham was not Thomas' son, that Thomas had mumps before he married Nancy.

Mumps, in young men, was known to cause genital issues. It could, in a minority of illnesses, cause orchitis, a painful inflammation of the testes that was sometimes accompanied by shrinkage or atrophy. This was usually in one teste rather than both. This is why Herndon was so interested in someone telling him the size of Thomas' genitalia. The condition could cause infertility for up to a year but rarely, very rarely was the condition ever permanent. In fact, more recent medical studies have concluded that mumps do not cause infertility and do not result in impotence.[159]

Abraham would have known these beliefs about mumps, and he could possibly have heard people saying a man who had mumps could not have children. Knowing Thomas had mumps could have caused Abraham to question his paternity but there is no record, outside Herndon's interpretation of Lincoln, that he did. Abraham would also have known men who had mumps who had no lasting effects and were very able to have children.

---

[158] Emanuel Hertz. *The Hidden Lincoln, From the Letters and Papers of William H. Herndon*, pages 118-119. Herndon letter to Weik dated January 1, 1886.
[159] Hal B. Jenson, M.D. and Charles T. Leach, M.D. www.pediatricweb.com. Dr. Jenson is the Chief of Pediatric Infectious Diseases at the University of Texas Health Science Center in San Antonio, Texas. Dr. Leach is Associate Professor of Pediatrics at the University of Texas Health Science Center.

Thomas Lincoln: Abraham's Father

Herndon would take his bias and proceed to develop his proof points, like a legal argument, that Thomas could not be Abraham's father. He sent those to Jesse Weik in a letter he marked as being "religiously private". His proof points would turn out to be weak because his facts were either errant (such as his point that Thomas and Nancy were married in September 1806 when they were actually married in June of 1806) or simply supposition twisted to make his belief sound plausible.

The facts are about as follows: Lincoln once told me that his mother Nancy Hanks was the illegitimate child of a Virginia planter; he told me never to tell it while he lived, and this I have religiously kept and observed. This is one fact in the chain of inferences. Thomas Lincoln, the father of Abraham, in the spring of 1805 commenced going to see Sally Bush; he courted this finely developed and buxom girl; she refused him, did not at all reciprocate his love. This lady, whom I knew, was far above Thomas Lincoln, somewhat cultivated and quite a lady. Mr. Lincoln, Thomas, then — say in the summer of 1806 — commenced going to see Nancy Hanks, Abraham's mother. Nancy Hanks accepted Thomas Lincoln's hand; they were actually married in Washington County, Kentucky. The marriage took place September 23, 1806, and the first child born to Mrs. Lincoln was on the tenth day of February 1807, a little less than five months from the day of the marriage. This is the second fact which you must carry along in order to draw correct inferences. About 1815 one Abraham Enloe was caught by Thomas Lincoln in such relations and under such conditions with his wife that he was convinced that his wife was not, like Caesar's wife, above suspicion. Thomas Lincoln jumped on and into Enloe for what he had been doing, as Lincoln supposed. Lincoln bit off Enloe's nose in the terrible fight. This is fact number three. Lincoln, Thomas, was so annoyed with Enloe's visits and conduct that he was driven from Kentucky; he moved from there, to Indiana, about 1816-17. While Mrs. Lincoln bred like a rat in

Kentucky, she had no more children in Indiana. This is fact number four. Mrs. Lincoln died about 1818-19 in Indiana. In about one year thereafter Thomas Lincoln went back to Kentucky to see Sally Bush, who had in the meantime – say in 1807-8 – married to one Johnston. Johnston and Mrs. Johnston had two children or more. I knew them both. Johnston died about the time that Mrs. Lincoln did – one died in Indiana and the other in Kentucky. Miss Bush, now Mrs. Johnston, was a finely developed woman and so was Mrs. Lincoln. The reputation of Mrs. Lincoln is that she was a bold, reckless, daredevil kind of a woman, stepping to the very verge of propriety: she was badly and roughly raised, was an excellent woman and by nature an intellectual and sensitive woman. Lincoln, Abraham, told me that his mother was an intellectual woman, sensitive and somewhat sad. I distinctly remember what Lincoln told me and the cause of the conversation. Lincoln said to me on that occasion this: 'All that I am or hope ever to be I got from my mother, God bless her' and I guess all this – what Lincoln told me – was the truth. Thomas Lincoln went back to see Mrs. Johnston, as said before, and they were married in Elizabethtown, Kentucky, about the year 1819. Remember that Mrs. Johnston had children by Johnston. This is a fifth fact. Mrs. Johnston, now Mrs. Lincoln, went to Indiana with Thomas and there had no children while in the prime and glory of her good life she was a good woman, a kind, clever, and polite one. I knew her. Mrs. Thomas Lincoln, his second wife, now took possession of things in Indiana, dressed up, taught, and kindly cared for Thomas Lincoln's two children by his first wife – Abraham and Sarah. Mrs. Lincoln, Thomas's second wife, had no more children while in Indiana, though she bred, had children, in Kentucky by Johnston. Here is the sixth fact. The two children by his first wife and the two by his last wife – Johnston the father – were raised up together and actually loved one another. In other words, Lincoln had two or three children by his first wife, and none by his last. Mrs. Johnston had two or three children by her first husband and none by Thomas Lincoln. The four children were raised up, vegetated together. In addition to all the above facts or supposed ones – for I give no opinion – Dennis Hanks told me that Thomas Lincoln, when tolerably young, and before he left Kentucky, was castrated. Abraham Enloe said, often said, that Abraham Lincoln was his child. All these facts, if facts they are, I received from different persons, at different times and places. I reduced much to writing at the time, have letters on the subject from Kentucky and some of the facts I remember, i.e., I well remember what was told me, though I did write all down.[160]

As time progressed, Herndon began to realize the damage he had done his own reputation by casting dispersion on the Lincoln family. He began to look for a way out of his predicament without surrendering his belief that Thomas was not the father.

She [Nancy Lincoln] cared nothing for forms, etiquette, customs, etc., etc., but burst through them without a care for consequences; she was a social creature, very much so, loved the company of men more than women, and by her peculiar nature she got up a bad reputation; and because she had a bad reputation it was, it is still, charged that Abraham Lincoln is the child of one Enloe. My own opinion, after a searching examination, is that Mrs. Lincoln, Nancy Hanks, was not a bad woman, was by nature a noble woman, free, easy, and unsuspecting. My own opinion after a sweeping and searching examination, investigation, is that Abraham Lincoln was the child and heir of Thomas Lincoln and Nancy Hanks Lincoln. I admit that all things are not perfectly clear to me; and yet I think that the weight of the testimony is in my favor on both of these grounds. Old Thomas Lincoln, Abraham's father,

---

[160] Emanuel Hertz. *The Hidden Lincoln, From the Letters and Papers of William H. Herndon*, pages 138-139. From a letter to Jesse Weik marked "Religiously private", dated January 19, 1886. See also: William H. Herndon, Douglas L. Wilson & Rodney O. Davis, Editors. *Herndon on Lincoln, Letters*, pages 203-204.

was castrated, fixed, cut, but no one can fix the exact time of the loss of his manhood. That event being uncertain, lets in the presumptions of chastity, virtue, and heirship, and on these hangs the weight of testimony alone. This is pretty close rubbing, is it not?[161]

In another letter, written not long after this one, Herndon would confirm that he did not believe Thomas to be Abraham's father and that his argument supporting Thomas was just legal fiction.

If the time of Lincoln's castration was before marriage, then Abraham is the illegitimate child of someone, but, if after Thomas, her youngest son, then Abraham was got in lawful wedlock. Under this state of facts, do you not see the importance of presumptions? The law conclusively presumes that all persons born in lawful wedlock shall be presumed to be the lawful child and heir of the husband and the wife unless it should be conclusively proved that the marriage was incapable of procreation by nature or accident. No one now living can fix the time when Thomas Lincoln was castrated. The presumption of law saves Abraham's paternity. This is close shaving on so important a subject.[162]

Herndon would say it much more plainly to Jesse Weik.

Being in a hurry when I wrote the first part of this letter, I forgot to say to you that you can safely say that, in law, Abraham Lincoln was the son and heir of Thomas Lincoln and Nancy Hanks Lincoln and be safe in the saying of it. The general reader will not notice the sharp point, in law. This may help us; L. was born in lawful wedlock and that

---

[161] Emanuel Hertz. *The Hidden Lincoln, From the Letters and Papers of William H. Herndon*, pages 204-205. Herndon letter to Truman H. Bartlett dated September 25, 1887. See also: William H. Herndon, Douglas L. Wilson & Rodney O. Davis, Editors. *Herndon on Lincoln, Letters*, pages 261-262.
[162] Emanuel Hertz. *The Hidden Lincoln, From the Letters and Papers of William H. Herndon*, page 206. Herndon letter to Truman H. Bartlett dated September 30, 1887. See also: William H. Herndon, Douglas L. Wilson & Rodney O. Davis, Editors. *Herndon on Lincoln, Letters*, pages 262-263.

is enough for us. Couch the idea somehow in general words.[163]

How could Herndon have gone so far wrong and fed the enemies of Abraham Lincoln with slander and libel readily available for their use? The answer is that Herndon lost esteem and respect without Abraham Lincoln as his law partner and he wanted to regain that by being the only person who could tell the true story of the President. Herndon needed a different story than others were telling if he was going to stand out from the crowd and reestablish himself in a place of prominence. So, when Herndon caught wind of a story that Lincoln had been illegitimate, he leapt at it and built on it, using intuition and some imagination to reach conclusions that could not be readily supported in fact.

As much as Herndon claimed Lincoln had told him things no one else knew, he revealed how he actually got his facts from Lincoln in a letter to Ward Lamon.

I do not think that Mr. Lincoln was a hypocrite and yet I know he scarcely trusted any man with his more profound secrets. I had to read them in his facts, acts, hints, face, as well as what he did not do nor say, however absurd this last expression may appear to be.[164]

Herndon even admitted to being a mind reader in a letter to Jesse Weik. He wrote, "I studied the man and think that I could read his thoughts clearly, distinctly, certainly in a general way."[165] He made that approach clear in another letter. "I judged the man [Lincoln] by his questionings, his manner, his nervousness, his unrest and the play of his features, with their colors, giving a significance to his thoughts and his wishes, a mind's revelation to

---

[163] Emanuel Hertz. *The Hidden Lincoln, From the Letters and Papers of William H. Herndon*, page 228. Herndon letter to Jesse Weik dated December 1, 1888.

[164] Emanuel Hertz. *The Hidden Lincoln, From the Letters and Papers of William H. Herndon*, page 77. Taken from Herndon's letter to Ward Hill Lamon on March 6, 1870. See also: William H. Herndon, Douglas L. Wilson & Rodney O. Davis, Editors. *Herndon on Lincoln, Letters*, page 104.

[165] Emanuel Hertz. *The Hidden Lincoln, From the Letters and Papers of William H. Herndon*, page 263. Taken from Herndon's letter to Jesse Weik on February 21, 1891. See also: William H. Herndon, Douglas L. Wilson & Rodney O. Davis, Editors. *Herndon on Lincoln, Letters*, page 338.

mind."[166] Herndon believed he understood Lincoln to a decree no else did even though he recognized that Lincoln did not think Herndon understood him. "Mr. Lincoln would doubly explain things to me that needed no explanation. However I stood and took it out of respect for the man: he was terribly afraid that I did not understand him when I understood even his thoughts at it."[167]

Much of the early argument for Thomas not being Abraham's father came from the fact that the marriage license of Thomas and Nancy was not found for many years. Herndon's early argument was based on the fact that Thomas and Nancy were not married. He hastily realigned his argument when the marriage bond was discovered but he did not let that fact turn him from the intuition he had come to from reading the hints in Lincoln's face and from reading Lincoln's thoughts.

Simple history shows that Abraham Enloe did not claim to be Abraham Lincoln's father. Others claimed that of him. Herndon had no documented evidence for his supposition, based on the lack of a marriage license and mind reading, for anyone other than Thomas Lincoln being Abraham's father, and no one had claimed to be Abraham Lincoln's father other than Thomas Lincoln. The claims of Lincoln being a bastard child were politically motivated and not based in fact or history.[168]

Another misrepresentation that has also been used repeatedly to try and cast doubt on Thomas being Abraham's father is physical resemblance. The Enloe family has published pictures of male relatives claiming the resemblance to Abraham Lincoln is undeniable while there is little resemblance between Thomas and Abraham. There is some truth in there being a lack of physical resemblance between Thomas and Abraham, but if that is proof of parentage then Abraham is proven to not be the father of his

---

166 William H. Herndon. *Herndon on Lincoln: Letters*, page 131. Taken from a Herndon letter to an unnamed New York clergyman on November 24, 1882.
167 William H. Herndon. *Herndon on Lincoln: Letters*, page 192. Taken from a Herdon letter to Jesse W. Weik dated from Springfield, Illinois on January 9, 1886.
168 For a detailed handling of the paternity of Abraham Lincoln, see William E. Barton's *The Parents of Abraham Lincoln*, Edward Steers Jr.'s *Lincoln Legends: Myths, Hoaxes, and Confabulations Associated with Our Greatest President*, and Louis A. Warren's *Lincoln's Parentage & Childhood*. The myth of Thomas not being Abraham's father has been refuted for decades by solid research and fact.

three sons. There is little resemblance between Abraham and Robert or Willie or Tad. Yet no one claims Abraham was not their father.

While there is a lack of physical resemblance between Thomas and Abraham, or Abraham and Robert, there is physical resemblance between Thomas and Robert.

When facts are put in place, history shows that Thomas was Abraham's father. There is no credible evidence to the contrary. The myths perpetuated to deny Thomas' paternal standing are based on oral traditions. They refuse to consider or take into account where Nancy was before Abraham's birth or when Nancy and the alleged father(s) were in close geographical proximity (if they ever were). The court records, tax records, census records, property records, and other documents provide incontestable support that Thomas Lincoln was the father of Abraham Lincoln.[169]

Life at Sinking Spring

In February of 1809, Thomas served Hardin County as a prison guard in Elizabethtown. Moving out of town had not diminished the demand for his help. Thomas served on two juries in March and listed two horses[170] in the tax census in addition to his farms and his holdings in Elizabethtown. In 1809 Thomas was a prosperous young man with a family. He owned 538 acres in two farms, two lots in Elizabethtown (one improved with a house).

March 1809 brought a settlement to the Geoghegan lawsuit Thomas had filed to recover wages. The settlement, in Thomas' favor allowed him to recover costs of the suit as well.[171]

In these early months of 1809, before the need to till and plant, Thomas worked in Elizabethtown and the surrounding area at carpentry and cabinetmaking and he hunted. Thomas delighted in hunting and bringing home fresh game for the family table. The land teemed with game. Deer, turkey, bear, wild cats, and an occasional panther provided plenty of targets. Thomas' reputation as a hunter and marksman meant the hunt rarely failed to provide

---

[169] J. G. De Roulhac Hamilton. "The Many-Sired Lincoln." *The American Mercury*, page 135.

[170] Louis A. Warren. "Abraham Lincoln's Father." *The Lincoln Kinsman*, pages 5.

[171] Louis A. Warren. "Abraham Lincoln's Father." *The Lincoln Kinsman*, pages 5.

food, resources, and income for the family.[172] Animal hides were used for clothing and bartering. The hunting also found hives with wild honey, a sweet addition to the pioneer table.

Life was not isolated or lonely on Sinking Spring farm. Neighbors were not close in modern terms of close neighbors, but pioneers did not see a mile or two as much distance at all. It was normal and the distance between homes did not prevent visiting and neighboring. During the days and evenings, neighbors and friends would gather. Travelers were often passing through. Thomas was known for his hospitality. He was a generous man who shared what he had, welcoming friend and stranger to his table.

Thomas' family shared their own company and that of friends who visited and stayed overnight. Days were filled with work, but the evenings were devoted to stories and laughter and rest. Thomas, the master storyteller, was in much demand for his humor and wit. Stories of family history, the Bible, anecdotes, local lore, and national pride – all were told around the fireplace or sitting under the stars at Sinking Spring.

Sometime not long prior to the move from Sinking Spring to Knob Creek, Dr. Daniel B. Potter died in Elizabethtown. His accounts showed, at the time of his death, his estate was owed $1560.35 ¾ from patients. A task force went about collecting. Thomas had a running account with the doctor, paid up except for $1.46. The records showed Thomas paid the amount due.[173]

Abraham did not remember the Sinking Spring farm. His earliest memories were of Knob Creek. In speaking of his birthplace, Abraham will show his lack of memory by saying "I was born Feb. 12, 1809 in then Hardin county Kentucky, at a point within the more recently formed county of Larue, a mile, or a mile & a half from where Hodgenville now is. My parents being dead and my own memory not serving, I have no means of identifying the precise locality. It was on Nolin creek"[174]

---

172 Douglas L. Wilson and Rodney O. Davis. *Herndon's Informants*, pages 27-28. From an Erastus Wright interview of Dennis Hanks and sent by letter to Herndon from Chicago, Illinois on June 8, 1865.
173 W. E. Barton, *Life of Abraham Lincoln Volume I*, page 7.
174 Ronald C. White. *Lincoln in Private*, page 228. From a fragment Lincoln wrote on June 14, 1860 regarding his birthplace.

The Sinking Spring Cabin

After Thomas left Sinking Spring farm, it passed through various owners, some who cared for it well and some who neglected it. A part of the farm would become part of the National Park Service as the Abraham Lincoln Birthplace National Historical Park. There is a cabin in the Memorial Building at the park, but it is not Thomas' cabin, not where Abraham was born. The cabin at the park was early on referred to as the birthplace cabin but it is now referred to as the Symbolic Cabin, a representation of Thomas' cabin. Thomas' actual cabin was lost while the family was living in Indiana, well before Abraham found fame and glory.

The story of what happened to the cabin Thomas built is fairly simple. The cabin was lost when Henry Brother owned the farm. His son Jacob told the tale.

> *My name is Jacob S. Brother. My father's name was Henry, but he was generally known as 'Harry.' I was born in Montgomery County, Kentucky, March 8, 1819. In the year 1827, when I was eight years old, my father purchased the old farm on which Abraham Lincoln was born. He purchased it of Henry Thomas. We lived in the house in which Lincoln was born. After some years, my father built another house almost like the first house. The old house was torn down, and, to my knowledge, the logs were burned for firewood. Later he built a hewed log house, and the second old house was used as a hatter-shop. My father followed the trade of making hats all his life. The pictures we often see of the house in which Lincoln was born are pictures of the first house built by my father.*[175]

Jacob Brother had his dates slightly off. Later property records show that Henry owned the farm from 1835 to 1840. In 1865, artist John B. Rowbotham went to the farm to document the place where Abraham Lincoln was born. He confirmed the birth cabin was no longer there. The spot where it stood was

---

[175] J. T. Hobson. *Footprints of Abraham Lincoln*, pages 14-15.

marked by a few stones from the chimney and two aging pear trees planted by Thomas. Most of the knoll on which Thomas had built his family's cabin was a barley field.[176]

The story of how the symbolic cabin came to be enshrined in the Memorial Building at the Abraham Lincoln Birthplace National Historical Park is a convoluted path. In 1894, the first cabin built by Henry Brother, the cabin later used as a hattery, was neglected and becoming dilapidated. An entrepreneur by name of A. W. Dennett, purchased the farm with an eye to turning it into a tourist site. The concept failed for lack of attendance, but that did not stop Dennett from believing he had something people would pay to see. He assumed the old cabin was the birthplace cabin, Thomas' cabin. He took the cabin apart and took it on the road as an exhibit, rebuilding it and tearing it down as he traveled the country. Dennett had also purchased a cabin that was claimed as the birthplace of Jefferson Davis. With Dennett's traveling roadshow, both cabins were displayed together.

Dennett was still wrong about what people would pay to see. He went broke. Both cabins were taken apart and put into storage. The logs intermixed and confused.

In 1906, the Lincoln Farm Association purchased the "sacred" logs of the supposed Lincoln cabin for $50,000.[177] They also purchased 110 acres of the Sinking Spring farm. $350,000 later, Abraham Lincoln's birthplace, Thomas' humble farm, was established as a national shrine. [178]

Knob Creek Farm

In 1811, as deed troubles cropped up without resolution, Thomas concluded the deed to Sinking Spring could not be supported and he sought out another home for his family. Along Knob Creek was land where several others were finding homes and farms. George Lindsey owned 228 acres on Knob Creek at the foot of Muldraugh's Hill, land on which he was no longer

---

[176] Hays, Roy. "Is the Lincoln Birthplace Cabin Authentic?" *Abraham Lincoln Quarterly*, page 128.

[177] Hays, Roy. "Is the Lincoln Birthplace Cabin Authentic?" *Abraham Lincoln Quarterly*, page 153.

[178] National Park Service. www.nps.gov/nr/travel/presidents/ lincoln_birthplace.html.

living. It was here that Thomas leased land and built a cabin for his family.[179] Complete records are lacking to show the exact arrangement Thomas made with Lindsey.

From tax records, it appears Thomas leased thirty acres of bottomland and not all the hills and gorges on Lindsey's land. Those hills were of little value to Thomas since they could not be profitably farmed or used in other ways. It is on the thirty acres that Thomas was taxed.[180] These thirty acres were the best of Lindsey's 228 acres. It was relatively good soil. The draw back was that it was bottomland. The Spring runoff from the hills and gorges surrounding it could quickly swell Knob Creek out of its banks, flooding the fields and washing out crops.

These conditions and the fact that Thomas continued to try and obtain clear title to the Sinking Spring farm indicate Thomas did not move to Knob Creek because it was a better location with better land but rather because he needed a place for his family while he attempted to keep Sinking Spring farm.[181]

The Knob Creek farm was ten miles northeast of Sinking Spring. The bottomland was surrounded by high hills resembling knobs which gave the creek its name. The area was heavily wooded with plenty of game for hunting. Knob Creek ran through ravines and gorges until it reached the Rolling Fork, a tributary of Salt River, at the northern edge of Lindsey's land.

Dennis Hanks, whose adoptive parents, Tom and Betsy Sparrow, lived on a neighboring farm described the Knob Creek farm in a very picturesque way. He spoke of the Lincoln farm being in a hollow with "high, tall, and peaky hills" surrounded by deep hollows and ravines and "bordered with cedar."[182]

Hanks described the land with accuracy, matching the descriptions others have given but he seems confused on other points. He said Thomas "owned the land in fee simple" but court

---

[179] Kent Masterson Brown. *Report on the Title of Thomas Lincoln to, and the History of, the Lincoln Boyhood Home along Knob Creek in LaRue County, Kentucky*, page 30.

[180] Kent Masterson Brown. *Report on the Title of Thomas Lincoln to, and the History of, the Lincoln Boyhood Home along Knob Creek in LaRue County, Kentucky*, page 42.

[181] Kent Masterson Brown. *Report on the Title of Thomas Lincoln to, and the History of, the Lincoln Boyhood Home along Knob Creek in LaRue County, Kentucky*, page 33.

[182] Douglas L. Wilson and Rodney O. Davis. *Herndon's Informants*, page 38. From a Herndon interview with Dennis Hanks in Chicago on June 13, 1865.

records show the land was leased and that the title was never in Thomas' name. Hanks also claimed the Knob Creek cabin was a double cabin (two cabins put together to form a two-room cabin).[183] No other records or descriptions report the Knob Creek cabin as being anything other than a standard one-room cabin of approximately sixteen by eighteen feet.

Life at Knob Creek

The Knob Creek farm was located along the Old Cumberland Trail, the Nolin-Bardstown Road, running from Louisville to Nashville. The road ran in front of Thomas' cabin, providing a variety of travelers passing through and stopping to chat.[184] Thomas traveled the Old Cumberland Trail north to the point where Knob Creek flowed into the Rolling Fork and then turned West on the Elizabethtown-Springfield Road to go to Elizabethtown to conduct business.

Being on the Old Cumberland Trail, the Knob Creek farm was far from isolated. The Trail was a main route of travel between Louisville and Nashville as well as points north and south of those cities. Thomas spoke with hundreds of travelers and pioneers making their way past his home. He heard their stories and their hopes. Thomas and Nancy had a steady stream of news and entertainment from those passing over the Trail. As pioneers headed to new land in Indiana, Thomas, with his experience of deed troubles in Kentucky, heard about the Indiana land system and the clean deeds offered.

With the pattern of pioneer hospitality and Thomas being a generous man, the Lincoln cabin was a good spot for travelers to stop for the night, pulling their wagons off the road and enjoying the stories Thomas had in his repertoire with which to pass a pleasant evening.

It was on these pioneer evenings, sitting around the fireplace or under the stars beside a campfire, that Thomas told tales and listened to the stories and news from visitors and neighbors. Thomas, an expert storyteller with a gifted memory for stories,

---

[183] Douglas L. Wilson and Rodney O. Davis. *Herndon's Informants*, page 36. From a Herndon interview with Dennis Hanks in Chicago on June 13, 1865.
[184] R. Gerald McMurtry. "The Lincoln Migration from Kentucky to Indiana. 1816. *Indiana Magazine of History*, page 12.

legends, and jokes would have been in his element. Sarah and Abraham began life in this culture and grew up with it. Watching this scene of sharing and happiness night after night impressed itself on Abraham's almost photographic memory and he adopted it as his own. Generosity, storytelling, mimicry – these were a gift from Thomas to Abraham.

Of this legacy, there are reports that Abraham told vulgar stories and jokes. Helen Nicolay, wife of Lincoln's secretary John Nicolay, saw that legacy in this way.

> *The life in which he grew up, the life of pioneer times, and of the small village communities which immediately followed it in the Middle West, was poor in culture and refinements of living, but strong in racy human nature. Hence over fastidious people, who like 'quarrying among the ancient,' found his stories coarse. Homely, would be a truer term, for they were never coarse in spirit, even when most sordid in detail. Ethically they always pointed a clean moral. They were of the soil – strongly of the soil – but never of the charnel-house.*[185]

1811

Knob Creek was a busy and happy place for Sarah's and Abraham's early years. The farm was like most pioneer farms. Thomas had outbuildings – barns and sheds – to handle the work needed to make a farm profitable. It is likely Thomas had a workshop to house his cabinetmaking tools and where he built cabinets and other furniture. Nancy may have had a small workshop for spinning and weaving, housing the spinning wheels and looms. Pioneer farms were home industries producing much of the necessities of life.

Soon after Thomas moved his family to Knob Creek, a stray horse showed up along the road. This was not a rare thing. Horses often strayed from their owners, frequently enough that the County courthouse maintained a record labeled the Certificate of

---

[185] Helen Nicolay. *Personal Traits of Abraham Lincoln*, page 19.

Strays.[186] The horse showed up at Knob Creek on May 11, 1811. Thomas, showing the honesty and integrity he was known for, took the time to travel to the county courthouse in Elizabethtown to advertise the horse he had found and was caring for. His listing read: "Taken up by Thomas Lincoln in Hardin County on Knob Creek, on the road leading from Bardstown to Nolin a gray mare, eight years old... appraised at twenty dollars."[187] What became of the horse is unknown.

Life at Knob Creek faired very similar for Thomas to his life at Sinking Spring. He farmed during farming months while working a busy carpentry and cabinetmaking business as well as fulfilling his civic duty when called upon. September of 1811 found him on another jury in Elizabethtown.[188] Living twenty miles from the county seat did not exempt Thomas. He remained very active in Elizabethtown at business and the county respected him and wanted him on juries and as a prison guard and performing other services when needed.

The New Madrid Earthquakes

In December of 1811, Thomas experienced one of the key geological events of the time, the New Madrid earthquake. The New Madrid earthquake was a series of three earthquakes and is one of the largest earthquakes on record since the beginning of European settlement in America.

The first quake struck on December 16, 1811 in the middle of the night, registering at M7.5. The epicenter was in northeast Arkansas. The second quake of the series hit at M7.3 on January 23, 1812 and the third with M7.5 on February 7, 1812. The quakes caused extensive damage in the surrounding 230,000 square miles and was felt for around 2 million square miles. Each main shock was followed by a series of aftershocks stretching the event from

---

[186] Kent Masterson Brown. *Report on the Title of Thomas Lincoln to, and the History of, the Lincoln Boyhood Home along Knob Creek in LaRue County, Kentucky*, page 31.
[187] Kent Masterson Brown. *Report on the Title of Thomas Lincoln to, and the History of, the Lincoln Boyhood Home along Knob Creek in LaRue County, Kentucky*, page 36.
[188] Louis A. Warren. "Thomas Lincoln Chronology". *Lincoln Lore*, page 1.

December 16, 1811 through March 15, 1812.[189] One estimate puts the number of moderate to large earthquakes over this three-month period at more than 200.[190]

Due to the main impact areas being more sparsely populated, loss of life was limited but land damage was extensive, raising some areas and dropping others by as much as 15 feet. Large waves pushed upstream on the Mississippi. Buildings, homes, and chimneys were toppled as far away as Cincinnati.[191] Kentucky felt all three major quakes.

Nothing records the reaction of Thomas or his neighbors to the New Madrid quakes but Thomas' home at Knob Creek felt each of the quakes and many of the aftershocks. Trees fell. Cabins and chimneys were damaged. Newspapers, preachers, and travelers would have shared many a tale as they passed Thomas' cabin and Thomas would have told his own experience of the quakes to friends and visitors.

Life at Knob Creek (Continued)

1812

As 1812 dawned, Nancy was again pregnant and Thomas' business was prospering. He was noted as an excellent craftsman, skilled in woodcraft of almost any kind. Thomas was called on to do the work of a joiner, to build various kinds of furniture, and to make the finishing touches in houses for mantels, doors, staircases, and windows. An examination of the furniture Thomas built gives much detail about his skill as a master wood craftsman.

> *First, the workmanship on all the pieces is of excellent quality. One piece has deteriorated badly over the years due to abuse and poor treatment. This is the wall cupboard which has been on display in recent years at the*

---

189 U. S. Geological Survey. *Summary of 1811-1812 New Madrid Earthquakes Sequence.* earthquake.usgs.gov/earthquakes/events/1811-1812newmadrid/summary.php

190 Carl W. Stover and Jerry L. Coffman. *Seismicity of the United States, 1568 – 1989 (Revised)*, page 68.

191 U. S. Geological Survey. *Summary of 1811-1812 New Madrid Earthquakes Sequence.* earthquake.usgs.gov/earthquakes/events/1811-1812newmadrid/summary.php.

Rockport, Indiana County Courthouse and the Lincoln National Memorial near Lincoln City, Indiana. The abuse and poor treatment of the cupboard occurred before it was acquired by these institutions. It should be mentioned that most of the other pieces of furniture have been refinished and probably repaired in some ways so that the contrast they provide to the wall cupboard is very marked.

Second, the designs of the pieces of furniture clearly show that Thomas Lincoln was familiar with fashionable furniture of the period in which the furniture was made. For example, he used inlaid flower and vine designs on some of his cupboards and he used narrow inlay strips of light-colored wood to outline the drawer fronts on some of his pieces, including cupboards and the chest of drawers. He also used dentil moldings below the crown moldings on some of his cupboards.

Finally, an examination of the furniture confirms the conclusion that Thomas Lincoln had a large number of woodworking tools and that he must have had a workshop of some kind. Furniture of this quality could hardly have been made on the kitchen table after the supper dishes had been cleared.[192]

In June of 1812, Thomas took another turn at jury duty in Elizabethtown as national and international politics became entangled leading to the opening of the War of 1812. Just over 25,000 Kentuckians served in the war effort. Kentucky sent 36 regiments, 4 battalions, and 12 independent companies.[193] Thomas was not among these. No record from the war department or military/veteran organizations list Thomas as having served even though he had served in the Kentucky militia. Perhaps it was because of the failure of his eyesight. Perhaps it was some other reason. Regardless, Thomas did not go on active

---

[192] Warren E. Roberts. *Thomas Lincoln: Cabinetmaker.* www.indiana.edu/~wer/about/documents/ Roberts-Lincoln.pdf, pages 4-5.
[193] A. C. Quisenberry. "Kentucky Troops in the War of 1812." *The Register of the Kentucky Historical Society*, page 13.

duty. He stood ready to serve in protecting Hardin County and Kentucky but the major efforts and battles of the War of 1812 were well away from Kentucky.

At some point before Thomas moved to Indiana, he lost sight in one eye. What caused Thomas to go blind in one eye is unknown. The timing of that loss of sight is also unknown. Details off the loss are frustratingly absent. Thomas' eyesight continued to decline for the remainder of his life.[194]

A possibility of a cause is found in family history. Robert Lincoln had right esotropia, a form of strabismus that cause the right eye to turn inward. Abraham had left hypertropia, an upward turning left eye.[195] Some have assumed that Abraham's eye issue was caused from the kick in the head he suffered at the mill as a child. Considering Robert's esotropia and that esotropia can be genetic, it is possible that Abraham's upward turned eye was the result of a genetic condition rather than a horse kick. We don't have details on Thomas. Esotropia can in some instances cause blindness. It is possible that Thomas suffered from esotropia and lost sight in one eye with family genetics passing the condition on to Abraham and Robert.

Thomas' loss of sight from whatever cause would explain the deterioration of his handwriting, his signature going from well-defined penmanship to what Abraham would refer to as Thomas bunglingly[196] signing his name. It could have been this that kept Thomas home and out of the war. It could also have been Nancy's third pregnancy, a time when joy turned quickly into sorrow.

Infant Thomas

Little is known of Thomas' third child. Many of those who knew the facts of Abraham Lincoln's life did not know there was a third child. Many Lincoln biographers skip any mention of little Thomas. The date of his birth is unknown. The date of his death is unknown. It is even unknown if 1812, the commonly accepted year for his birth and death, is when he was born and died. It is

---

194 Richard E. Hart. "Thomas Lincoln Reconsidered." *For the People*, page 9.
195 David S. Reynolds, *Abe*, page 396.
196 Roy P. Basler. Editor. *The Collected Works of Abraham Lincoln*, volume 4, page 61. From the Scripps autobiography.

certain that Thomas and Nancy had a third child and the child died soon after birth.

When Nancy gave birth to a son, he was named after his father, Thomas, and called Tommy. He was sickly. The family sent to Elizabethtown for Dr. Daniel B. Potter. The physician hurriedly went to the Lincoln home at Knob Creek and did his best, but the child could not be saved. Dennis Hanks tells that Tommy did not live three days. Dr. Potter's records show that Thomas paid him $1.46 for his services.[197]

The next scene is heartbreaking. As Nancy held and tended the body of her lost baby, Thomas picked up his tools and made a small casket to hold the body of his son.[198] Some coffins were simply wood and nothing more. Sometimes families provided linen for lining the coffins and a bed of wool to soften where the deceased lay. Nancy did such for little Thomas. She brought out some of her home-spun flax cloth and a basket of wool for Thomas to use in making his baby a coffin.[199]

No doubt there were friends and family around them during this time. That was the pioneer way. But how does a father make a coffin for his child without wetting the wood with his tears? In addition to making Tommy's coffin, tradition says Thomas selected a stone for a grave marker and carved the initials T L into it.

Tommy was buried in the family cemetery of neighbor George Redmon.[200] The Redmon cemetery was a half mile from the Lincoln home, atop a knoll overlooking the Lincoln farm. Friends and family walked with Thomas and Nancy from their Knob Creek cabin to the cemetery. The procession was a solemn affair as the Baptist Association considered singing inappropriate.[201] George Redmon placed Tommy's small casket on his shoulder and carried it for the family.[202]

---

[197] Roger Norton. rogernorton.com.

[198] R. Gerald McMurtry. "Re-Discovering the Supposed Grave of Lincoln's Brother". *Lincoln Lore*, page 1.

[199] William E. Barton. *The Women Lincoln Loved*, page 87.

[200] George Redmon's last name is sometimes spelled Redmond or Redman.

[201] William E. Barton. *The Women Lincoln Loved*, page 88.

[202] William E. Barton. *The Women Lincoln Loved*, page 88.

The Lincolns were members of the Little Mount Church. Elder William Downs preached Tommy's funeral. Williams Downs' brother would later help start the Little Pigeon Church in Indiana where Thomas and Nancy would join.[203]

The Redmon cemetery and Tommy's grave were nearly lost to history until 1933 when a crew from the Works Progress Administration began work to clear the site. In their work, they uncovered Tommy's grave marker where it had been covered over. Whether the stone was still lying on Tommy's grave or if it had been moved at some point is uncertain, but the spot was marked and is now honored as the site of Tommy's grave. Boy Scout Troop 15 of Des Moines, Iowa donated a new tombstone for Tommy on August 18, 1959.[204] That stone now marks the grave and the original stone with the initials carved by Thomas is on display at the Abraham Lincoln Birthplace National Historical Park.

Oddly enough, the marker from the Boy Scouts lists little Tommy's dates as 1811 and 1815 rather than simply 1812. It is unknown as to why they put those dates.

Life at Knob Creek (Continued)

In the 1812 tax census, Thomas listed three horses for taxation.[205] Thomas may have tried his hand at breeding horses. His brother Mordecai, who visited with the family, was a well-known horse breeder. He could have encouraged Thomas toward it. It is known that Thomas loved horses and kept good ones. Racing horses was popular sport and Thomas was known to join in a friendly contest, but he did not race his horses for wagers or bet on horse races.[206]

When Thomas built furniture, he built special items for his family. One such was a small, child size ladderback chair made out

---

[203] John F. Cady. "The Religious Environment of Lincoln's Youth." *Indiana Magazine of History*, page 17.

[204] William L. Kent. "Tommy Lincoln's Grave Marked," *Lincoln Herald*, pages 51-53.

[205] Louis A. Warren. "Thomas Lincoln Chronology". *Lincoln Lore*, page 1.

[206] William E. Barton. *The Women Lincoln Loved*, page 70.

of hickory with a hickory strip woven seat for three-year-old Abraham.[207]

It was at Knob Creek that Thomas almost lost Abraham. Abraham was young and playing with a friend (Austin Gallagher) along a swollen and rushing Knob Creek. Attempting to cross the creek on a log, Abraham fell into the rushing water. Austin managed to grab a stick and reach it out for Abraham to grab. Austin pulled Abraham from the creek, saving his life.[208]

Abraham tells a fishing story from this time period. He was asked what he remembered of the war with Great Britain in 1812. He answered, "Nothing but this. I had been fishing one day and caught a little fish which I was taking home. I met a soldier in the road, and having always been told at home that we must be good to soldiers, I gave him my fish!"[209] It is a simple story but it gives us a solid glimpse into some of the things Thomas was teaching his son.

1813 – 1815

It was in 1813 that the Mather estate brought the suit against Thomas and Bush and Vance for the Sinking Spring farm. Thomas offered to pay the balance owed by Vance but, the Mather estate refused to accept payment. In late 1813 the court ordered the land sold and Thomas lost all claim to the farm, but the case did not end with that decision. An appeal was filed.[210]

In September of 1813, Thomas served as a special bailsman for Cobie Scott,[211] one of the opportunities Thomas' received from being a prison guard.

As the year wound down and 1814 began, the Old Cumberland Trail was heavily travelled with soldiers and militiamen returning from the War of 1812. As they passed the Lincoln home, Thomas invited them to stop and rest. He fed them and entertained them with his stories. He listened to their stories. The number of militia Thomas cared for is unknown but there

---

[207] From the records of the Lincoln Financial Foundation Collection.

[208] Ida M. Tarbell. *In the Footsteps of the Lincolns*, page 103.

[209] W. E. Barton. *Life of Lincoln Volume I*, page 87.

[210] Kent Masterson Brown. *Report on the Title of Thomas Lincoln to, and the History of, the Lincoln Boyhood Home along Knob Creek in LaRue County, Kentucky*, page 30.

[211] Louis A. Warren. "Thomas Lincoln Chronology". *Lincoln Lore*, page 1.

were whole companies of troops coming by the Knob Creek farm on their way home and Thomas welcomed them.

On April 23, 1814, Thomas went to the Hardin County courthouse to obtain the deed for the Mill Creek farm. The Brumfield's, Thomas' sister Nancy and her husband William, were purchasing their own farm and were moving from the Mill Creek farm. Bathsheba Lincoln was moving with them. Without their help at Mill Creek, it was impossible for Thomas to continue to run that farm while tending his Knob Creek farm and maintaining his woodworking trade. Thomas made preparation to sell Mill Creek after the 1814 harvest.

On May 9, Thomas was appointed to serve as an appraiser for the Joseph estate.[212] The Joseph estate included slaves.

The relation of Thomas and slavery is blurred. Kentucky was a slave state. Thomas lived and worked around people who fully supported slavery. The reported number of slaves in Hardin County varies from just under a thousand to over a thousand depending on the record being used. Thomas' brother Mordecai owned a slave. His uncle Isaac owned as many as 40.[213] In his woodworking business, Thomas worked for people with slaves. The Berry family with whom the Lincolns were very close and with whom Nancy had lived, were slave owners. Thomas served as a patrolman and the main responsibility of a patrolman was to patrol for runaway slaves. There is nothing easy in discerning Thomas' position and dealings with slavery during his years in Kentucky. Thomas developed a strong aversion to slavery before moving to Indiana but in his early life he appears to have tolerated slavery. That would change and his opposition to slavery would become an established and firm position for him.

Slavery was very controversial in the area of Kentucky where Thomas and Nancy started their family. People were splitting over the issue. The South Fork Baptist Church, just two miles from the Sinking Spring farm, split over slavery in 1808.[214] Thomas and Nancy affiliated themselves with the founding of the Little Mount

---

[212] Louis A. Warren. "Thomas Lincoln Chronology". *Lincoln Lore*, page 1.

[213] National Park Service. www.nps.gov/libo/learn/historyculture/thoughts-on-slavery.htm.

[214] Louis A. Warren. *Lincoln's Youth Indiana Years Seven to Twenty-one 1816-1830*, page 13.

Church, a Separate Baptist church approximately three miles from Knob Creek, a church in which slavery was considered anathema, an evil, a sin, and was preached as such on a very regular basis. Abraham Lincoln's earliest memories of church and sermons were at Little Mount, hearing slavery condemned in no uncertain terms.

When it came time for Sarah and Abraham to attend school, Thomas sent them to a school where they were taught by an abolitionist teacher, Caleb Hazel. Abraham, from his earliest memory, will be opposed to slavery. He learned that from Thomas' influence.

When and where Thomas turned against slavery and began associating with abolitionists is unknown. It is known that his opposition to slavery was part of the reasoning behind his move out of Kentucky to a free state where he would continue to associate with abolitionists. What continues to blur the line for Thomas and slavery in history is the fact that while in Kentucky he did compromise with that belief to earn a living, doing work for slave owners. Somewhere, for reasons that are not fully clear, Thomas came to believe strongly that slavery was wrong. He may not have always been clear in his actions to match that belief while he was in Kentucky, but the belief became stronger and stronger with him and he passed that opposition to slavery on to his son Abraham.

Following the appraisal for the Joseph estate, with its slaves, Thomas attended the estate sale. On July 18, he purchased a currycomb and the highest priced calf in the sale. On the 19th of July, Thomas attended the estate sale of Thomas Hill and purchased a toy wagon, a truck wagon, a toy for his children.[215] In addition to any purchased toys, Thomas had a habit of making toys for Abraham and Sarah out of whatever materials – corncobs, sticks, cornsilk – he had handy.[216]

In September of 1814, Thomas was at the county courthouse to sign an amended document in the Mather suit over Sinking Spring. In October, he bought a heifer and a currycomb.[217] Also

---

[215] Kent Masterson Brown. *Report on the Title of Thomas Lincoln to, and the History of, the Lincoln Boyhood Home along Knob Creek in LaRue County, Kentucky*, page 37.
[216] David S. Reynolds, *Abe*, page 78.
[217] Louis A. Warren. "Thomas Lincoln Chronology". *Lincoln Lore*, page 1.

in October, he sold the Mill Creek farm.[218] Thomas' brother-in-law and sister, William and Nancy, purchased their own farm in 1814. Thomas had provided them a place to live and work. Mill Creek had profited them to the point they could purchase their own farm. They moved there with Thomas' mother, Bathsheba, and Thomas sold Mill Creek. Charles Melton purchased the farm for $486.[219] In the sale process, Thomas discovered there had been a clerical error in recording the deed. He could only guarantee the farm to have 200 acres rather than the 238 he had purchased. Due to that error, Thomas lost money on the sale.[220]

Thomas's father and grandfather and great-grandfather had all worked to increase their wealth by gaining land. Thomas tried that but the Kentucky deed system worked against him. He never became a large landowner. Despite that, he was prospering. In 1814, Thomas listed three horses for the tax census.[221] The total value of his listed property was $510. It was not a great sum but in 1814 it was a good accumulation and far from poverty. There were ninety-eight persons listed on the Hardin County tax census. Only fifteen of those ninety-eight had more property than Thomas.[222] It is also worth noting that Thomas' name never appeared on the list of delinquent taxpayers.[223]

In a time when bartering remained the major method for business and income, Thomas' woodworking skills put him in a position to have cash money when there was little in circulation. He was respected and successful, a skilled laborer in demand. The year 1814 was a high mark for Thomas. He would never be destitute or go hungry but in financial terms, 1814 was the best

---

[218] The Mill Creek farm is now part of the Nall-Lincoln subdivision with an Elizabethtown, Kentucky address. It is located on the Battle Training Road (Highway 434), north of Elizabethtown, east of the Dixie Highway (Highway 31W). The subdivision can be found by locating Lincoln Road, Nall Avenue, Lincoln Avenue, and Melton Avenue along Battle Training Road. There is a stone quarry located across the road from the former Mill Creek Farm. The section of the 238 acres of the Mill Creek farm where the subdivision is now found is the area where the original farm cabin and buildings were located. See Gerald R. McMurtry and Louis A. Warren: *The Thomas Lincoln Mill Creek Farm*.
[219] Louis A. Warren. "Abraham Lincoln's Father." *The Lincoln Kinsman*, page 6.
[220] R. Gerald McMurtry. *The Thomas Lincoln Mill Creek Farm*, page 3.
[221] Louis A. Warren. "Thomas Lincoln Chronology". *Lincoln Lore*, page 1.
[222] R. Gerald McMurtry. *The Lincolns in Elizabethtown, Kentucky*, page 14.
[223] D. M. Coleman. *Thomas Lincoln, The Father of Abraham Lincoln*, page 13.

year of Thomas' life. Circumstances and failing eyesight would financially limit him for the rest of his life, especially in Illinois.

On Knob Creek farm, Abraham went from toddler to young child. Farm life was typical of other settlers in the area with the exception that Thomas had a workshop for making quality furniture and cabinets. Sarah learned cooking and weaving and sewing from Nancy. Abraham learned farming and woodworking from Thomas.

The chores were routine. Abraham carried wood to fill the wood box and water for the water troughs. Nuts and berries were gathered in season. Thomas plowed the fields and prepared the furrows. Abraham and Sarah followed, dropping seeds for the garden plants and field crops. Such made up what Abraham called his earliest memories.

The ground was put to good use. In the big field where Thomas planted seven acres of corn, pumpkin was planted every other hill and every other row to grow and entwine among the corn stalks. Bloody butcher corn, scarlet runner pole beans, Connecticut field pumpkins, Indian corn, old Dutch half-runner beans, dipper gourds, wheat, oats, tobacco, squash, potatoes — such were the crops Thomas and his family raised. The farm had good soil and the three fields on the farm were better for farming than the ground at Sinking Spring had been. However, there was a major drawback for Knob Creek, and it was substantial.

Being on low ground, Spring rain meant Spring floods. The floods were a danger to people, as when Abraham nearly drowned in the flood swollen stream, and crops. Preparing fields and planting crops was frequently followed by repairing flood washed fields and replanting crops. The ground may have been good but losing crops and labor to floods was not.

Dr. D. J. Wright[224], an Indiana physician, visited Abraham Lincoln at the White House in 1864 and asked him about going back to Kentucky someday after the war and seeing his old home at Knob Creek. He recorded Lincoln's answer.

> *I would like that very much. I remember that old home very well. Our farm was composed of three fields. It lay in*

---

[224] The Fehrenbacher's list the Doctor as J. J. Wright but Ida Tarbell lists him a D. J. Wright.

the valley surrounded by high hills and deep gorges. Sometimes when there came a big rain in the hills, the water would come down through the gorges and spread all over the farm. The last thing that I remember of doing there was one Saturday afternoon. The other boys planted corn in what we called the big field – it contained seven acres – and I dropped the pumpkin seeds. I dropped two seeds every other hill and every other row. The next Sunday morning there came a big rain in the hills. It did not rain a drop in the valley, but the water coming down through the gorges washed ground, corn, pumpkin seeds and all clear off the field.[225]

Despite the hardships, Thomas persevered. He and Nancy had a strong marriage and a happy home. Their faith was a big part of that. Nancy sang hymns and taught her children the Bible. Daily Bible reading was a routine part of life in the Lincoln cabin. Thomas prayed before every meal.

In the Fall of 1815, Thomas sent Abraham and Sarah to school. It was normal for children to attend school, if there was a school, once crops were harvested and stored away. It is probable that Sarah, being two years older than Abraham, had attended school before.

In 1815, Zechariah Riney[226] was the schoolmaster in a fifteen-by-fifteen foot, one-room, log schoolhouse located two miles from the Lincoln home. Riney's school was known as an ABC school or blab school where the basics of reading, writing ('riting), and arithmetic ('rithmetic) – the three R's – were taught by the children all repeating their lessons out loud at the same time.[227] Sarah and Abraham walked to school though Thomas did on occasion ride them to school on horseback or in a wagon.

Riney's school was a standard one-room cabin with a dirt floor located approximately two miles northeast of the Knob Creek Farm. The schoolhouse was close to a ferry, mill, and distillery on

---

[225] Don E. and Virginia Fehrenbacher. *Recollected Words of Abraham Lincoln*, page 508. From a memorandum of a statement by Wright dated April 18, 1896 in the Tarbell Papers.
[226] Riney was Catholic by faith.
[227] Ida M. Tarbell. *In the Footsteps of the Lincolns*, page 106.

the Rolling Fork River owned by Peter Atherton. Atherton owned eight slaves between the years of 1814 and 1816.[228] Sarah and Abraham would have been able to observe the slaves at work while attending Riney's school.

In addition to being able to see slaves at work, with the Old Cumberland trail running adjacent to the Knob Creek farm, while it is not recorded, this was very likely the first time Abraham encountered the slave trade. The Trail was an overland route used routinely by slave traders to transport slaves in chains to the markets in Nashville and points south.[229]

During the Fall and Winter, Thomas did some work for Wattie Boone at his distillery which was located near the school.[230] Thomas, being a cooper, made barrels for Boone and did other work as well.

On the tax records for 1815, Thomas listed the thirty acres of the Knob Creek farm and four horses.[231] This payment of taxes on the leased land has caused confusion in Lincoln biography with some assuming, wrongly, that Thomas owned the farm outright.

It was in the Fall of 1815 that Thomas had more deed problems. On September 15, a suit for ejectment was brought against him. The formal bill of ejectment was delivered to Thomas on December 27.[232] The suit was brought by the descendants and heirs of Thomas Middleton of Philadelphia. Middleton had title to 10,000 acres of ground on the southside of Rolling Fork River[233], a deed the heirs contended included Knob Creek farm. Thomas' landlord, George Lindsey, defended vigorously against the Middleton suit but it would not be settled until 1818, after Thomas had moved to Indiana. Lindsey won the suit and kept his land.[234]

As 1815 closed, a world impacting event occurred. Mount Tambora, in Indonesia, erupted in April of 1815, spewing tons of volcanic dust, ash, and sulfur dioxide into the atmosphere. The

---

228 Richard Hart. "Slavery in Lincoln's Hardin County, Kentucky", page 6.

229 Richard Hart. "Slavery in Lincoln's Hardin County, Kentucky", page 6.

230 Ralph Gary. *Following in Lincoln's Footsteps*, pages 217-218.

231 Louis A. Warren. "Abraham Lincoln's Father." *The Lincoln Kinsman*, pages 6-7.

232 Louis A. Warren. "Thomas Lincoln Chronology". *Lincoln Lore*, page 1.

233 Kent Masterson Brown. *Report on the Title of Thomas Lincoln to, and the History of, the Lincoln Boyhood Home along Knob Creek in LaRue County, Kentucky*, page 41.

234 Kent Masterson Brown. *Report on the Title of Thomas Lincoln to, and the History of, the Lincoln Boyhood Home along Knob Creek in LaRue County, Kentucky*, pages 42-46.

atmospheric damage cooled the earth, dropping the average global temperature. Impact in American in 1815 was mostly unnoticed but 1816 would be a different story. 1816 became known as the Year with No Summer or Eighteen-Hundred-and-Froze-to-Death.

1816 / The Year with No Summer

The winter of early 1816 turned into Spring. Thomas, like other farmers in the area, began tilling and planting. As planting season turned into growing season, the impact of Mount Tambora was felt in Kentucky. Spring arrived and then the weather turned backward. The Earth was in the final decades of the Little Ice Age. The Mount Tambora eruption served to aggravate the global cooling and send the world back into colder temperatures and conditions. The global temperature dropped by as much as 3 degrees. The colder than normal weather led to crop failure and, in some areas, famine. The global cooling brought outbreaks of disease, caused migrations as people moved to find better conditions, and stirred religious revival as people struggled to understand the bizarre weather.[235]

Northeastern states were hit the hardest. Lakes were frozen as far south as Pennsylvania. There were heavy snows in New England. In Vermont, there was snow in June, below freezing temperatures in July, and a killer frost in August.[236] Winter clothing was being routinely worn in July and brought out occasionally in August.

The year 1816 is not the coldest year on record but the year's prolonged cold spell overlapped the growing season for farmers. Crops failed and many areas faced food shortages. Even where temperatures warmed enough to keep snow and killer frosts away, the skies were overcast causing crops to fail for lack of sun. Prices spiked. The price of oats rose from twelve cents per bushel to ninety-two cents per bushel with other grain crops doing

---

[235] Doyle Rice. "200 Years Ago, We Endured a 'Year Without a Summer'". *USA Today*. www.usatoday.com.
[236] Doyle Rice. "200 Years Ago, We Endured a 'Year Without a Summer'". *USA Today*. www.usatoday.com.

similar.[237] Where crops were brought in, the cold in the rivers and the unpredictable weather hindered food transportation. As far south as Virginia, Thomas Jefferson reported crop failures, failures that pushed Monticello into debt. Savannah, Georgia had a high temperature of 46 degrees on July 4th. Farmers suffered one of the shortest growing seasons in North American history.

One interesting side-effect of the Year with No Summer was a group of writers who challenged each other to write dark tales that would reflect the gloomy weather. Mary Shelley wrote what would become a classic of horror literature, *Frankenstein*.[238]

There is no question that Kentucky was impacted by the strange and cold weather of 1816's chilly Summer. The full impact on Thomas at Knob Creek is unknown. Kentuckians were able to bring in some crops and they received the benefit of higher prices for the foodstuffs they grew. The growing season of 1816 would not have been one of Thomas' best for produce but the higher prices could have offset the smaller harvest and kept him from losing money.

On May 18, Thomas was appointed road surveyor for a section of Old Cumberland Trail near Knob Creek farm. George Redmon had held the position but his death left a need and the County turned to Thomas to fill that need.[239] Being road surveyor, Thomas was required to keep the road in good condition for travelers and daily use.

In the Fall of 1816, Thomas and Nancy sent their children to school with Caleb Hazel as schoolmaster. Zechariah Riney had moved and Hazel stepped up to provide the children with lessons. Hazel owned the farm bordering Knob Creek. He was a friend and neighbor of the Lincolns.[240] He was a close enough friend that on October 16 Thomas signed as witness for Hazel's marriage bond to Mary Stevens.[241] Hazel was a known abolitionist and

---

[237] Robert McNamara. *The Year Without a Summer Was a Bizarre Weather Disaster in 1816*. www.history1800s.com.

[238] Robert McNamara. *The Year Without a Summer Was a Bizarre Weather Disaster in 1816*. www.history1800s.com.

[239] R. Gerald McMurtry. "Re-Discovering the Supposed Grave of Lincoln's Brother". *Lincoln Lore*, page 2.

[240] Ida M. Tarbell. *In the Footsteps of the Lincolns*, page 106.

[241] Louis A. Warren. "Abraham Lincoln's Father." *The Lincoln Kinsman*, pages 6-7.

taught the children abolitionism. Whatever position Thomas had held earlier in life, he was now firmly supportive of a church teaching abolition and a schoolmaster teaching abolition.

In September, the Mather case to reclaim Sinking Spring and other land was finally complete. What Thomas had seen as the probable result when he left the Sinking Spring farm was proven. Mather won the case and Thomas lost his last chance to regain the farm.[242] Some good news from the settlement was an order for Isaac Bush to repay Thomas with interest. The bad news is that Bush did not pay and Thomas was forced to take him to court in November to obtain payment.

Thomas listed four horses for taxation in 1816 and no land.[243] With the decision in the Mather case and the ejectment suit against his tenancy at Knob Creek, Thomas set his eyes firmly on Indiana. Along with him, nine of his Knob Creek neighbors lost their land due to title problems.[244]

A saying Thomas said often enough that Abraham quoted it and followed the advice was "if you make a bad bargain, hug it the tighter."[245] This Thomas did with his struggle with Kentucky land titles. He worked hard and kept at it, hugging the bargain the tighter to try and get good from the bad, but the Kentucky deed system was gravely flawed and was a key reason Thomas packed up for Indiana where the deed system worked and land titles were clear.

On a bit of a side note regarding Abraham learning this from Thomas, when Lincoln was elected to the U. S. House of Representatives in 1846 he had an agreement with colleagues that they would each take one term and then let one of the others take a turn. Abraham was tempted to break that agreement because he wanted a second term.

---

[242] Kent Masterson Brown. *Report on the Title of Thomas Lincoln to, and the History of, the Lincoln Boyhood Home along Knob Creek in LaRue County, Kentucky*, page 47.
[243] Louis A. Warren. "Abraham Lincoln's Father." *The Lincoln Kinsman*, pages 6-7.
[244] R. Gerald McMurtry. "The Lincoln Migration from Kentucky to Indiana. 1816. *Indiana Magazine of History*, pages 387-388.
[245] Roy P. Basler. *The Collected Works of Abraham Lincoln*, volume 1, page 280. Taken from a letter from Abraham Lincoln to Joshua Speed dated February 25, 1842.

I made a declaration that I would not be a candidate again, more from a wish to deal fairly with others, to keep peace among our friends, and to keep the district from going to the enemy, than from any cause personal to myself; so that if it should happen that if nobody else wishes to be elected, I could not refuse the people the right of sending me again. But to enter myself as a competitor of others, or to authorize any one so to enter me, is what my word and honor forbid.[246]

The bargain Abraham had made turned out to not be what he wanted but it was his word. He had made a bad bargain. He regretted the arrangement he had made but his word was given. He stood by it. He made a bad bargain but hugged it the tighter to find a way forward.

The Cabin at the Lincoln Boyhood Home at Knob Creek

The land Thomas leased at Knob Creek is now under the authority of the Abraham Lincoln Birthplace National Historical Park. The cabin Thomas built was long ago destroyed and lost. As a stand in, the park brought in a cabin reputed to be the birth cabin of Abraham's playmate and rescuer, Austin Gallagher.

Moving to Indiana

Thomas was reasonably successful in Kentucky. He became a skilled woodcraftsman, respected in his community and church. Still, Kentucky did not provide what he wanted. He purchased two farms. One, Mill Creek, he sold at a loss due to a title discrepancy. The second, Sinking Spring, he lost due to the poor Kentucky surveying and deed records. He leased a third farm, Knob Creek, but the bottomland, while good soil, was too prone to flooding and, once again, deeds were disputed. Something more was needed.

The Old Cumberland Trail running directly past Thomas' front door at Knob Creek gave him the opportunity to talk to hundreds of travelers. He heard of Indiana, a place with good land,

---

[246] Letter from Abraham Lincoln to William Herndon from Washington, dated January 8, 1848. Collected Works of Abraham Lincoln, Volume 1, page 431.

a land where the surveys were done correctly and the deed records were accurate. There is little doubt this was a big part of the reason Thomas moved his family to Indiana. Thomas would have his choice of land and he would know the money spent gave him a clear title. The land ordinance of 1785 assured him of this.

Indiana was also a free state. The Northwest Ordinance made it so. This was the second reason Thomas moved. He was associated with abolitionists and attended an abolitionist church in a state where slaves were welcome. As Thomas became more opposed to slavery, living among slaveowners was more and more difficult for him. The economy of the move with the promise of a good deed for land paid for may have been the main factor in Thomas' move but being away from slavery was also a major factor. Thomas' brother Josiah had already moved to Indiana. That encouraged Thomas to move also. The men of the Lincoln family were known for increasing their holdings and wealth by land trades. The thought of being able to succeed at that in Indiana as he was not able to do in Kentucky played strongly on Thomas. Indiana was an opportunity.

Sometime in the Fall of 1816, Thomas made his first known journey to Indiana to inspect the land for himself. This research trip led him to his future home. He found a quarter-section of land in Hurricane Township of Perry County. It was the southwest quarter of Section 32, Township 4 S, Range 5 W. The parcel later became Section 32 of Carter Township in Spencer County when Perry County was divided into smaller counties in 1818. Federal surveyors had been through the land in 1805, settling boundaries and property lines. Thomas found all of this in the records office. The tract Thomas chose for his future home was surveyed in 1805 by David Sandford and Arthur House.[247]

Surveyors described the land as level, surprisingly, even though the land is hilly, but not as hilly as other parts of southern Indiana. It was land with thick brush under oak and hickory trees. There was a stream close by for water. Thomas liked the section of land and followed the tradition of piling brush at the four corners to show others the land was claimed. He also built a

---

[247] Wayne C. Temple. *Thomas and Abraham Lincoln As Farmers*, page 18.

makeshift shelter[248] to provide himself a dwelling while he was there as well as being another indicator to other settlers that this parcel of land was claimed. The shelter was the half-face camp his family would settle into while their cabin was being built.

Returning to Kentucky, Thomas told his family of the new home and they began preparations to move. Thomas had a surplus from his farming. He arranged to leave 200 bushels of corn in the loft of one of neighbor Caleb Hazel's cabins until he could sell it.[249]

As the family prepared to leave Kentucky, Thomas built a flatboat to carry belongings. He converted the payment for the Mill Creek farm and possibly the Bush settlement for the Sinking Spring farm into whiskey. Whiskey was a common form of barter and commerce. He received 400 gallons, ten barrels of whiskey.

When the raft was ready, Thomas loaded it with furniture, farm tools, woodworking tools, and household goods. He rafted down the Rolling Fork toward the Salt River. He most likely had help with him from family and friends, but names are not recorded and tradition has Thomas making the flatboat trip alone. Somewhere on the Rolling Fork, the raft partially capsized, tilting some of the load into the water.

Thomas saved most of the whiskey and most of the household goods. He did lose some farm tools and woodworking tools that sank to the river bottom. He lost a barrel of nails that he was unable to replace until a blacksmith moved into the area near the Pigeon Creek farm. Additionally, Thomas was unable to salvage a cabinet which he left in the river. Later, the cabinet was retrieved by nearby residents.[250] It was restored by John T. Crowley and is now on display in a Harrogate, Tennessee museum.[251]

With his belongings reloaded and arranged on the flatboat, Thomas continued down the Rolling Fork to the Salt River and

---

[248] Edward Murr. "Lincoln in Indiana." *Indiana Magazine of History*, page 320.

[249] Louis A. Warren. *Lincoln Association Papers.* "The Environs of Lincoln's Youth", page 130.

[250] Kathy Tretter. "Lincoln Family Corner Cabinet Hidden for Years in Southern Indiana." *Ferdinand News.*

[251] Abraham Lincoln Association. *Thomas Lincoln: Carpenter and Cabinetmaker 2016 Calendar*, July.

along the Salt River to the Ohio River. There he crossed the Ohio and safely landed at Thompson Ferry where he stored his goods with a man by name of Posey to whom he sold the flatboat.[252]

Returning to Kentucky, Thomas completed preparations and began the move to Indiana with his family. At the time of the move, Thomas had hogs, horses, and cattle. Some of these he may have traded. Others he took with him to start his new Indiana farm. While there may have been several helping in the family's move, two names are recorded. Ralph Crume, Thomas' brother-in-law by marriage to Thomas' sister Mary, worked with Dennis Hanks to herd the animals on the journey.[253]

The latter part of November, the month the Indiana move began, was cold and sometimes stormy but as December arrived, the first half of the month was the most pleasant weather of the 1816-1817 Winter season.[254]

The trip from Knob Creek to Pigeon Creek is only fifty miles in a straight line but with the hills and creeks, rivers and woods, the distance Thomas traveled with his family was nearly double that. The Lincolns moved from an area of Kentucky with ten people per square mile on average to the Little Pigeon Creek area of Indiana that averaged only three people to the square mile.[255]

From Knob Creek to the Ohio River, Thomas' family traveled by horseback, traveling slowly with the livestock being herded along with them. Varying traditions have them using a small cart or a small wagon to carry their remaining household items and supplies for the journey. One of these goes into detail that Thomas was driving an ox cart pulled by two huge oxen with a cow in tow.[256] This story is often rejected because Thomas was known to

---

[252] Douglas L. Wilson and Rodney O. Davis. *Herndon's Informants*, pages 98-99. Statement by A. H. Chapman dated September 8, 1865.

[253] Douglas L. Wilson and Rodney O. Davis. *Herndon's Informants*, page 98. Statement by A. H. Chapman dated September 8, 1865..

[254] R. Gerald McMurtry. "The Lincoln Migration from Kentucky to Indiana. 1816. *Indiana Magazine of History*, pages 391. The weather information was found in a newspaper clipping in a scrapbook. The newspaper referencing the scrapbook weather report was the Grandview Monitor of Grandview, Indiana. Exact date of the scrapbook newspaper clipping is unknown.

[255] Carl Sandburg. *Abe Lincoln Grows Up*, page 68.

[256] Breckinridge-Perry County Lincoln Highway Association. *At the End of the Trail*, page 4.

own horses in Kentucky but not oxen. This ox cart tradition is from the same source however, as an accepted story of Minerva — a slave owned by Colonel David R. Murray, providing buttered bread and milk for the Lincoln children.

The journey was slower at the start because the Lincolns stopped to visit and say farewell to friends and neighbors and family. After going only a short way on the first day of travel, they stopped at the home of Rollie Thomas and other neighbors came there to wish the Lincolns well.[257] That first night was spent at the farm of William Atherton, another friend and neighbor who lived just a little farther along the road from Rollie Thomas.[258]

The next known stop was Elizabethtown[259] where Thomas had lived and worked, where he had continued to do a lot of work after moving from the town. Thomas and Nancy had family in Elizabethtown. They were greeted by many while there and sent on their way with love and probably a fresh supply of home-cooked food for the road.

From Elizabethtown, Thomas turned his family off the most direct route to Indiana to go to William Brumfield's farm, not far from Mill Creek farm. This was another road where Thomas and Nancy knew most of the people living along the way and where they made at least brief stops at almost every farm.

Thomas stayed at the Brumfield farm for several days, visiting with his mother Bathsheba and his sister Nancy's family.[260] No doubt other friends came there as well. The Mill Creek community was filled with relatives and long-time friends. The days and evenings were filled with stories and memories, love, and a touch of sadness at parting.

From the Brumfield farm, Thomas led his family north through Big Spring to Hardinsburg to Yellow Banks along the wagon trail. From Yellow Banks, Thomas followed the Yellow

---

[257] R. Gerald McMurtry. "The Lincoln Migration from Kentucky to Indiana. 1816. *Indiana Magazine of History*, page 397.

[258] R. Gerald McMurtry. "The Lincoln Migration from Kentucky to Indiana. 1816. *Indiana Magazine of History*, page 400.

[259] R. Gerald McMurtry. "The Lincoln Migration from Kentucky to Indiana. 1816. *Indiana Magazine of History*, page 400.

[260] R. Gerald McMurtry. "The Lincoln Migration from Kentucky to Indiana. 1816. *Indiana Magazine of History*, pages 402-403.

Banks Road to Pellville. At Pellville, they took a direct route north to the Ohio River.[261]

Somewhere in the trek to Indiana, Thomas took his family by his brother Mordecai's home to say goodbye. Despite the distance put between them by the move, Mordecai and Thomas stayed in communication and Mordecai visited Thomas in Indiana. The families stayed close enough that Abraham invited his cousins to his inaugural even though they were staunch Democrats.[262]

Almost every tradition and historian have the Lincolns crossing the Ohio at Thompson's Ferry with a landing near where Anderson Creek flows into the Ohio River. The ferry flatboat would have been of more substantial construction, able to carry larger loads and built for daily use in ferrying travelers across the river.[263] Thompson's Ferry, owned and run by Ephraim Thompson, was two and a half miles west of Troy, Indiana, the county seat for Perry County. It is likely Thomas went through Troy to pick up supplies before going to the new farm.

There is a lesser-known historical alternative to Thomas' route being through Thompson's Ferry. The report of the Breckinridge-Perry County Lincoln Highway Association, which was not accepted by other groups, reports that Thomas went from Hardinsburg to Joeville (now Cloverport) where they crossed the Ohio River landing at Tobin's Bottom (now Tobinsport) in Indiana. According to this tradition, there was no ferry boat, so a raft was constructed at the crossing on which the ox cart and family crossed with the cattle swimming. This somewhat unlikely scenario had a canoe pulling and guiding the raft across the river. There was also a man on the raft poling the craft as the river was low at the time of crossing.[264]

---

[261]R. Gerald McMurtry. "The Lincoln Migration from Kentucky to Indiana. 1816. *Indiana Magazine of History*, pages 404-408. More detail of this journey to the Ohio River can be found in McMurtry's article and in the records of the Lincoln Memorial Highway Commission.

[262] Marcy G. Bodine. "Story of the Lincolns of Hancock County." *Macomb Daily Journal*.

[263]R. Gerald McMurtry. "The Lincoln Migration from Kentucky to Indiana. 1816. *Indiana Magazine of History*, page 409.

[264] Breckinridge-Perry County Lincoln Highway Association. *At the End of the Trail*, page 4, 8-9.

In Indiana, following the more traditional route, the family retrieved their belongings from storage and Thomas hired wagons and teams[265] to carry belongings and family to Pigeon Creek, one and a half miles from Gentryville. It was roughly sixteen miles to the new home site. Thomas followed the Vincennes-Troy Road to a point near his land.

From that point, travel became more difficult. There were trails and traces but no true roads leading to Thomas' land. Thomas used his axe and, with the help of his friends and family, he began cutting a road for the wagons to follow. The forest was thick with brush to be cleared, making the going slow. Bridges had to be constructed for streams or low areas where the wagons could get bogged down.[266]

After much visiting, traveling, and clearing a road, Thomas arrived at Pigeon Creek. It was time to build a new farm.

---

[265] Douglas L. Wilson and Rodney O. Davis. *Herndon's Informants*, page 99. Statement by A. H. Chapman dated September 8, 1865.
[266] Douglas L. Wilson and Rodney O. Davis. *Herndon's Informants*, page 93. Letter from Nathaniel Grigsby to Herndon dated September 4, 1865.

Indiana

As Abraham Lincoln looked back on his life, he described Thomas moving the family to Indiana.

He removed from Kentucky to what is now Spencer County, Indiana, in my eighth year. We reached our new home about the time the State came into the Union. It was a wild region, with many bears and other wild animals still in the woods. There I grew up.[1]

The Treaty of Vincennes (1804) ceded Native American (Delaware and Piankeshaw) land in southern Indiana along the Ohio River to the United States. This included the land Thomas bought for the Pigeon Creek farm. Most Native Americans had left the area by the time the Lincolns moved to Spencer County.

Thomas arrived in Indiana with statehood. He moved into Spencer County in early December 1816. Indiana became the 19th State on December 11, 1816.

In the 1860's, Ernest Duvergier de Hauranne, would describe southern Indiana poetically.

There are some very pleasant landscapes in southern Indiana – mountainous areas covered with large stands of timber, varied here and there by broad cornfields. It is a delight to let one's eyes roam over these beautiful, rolling, golden fields, which lie partly in the shadow of tall trees that cover the lower slopes of the hills. The rivers are sluggish and yellow with clay; they flow through valleys full of lush vegetation between rows of century-old trees – plane trees, sycamores with shiny leaves, slender elms that rise to a noble height, cottonwoods with pale streamers, cork-oaks whose delicate brown limbs hang out over the water and trail their tips in it. In the depths of these forests there are damp, shady dells where small,

---

[1] Roy P. Basler. *The Collected Works of Abraham Lincoln*, volume 3, page 512. Taken from a letter from Abraham Lincoln to Jesse W. Fell enclosing an autobiography for use in campaigning.

dark brooks slip quietly along, nearly covered by dead leaves.[2]

The cornfields de Hauranne mentions were not so easily seen when Thomas moved to Indiana but the century old trees with the lush vegetation in virgin forests among the rolling hills of southern Indiana were there. It was through this terrain that Thomas and Ralph and Dennis cut their way while Nancy and Sarah and Abraham pulled away the brush and limbs to make a road.

Southern Indiana was covered by hardwood forests with large trees. Mixed in were cherry trees, apple trees, and grape vines along with an abundance of wild strawberries. The land was full of wildlife. Deer, antelope, rabbits, turkey, mink, weasels, groundhogs, possum, bear, wolves, mink, fox, and wildcats were in abundance. The nearby stream was Little Pigeon Creek, so named because of thousands of passenger pigeons who made the area their home.

Thomas claimed 160 acres of good ground. He had marked the boundaries by notching trees with his axe and piling brush. Because he would not register his claim until months later, some have assumed he squatted on the land, but Thomas was following standard practice in the land laws of the time. He marked his land and registered it after making improvements.

At the time Thomas came to Indiana, it was mainly populated by Southerners. Over half the settlers came from Kentucky, from the same area as the Lincolns. [3] Being near the Ohio River, the infant Indiana economy was built on river trade. In the Pigeon Creek community, the economy continued the pioneer pattern of being an agricultural subsistence economy very similar to what Kentucky had. Each family produced what they needed to survive with neighbors contributing skills and help in exchange for the same in return. Barter was the standard of trade as cash was scarce.

Into this environment Thomas came with his family in 1816. Thomas was 37 years old, Nancy 32, Sarah 9, Abraham 7, and Dennis Hanks was 17. The fourteen years Thomas lived in Indiana

---

[2] Ernest Duvergier de Hauranne. *A Frenchman in Lincoln's America*, Volume 1, pages 339-340.
[3] Kenneth J. Winkle. *The Young Eagle*, page 12.

would be the formative years for Abraham, the years building the foundation of Abraham's life and thought.

There is one odd note in Thomas' history at this early period in Indiana that says Thomas remained at the mouth of Anderson River until the Fall of 1817. This record says Thomas worked a ferry established originally by Judge McDaniel but then owned by James Taylor.[4] There is no corroboration for this deviation in Lincoln history. The record of Thomas living for a time at Anderson Ferry appears to confuse Thomas with Abraham later working for James Taylor and running the ferry. Weston Goodspeed, in his history of Spencer County, prints a definite denial. "It is not true that Thomas Lincoln lived for a time at the mouth of Anderson Creek where he kept a ferry. He did not live there, and hence kept no ferry. He lived nowhere in the county except on his farm at what is now Lincoln City."[5]

Pigeon Creek Farm

1816 - 1817

As the Lincolns arrived at the new Pigeon Creek farm, Thomas unloaded family possessions and covered them to protect them from the weather. What they needed for daily living and work was put into the half-face camp. It is likely Thomas sent Ralph Crume and Dennis Hanks back to Thompson's Ferry to return the wagons and teams he had hired. Crume then returned to Kentucky.

Many pioneers moving into a wilderness area to settle first lived in tents. Tent living was often for weeks and, dependent on the timing of the move, some lived in tents through winter. Thomas decided against a tent. He chose the other oft used pioneer shelter, the half-face camp.

The standard half-face camp was constructed by choosing two strong, straight trees about fourteen feet apart east to west. Using these trees, trimmed and hewed, other logs (smaller and easier to work with than the logs used for cabin construction) were placed

---

[4] B. N. Griffing. *An Illustrated Historical Atlas of Spencer County, Indiana,* page 10.
[5] Selwyn A. Brant and Weston A. Goodspeed. *History of Warrick, Spencer, and Perry Counties, Indiana,* page 273.

to enclose the east, west, and north sides. These small timbers were put together in the same way a log cabin was built. Logs were then laid across the top of the shelter and covered with sod and tree branches to form a roof. The sides were made tight from the weather using a clay mix. A large fire was kept burning day and night in front of the open south side (which on occasion was partly enclosed with skins or branches).

If properly constructed, and Thomas was skilled at such, a half-face camp was a sturdy and reliable temporary shelter though it could be uncomfortable at times when the wind came out of the south, blowing smoke into the shelter from the fire or when heavy rain soaked through the roof and dripped on the occupants sheltering below. Fortunately for the Lincolns, December of 1816 was mild and warmer than usual.[6] The time the Lincolns spent in the half-face camp was not nearly as cold or desperate or uncomfortable as often pictured. Adding to the shelter and comfort for the Lincolns is the fact that Thomas built his half-face camp using the excavated bank of a hillside as the back.[7]

Surveying the land and setting it up for sale had led to a move to settle Indiana only a matter of years before Thomas moved his family.[8] The land was still mostly forested wilderness with a sparse population. Indiana cities and centers of government were more large villages than actual cities. Perry County was large and undivided. What would become Spencer County was still a part of it. In 1815, the year prior to Thomas' arrival, in all of Perry County, only 318 names were listed for taxes. [9]

At the time the Lincolns came to Indiana, most of the population lived within one hundred miles of the Ohio River. Thomas' brother Josiah was in Indiana as were two of Hananiah Lincoln's sons, Austin and David.[10] Many coming to the Pigeon Creek area or planning to were friends and relatives.

Land records show Pigeon Creek was a growing community when Thomas arrived. The Carters, Grigsbys, Gentrys, Wrights,

---

[6] William E. Bartelt. *There I Grew Up*, page 11.

[7] William E. Barton. *The Women Lincoln Loved*, page 91.

[8] The land was surveyed by David Sandford and Arthur House in 1805. Wayne C. Temple. *Thomas and Abraham Lincoln As Farmers*, page 18.

[9] R. Gerald McMurtry. *Lincoln Highlights in Indiana History*, page 3.

[10] R. Gerald McMurtry. *Lincoln Highlights in Indiana History*, page 3.

and Gordans were there. The extended families of these settlers owned tracts of land and farms near or next to Thomas. Farms and businesses were being established. When Thomas and Nancy moved to Indiana, they had neighbors with more coming. By 1818, when the schoolhouse was built, there were over 130 children in the area, aged 17 and younger. By 1820, there were forty families settled within five miles of Thomas' Pigeon Creek farm. By pioneer standards, those were close neighbors.

This was the area Thomas chose for his family. In December 1816, they established themselves in a sturdy half-face camp and immediately began preparing for long term residence. The first task was a new home. During the Winter of 1816-1817, Thomas and Dennis, with help from Abraham, cut trees, cleared underbrush, and put up their log home. It was a standard eighteen-by-twenty-foot cabin, one story with a loft, one door, and one window. The loft was a large bedroom. It was reached with a peg ladder. Holes were bored into the log wall and pegs inserted, pegs of sufficient size and strength to allow a person to climb them like a ladder.[11]

Building a log cabin did not take long. Large stones were placed at the four corners to serve as a foundation. Logs were cut, trimmed, and notched and then laid on the stones. More logs were added until the walls were in place. A loft was built by laying small logs across the lower walls as rafters. The roof was placed above the loft walls and sheathed with clapboard to make it tight. Wood shingles covered the roof. The loft floor was made from clapboard. The cabin floor could be hard-tamped earth at first with a puncheon floor added later or the floor could be put in as the cabin was raised. Openings were cut into the logs for the door, window, and chimney. Spaces between the logs were chinked with sticks and rocks and plastered over with mud or clay. Thomas was known for his finishing work, so the cabin had a framed in door and window with planks. It sounds like a lot of work, and it was, but it was quick work, especially with the help of family and neighbors.

---

[11] Douglas L. Wilson and Rodney O. Davis. *Herndon's Informants*, page 40. From Dennis Hanks interview with Herndon on June 13, 1865.

Being winter and farming chores over, the neighbors – by common custom of the time – came to both welcome Thomas and help the family settle in. That help included assisting in building the cabin. Some historians have the Lincolns hunkered down in the half-face camp for the entire winter. That is very unlikely. Thomas and Dennis, with the help of Nancy, Abraham, and Sarah, could have put up the cabin by themselves in a matter of days. With the neighbor's help, it would have been quicker, possibly even a day. It is very probable that Thomas had his family comfortable in their new cabin home within the first week they were in Indiana.[12]

Tradition has the Lincolns living in a cabin with a hard-tamped dirt floor until Sarah had Thomas put in a floor when she came to the Indiana home. In all likelihood, Thomas put in a puncheon floor, a wood floor made with logs flattened on one side to form a level surface not long after putting up the cabin. Neighbor Nathaniel Grigsby remembers the floor.[13]

The cabin was situated on a rise with the ground descending from the front door. The cabin sat with the chimney on the east wall, the door in the south wall along with a window. Neighbor Elizabeth Crawford remembers the cabin also having a window in the north wall. Ground was cleared in front of the door for a garden.[14]

As the cabin and outbuildings (workshops, livestock sheds, barn) were raised, it is likely the neighbors helped in that construction also and in clearing land ready for Spring planting. Cutting logs for the cabin was done with an eye on taking out trees to make a field. Pioneers were efficient in clearing land quickly. Smaller trees, a foot to a foot and half in diameter or smaller, were cut down and the stump and roots grubbed out. Larger trees that were not cut for logs were girdled. Girdling a tree meant cutting a ring around the trunk with an axe, removing the bark and blocking the sap from flowing. The tree died and sunlight was not blocked

---

[12] Louis A. Warren. *Abraham Lincoln Association Papers.* "The Environs of Lincoln's Youth", page 132.
[13] Douglas L. Wilson and Rodney O. Davis. *Herndon's Informants*, page 93. Letter from Nathaniel Grigsby to Herndon dated September 4, 1865
[14] Douglas L. Wilson and Rodney O. Davis. *Herndon's Informants*, pages 261-262. From an Elizabeth Crawford letter to Herndon dated July 22, 1866.

by leaves. This allowed crops to be planted around the dead trees which would be taken out later as time allowed. As the trees were taken out or girdled, underbrush was cleared and burnt.[15] Large fields were cleared quickly in this manner.

Not long after the Lincolns settled into their new home, Nancy's aunt and uncle, Thomas and Betsy Sparrow, moved to Indiana. Thomas and Betsy moved into the half-face camp while they looked for land of their own. They sheltered in the Lincoln cabin when weather was foul.

The Sparrows had raised their nephew Dennis and, when they arrived, he lived with them. An often-overlooked member of the family is Sophie Hanks. Tom and Betsy were kindly folks who took in children to raise. They took Dennis Hanks in and, in similar fashion, took in Sophie.

Sophie was one of six illegitimate children born to Sarah Hanks. Sarah was a sister or half-sister to Nancy Hanks Lincoln. Sophie was Thomas and Nancy's niece. Born on March 14, 1809,[16] she was a month younger than Abraham.

Sophie Hanks is an enigma in Lincoln history. There is little doubt she had a close connection with Thomas' family. Her stories and history confirm details and add details to the lore, but her place is difficult to determine.

A small portion of Lincoln historians include her as living in Thomas' home from the deaths of Tom and Betsy Sparrow until Sophie married Dillings Lynch in 1827. They place her as the ninth person in the Lincoln cabin with Thomas and Sarah, their children, and Dennis Hanks. This is at issue with known history. In all his interviews and research, William Herndon did not hear of or include Sophie Hanks as he documented the early years of Abraham Lincoln. Dennis Hanks, who corresponded with Sophie after she was married and living outside Indiana, never mentioned her name in relation to the Lincoln home.

When Sarah came to Indiana with her children, Dennis Hanks speaks of eight people living in the cabin. Sophie living there would have made nine. The 1820 census lists eight people in the

---

[15] Edwin Coles Bearss. *Lincoln Boyhood – As a Living Historical Farm*, pages 73-74.
[16] Arthur E. Morgan. "New Light on Lincoln's Boyhood." *The Atlantic Monthly*, pages 208-218.

Lincoln household. Sophie is not included. Descendants of Sophie Hanks speak of her being close with the Gentry family and Sophie living with the Gentry's for a period of time.[17] The 1820 census lists only James Gentry's seven children.

Where Sophie Hanks lived and when she lived there may well remain a mystery. That she is related and that she was very familiar with Thomas' home and family is clear and the stories she left with her family add valuable information, but she is a puzzle in Lincoln history that is yet to be solved.

As Thomas prepared the land and settled his family, tradition provides an added reason for Thomas choosing to buy the section of land he chose. He was establishing himself in an area where he would have a good start in business. In addition to being a carpenter, cabinetmaker, and wheelwright, Thomas was a cooper, making barrels. Near Thomas' new home were at least three distilleries, more commonly called stills. In Kentucky, Thomas made barrels for Thomas Carter and Carter was now living in Indiana, not far from Thomas.[18] Neighbor Noah Gordon, in addition to his horse mill, operated a distillery. Distilleries needed barrels and Thomas was skilled in making them. As he started up a new farm, Thomas reached out to engage in business and trade with his neighbors. It did not take long for Thomas to be a sought-after carpenter, cabinetmaker, and cooper.

Thomas' farm and business were a welcome addition to a growing community. James Gentry established Gentryville not far from Thomas' Pigeon Creek farm. Near Gentryville there were the distilleries, Gordon's mill, Peter Whittinghill's mill, Gentry's cotton mill, William Whittinghill's tannery, Gentry's store, and Shadrack Hall's tannery.[19] Thomas brought a grouping of much needed skills to the community. As in Kentucky, those skills would provide the main living for Thomas and his family. "John Romine of Spencer County related that Thomas Lincoln practiced his carpentry trade there, 'relied on it for a living, not on farming.'"[20]

---

[17] Arthur E. Morgan. "New Light on Lincoln's Boyhood." *The Atlantic Monthly*.
[18] William E. Bartelt. *There I Grew Up*, pages 112-113.
[19] William E. Bartelt. *There I Grew Up*, page 113.
[20] Wayne C. Temple. *Thomas and Abraham Lincoln As Farmers*, page 18.

In the Spring of 1817, Thomas planted his first crops at Pigeon Creek farm. Wheat, flax, cotton, corn – these were planted for both the family's use and for sale and barter. Six acres of ground was cleared for crops. Over the course of the next two years, the acreage being planted would nearly triple to ten acres for corn, five acres for wheat, two acres for oats, and an acre of meadow. Additionally, there was land around the house which included a large garden. The kitchen garden that Elizabeth Crawford remembered being in front of the Lincoln cabin had melons, squash, pumpkins, beans, potatoes, and other vegetables, planted from the seed Thomas brought from Kentucky. The meadow included log pens and sheds for safely housing livestock at night. The numerous wolves in the Indiana forest made it difficult to raise sheep, pigs, and small livestock. The meadow's pens and sheds were the only way to protect them.[21]

The Pigeon Creek farm had access to a good, clear spring for water at the foot of the hill on which the cabin sat. Abraham carried water from the spring to the house every day. It was a long walk and a heavy load, but Abraham was large for his eight years. With Spring, Thomas dug a well. This turned into a problem. Thomas dug several locations but was not able to find a good well. The best he had was a well where the water had to be strained in warm weather before drinking.[22] The spring at the bottom of the hill became the main source of water for the family.

From the crops Thomas raised, cotton and flax, Nancy made clothing. Nancy was a skilled seamstress, but everyday pioneer clothing did not require her full skill. From cotton and flax, Nancy, with Sarah's help, made homespun and handmade clothing. She supplemented the cotton and flax with wool from the sheep and animal skins that Thomas cured from his hunting and bartered for at the tanneries.

Buckskin pants were standard wear for pioneer men. The seams were sewn with dressed deerskin, often providing a fringe. Hats were made from coonskin or fox skin with the tails kept as a standard ornament hanging from the back. The women wore

---

[21] B. N. Griffing. *An Illustrated Historical Atlas of Spencer County, Indiana*, page 10.
[22] Douglas L. Wilson and Rodney O. Davis. *Herndon's Informants*, page 98. Statement by A. H. Chapman dated September 8, 1865.

bonnets said to resemble the covering of a Conestoga wagon. It was functional if not stylish. Nancy clothed her family with clothing made from flax and cotton raised by Thomas. The homespun was comfortable though it may have lacked pattern and color. She made flax and cotton clothes for warmer weather and wool clothing for cold weather.[23]

During his presidency, Abraham used a story from the farm to illustrate a point he was making to his cabinet. He does not say which farm he is speaking of. It could have been the Knob Creek farm or the Pigeon Creek farm, but either way the story provides a glimpse of Thomas' farm.

> *I remember when I was a lad, there were two fields behind our house separated by a fence. In each field there was a big bulldog, and these dogs spent the whole day racing up and down, snarling and yelping at each other through that fence. One day they both came at the same moment to a hole in it, big enough to let either of them through. Well, gentlemen, what do you think they did? They just turned tail and scampered away as fast as they could in opposite directions.[24]*

While many portray pioneer life as isolated and lonely, time spent in long stretches with only family around, that is not reality. Universal custom of pioneer life was to be neighborly. When there was a need, neighbors gathered. The only thing needed was to send out word to let the community know what was needed and when. This was not considered charity or being weak. It was neighboring. It was socializing.

Work was turned into festivity. The men competed to complete the work and show their skill, strength, and endurance. Women did the same as they worked. Jokes and stories and laughter were the order of the day along with accomplishing whatever was needed. Cabins and barns and animal pens were built in one day. Fields were cleared. Harvests were brought in. The women cooked feasts and did a week's worth of quilting, spinning, and clothes-making in a day. Chores that would take a

---

[23] B. N. Griffing. *An Illustrated Historical Atlas of Spencer County, Indiana*, page 10.
[24] Donald T. Phillips. *Lincoln on Leadership*, page 35.

single pioneer family weeks or even months to do by themselves were finished by sundown. While men and woman worked, children helped and played. After the day's work was finished, it was time for music and dancing and storytelling.[25] Pioneer life was not easy, but neither was it solitary. Dennis Hanks remembered the early days in Indiana and put it simply. "It was pretty pinching times at first in Indiana, getting the cabin built, and the clearing for the crops; but presently we got reasonably comfortable."[26]

The Lincoln table was never short of food. Between what they grew on the farm, the livestock they raised, the natural bounty of the forest in berries, nuts, and honey, and the abundance of game, food was not a problem. Thomas loved to hunt and it was said he never came home empty-handed. Such was not true of Abraham.

As all pioneer boys, Thomas taught Abraham to shoot and Abraham became a fair shot, but hunting was not something the kind-hearted boy took to. He told the story simply in the third person for a campaign biography. "A few days before the completion of his eighth year, in the absence of his father, a flock of wild turkeys approached the new log-cabin, and Abraham with a rifle gun, standing inside, shot through a crack, and killed one of them. He has never since pulled a trigger on any larger game."[27] This would have been in 1817, some days ahead of Abraham's eighth birthday in February. Sighting down the turkey and killing it was a feat not all eight-year-olds could emulate. Seeing the dead animal and knowing he had taken its life struck Abraham in the heart. He turned from hunting and never "pulled a trigger on any larger game" afterward.

This turkey story also provides information on the building of the cabin. Abraham shot the turkey through a chink in the logs of their cabin, not he half-face camp. That means the cabin was built, though not fully chinked (a task not easily completed in winter) and the Lincoln's did not spend the entire winter in the half-face camp.

---

[25] Donald T. Phillips. *Lincoln on Leadership*, page 35.

[26] Allen Thorndike Rice. *Reminiscences of Abraham Lincoln by Distinguished Men of His Time*, page 457.

[27] Roy P. Basler. *The Collected Works of Abraham Lincoln*, volume 4, page 62. From Abraham Lincoln's Autobiography written for John L. Scripps.

It was on October 15, 1817 that Thomas went to the land office in Vincennes to register his claim. The law allowed a settler time to develop the land and make improvements before officially registering a claim. Thomas was within the timeframes specified in the law. In Vincennes, Thomas paid $16 down. The claim was for 160 acres at $2 per acre. The full price for the land was $320. Thomas received receipt number 8499 and the clerk spelled Thomas' last name phonetically as pronounced in the local dialect, "Linkern".[28]

On December 26, 1817, Thomas returned to Vincennes and paid an additional $64 on his claim, receiving receipt number 9205.[29] With this payment, Thomas had paid for one fourth of his land.

1818

As 1818 came, Thomas had his family settled in. The Sparrows laid claim to a plot of land near Thomas', a cabin was raised, and land cleared. Tom and Betsy moved there with Dennis and Sophie.

Thomas established a pattern he would follow through all the Indiana years. In the warm months, he farmed and did woodworking on the side as time allowed. In the non-farming months, he worked as carpenter, cabinetmaker, furniture maker, and cooper.

As in Kentucky, Thomas' skill and hard work gave him plenty to do. The forest provided plenty of wood. Thomas worked mainly with walnut, cherry, and poplar. He did business with a local sawmill to get the lumber sawed down. From there Thomas brought the wood to his workshop where he produced mostly Federal style furniture with tapered legs, contrasting veneers, meticulously done inlays in patterns of vines and hearts or whatever the customer might want. The style and level of detail depended on what the customer paid for or bartered in trade.

---

[28] William E. Bartelt. "The Land Dealings of Spencer County, Indiana, Pioneer Thomas Lincoln." *Indiana Magazine of* History, page 213.

[29] William E. Bartelt. "The Land Dealings of Spencer County, Indiana, Pioneer Thomas Lincoln." *Indiana Magazine of* History, page 213.

Some of Thomas' pieces sold for a mere $5 while others were more than $40.[30]

Neighbor William Woods told of Thomas' work. "Thomas Lincoln often and at various times worked for me, made cupboards, etc., other household furniture for me; he built my house, made floors, ran up the stairs, did all the inside work for my house."[31]

Nancy's work was also seasonal. During farming months, she worked with the crops and garden. She prepared cotton and flax from the fields for later spinning and weaving and making clothes. She sheered the sheep and worked the wool. Starting in the Fall, much of her time was spent in her workshop where her spinning wheels and loom were set up to spin and weave the cotton and flax and wool material into cloth and the cloth into clothes and quilts and whatever else her family needed.[32]

The Hall family lived about four miles from the Lincolns. Mr. Hall operated a large farm and a tannery. He was very successful in his business and prosperous in the community, employing many of the men at various times to support his businesses. Both Thomas and Abraham did work for him. His son, Wesley, was interviewed later in life and provided a picturesque story of life in the Lincoln cabin.

> *On one occasion during the early winter Wesley Hall was sent to mill beyond Gentryville, a short distance from the Lincoln cabin, but since the Halls lived to the east some four miles it was more than a five miles journey. According to the pioneer custom, no favors were shown youth or age in certain things, and the rule especially obtained in the matter of going to mill, for each one had to "take his turn." Such was the law.*
>
> *Young Hall found upon his arrival on this occasion that a number of men and boys had preceded him, and by the*

---

[30] Rich Davis. "Teacher Quickly Becoming a Lincoln Furniture Expert". *Evansville Courier-Press.*

[31] Emanuel Hertz. *The Hidden Lincoln, From the Letters and Papers of William H. Herndon*, page 343. From a William Wood's letter dated September 15, 1865.

[32] Kenneth J. Winkle. *The Young Eagle*, page 47.

time his turn came the entire day had almost passed. During the last half of the afternoon a severe snow storm had set in, and by the time the miller carried out his "grist" and assisted him to mount preparatory to making the homeward journey some inches of snow had fallen. This alarmed the pioneer lad, lest some mishap should befall him, and he should lose his way through the forest, become a prey to wild animals, or succumb to the cold. More especially was he so impressed since nightfall was fast approaching and the snow was driving furiously in his face. On reaching the turn in the road leading up to the Lincoln cabin he decided to go there for the night. Riding up in front of the silent, snow-mantled house, he hallooed in true pioneer fashion a time or two: "Hel-lo! Hel-lo!" Just here it will be proper to permit Mr. Hall to tell the remainder of his story:

"Bye and bye I heard the door begin to creak on its wooden hinges, and then through the storm I saw old Tom a shadin' his eyes with his hand a tryin' to see who I wuz. And purty soon, satisfying himself that it wuz me, he leaned back and laughed a big broad laugh, and then a startin' out to where I wuz he says, says he: 'Is that you Wesley? You get down from thar and come in out of the weather.' So I commenct to git ready to slide off my sack and by the time I got ready to light, old Tom wuz there and helped me down. Then a turnin' around lookin' towards the cabin, he calls out a time or two, big and loud: 'Abe! O Abe! Abe!' And he aint more'n called till I seen him a comin' through the door, and when he asked what wuz wanted, and seein' who I wuz at the same time, old Tom says: 'Come out here and git Wesley's grist while I put his hoss in the stable. Wesley's mighty nigh froze I reckon.' Then he laughed again. Well, I wuz cold I c'n tell you fer I hadn't had anything to eat ceptin' parched corn since mornin'. Well, as I say, old Tom told Abe to come and get my sack, and I noticed as Abe come out to where I wuz he hadn't but one shoe on, and thinks I to myself, what's up

with Abe fer I saw Abe wuz a walkin' on the ball of his heel so's to hold his big toe up which wuz all tied up, and by this time I reckon there wuz mighty nigh six inches of snow on the ground. Yit Abe's foot wuz so big and long it didn't make no difference if the snow wuz that deep. Abe hadn't any trouble about a keepin' his sore toe above the snow line. When I asked him what wuz the matter with his foot he told me he'd split his big toe open with an ax out in the clearin' that day. Well, Abe then wuz as big and stout as he ever wuz, and so he jest reached over and took that sack of meal with one hand and layin' it across his arm, him and me went into the house while old Tom put the hoss in the pole stable.

"I set down in front of the fireplace and commenct to thaw out, and in a little bit old Tom come in, and a settin' down by me a slappin' his hands together and then a rubbin' em so, like he allus' done, he says, says he: 'Wesley, you got purty cold I reckon, did you?' And when I commenct to say I did, Mrs. Lincoln come in and she says, after we'd passed the time of day, she says, says she: 'Wesley, I reckon you're hungry.' And I told her I wuz; and then I told her about the parched corn. And she says: ''We haint got no meal to bake bread. We're out just now', but a pointin' to the big bank of embers that I'd already noticed in the fireplace and of course knowd what it meant, she says, says she, 'we've got some potatoes in thar a bakin' and we'll git a bite fer you purty soon.' At that I spoke up and I says, says I: 'Mrs. Lincoln, jist help yerself out of my sack thar.' And so she done as I told her.

"Well, old Tom and Abe and me went on a talkin' and purty soon I heard a funny grindin' noise back of me, and I looked around to see what it wuz, and it wuz Mrs. Lincoln a hollerin' out a big turnip."

Just at this point in Mr. Hall's narrative he paused and asked the writer if he could guess what Mrs. Lincoln was "hollerin' out that turnip fer". When some two or three attempts had been made to solve this mystery and all proved to be clearly wrong, to the evident amusement of the old gentleman, he resumed his narrative by saying: "She was makin' a grease lamp. Course I'd seen a many one. She hollered it out and cut a small groove in it on the lip, and after she'd filled it with hog's lard and laid a wick in the notch, and lit it, she handed it to' me, and a butcher knife to Abe, and she says: 'Boys, go and get me some bacon.' So me and Abe went out to a little pole smoke house and I held up the light while Abe cut a half moon out of a side of bacon. So Mrs. Lincoln went on with gittin' supper, and bye and bye she says: 'Supper's ready.' So when we set down to it we had corn cakes, baked potatoes and fried bacon. After the supper dishes was washed up old Tom, a slappin' his hands together and a rubbin' em like I say, he says, says he: 'Now, Abe, bring out your book and read fer us.' Old Tom couldn't read himself, but he wuz proud that Abe could, and many a time he'd brag about how smart Abe wuz to the folks around about. Well, Abe reached up on a shelf where he kept his books and then a stirrin' up the fire on the hearth with some dry stuff he had piled in one corner by the jamb, he commenced to read."

When the writer asked as to whether the narrator remembered what book it was that Abe read from, he straightway replied:

"Oh, yes! It wuz the life of Ben Franklin. He read to us till bed time, and that night Abe and me slept together up in the loft. We got up there through a scuttle hole in one corner of the ceilin', and to git up to it we had to climb up a peg ladder made by boring holes in the logs and insertin' wooden pins. I remember the bedstid which of course I saw many a time. It wuz a mighty sorry affair; still it answered the purpose. A hole wuz bored in the north wall and a rail-like piece wuz sloped off to fit this. The same thing wuz done on the west wall, and these two rails wuz brought together and fastened in the same way to an

> *upright post out in the floor and then across these wuz laid split boards or whipped plank, or some thin slats rived out, and on these wuz a gunny sack filled with leaves gathered from the woods. On this Abe and me slept covered with bear skins." [33]*

This story provides good insight into Thomas, old Tom, from someone who knew him and the family well. It shows the cabin had a good size loft and that along with his and Nancy's workshops and the animal pens, Thomas had a stable and a smokehouse. It also shows how proud and supportive Thomas was of Abraham's education. He bragged about him to all who would listen. The story shows that Thomas provided Abraham with books and a shelf to keep them on. The story provides information that Abraham had a bed in the loft and did not sleep on the loft floor.

In 1818, Thomas moved to Spencer County without moving an inch. Perry and Warrick Counties were divided out and Spencer County was formed. Thomas' farm was part of the new county. [34]

When Thomas' brought his family to Indiana, there was not a church building. Congregations met in homes and traveling preachers, such as Parson David Elkin of the Baptist Church, went from home to home gathering the community and preaching. Thomas and Nancy attended the Little Pigeon Baptist Church.

Little Pigeon Church was a Regular Baptist Church that started with thirteen charter members on June 8, 1816, six months before the Lincolns moved to Indiana. John Weldon and Thomas Downs, from Kentucky, established the church with six men and seven women. Samuel Bristow was the pastor. [35] The church met in members' homes. Thomas and Nancy joined the church by letter from the Little Mount Church as members in good standing in 1818.

Thomas' Religion

Thomas lived during the historical period known as the Second Great Awakening. The Awakening was a series of religious

---

[33] Edward Murr. "Lincoln in Indiana." *Indiana Magazine of History*, pages 322-325.

[34] J. T. Hobson. *Footprints of Abraham Lincoln*, page 17.

[35] B. N. Griffing. *An Illustrated Historical Atlas of Spencer County, Indiana*, page 10.

revivals that swept across the United States from the late 1700's through the mid 1800's.[36] At the time of the American Revolution, Congregationalists (Puritans), Quakers, and Episcopalians (Anglicans) were the mainstay of religion in America. By 1800 that changed. The Awakening brought an evangelical surge to America led by Methodists and Baptists. These two movements were the fastest growing religious groups in the country.

The Second Great Awakening was driven by camp meetings, some of which were very large. At these camp meetings, thousands of people were converted through the enthusiastic preaching and singing and the evangelical fervor that permeated the meetings. One such meeting was held at Cane Ridge, Kentucky in 1801. Cane Ridge was 80 miles east of the Beechland community where Bathsheba Lincoln's cabin was located. There is no record that Thomas went to the Cane Ridge Communion, but twenty thousand people did. At Cane Ridge, several preachers preached at the same time in different locations in the Camp. People wept and prayed, shouted and danced. Hundreds experienced conversion. Word of the Cane Ridge meeting would have been known in Beechland. It was the kind of meeting that both Thomas and Nancy would have felt at home in.

An old story has been told for many years regarding Thomas and Nancy meeting at a similar camp meeting. The story lacks accuracy, but it illustrates a long tradition of Thomas being in and fitting in gatherings like the Cane Ridge Camp Meeting. The story is that a camp meeting was being conducted in Kentucky in 1809 by Peter Cartwright. In the midst of a prayer meeting, a young man leaped to his feet and began to dance and sing. Moments later a young woman joined him. The couple was said to be Thomas Lincoln and Nancy Hanks, who were soon introduced and shortly married. [37] While this is a fun story and it correctly reflects the passion exhibited during the Second Great Awakening's camp meetings and revivals, the history for Thomas and Nancy not meeting until a religious revival when both were adults is errant as is the date in the story.

---

[36] http://www.ushistory.org/us/22c.asp.
[37] D. James Kennedy. *What They Believed: The Faith of Washington, Jefferson, and Lincoln*, page 2.

Thomas did participate in such meetings. That is the truth behind such stories. Nancy also participated and her family was well known for its fervor. The Hanks were said to be the best singers and shouters in the Elizabethtown area.[38] William Herndon related a story that was told him about Thomas and Nancy in a camp meeting in Elizabethtown prior to their marriage in 1806.

> *It was at a camp-meeting, as before said, when a general shout was about to commence. Preparations were being made; a young lady invited me to stand on a bench by her side where we could see all over the altar. To the right a strong, athletic young man, about twenty-five years old, was being put in trim for the occasion, which was done by divesting him of all apparel except shirt and pants. On the left a young lady was being put in trim in much the same manner, so that her clothes would not be in the way, and so that, when her combs flew out, her hair would go into graceful braids. She, too, was young not more than twenty perhaps. The performance commenced about the same time by the young man on the right and the young lady on the left. Slowly and gracefully they worked their way towards the center, singing, shouting, hugging and kissing, generally their own sex, until at last nearer and nearer they came. The center of the altar was reached, and the two closed, with their arms around each other, the man singing and shouting at the top of his voice. "I have my Jesus in my arms Sweet as honey, strong as bacon ham." Just at this moment the young lady holding to my arm whispered, "They are to be married next week; her name is Hanks."* [39]

Thomas grew up and lived his life in the midst of the religious fervor and style of the Second Great Awakening. It dominated the revivals and camp meetings. The preachers Thomas knew and associated with were the Methodists and Baptists finding their

---

[38] William H. Herndon & Jesse W. Weik. *Herndon's Life of Lincoln*, page 15.
[39] William H. Herndon & Jesse W. Weik. *Herndon's Life of Lincoln*, page 15.

direction and style from the Awakening. At some point during the Awakening, a young Thomas Lincoln made a commitment to the Baptists. His family background was from the staider approach of Congregationalists and Quakers, but when Thomas turned his life over to Jesus, it was to be a Christian of the Baptist persuasion. Nancy stood with him in this choice. It is possible the move toward the Baptists began with Captain Abraham and Bathsheba. The Baptists had a strong impact in the Shenandoah Valley prior to and during the Revolution, a time period where they could have influenced the Lincoln family. This strong push followed and continued with the pioneers moving from the Valley into Kentucky.[40] There is not enough information to know if Thomas converted to the Baptists in his youth or if he was raised Baptist because his parents had converted.

Following their marriage, Thomas and Nancy joined and held membership in Separate Baptist churches. Separate Baptists were one of several denominations claiming to have no creed but the Bible[41] and the Bible was considered the only rule of faith and practice. The Lincolns were founding members of the Little Mount Church in Kentucky and very early members of the Little Pigeon Church in Indiana, both of which were Separate Baptist.[42] The minutes of the Little Pigeon Church from 1816 through the 1830's have been preserved and provide insight into the Lincoln's church. [43]

Separate Baptists have been called Primitive Baptists and Hard Shell Baptists. The Separate Baptist churches to which the Lincolns belonged refused to have or accept any written creed, but they followed Calvinist theology, believing strongly and strictly in predestinarian doctrine. It has been said the Separate Baptists out-

---

[40] Richard F. Nation. *At Home in the Hoosier Hills*, page 45.

[41] Many congregations and some denominations still proudly claim to have no creed but the Bible; however —no disrespect intended – all of these groups can generally be traced to a specific theological tradition and they follow that tradition's interpretation of the Bible even though they may not recognize they are doing so.

[42] The Little Pigeon Church later became a part of the United Baptist Association when the Regular Baptists and the Separate Baptists merged but the merger little changed Separate Baptist beliefs and practices.

[43] Allen C. Guelzo. "Abraham Lincoln and the Doctrine of Necessity. *Journal of the Abraham Lincoln Association.*

Calvined Calvin in their rigid interpretation of Biblical doctrine. They believed God was in control of human affairs and all things hinged upon his decisions and actions. What God predestined to be, would be.

They were so strong in this belief that they rejected evangelism and missionary work. The records of Little Pigeon during the time when Thomas was a member show votes declining responsibility to help missionary organizations and track societies.[44] Separate Baptists believed in the sacraments of the Lord's Supper, Baptism (by immersion), and Foot Washing. They believed and followed a very strict standard of morality and behavior. All members were expected to maintain the doctrine in purity and to live their lives in accord with church practice and polity. Members were expected to raise their children respecting the rules and life of the church. To step outside these rules and requirements would cause a member to stand accused before the church and the resulting deliberations would either clear the member or order them to be disciplined.

Church discipline could involve corrective actions to show repentance and, if repentance was not shown, membership in good standing could be revoked and the member put out of the church. Thomas Lincoln served several times for the Little Pigeon Church on the committee investigating charges brought against members for violating Christian and church standards.

Separate Baptists took living a Christian life very seriously. Thomas and Nancy Lincoln agreed to this standard for themselves and their children. Thomas Lincoln was one of the leading men among the Separate Baptists of Indiana.[45] He was chosen for leadership positions and selected to sit in judgment of other members when accusations were brought. His integrity and moral behavior were highly respected.

Early frontier churches were not lax in church discipline or in expectations of how their members should live. The Separate Baptist Church had a strict code of conduct members were expected to fulfill. If a member's conduct and way of life

---

44 W. E. Barton. *Life of Lincoln, Volume I*, page 129.
45 Allen C. Guelzo. "Abraham Lincoln and the Doctrine of Necessity. *Journal of the Abraham Lincoln Association*, page 67.

conflicted with this code, other members could and did bring accusation against the member. The records of the churches are clear on this point. If a member did not live up to the Christian standard set by the church, that member would not long be in good standing. To maintain membership in good standing was an achievement that was not achieved if one's life was undisciplined. Thomas Lincoln was always a member in good standing. There is no existing record that Thomas' morals or principles were called into question and there are several records that he stood in high regard with his pastors and fellow members.[46] In Indiana, Thomas was considered to be one of the five or six most important men in his denomination.[47]

In Thomas' family, the Bible was their first book.[48] They had other books and they read from those, but the Bible was first and most important. From their church teaching, the Bible was their guide in life. Daily Bible reading was a part of life for the Lincolns. Nancy taught Sarah and Abraham their letters and used the Bible to teach them to read. She sang Bible songs and taught them to her children. She memorized Bible verses and repeated them, teaching her children to memorize them. These lessons stayed with Abraham his entire life and references to the Bible was part of his daily speech and standard fare in his public speeches and thought.

No meal was served in the Lincoln house without a blessing before eating.[49] Thomas' standard prayer before eating was, "Fit and prepare us for life's humblest service, for Christ's sake, Amen."[50]

Learning the Bible and learning about God's salvation in Jesus was the foundation on which Thomas raised his family. The family went to church, or when the church met in homes, hosted the gathering at their home. If there was a church meeting, the

---

[46] Louis A. Warren. *Lincoln's Parentage & Childhood*, pages 134-135.
[47] Allen C. Guelzo. "Abraham Lincoln and the Doctrine of Necessity." *Journal of the Abraham Lincoln Association.*
[48] Louis A. Warren. *Lincoln's Youth Indiana Years Seven to Twenty-one 1816-1830*, page 30.
[49] Louis A. Warren. *Lincoln's Youth Indiana Years Seven to Twenty-one 1816-1830*, page 115.
[50] D. M. Coleman. *Thomas Lincoln, The Father of Abraham Lincoln*, page 21.

Lincolns were there. When problems arose, Thomas turned to prayer. It was a pattern he followed his entire life.

Little has been written or told relating to Thomas and Nancy influencing Sarah's life but it is known that when Sarah was preparing to be wed, she joined the Little Pigeon Church on confession of faith. The normal pattern for the Separate Baptists was for men and women to join when they were adults and preparing to wed. Sarah followed this tradition.

With Abraham, the influence of Thomas' beliefs set a lifelong pattern. Even when Abraham stepped away and looked for something deeper than the simple fare provided by most of his childhood preachers and the simple lessons of his parents, having the Bible at hand, reading it, and quoting from it was always a part of Abraham Lincoln.

Thomas and Nancy taught Abraham the Bible and they took him to meetings where he would learn it. The books in the home from which Abraham read extended this religious influence. Nancy used Dilworth's Speller to teach her children. This speller contained a large number of Bible selections along with stories having Scriptural morals about behavior and faith. David Turnham, an Indiana neighbor and playmate of Lincoln, later told Herndon that Abraham read the Bible, and that "What Lincoln read, he read and re-read, read and studied thoroughly."[51] The Lincoln family Bible from which Abraham read as a child was an edition from 1799 that included notes on each book plus commentary. The preface of the Bible stated, "The Scriptures therefore are the most valuable blessings God ever bestowed upon us except the sending of his son into the world." [52] This statement is very similar to what President Lincoln said in thanks for the gift of a Bible he was presented while president. Regarding this influence of the Bible on the Lincoln family, Dennis Hanks wrote to Herndon. "Lincoln's mother taught him to read the Bible, study it and the stories in it and all that was moral and affectionate in it, repeating it to Abe and his sister when very young. Lincoln was

---

[51] Douglas L. Wilson and Rodney O. Davis. *Herndon's Informants*, page 121. Taken from Herndon's notes from interviewing David Turnham on September 15, 1865.
[52] Louis A. Warren. *Lincoln's Youth, Indiana Years Seven to Twenty-one 1816-1830*, page 31.

often and much moved by the stories."[53] Thomas' home was a strong Christian environment.

President Lincoln spoke of this in his autobiographical statement for Scripps. "This practice [family Bible reading and devotions], continued faithfully through a series of years, could not fail to produce certain effects. Among other things, its tendency was to impart an accurate acquaintance with Bible history and Bible teachings; and it must also have been largely instrumental in developing the religious element in the character of the younger members of the family. The facts correspond with this hypothesis. There are few men in public life so familiar with the Scriptures as Mr. Lincoln, while to those pious labors of his mother in his early childhood are doubtless to be attributed much of that purity of life, that elevation of moral character, that exquisite sense of justice, and that sentiment of humanity which now form distinguishing traits of his character."[54]

Another important part of church and faith for Thomas was his opposition to slavery. While some southern (and northern) churches capitulated their honor and integrity to defend the vile institution of slavery, Thomas chose not to be a part of them. The Lincolns' churches were opposed to slavery and preached opposition. The preacher Thomas and Nancy chose to perform their marriage ceremony was a staunch opponent to slavery. The preachers the family associated with stormed against subjecting any human being to slavery. They preached the Bible as opposed to slavery and they preached the Declaration of Independence that "all men are created equal." This preaching was a strong influence on Abraham and these sermons would have been among those he mimicked.

"I am naturally anti-slavery. If slavery is not wrong, nothing is wrong. I cannot remember when I did not so think and feel."[55]

---

[53] Emanuel Hertz. *The Hidden Lincoln, From the Letters and Papers of William H. Herndon*, page 276. Taken from a letter from Dennis Hanks to Herndon on June 13, 1865.

[54] John Locke Scripps. *The First Published Life of Abraham Lincoln*, page 18. This campaign biography went through edits by Lincoln and was approved by Lincoln.

[55] Roy P. Basler. *The Collected Works of Abraham Lincoln*, volume 7, page 281. Quoted from a Lincoln letter to A. G. Hodges on April 4, 1864.

The influence on Abraham is clear. The churches Thomas and Nancy chose to affiliate with were strongly emancipationist in belief. Thomas and Nancy believed and taught opposition to slavery to their children. There can be little doubt that President Lincoln's anti-slavery views were the product of his religious upbringing.

Outside the home, going to church and preaching services was a regular event in Lincoln family life. From the records of the Little Pigeon Church and the standards of the Separate Baptist denomination, it is known that attendance and Christian discipline was required of members. While services were somewhat irregular around the Knob Creek home, the Lincolns were in attendance when services were held. Services were more regular at the Little Pigeon Church and the Lincolns were there. If they had not been regular in attendance, the elders would have visited them to inquire and church records would have recorded their names as under investigation. No such listing was ever made against Thomas and Nancy.

We know from friends and family that these services had an impact on Abraham. He paid close attention to the sermons and committed them to memory. Later in the week, he would gather a crowd of friends and family and re-preach the sermon to them, mimicking the preacher's habits and voice, and coming very close to the very words used in the sermon on Sunday. This impressed and amused the community. Some have reported this as mocking the church and the preachers and Christianity. They have said Abraham was highly disrespectful of the preachers and put them to shame and ridicule in his reenactments. That interpretation does not hold up to historical fact. Mimicry was a part of pioneer life.

"The pioneers were great yarn spinners and often acted out the things they told. They enjoyed practical jokes and were great mimics. All these things Abraham absorbed in his boyhood before he left Indiana for Illinois."[56] Mimicry was common. Abraham mimicking preachers was not a mockery or ridicule as some have read into it. It was part of frontier life. Had Abraham been mocking and ridiculing the church and its preachers, the records

---

56 Bess V. Ehrmann. *Lincoln and His Neighbors*, page 19.

of the Little Pigeon Church would show that Thomas and Nancy were called to account for such lax discipline in their family. They were not so accused. The church and the people who heard Abraham re-preaching the sermons and mimicking the preachers did not see it as ridicule. Abraham was not mocking or disrespecting the church in his youth. Neither Thomas nor Nancy would have tolerated such a performance.

This is further supported by the fact that as a teenager, Abraham was appointed a sexton at the Little Pigeon Church. We do not know what the exact duties of the sexton were, but we know from church records that part of the sexton's duties were keeping the church clean, doing general maintenance, and providing firewood and candles for services. There is a receipt for candles which Abraham signed, recording his name as Abraham Lincoln, Sexton. An open mocker of the faith would not have been accorded a position in the church. However, neither do we have anything to show that Abraham made a statement of faith to receive this position. Receiving this employment at age fourteen and fulfilling his responsibilities simply shows that Thomas and his family were in good standing with the church.[57]

Little is recorded of Sarah Bush Lincoln's religious beliefs. It is known she joined the Little Pigeon Church on confession of faith. She was active in churches for the remainder of her life.

When Thomas moved his family to Illinois, he led his family in a move away from the Baptists as the fervor of the Second Great Awakening began to fade. Members of the Hanks family had moved to Charleston, Illinois, about ten miles from Thomas' Goosenest Prairie farm. The families visited one another. One such visit was on the occasion of a large Campbellite (Disciples of Christ) revival being held in the Coles County Courthouse. The result of the revival was that the Hanks and Lincoln families joined the Campbellite church. Thomas faithfully attended that church to the end of his life. During those last years of his life, the Bible remained his constant support. He read from the Bible daily.[58]

---

[57] Alan T. Nolan. "Abraham Lincoln and Indiana." *Traces of Indiana and Midwestern History*, page 8.

[58] H. B. Glasco. "Thomas Lincoln. His Tomb – The Old Cabin in Which He Died – His Religion – Some Stories of His Life." *The Independent.*

Nancy Lincoln's Death

The early part of 1818 was just a normal pioneer year. Thomas worked at his carpentry until the winter passed. He had expanded the size of his fields from the previous year and more crops were planted, providing more for the family, more for sale, and more for barter. The community was larger with more neighbors moving in and more cabins being raised. The Lincolns were part of the festivities around those raisings and in welcoming new neighbors, new friends.

Spring came and the plows turned up the furrows where the seeds were planted. Nancy and Sarah worked in the large garden. Thomas and Abraham took care of the livestock and worked the fields. Spring gave way to Summer and Summer turned toward Fall and harvest. With the harvest came sickness.

On pioneer farms, many animals fed by grazing the wooded areas outside the fenced meadows. In the Fall of 1818, most of the usual forage plants had dried up and the main vegetation found was in wet areas. One of the plants that grew in these wet areas was white snakeroot, a perennial herb plant that pioneers tried to keep cleared out of pasture areas and wooded areas where animals grazed. Pioneers knew the plant was trouble. It was poison, a poison that a cow could ingest but whose symptoms would not show up until the poison had already spread through the milk.[59]

White snakeroot contains tremetol, a poisonous substance that caused the "milk sick".[60] In the early 19th century in the Ohio River Valley, hundreds died from milk sickness.

In human beings the first symptoms are weakness, dizziness, and loss of appetite, followed by nausea and persistent vomiting. There is pain in the region of the stomach and great thirst. The tongue is swollen and coated white, and the skin is dry. There is an odor of acetone on the breath, no peristalsis [the involuntary constrictions of the bowels that move bodily waste products through the intestines], obstinate constipation, weak pulse, slow respiration, subnormal temperature,

---

[59] William E. Bartelt. *There I Grew Up*, page 20.
[60] James Fitton Couch. *Trembles (or Milk Sickness)*, page 4.

great prostration, and frequently collapse. As the disease progresses coma develops and continues until death, which is quiet. In nonfatal cases recovery is slow. The weakness and lassitude persist for weeks, and slight exertion is very fatiguing. Relapses with fatal termination often occur during convalescence. The patient misjudges his strength and overexerts by taking a long walk or performing some laborious task about the farm, returning home to collapse and often to die within 2 or 3 days. [61]

As milk sickness spread in the Little Pigeon Creek community, Thomas was kept busy making coffins. Abraham whittled the pegs that held the boards together. There is no record of what Thomas charged for the coffins, but it is likely he followed the usual standard of a dollar a foot. A child's coffin averaged three dollars, a woman's six dollars, and a man's seven dollars. [62]

There was not an established cemetery for the community so John Carter, owner of the farm adjacent to the Lincolns, offered a hilltop on his land as a cemetery. [63] This burial ground became a frequently visited site as a horse-pulled sled carried the coffins of the dead.

As the community pulled together to care for the sick and to bury the dead, Nancy Lincoln was one of those who went from home to home nursing those sick and dying. There are specific records of Nancy serving as nurse in two homes, the Brooners and the Sparrows.

Peter and Nancy Brooner lived a half mile from Thomas' cabin. They were living in the Little Pigeon Creek community before Thomas and Nancy arrived. Not long before her sickness, Nancy Brooner gave birth to a daughter, Sarah. When she contracted milk sickness, Nancy Lincoln frequently visited the Brooner home to care for the sick woman and to help tend the family. The Brooners' oldest son, Henry, was fourteen when his mother died. He was a frequent visitor and overnight guest in the Lincoln cabin. It is from his memories that the story of Nancy Lincoln being a nurse to Nancy Brooner is recalled.

---

[61] James Fitton Couch. *Trembles (or Milk Sickness)*, page 7.
[62] William E. Barton. *The Women Lincoln Loved*, page 86.
[63] William E. Bartelt. *There I Grew Up*, page 21.

Tom and Betsy Sparrow, who had stayed for a time in Thomas' half-face camp, had set up their own farm not far from the Lincoln cabin. Both Tom and Betsy came down with the milk sick at the same time. This was prior to Nancy Brooner's sickness as Nancy Lincoln only survived Nancy Brooner by a week.[64]

Nancy took care of her relatives, no doubt staying in the home overnight as much as possible. Dennis Hanks told of Nancy's care for his adoptive parents. Sophia Hanks was eight years old. When the Sparrows died, Thomas and Nancy took in Dennis and Sophia as their own.[65]

Where Nancy contracted the milk sick is not known, but somewhere in late September 1818, the symptoms became clear. Nancy Lincoln had the milk sick. There was no known cure.

Nancy was a strong woman and a woman of strong faith. She knew she was dying. Tradition tells of her calling her children to her bedside where she shared the final wisdom she would give them. It was custom in the 19th century for families and friends to gather at the deathbed to hear the final words of the dying. These words were remembered and passed down. Sarah was eleven and Abraham was nine when their mother called them to her side. To Abraham she said, "I am going away from you, Abraham, and I shall not return. I know that you will be a good boy, that you will be kind to Sarah and to your father. I want you to live as I have taught you, and to love your Heavenly Father."[66]

Nancy Lincoln died on October 5, 1818. She was 34 years old.[67]

As Nancy had gone to other cabins to nurse the dying and help prepare the dead for burial, friends now came to the Lincoln cabin to prepare Nancy's body for burial. Preparations were simple as there was no embalming and burial was as soon after death as possible. The women washed Nancy and dressed her in

---

[64] J. T. Hobson. *Footprints of Abraham Lincoln*, page 18.

[65] J. T. Hobson. *Footprints of Abraham Lincoln*, page 18.

[66] Louis A. Warren. *Lincoln's Youth, Indiana Years Seven to Twenty-one 1816-1830*, page 54.

[67] Nancy Hanks Lincoln's tombstone is marked saying she was 35 years old when she died. Nancy was born February 5, 1784 and died on October 5, 1818. She was four months shy of her 35th birthday and only 34 years old when she died.

her Sunday best. After that, there was a short time for family and friends to pay a final visit before she was placed in her coffin.

It is a hard thing to express the pain of a husband losing his wife or to put in words the sorrow of children whose mother has died. It is even more difficult to imagine the anguish Thomas must have felt as he not only faced Nancy's death but also went to his workshop to whipsaw the boards from which he would build her coffin. Abraham whittled the pegs.

There is little in Abraham's writing and speeches to indicate the depth of his grief over the loss of his mother. Later, President Lincoln provides a glimpse into what he felt and learned through the death of his mother. In 1862, he wrote Fanny Washington to console her on the death of her father in the war.

> *It is with deep grief that I learn of the death of your kind and brave Father; and, especially, that it is affecting your young heart beyond what is common in such cases. In this sad world of ours, sorrow comes to all; and, to the young, it comes with bitterest agony, because it takes them unawares. The older have learned to ever expect it. I am anxious to afford some alleviation of your present distress. Perfect relief is not possible, except with time. You cannot now realize that you will ever feel better. Is not this so? And yet it is a mistake. You are sure to be happy again. To know this, which is certainly true, will make you some less miserable now. I have had experience enough to know what I say; and you need only to believe it, to feel better at once. The memory of your dear Father, instead of an agony, will yet be a sad sweet feeling in your heart, of a purer, and holier sort than you have known before. Please present my kind regards to your afflicted mother.*[68]

Nancy' body was conveyed by horse-drawn sled to the hilltop cemetery. The burial rites were overseen by Lamar Young, an elder

---

[68] Roy P. Basler. Editor. *The Collected Works of Abraham Lincoln*, volume 6, pages 16-17. From a letter of Abraham Lincoln to Fanny Washington dated December 23, 1862 from Washington, D.C.

of the Little Pigeon Church.[69] After the burial, Peter Brooner reached his hand out to Thomas and said, "We are brothers, now." Both had lost their wives and the mother of their children. They were bonded in grief.[70]

Nancy's funeral was preached later, after word could be sent to friends and family farther away and they had time to gather. Tradition tells the story of Abraham writing to Pastor David Elkins of the Little Mount Church in Kentucky to have him come and preach Nancy's funeral. The story is fanciful and touching but probably not accurate. Pastor Elkins did come to preach Nancy's funeral, but it was most likely because of Thomas sending for him and making the arrangements. It was nearly a year past Nancy's death when the pastor came to Indiana to preach her funeral. Pastor Elkins preached the funeral sermon at Nancy's grave and spoke of her "staunch Christian faith and the virtues she exemplified as a faithful wife and revered mother."[71]

Such a delay between death/burial and the funeral seems odd to modern ways but it was frontier custom to defer the funeral (sometimes as long as a year) to allow for a decent period of mourning and grieving.[72]

Nancy Hanks Lincoln Remembered

Much of Nancy Hanks Lincoln's life will remain shrouded in mystery. Historical documents are limited, and complete facts of her life are unavailable.[73] However, enough is known to give a good picture of the woman she was.

Nancy, for the time and place where she lived, was educated better than most women. She could read and was able to teach her

---

[69] Roy P. Basler. Editor. *The Collected Works of Abraham Lincoln*, volume 6, pages 16-17. From a letter of Abraham Lincoln to Fanny Washington dated December 23, 1862 from Washington, D.C .

[70] J. T. Hobson. *Footprints of Abraham Lincoln*, page 18

[71] J. T. Hobson. *Footprints of Abraham Lincoln*, page 55.

[72] David S. Reynolds, *Abe*, page 85.

[73] Lincoln historians owe a great debt to those like Louis A. Warren, William Barton, and Ida Tarbell who spent countless hours scouring old legal records in dusty archives and traveling to all areas Lincoln related to find the truth about Lincoln's parents and family. Modern scholarship is building on what they did, adding new information and detail, but without the foundation these early scholars laid, much would have been lost.

children to read. She was a skilled seamstress and a woman who was productive in clothing and feeding her family. She was respected and loved by friends and family. Those who knew her held her in high regard.

Most of the testimony to Nancy's character comes from friends and neighbors in Indiana. Neighbor Isaac Arnold reports that Nancy "was a woman of deep religious feeling, of the most exemplary character and most tenderly and affectionately attached to her family. Her home indicated a degree of taste and love of beauty exceptional in the wilderness settlement in which she lived."[74]

Another Hoosier neighbor takes the description further, stating Nancy "was a very smart, intelligent and intellectual woman; she was naturally strong-minded; and a gentle, kind and tender woman, a Christian of the Baptist persuasion. She was a remarkable woman."[75]

Neighbor and friend Nat Grigsby reported, "She was a brilliant woman, a woman of great good sense and morality."[76] "Mrs. Lincoln, the mother of Abe Lincoln, was a woman known for the extraordinary strength of her mind among the family and all who knew her…She was a brilliant woman, a woman of great good sense and morality…Thomas Lincoln and his wife were really happy in each other's presence, loved one another."[77]

One story reports Nancy's physical prowess. Nancy "…was said to be a very strong-minded woman, and one of the most athletic women in Kentucky. In a fair wrestle, she could throw most of the men who ever put her powers to the test. A reliable gentleman told me he heard the late Jack Thomas, clerk of the Grayson Court, say he had frequently wrestled with her, and she invariably laid him on his back."[78]

---

[74] Louis A. Warren. *Lincoln's Youth, Indiana Years Seven to Twenty-one 1816-1830*, page 56.

[75] Alan T. Nolan. "Abraham Lincoln and Indiana." *Traces of Indiana and Midwestern History.*

[76] Emanuel Hertz. *The Hidden Lincoln, From the Letters and Papers of William H. Herndon*, page 355.

[77] Emanuel Hertz. *The Hidden Lincoln, From the Letters and Papers of William H. Herndon*, page 355. Statement by Nat Grigsby (neighbor and friend) to Herndon dated September 12, 1865.

[78] F. Linder Usher. *Reminiscences*, page 39.

Many other neighbors and friends and family could be quoted to the same effect. Nancy Lincoln was a woman of intelligence, a spiritual woman, a woman of good moral values and integrity. Her memory became a precious treasure to Abraham.

Lucius E. Chittenden, who served in the Lincoln administration and was very well acquainted with Lincoln, wrote in his reminiscences, "Except for the instruction of his mother, the Bible more powerfully controlled the intellectual development of the son than all other causes combined."[79]

This held to what Abraham Lincoln said when talking of his mother. She had interested him in the Bible and Bible stories before he learned to read. Later in life, as he read verses memorized as a boy through hearing his mother repeat them, in his mind he could hear the tones of her voice, hearing her again in his memory. Her instruction and love guided him his entire life. The President cherished his mother's legacy, holding her with love in his heart. "All that I am, or hope to be, I owe to my angel mother." [80] Such is the legacy of Nancy Hanks Lincoln.

Between Marriages

1818 - 1819

The winter of 1818-1819 was a long and dreary time period for Thomas and the family. The home was completely changed. Nancy, the loving mother who had run the household with tenderness and grace was no longer there. Dennis Hanks, nineteen years old and having inherited the Sparrow cabin and land, lived mainly with the Lincolns over that winter. Sarah, eleven years old, took over Nancy's work as the woman of the family. Sophie Hanks, nine years old, was able to help Sarah but the two young girls were no replacement for all that Nancy had done and meant

---

[79] Emanuel Hertz. *The Hidden Lincoln, From the Letters and Papers of William H. Herndon*, page 212. Statement by Nat Grigsby (neighbor and friend) to Herndon dated September 12, 1865.

[80] J. G. Holland. *Holland's Life of Abraham Lincoln*, page 23. Following Herndon's denigration of Nancy's character, many have said that Lincoln's memory of Nancy faded away with time and that this quote referenced Sarah Bush Lincoln. But what nine-year-old forgets sitting at his mother's deathbed? Abraham's remarkable memory would not have lost Nancy to fading.

to the family. Abraham, nine years old, was devastated by the loss of his mother.

Thomas was not able to be both father and mother to the family. The pioneer way of life required the skills of both the man and the woman to fulfill the needs of the subsistence farm economy. Labor and chores were divided according to man's work and woman's work in the 19th century. One adult, no matter how skilled in the work of the other sex, could not do all the cooking, gardening, farming, weaving, sewing, hunting, and daily chores that took two adults full time. Thomas was overwhelmed and his family suffered.

Nancy had the winter clothing prepared and ready along with food put away and stored. Thomas and Dennis spent the time tending to the repair of farm tools and to hunting, things the men would normally do. Hunting was a necessity for pioneer life. It was a main source of food and the hides served many purposes. Thomas spent time in his workshop making furniture and cabinets. Winter was the time for his woodworking businesses to be the focus of his labor.

Sarah did her best but the weight of filling in for Nancy overwhelmed the young girl who turned twelve in February of 1819, as her brother Abraham turned ten. The food was not the same as Nancy made. The work on the clothing for Spring and Summer did not come close to being ready or as capably done. There were times all Sarah could do was sit by the fire and cry. Dennis and Abraham tried to cheer her up by bringing her a baby raccoon and a turtle for pets. They even tried to catch a fawn but were unsuccessful at that.[81]

Somewhere in 1819, Thomas made a venture at making money through taking a load of pork to New Orleans via flatboat down the Ohio and Mississippi Rivers. Thomas was speculating in pork the way the Lincoln family had often speculated in land. Pigs were cheap and if the pork could be gotten to New Orleans, there was good money to be made. Thomas built a flatboat and bought, mainly on credit, as much pork as the flatboat could carry. He did well until he got on the Ohio River somewhere near Devil's Island. There, the flatboat capsized, and he lost everything

---

[81] David Herbert Donald. *Lincoln*, page 26.

including the flatboat, barely avoiding drowning. He traveled back home on foot and went back to work at carpentry and farming, paying off the credit on which he had bought the pork. He paid everyone for everything he owed but lost everything he had put into the venture.[82]

As planting and farming began in 1819, the family relied on clothing from the previous year. Thomas and Dennis got along somewhat well but the children had grown, and their clothing was small and becoming ragged. The cleanliness and care Nancy had brought to the family was not kept up. What had been a well-clothed and well cared for family under Nancy's watchful eye became wild and ragged and dirty. Something needed to be done and Thomas pondered out a plan.

In the pioneer subsistence economy, life without a spouse made running a household extremely difficult. The normal thing was for a widow and widower to seek out each other and merge their families into a new family to meet the rigors of life. As the 1819 harvest was completed, Thomas had his plan made. In November, he left his children in the care of Dennis Hanks and, no doubt, with the promise of neighbors to look in on them, Thomas went to Elizabethtown, Kentucky in hopes of returning with a new wife.

Sarah Bush Lincoln

Thomas went to Elizabethtown to ask Sarah Bush Johnston to marry him. The Lincolns had kept in touch with their friends and family in Kentucky. Thomas knew that Sarah's husband had died, and she was now a widow with three children.

Sarah Bush was born on December 13, 1788 in Hardin County, Kentucky. She was the third daughter of Christopher and Hannah Bush. The Bushs moved to Elizabethtown in 1790. Christopher and Hannah had a large family with nine children. He served as a patrol captain searching and watching for runaway slaves. The family was comfortable financially.

Sarah is described as light-skinned with blue-gray eyes. She was known to be hard-working and very neat in her habits.

---

[82] Arthur E. Morgan. "New Light on Lincoln's Boyhood." *The Atlantic Monthly*.

Despite the family being financially stable and Elizabethtown offering some good schools, Sarah could neither read nor write.

Thomas knew the Bushs and was a friend of the family when living in Elizabethtown and Hardin County. Nancy had also been a friend of the Bush family. Thomas worked with Sarah's brother Isaac to take produce down the Ohio and Mississippi to New Orleans. Isaac was the person that sold Thomas the ill-fated Sinking Spring farm without a clear title to the land.

Sarah married Daniel Johnston on March 13, 1806, three months earlier than Thomas married Nancy. With Daniel she had three children: Sarah Elizabeth (born January 9, 1807), John D. (born in 1810), and Matilda (born in 1811). Unlike Sarah's life under her father's roof, Daniel and Sarah struggled financially. In the Hardin County tax census, Daniel listed little or no taxable property. He incurred debts that his brothers frequently settled for him. In 1814, Daniel was hired as the county jailer, in which position he frequently hired Thomas as an assistant jailer. The position included housing for Daniel and Sarah and their children. Sarah took on being the jail cook, housekeeper, and janitor. This time period was as comfortable financially as the family ever was during the marriage even though they did not own their own home.

In 1816, a cholera epidemic swept through Elizabethtown. Daniel succumbed to the disease, leaving Sarah a widow with three children to cloth and feed. Somehow, possibly with savings from the previous two years of steady employment, possibly with help from her family and the Johnstons, Sarah bought a cabin[83] and settled there with her children. She continued working as cook and cleaner at the jail to keep her family clothed and fed.

Tradition says that at an earlier point in his life, when he lived in Elizabethtown, Thomas had courted Sarah. Nothing is said of the feelings they had for each other or of why the courtship did not work out, but both went their separate ways in marriage. Thomas with Nancy and Sarah with Daniel.

---

[83] This cabin was later allowed to get run down and was used as a slaughterhouse. It was moved two or three times, which did not help its condition. At that point, Samuel Haycraft reported to Herndon and others that the run-down shanty cabin was the "best" house Thomas could provide for Nancy when they lived in Elizabethtown. He was mistaken.

History records Thomas' proposal to Sarah as straight forward and to the point. "Well, Mrs. Johnston, I have no wife and you no husband. I came to propose to marry you. I knowed you from a gal and you knowed me from a boy. I have no time to lose, and if you are willing, let it be done straight off." Sarah hesitated in her reply. "Tommy, I know you well, and have no objections to marrying you; but I cannot do it straight off, as I owe some debts that must be paid first." Sarah was a woman of principle. She would not consider marrying Thomas and leaving debts behind her. She told Thomas, "I owe too much." Thomas asked the simple question. "How much?" Sarah replied, "Two dollars and a half." This was the amount that she considered "too much". Considering this amount as too much and an obstacle to marrying shows that Sarah's finances were tight, but Thomas took it in stride. "If that's all, I'll pay that."[84] For Thomas, the amount was no problem.

Thomas got the names of Sarah's creditors and went immediately to pay the debts. Sarah readily accepted Thomas' proposal and began preparation to marry and move her family. Thomas and Sarah were married on December 2, 1819 by Rev. George L. Rogers of the Methodist Episcopal Church. The wedding was conducted at the home of one of Sarah's neighbors, Benjamin Chapeze, a local lawyer.[85] Thomas had signed the marriage bond the morning of the wedding with Christopher Bush, Sarah's father, signing for Sarah.[86]

Later, explaining the quick nature of Thomas' trip to Kentucky and the speed with which the marriage was arranged, Dennis Hanks said, "Tom has a kind of way with women, and maybe it was something she took comfort in to have a man that didn't drink and cuss none."[87]

Samuel Haycraft also told of the short, quick trip Thomas made from Indiana to Kentucky to wed Sarah. "Old Mr. Lincoln (whose name was generally pronounced Linkhorn) made a very short courtship. He came to see her on 1 Dec 1819 and in a plain straight forward manner told her that they knew each other from

---

[84] Arthur E. Morgan. "New Light on Lincoln's Boyhood." *The Atlantic Monthly.*

[85] R. Gerald McMurtry. *The Lincolns in Elizabethtown, Kentucky*, page 6.

[86] R. Gerald McMurtry. *The Lincolns in Elizabethtown, Kentucky*, page 14.

[87] Joe Wheeler. *Abraham Lincoln: A Man of Faith and Courage*, page 47.

childhood, that he had no wife and she no husband and that he came all the way to marry her and if she was willing, he wanted it done right off. She replied that she could not right off as she owed some little debts which she wanted to pay first. He replied give me a list of them. He got the list, paid them off that evening. Next morning, I issued the license and they were married in 60 yards of my house and left right off."[88] Thomas had left his children in care of Dennis Hanks and neighbors at the start of winter. He wasted no time in getting to Kentucky and returning to Indiana to tend to his family.

After the wedding, Thomas once again hired his brother-in-law, Ralph Crume to help move the new additions to Thomas' family to Indiana. Sarah and her children were moved in a wagon drawn by a four-horse team.[89] The group most likely followed many of the same roads Thomas had followed with Nancy.

Thomas wanted Sarah to sell much of her household goods as he had a cabin already furnished with furniture he had made and household goods that he and Nancy had used. Sarah was loath to part with her goods. It is understandable that a woman would not want to sell all her possessions and then use the possessions of the deceased wife. Thomas did not understand that, but Sarah made it clear she would take her things with her to Indiana. A. H. Chapman provided a summary of the items Sarah loaded onto the wagon. She had "1 fine bureau, 1 table, 1 set chairs, 1 large cloth chest, cooking utensils, dishes, knives, forks, spoons, 1 spinning wheel, clothing, 2 beds and bedding, and other articles."[90]

Sarah also kept the home and property she owned in Elizabethtown (an acre and a quarter plus the cabin). There is no record on whether she rented it out or let others use it free of charge.

Thomas' second wife was another good choice in his life. Nancy was a wonderful wife and mother. Sarah was the same.

---

[88] Douglas L. Wilson and Rodney O. Davis. *Herndon's Informants*, page 503. From a letter to Herndon from Samuel Haycraft dated December 7, 1866 from Elizabethtown.

[89] Douglas L. Wilson and Rodney O. Davis. *Herndon's Informants*, page 98. Statement by A. H. Chapman dated September 8, 1865.

[90] Douglas L. Wilson and Rodney O. Davis. *Herndon's Informants*, page 99. Statement by A. H. Chapman dated September 8, 1865.

Neighbor Elizabeth Crawford described Sarah as a "strong, healthy woman, was cool, not excitable, truthful, shy, shrinking."[91] Her granddaughter, Harriet Hanks Chapman, said Sarah was "a very tall woman, straight as an Indian, of fair complexion, and was, when I first remember her, very handsome, sprightly, talkative, and proud. She wore her hair curled till gray; is kindhearted and very charitable, and also very industrious." She wasn't educated but she made up for the lack of education in spirit.[92]

As Sarah left Elizabethtown with Thomas, heading for her new home, her experience would have been similar to that of another pioneer family who moved in 1812 to a cabin near Brookville, Indiana. Maria Test told of her family traveling through wilderness territory on a new road that was full of tree stumps cut just enough for a wagon to get by. The family had expected a town like the one they left in Pennsylvania, but they found their cabin and land surrounded by thick forest with no other human habitation in site. Disheartened by their new home, Maria's father had the family freshen up from their journey. He would take them into Brookville so they could dine at the hotel. The town turned out to be a few log cabins in a larger clearing by the road. One of these cabins was the hotel and the dining area a few homemade chairs around a homemade table. The new reality was quite different from the home they had left. Their meal, though, was quite good: fried squirrel and wild turkey, cornbread, bacon, eggs, potatoes, and coffee.[93]

The road experienced by the Tests would have been what Thomas and Nancy experienced on coming to Indiana. The Lincoln cabin location and the town of Gentryville was similar for Sarah to what the Test's found in Brookville.

With Sarah's arrival in Indiana, her new home was a cabin about the same size as her Elizabethtown cabin. But the Indiana cabin, was much more crowded. Thomas' cabin was now home to eight people: Thomas (age 40), Sarah (31), Dennis Hanks (19),

---

[91] Emanuel Hertz. *The Hidden Lincoln, From the Letters and Papers of William H. Herndon*, page 367. Statement of Elizabeth Crawford, neighbor, to Herndon dated September 16, 1865.
[92] Charles H. Coleman. *Abraham Lincoln and Coles County, Illinois*, page 58.
[93] Indiana Public Media.
http://indianapublicmedia.org/momentofindianahistory/ adapting-life-frontier/.

Sarah Elizabeth "Betsy" Johnston (12), Sarah Lincoln (12), Abraham Lincoln (9), John D. Johnston (9), and Matilda Johnston (8).

There are two stories of Sarah's reaction to Thomas' home when she reached Indiana. One is completely negative, implying Thomas misled her about his home and that she found it deficient in all ways, immediately putting Thomas to work to fix the cabin to be a fit habitation instead of a hovel. In this version Sarah was shocked to see a cabin with no floor, no door, and no windows so she put Thomas to work making the home more like a city dwelling than a backwoods abode.[94] In this version, the furniture and furnishings Sarah found were of such poor quality that she replaced them with her own.

The truth flows more in other reports. Herndon interviewed Sarah and she reported no shock. In her own words, "When we landed in Indiana, Mr. Lincoln had erected a good log cabin, tolerably comfortable."[95] She did consider the country to be wild and desolate compared to her years living in Elizabethtown. Even though the cabin was "tolerably comfortable", Sarah saw some improvements she wanted. The rougher puncheon floor of the cabin was replaced with a floor of whipsawed and planed planks. More beds were needed, and these Thomas made at Sarah's direction along with more chairs. She also had Thomas do more work on the roof so snow did not seep in.[96] With all these improvements, Dennis Hanks claimed the Lincolns had the best house in the country.

Sarah did the same kind of reclamation of Dennis Hanks and Thomas' children. Sarah found them with ill-fitting clothes and a ragged, dirty appearance. A year without Nancy in the cabin was evident. Sarah found young Sarah Lincoln and Abraham ragged and dirty and thought her new stepson "the ugliest chap that ever obstructed [her] view".[97] She soon set things right for the children and Dennis, getting them cleaned up and in proper clothing that

---

[94] Douglas L. Wilson and Rodney O. Davis. *Herndon's Informants*, page 99. Statement by A. H. Chapman dated September 8, 1865.

[95] Douglas L. Wilson and Rodney O. Davis. *Herndon's Informants*, page 106. From Herndon's interview with Sarah Bush Lincoln on September 8, 1865.

[96] Richard Lawrence Miller. *Lincoln and His World, Volume 1*, page 46.

[97] Michael Burlingame. *Abraham Lincoln: A Life*, volume 1, page 26.

fit their growing frames. She could not change the fact that Abraham was homely, but her love would soon draw the two together for life.

Sarah brought a new touch to the Lincoln cabin. Where Thomas and Nancy had been fine with living rough as pioneers, Sarah – though poor herself and in debt – wanted more than just enough to get by on. She wanted some comfort items in her home, and she shared that desire with her children. This may be where Abraham began to let his ambition for a better life grow.

One of the things Sarah brought to the cabin were more books that Abraham latched onto for reading. While it is doubted Sarah could read or write (she signed documents by making her mark), she still had books to bring with her. One of those sometimes credited to her is *Pilgrim's Progress*. But there is another story of how *Pilgrim's Progress* came into Abraham's hands. It is said Thomas saw the book at a neighbor's house and knew his voracious reader of a son would love it. Thomas either bartered or bought it and gave it to Abraham.[98]

Sarah found the Lincoln farm well stocked with horses, cattle, sheep, chickens, and hogs. The workshop where Nancy had done the spinning and weaving was now Sarah's to fix up as she desired. The fields where Thomas had brought in a good harvest of corn and wheat, flax and cotton were cleared, and more were being added. The garden was cleared and awaiting the next Spring planting.

It was not the city. Thomas and Nancy lived in a subsistence pioneer economy where they raised or made or hunted or bartered for what they needed. It was a life Thomas loved and was very comfortable with. It was a life far different from what Sarah had known in Elizabethtown where she raised a small garden but otherwise worked for money and bought what was needed at the stores.

Gentryville was new and close to Thomas' farm. There was a store there and a few other businesses. The town was growing but it was not Elizabethtown. Sarah made a big adjustment to her life when she married Thomas. She went from the city to a pioneer setting and into that setting she brought her great energy, her good

---

[98] Fred Kaplan. *Lincoln*, page 18.

sense, and her passion for cleanliness. Sarah left Thomas to his carpentry, hunting, and farming while she took over trading for the family, managing the house and garden, and raising the children.

Thomas and Sarah did not have any children from their marriage because of circumstances Dennis Hanks referred to somewhat mysteriously. "Thomas Lincoln and Mrs. Lincoln [Sarah] never had any children, accident and nature stopping things short"[99] but the house was full of children, laughter, and love.[100] Dennis recorded nothing to explain what accident and nature were or if accident and nature limited Thomas or Sarah or both.

Pigeon Creek Farm (Continued)

Panic of 1819

As Thomas began his second marriage, the economy changed. Following the War of 1812, there was a period of rapid inflation raising the value of land, increasing the cost of manufactured goods, and inflating the price of agricultural items. The danger of war with Native Americans was minimal. New land was opened for settlement. Thousands of people, including Thomas and his family, moved into the lands of the Northwest Territory. Steamboat transportation was beginning to flourish, encouraging travel and commerce.[101] The economy was beginning the transformation from an agricultural subsistence economy, which was Thomas' way of life, to an industrial economy. The industrial revolution was reaching Indiana. Credit was easy and land speculation and purchase was a major form of investment.

Banks, including the highly influential Second Bank of the United States, issued paper money with little to back it. It was based on the inflated prices and with paper money that many settlers obtained their land, established their towns and villages,

---

[99] Douglas L. Wilson and Rodney O. Davis. *Herndon's Informants*, page 41. Letter from Dennis Hanks on June 13, 1865.

[100] Hanks does not elaborate on whether the "accident and nature" were related to Thomas, Sarah, or both.

[101] Thomas H. Greer. "Economic and Social Effects of the Depression of 1819 in the Old Northwest". *Indiana Magazine of History*, page 231.

and started their businesses. When the United States Treasury began refusing the paper currency, things turned bad for Indiana and the entire Northwest Territory. The Panic of 1819 ensued. Settlers took their paper currency to the banks to get hard money, gold and silver and copper. Banks did not have the reserves to back their paper currency and supply these demands. They began to call in loans. Trade was depressed. The rapid inflation turned into rapid deflation.[102] Property and investments began during inflationary times at high prices were suddenly worth less than what was paid for them. Businesses failed. Banks closed.

Settlers were unable to pay for the land they had purchased. In 1819 153,000 acres of land in the Northwest Territory was defaulted on. Landowners became squatters or were forced to find other homes. By 1820 in the Northwest Territory there was over $6.5 million of unpaid, overdue land payments. Agricultural and trade prices fell to levels so low that obtaining the money to make payments was impossible. The Panic of 1819 was the start of a six-year depression.[103] Abraham Lincoln considered his childhood a time of poverty. It was, and not just for his family. He lived from age ten to age sixteen during a time of deep economic depression.

Thomas had purchased land at the inflated prices, just like hundreds of others. His carpentry business and cooper business provided him a good income as he opened fields and worked to make his farm productive. In 1819 he found himself caught in the Panic and the depression hit him as it hit thousands of others.

The family did not go hungry nor were they without proper clothing. Thomas grew crops on the farm to feed his family and he hunted abundant game in the forest. The Lincoln table had plenty of food. Flax and cotton and animal skins were turned into clothing by Sarah's capable hands. The family had what they needed to live but the trade that had improved their lives collapsed. Thomas was unable to sell his furniture and other goods because money was scarce. The market for his surplus crops was deflated. Prices he could get for his work and furniture and cabinets and barrels was minimal. Thomas was among 150,000

---

[102] National Park Service. *Lincoln Boyhood: Historic Resource Study.*

[103] ushistory.org. *U. S. History Online Textbook.* "Economic Growth and the Early Industrial Revolution".

people in Indiana suffering from the depression that grew out of the Panic of 1819.[104]

Payment was due on Thomas'. The land office would only accept coin, United States Treasury notes, or currency issued by banks approved by the government.[105] Thomas, as most of the settlers, did not have that. The payments were missed, and Thomas fell behind in his obligation. He requested and received an extension on his debt but even that extension would prove difficult to meet.

Life at Pigeon Creek

1819 - 1820

In 1819, one of Abraham's chores nearly turned into another tragedy. Thomas had Abraham take corn to the mill for grinding. In his autobiography for Scripps', Abraham related the story in one sentence. "In his tenth year he [Abraham] was kicked by a horse, and apparently killed for a time."[106] The full story is much more interesting.

Noah Gordon's mill was two miles from the Lincoln cabin and Abraham rode one of Thomas' horses to the mill with a sack of corn for grinding. The mill was a horse mill where each customer hitched his own horse or mule to the gristmill arm. The customer would then make the horse walk in circles, pulling the arm and driving the millstone to grind the grain.

When his turn came, Abraham hitched his mare to the gristmill arm and began walking behind her, hitting her with a whiplash to keep her moving at a pace Abraham considered acceptable. As he drove the horse, he was loudly telling the mare to "git up, you old hussy". In his desire to be finished and on his way home, Abraham drove the mare hard and the mare took exception to being hit repeatedly. As Abraham once more exhorted the horse, he got as far as saying "git up" when the horse kicked back at him, hitting him in the head.

---

104 Thomas H. Greer. "Economic and Social Effects of the Depression of 1819 in the Old Northwest". *Indiana Magazine of History*, page 228.
105 Thomas H. Greer. "Economic and Social Effects of the Depression of 1819 in the Old Northwest". *Indiana Magazine of History*, pages 232-233.
106 John Locke Scripps. *The First Published Life of Abraham Lincoln.*

Abraham was bloodied and unconscious from the kick. Noah Gordon rushed to him and took the boy into the house. Dave Turnham, a neighbor boy who went to the mill with Abraham, ran the two miles to the Lincoln home to get Thomas. Thomas rushed to the mill, picked Abraham up, and took him home in a wagon. Neighbors gathered. Everyone expected Abraham to die. He was unconscious overnight but the next day he began to jerk and wake. As he woke, he finished what he had been saying and yelled out, "you old hussy!"[107]

There is no record of Thomas' thoughts or what he said during this time but there can be little doubt that he was in anguish. The Lincoln men were noted as suffering from depression or the melancholy. Thomas was no exception to this condition, and it was a characteristic Abraham inherited. Thomas watched his father die, buried his infant son, and lost Nancy to an untimely death. Now he watched his son lying unconscious from a kick to the head with the neighbors surrounding him and already mourning the boy's passing. As Abraham awoke and came back to life, Thomas being Thomas, there must have been an exuberant release of joy in the form of shouting and praying and praising God. Abraham recovered from this injury, but he was left for life with occasional double vision and a left eye that sometimes wondered upward.

On July 3 of 1819, Luther Greathouse assigned 139.36 acres of land to Thomas. This assignment was prior to Thomas' marriage to Sarah and likely a result of the beginning Panic. Greathouse was a neighbor adjacent to the southwest corner of Thomas' land. He assigned a "short" section, not a full 160-acre section, the northeast quarter of Section 6, Township 5 South, Range 5 West.[108] Assigning land was a common method of getting rid of land that was no longer wanted or could not be paid for by the owner. The assignee accepted title to the land along with any debts and obligations still owed. There is no record of Thomas giving anything in exchange for the land. Considering the devaluation of land in 1819 it is likely the debt owed was all the land was worth and Greathouse was simply getting out from under

---

[107] Roger Norton. ww.rogernorton.com.
[108] William E. Bartelt. *There I Grew Up*, page 26.

the debt. Thomas, from a family of land speculators and not knowing the Panic would turn into a six-year depression, took on the land as an investment and a way to increase his wealth and holdings.

There is record of Thomas voting in August of 1819. The vote was taken at the home of Jonathan Greathouse. The votes of thirty-one men were cast.[109] Though votes in that period of history were announced and public, there is no record of who Thomas voted for.

In December, as 1819 came to a close, Noah Gordon donated land to the Little Pigeon Creek Baptist Church and the church determined to put a building on the land once planning was complete. Thomas was chosen to oversee the planning and construction. On February 12, 1820, the church approved the building plan, but construction did not begin. Evidently there was still some discussion going on and the unity needed to begin construction was not there despite the plan's approval.[110]

When he came to Indiana, Thomas took advantage of the credit system offered to claim land. Hundreds of pioneers did as he did. The Panic of 1819 left many of them in dire straits financially, owning land and unable to make payments. Seeing the difficulty, the government offered relief in the form of extensions before forfeiture was applied. Thomas applied for and received this relief. Unfortunately, this extension did nothing to lessen the impact and problems of the economic depression that came as a result of the Panic. At that time the government also changed the system to try to prevent the same problems recurring. Starting in July 1820, it was no longer a requirement to lay claim to a full section of 160 acres. Settlers were allowed to purchase a minimum of 80 acres at $1.25 per acre, payable in cash only.[111] This change did little to help Thomas or others who were holding the previous minimum of 160 acres under the old rules.

---

[109] William E. Bartelt. "The Land Dealings of Spencer County, Indiana, Pioneer Thomas Lincoln." *Indiana Magazine of History*, page 273.

[110] Louis A. Warren. "Pigeon Creek Church." *Bulletin of the Lincoln National Life Foundation.* The information and detail comes from the Minute Book of the Little Pigeon Creek Baptist Church.

[111] Selwyn A. Brant and Weston A. Goodspeed. *History of Warrick, Spencer, and Perry Counties, Indiana*, page 213.

There are differences of opinion as to when and how schooling was conducted in Indiana. Abraham wrote of the schools. "There were some schools, so called; but no qualification was ever required of a teacher, beyond '*readin, writin,* and *cipherin,*' to the Rule of Three. If a straggler supposed to understand Latin, happened to sojourn in the neighborhood, he was looked upon as a wizard. There was absolutely nothing to excite ambition for education. Of course, when I came of age I did not know much. Still somehow, I could read, write, and cipher to the Rule of Three; but that was all. I have not been to school since. The little advance I now have upon this store of education, I have picked up from time to time under the pressure of necessity."[112]

In the winter of 1819-1820, Andrew Crawford, a neighbor of the Lincolns, conducted a school in his home. It is possible Crawford held school in the previous winter as well, but it is uncertain if Thomas sent his children to school during the time following Nancy's death and prior to marrying Sarah.

Crawford's school was a subscription school for which parents paid two dollars per child attending. Crawford was the Pigeon Creek Justice of the Peace. His qualifications to teach exceeded those qualifications described by Abraham. Crawford taught the three R's, etiquette and manners, and some history. It is Crawford who will later loan Abraham Weem's *Life of Washington*, the book which Abraham said gave him much inspiration.[113]

In Crawford's school, the Lincoln children were in regular attendance. All five children attended: Sarah, Betsy, Abraham, John D., and Matilda. Dennis Hanks did not attend. The Crawford school was small with only a few students. Oddly enough, it is reported that Abraham, around eleven years of age, did not like school in his early years.[114]

At this point in time, Thomas' work was hampered by his being blind in one eye with the other eye being weak. The

---

[112] Roy P. Basler. *The Collected Works of Abraham Lincoln*, volume 3, page 512. Taken from a letter from Abraham Lincoln to Jesse W. Fell enclosing an autobiography for use in campaigning.
[113] Louis A. Warren. *Abraham Lincoln Association Papers*. "The Environs of Lincoln's Youth", page 134.
[114] Arthur E. Morgan. "New Light on Lincoln's Boyhood." *The Atlantic Monthly*.

handicap slowed Thomas. Most of his woodworking was done by feel. Neighbor Elizabeth Crawford, Andrew Crawford's wife, said that Thomas "felt his way on the work much of the time; his sense of touch was keen."[115]

It is hard to picture doing so much work by feel rather than sight and Thomas had a lot of work making small spinning wheels using his skill as a wheelwright. Families usually had several small spinning wheels, one for each female member of the family that was old enough to spin.[116] It was good work and Thomas' skill in making them was in demand as the population grew. It was slow work to do by feel.

Following Thomas' marriage, the Lincoln cabin was very crowded during the winter of 1819-1820. The replica home of Thomas Lincoln at the Lincoln Boyhood National Memorial has a standard one room cabin but there is strong probability that Thomas built a larger cabin with the expanded size of his family. Eight people needed more room. Sophie Hanks told her family that Thomas built a new home.[117] Building a new cabin was not an unusual event. It was normal for pioneers to build a better cabin and either tear down the old or use it for other purposes. Thomas' new cabin had two rooms downstairs and a large loft where the boys slept.[118]

Toward the close of 1820, on September 27, Thomas Barritt assigned 160 acres of land to Dennis Hanks. This was a similar situation to the one where Luther Greathouse assigned land to Thomas. The land assigned to Dennis was the quarter section bordering the east boundary of Thomas' land.

As the economic depression continued, more settlers defaulted on their claims and lost their land. Businesses failed and the growth envisioned for Indiana and the Northwest stagnated. Congress stepped in again.

---

[115] Emanuel Hertz. *The Hidden Lincoln, From the Letters and Papers of William H. Herndon*, page 367. Statement of Elizabeth Crawford to Herndon dated September 16, 1865.
[116] Arthur E. Morgan. "New Light on Lincoln's Boyhood." *The Atlantic Monthly*.
[117] Arthur E. Morgan. "New Light on Lincoln's Boyhood." *The Atlantic Monthly*.
[118] Louis A. Warren. *Lincoln Association Papers*. "The Environs of Lincoln's Youth", page 137.

1821 - 1822

The 1820 land law had not provided relief to landowners like Thomas. These landowners were at high risk to lose their land investment and homes. Westerners came together and petitioned the government for relief. In response, on March 2, 1821 Congress passed the Relief Act of 1821. This Act allowed landowners who were behind in their payments to surrender part of their land with any previous payments applied to the land they kept. In addition to this provision, the Act also forgave interest accrued prior to September 30, 1821.[119]

Unlike the earlier attempts to provide relief and recovery from the Panic of 1819, the Relief Act of 1821 provided relief to thousands of settlers, including Thomas. By the end of 1821, pioneer indebtedness to the federal government was reduced by half.[120] Pioneers were enabled to keep their land and improvements and the government received back land with clear title to sell to other pioneers.

To be eligible to benefit from the Relief Act, written consent had to filed before September 30, 1821. Thomas went to the Vincennes Land Office on September 12. At that time, Thomas took advantage of the provision allowing landowners who had paid one fourth of the price of their land to have eight more years to pay. Thomas still owed $240 that was due in eight installments of $30 each plus 6% interest. The first installment was scheduled for March 31, 1822. To document his transaction, Thomas received declaration number 1624 from the Vincennes Land Office. He was listed as "Thomas Lincorn", but his signature is "Thomas Lincoln". Under his name a clerk wrote "alias Linkern".[121]

In addition to taking advantage of the Relief Act, 1821 was an eventful year for Thomas. On March 10, the minutes of Little Pigeon Creek Baptist Church documented the appointment of

---

[119] William E. Bartelt. "The Land Dealings of Spencer County, Indiana, Pioneer Thomas Lincoln." *Indiana Magazine of History*, page 215.
[120] National Park Services. www.nps.gov/parkhistory/online_books/libo/hrs/hrs5a.htm
[121] William E. Bartelt. "The Land Dealings of Spencer County, Indiana, Pioneer Thomas Lincoln." *Indiana Magazine of History*, page 215.

five people as a committee with authority to set the building plan and employ workers to build the church.[122] Despite this progress, haggling on the building plan continued.

June brought a celebration for Thomas' family and his neighbors. On June 9, 1821, Dennis Hanks married (Sarah) Elizabeth "Betsy" Johnston.[123] Following the joyous celebration, Dennis and Betsy lived on Dennis' farm which bordered Thomas'.

In the early months of the Thomas and Sarah marriage, the two families merged into one. Daughter Sarah grew close to both Betsy and Matilda. Abraham developed a strong friendship with John. John was a year younger than Abraham. John was noted as kind and generous on the good side, lazy and argumentative on the bad. In contrast to Abraham, John was considered handsome and dashing. Where Abraham disliked hunting; John loved hunting. Where Abraham was studious and read everything he could find, John spent his time socializing with the youth of Pigeon Creek. Abraham was shy and backward with girls; John used his good looks to woo them. Abraham stood up for John and defended him when needed, when John was in the right. When Abraham thought John was in the wrong, John had to face the consequences without Abraham to back him up.[124]

Some of John's indolence in working could be attributed to Abraham's influence on him. Young Abraham would work when he had to, but he preferred not to. As he would later say, "My father taught me to work, but he did not teach me to like it."[125] This tendency is illustrated by a story of Abraham and Dennis Hanks being sent to pull fodder one day. They put the work off all morning, playing marbles. Around midday, Dennis thought of the work they should be doing and reminded Abraham of their responsibility. Abraham responded that he would rather play marbles than pull fodder.[126] Abraham was known for leading others to play and shun work. He used his stories to distract from labor and pulled pranks to get others to join him in play.

---

[122] Louis A. Warren, Editor. "Pigeon Creek Church." *Bulletin of the Lincoln National Life Foundation.*

[123] Louis A. Warren. "Abraham Lincoln's Father." *The Lincoln Kinsman,* page 7.

[124] Michael Burlingame. *Abraham Lincoln: A Life. Volume One,* page 29.

[125] Don Davenport. *In Lincoln's Footsteps,* page 36.

[126] Michael Burlingame. *Abraham Lincoln: A Life. Volume One,* page 45.

Abraham wanted to use his intellect to earn a living and move away from manual labor as a career. John did not have that ability or that drive. John's life became one scheme after another to get easy money but, without the intellectual prowess of Abraham, he failed. Later in life Abraham would scold John for his ways but the truth may be that John tried to follow what Abraham did, what Abraham had taught him when they were kids, but John did not have the intellectual skillset to pull it off as Abraham had.

Thomas taught Abraham and John how to build furniture and do carpentry. Abraham's work does not show the skill or care evident in Thomas' pieces. The inlays are not as consistent.[127] Abraham learned the skills, but he did not practice perfecting them. Thomas taught him to work but Abraham's mind was on learning and reading and moving away from the subsistence agricultural existence his family was leading. Abraham wanted something more than Thomas had ambition for.

On September 11, 1821, Thomas assigned the land he had received from Luther Greathouse to James Gentry. The financial details of the transaction are unknown.[128]

In 1822 the meeting house for the Little Pigeon Creek Baptist Church was finally built. Agreement was reached on the plans after much debate. The meeting house was a large log cabin, twenty-six by thirty feet with two chimneys, one on each end of the building. Windows, twenty inches by thirty-two inches were placed along the walls to allow plenty of light.[129] Thomas was the general contractor in charge of the work, and he applied his own skills in personally framing out the doors and windows along with using his woodworking skill to make the pulpit.[130] Split log benches were made for seating. The loft of the church was tall and designed to serve as sleeping quarters for those who came to church meetings from a distance and could not easily make the trip home after the close of meetings.[131] There is documentation that bricks were also

---

[127] Rich Davis. "Teacher Quickly Becoming a Lincoln Furniture Expert". *Evansville Courier-Press.*

[128] William E. Bartelt. *There I Grew Up*, page 26.

[129] B. N. Griffing. *An Illustrated Historical Atlas of Spencer County, Indiana*, page 10.

[130] John Y. Simon. *House Divided: Lincoln and His Father*, page 7.

[131] Louis A. Warren. *Lincoln Association Papers*. "The Environs of Lincoln's Youth", page 140.

used in the construction, probably for the chimneys and fireplaces. David Turnham made the bricks using a mold Thomas made.[132]

Thomas and Sarah were important members of the church. Thomas was a pillar in the Little Pigeon Creek Baptist Church. He was a leader of the congregation, serving on committees, as a trustee, as an arbitrator of disagreements and questions on church discipline, and even representing the church at a denominational conference.[133] Thomas was well respected, trusted, and liked in his church and in the Little Pigeon community.

A major event in Thomas' life occurred in 1822. He became a grandfather. Dennis and Betsy Hanks had their first child, a girl, Sarah Jane Hanks. One can only imagine the joy in Thomas' heart as he held the little girl and prayed over her as she began her life.

The economic depression was still ongoing, but things were beginning to improve. Trade was picking up. For the Lincolns, the closest trading point was the town of Troy on the Ohio River. To get there Thomas had to cross the Anderson River by ferry. The ferry was owned and operated by James Taylor.[134] Taylor also ran a shipping business. Thomas did business with him during his Indiana residence and Abraham would work for Taylor when he was older.

In an agricultural subsistence economy, farm surplus was traded to merchants for things that could not be raised, made, or hunted. Coffee and sugar were such items. In addition to farm surplus, Thomas traded furniture, cabinets, barrels, and other items produced in his workshop.

As Gentryville grew and developed, Thomas bartered and traded with James Gentry, doing business at the Gentry store. Gentry brought in sugar and coffee and other items and took in farm surplus, furs, livestock, furniture, cabinets, and whatever else Thomas might have bartered. Dealing with Gentry removed the need to travel to Troy as often though Thomas continued to trade with Taylor and in Troy as well as with Gentry.

---

[132] Selwin A. Brant and Weston A. Goodspeed. *History of Warrick, Spencer, and Perry Counties, Indiana*, page 426.
[133] John Y. Simon. *House Divided: Lincoln and His Father*, page 7.
[134] Louis A. Warren. *Lincoln Association Papers.* "The Environs of Lincoln's Youth", page 137.

This time period was the start of the estrangement that would grow over the years between Abraham and Thomas. The economic depression and the slow return of vibrant trade along with the beginning industrial revolution were enticing to Abraham. He wanted to become something more than a farmer/tradesman, something more than the life with which Thomas was content. Thomas loved the pioneer life. He worked to better his family and to attain financial success, but his striving was in tune with pioneer life, not the changing times.

Sophie Hanks, in her reminiscences, explained it simply. She said Thomas was like other people, like other pioneers. He did not work hard to get ahead because there was no market for products locally. The market was in trade with other states. He raised what he needed and was content with that.[135] In Kentucky, Thomas was a rising man, a man who was gaining on life and becoming financially successful. Following the Panic of 1819 with the ensuing economic depression and his failing eyesight, Thomas still worked hard at his farm and workshop, he still traded surplus and products, but his ambition settled into the subsistence economy and the pioneer life. He did not have the ambition Abraham did. He became content with his life as it was.

Growing Distance Between Thomas and Abraham

It was also during this time that Thomas began to grow close with his stepson, John D. Johnston. Many historians state that Thomas favored John over Abraham. It is possible he did so. Abraham was a personality Thomas did not completely understand. Abraham spent time with books and in study. Abraham shunned chores and doing what was needed to put food on the table. Abraham did not hunt. John hunted with Thomas and he worked the farm and workshop side-by-side with Thomas. Thomas and John were very similar in their outlook on life and what they wanted from life. Both were content with their family and the pioneer circle of friends. Abraham was looking for something different, something beyond the day-to-day struggle of subsistence farming.

---

[135] Michael Burlingame. *Abraham Lincoln: A Life. Volume One*, page 9.

Abraham understood the way of pioneer subsistence living. His resistance to it made things difficult. "Biographers sometimes quote Lincoln's phrase 'I used to be a slave' to suggest that he felt terribly oppressed by his father, who put him to work on the farm in various activities. But that was par for the course on the frontier in that era. Social historians have shown that all members of a frontier family except toddlers were expected to contribute to the family's survival."[136]

Another part of the change between Thomas and Abraham is credited to Thomas being abusive of Abraham. The accusation of abuse is based on Thomas' disciplining Abraham. It is true that Thomas disciplined Abraham. Thomas and Sarah disciplined all their children. Today's world looks down on corporal punishment, but the world Thomas lived in did not.

Etiquette in the early 1800s was set in deference to adults. Andrew Crawford taught this etiquette in his school and the Lincoln children learned those lessons. History notes that Abraham did not follow that etiquette. Etiquette required that children remain quiet until adults had spoken. Children were not to interrupt adults. Abraham took delight in breaking these conventions.

When a stranger came to the Lincoln home, the expectation was that Thomas would take the lead to greet and speak with the stranger. Abraham frequently spoke to the stranger first, questioning them as to what they needed or where they were going.[137] Thomas did as most parents did when that happened. He struck Abraham to remind him of his manners.

History tells us that Abraham became quick to correct his father in front of others. Abraham was a very intelligent child and his reading gave him knowledge that most on the frontier did not have. When Thomas said something Abraham did not agree with, Abraham interrupted the conversation to correct his father. When Thomas was telling a story and Abraham thought he was missing details or getting details wrong, Abraham interrupted to set things straight. No doubt, at times Thomas was wrong and Abraham

---

[136] Sara Gabbard. *Interview with David S. Reynolds*, page 5.
[137] Doug Pokorski. *The Sad Tale of Thomas Lincoln*. Springfield, Illinois: The State Journal Register Online.

right and other times Abraham was wrong, and Thomas was right, but it did not change the fact that the child Abraham was breaking accepted social etiquette with his behavior and Thomas stepped in to discipline Abraham, slapping him and whipping him.

Even in this, normal pioneer era actions which we now consider harsh, Thomas was patient with Abraham. Where it was normal for children to be disciplined quickly when they made a mistake, often in front of others, Thomas usually waited. Family tradition is that "Uncle Tom would not whip Abe or scold him before folk, but he would take him by himself and tend to him after they was gone. People in them days believed that whipping was good for children."[138] The remembrances passed on by Sophie Hanks tell us that while Thomas did whip Abraham, and the other children, he also talked to them about what they did and why it was wrong.[139] This talking and explaining made Thomas different from many pioneers who used corporal punishment but did not take the time to talk to their children about what was wrong.

What we today judge to be abusive, pioneers viewed as normal. Thomas was not seen as abusive. For his time in history he was likely seen as lenient because he often waited to discipline Abraham in private and he sometimes just talked rather than applying the rod. Of note is the fact that Abraham, while critical of many things in his childhood, did not criticize Thomas' discipline. It is true that later in their marriage, Abraham and Mary became very indulgent of their younger sons' behavior but that was not always the case. They used corporal punishment early on.

> *We have another boy, born the 10th. of March last. [1846] He is very much such a child as Bob was at his age – rather of a longer order. Bob is "short and low," and, I expect, always will be. He talks very plainly – almost as plainly as anybody. He is quite smart enough. I sometimes fear he is one of the little rare-ripe sort, that are smarter at about five than ever after. He has a great deal of that sort of mischief, that is the offspring of much animal spirits. Since*

---

[138] Arthur E. Morgan. "New Light on Lincoln's Boyhood." *The Atlantic Monthly*.
[139] Arthur E. Morgan. "New Light on Lincoln's Boyhood." *The Atlantic Monthly*.

I began this letter a messenger came to tell me, Bob was lost; but by the time I reached the house, his mother had found him, and had him whipped – and, by now, very likely he is run away again.[140]

The thought that Thomas' discipline of Abraham caused him to go completely in the opposite direction and allow his children to run free, binding and disciplining them only with love and not with physical punishment is dispelled by this letter. Abraham did not see physical punishment as a problem prior to the death of Edward Lincoln. The change in discipline habits followed that tragedy. Early in his parenting, Abraham used whippings as a means of discipline and he even joked about doing so. It is even possible that allowing the younger boys to get away with things for which Robert was whipped may have caused some of the separation and distance that came between Abraham and Robert, a situation very similar to the distance that developed between Thomas and Abraham.

Life at Pigeon Creek (Continued)

1823 - 1824

In 1823, the task of being schoolmaster fell to James Swaney. Swaney ran the second known Indiana school to which Thomas sent his children. The Swaney school was 4.5 miles southwest of the Lincoln farm on John Hoskins' land. In size, the Swaney schoolhouse was a little bigger than the building used by Andrew Crawford and it had two chimneys instead of one which meant the schoolroom was warmer during the winter school months.[141]

Schoolmaster Swaney was orphaned early in life. Azel Dorsey took James and his sister in, becoming their guardian. Dorsey, himself a schoolmaster, taught Swaney. Swaney was only nine years older than Abraham and barely older than some of his oldest students. It was under Swaney that Abraham became familiar with Murray's *English* Reader, a book Abraham would toil over until he

---

[140] Roy P. Basler. Editor. *The Collected Works of Abraham Lincoln*, volume 1, page 391. From a Lincoln letter to Joshua Speed dated October 22, 1846.
[141] Louis A. Warren. "Lincoln's Indiana Schoolmasters." *Indiana Magazine of History*, page 113.

acquired all the knowledge it could teach him. Swaney taught in the Little Pigeon community for two or three years, until he married and moved. Due to the distance of the schoolhouse from the Lincoln farm, Thomas' children were irregular in attendance.

For pioneers, work to make and grow what was needed to live usually took priority over school. Thomas' children, as all pioneer children, were put to work earning what the family needed. While Thomas did as most pioneers in prioritizing work over school, Thomas was proud of Abraham's intelligence and learning and did what he could to keep Abraham, and his other children, in school. There is an often-repeated story in Lincoln biography about a time Thomas cosigned a note for a friend and the friend defaulted on payment leaving Thomas liable. The standard telling has Thomas pulling his children, including Abraham, from school to work off the debt. This story could easily have been true but the context from which the original story was taken is false.

The story comes from a letter of Leonard Swett, an Illinois attorney who knew Abraham well, to Josiah H. Drummond. Swett told it this way:

> *His [Abraham's] father was a native of Kentucky, and when Lincoln was eight years old, moved to Indiana. As he grew up, his father designed to provide him the limited education common to western men; but becoming involved by surety for a friend, lost his property and was compelled to take him from school when he had been there only six weeks. He never went to school again but worked during his minority to acquire for his father a new home. When he was twenty-one, they had gathered money enough to enter 80 acres of land, at $1.25 per acre; and they then moved to Coles County in this state.*[142]

From this story, historians made Thomas out as opposed to education and thriftless in handling money. Yet when all the details given by Swett are reviewed, it is clear he does not have his facts correct. Thomas never lost his property in Indiana. Thomas'

---

[142] Allegheny College. *Documents of Ida M. Tarbell. The Ida M. Tarbell Collection of Lincolniana.* dspace.allegheny.edu/handle/10456/13717. From a letter of Leonard Swett to Josiah H. Drummond dated May 27, 1860.

children attended three schools during the time Thomas owned his Pigeon Creek farm. Abraham did attend school well past that first six weeks in Indiana. Thomas' children did not have to work to acquire him an Indiana home. Thomas paid off his farm well before Abraham turned twenty-one.

Thomas did cosign notes and he did have to stand surety on some of them when his friend or family member defaulted. That is correct history. That Thomas may have taken his children from school when work was needed is also very likely. That was common practice for all pioneers. Those parts of the story hold true. The other details are blatantly incorrect and have been used to portray Thomas in a manner he does not deserve.

At some point in 1823, Thomas' brother Mordecai travelled through Indiana on a visit.[143] How frequent these visits were is unknown but from Abraham's letters and reminiscences later, it is clear he knew his uncle fairly well. How often, if ever, Thomas and Sarah returned to Kentucky to visit family and friends is also unknown.

Travel to and from the Pigeon Creek farm was not easy. The area remained rugged with rough roads for many years after Thomas moved in. But just as his land in Kentucky had been on a major road, soon the Pigeon Creek farm gained traffic. A road from Corydon to Evansville was opened and ran by Thomas' farm on the south side and through Gentryville. In 1823 another road was put through Gentryville connecting Rockport and Bloomington.[144] These roads made travel to and from the Pigeon Creek farm easier and it also brought more trade and travelers through the region.

On May 5, 1823, Thomas became a grandfather for the second time. This time to a grandson. Dennis and Betsy Hanks had their second child, John Talbot Hanks.

In June of 1823 Thomas and Sarah officially joined the Little Pigeon Creek Baptist Church. They had been attending and helping the church but for some reason had not joined. It may have been because the Little Mount church from which they came

---

[143] Douglas L. Wilson and Rodney O. Davis. *Herndon's Informants*, page 121. From Herndon's interview of David Turnham on September 15, 1865.
[144] Douglas L. Wilson and Rodney O. Davis. *Herndon's Informants*, page 217. From a David Turnham letter to Herndon dated February 21, 1866.

was a Separate Baptist church and Little Pigeon was Regular Baptist. Around the time Thomas joined Little Pigeon Church there was a movement uniting Regular and Separate Baptists into one association. Thomas joined by letter and Sarah joined by confession of faith on June 7.[145] Thomas' letter of good standing from the Little Mount Separate Baptist Church in Kentucky put him in immediate good standing with the Little Pigeon Church. Sarah joining by experience implies that she had not been a member of a church in Elizabethtown or had not had time to get a letter with the quickness of her marriage to Thomas and move to Indiana.

With Thomas joining the church and taking on responsibilities to the congregation, the church reached out to young Abraham who was fourteen years old in 1823. The church appointed the boy as sexton. The young Lincoln took after his father in being a good-natured and happy person, though he was also considered lazy by some. Still, he was likeable, and he had good standing in the church. As sexton he was required to keep the church clean, do general maintenance, and provide firewood and candles.[146]

There is no record that Thomas ever preached at his churches, but he was known to enjoy church services and camp meetings from start to finish and when called on he could follow a sermon with an eloquent and effectual prayer.[147] His gift for humor and storytelling was well known and he was able to make the journeys to church and the long days at meetings entertaining for everyone.

Like his father, the young Lincoln was gifted in storytelling and mimicry. With his excellent memory, Abraham was able to outdo most of the others in the frontier habit of imitation. Abraham developed the habit of returning home from church and gathering friends and family who would sit and listen to the boy repeat the sermon, the text, and even the gestures of the preacher. On occasions when his stepmother could not make it to service, Abraham would make up for the loss by delivering the sermon to

---

[145] Louis A. Warren. *Lincoln's Youth, Indiana Years Seven to Twenty-one 1816-1830*, page 115.
[146] Alan T. Nolan. "Abraham Lincoln and Indiana." *Traces of Indiana and Midwestern History*, page 8.
[147] Herring Chrisman. *Memoirs of Lincoln*, page 16.

her and the family once they were home. Thomas and Sarah enjoyed Abraham's skill. Sarah is said to have told folks she got more out of and benefited more from Abraham's renditions than she did from the preachers themselves.[148]

The year 1824 was a routine year for Thomas as he worked his land and his trade. On April 10, he was appointed by Little Pigeon Church to represent the congregation at a church conference. On October 9, Thomas served on a disciplinary committee sent to visit a member who had separated from his wife.[149] Church discipline was strict, and members were expected to follow doctrinal guidelines and were called to provide an explanation if they did not.

Somewhere in this time period, James Gentry hired Thomas to make a wagon. Thomas, with Abraham's help, made the wagon entirely from wood including hickory rims on the wheels.[150] It is probable that John Johnston also helped.

Thomas had more help, and an additional mouth to feed, from 1822 to 1824. Dennis Hanks' half-brother John Hanks lived with Thomas over those years.[151] It was John Hanks who, for lack of success in settling in Indiana and finding livelihood, was one of the first of the family to move to Illinois. It was John Hanks who worked hard at and finally persuaded the extended Lincoln family to leave Indiana for Illinois.

With the economic depression following the Panic fading, the population of Pigeon Creek was again growing. One of Thomas' new neighbors was Elizabeth Crawford. Thomas helped her family with their home and built furniture for them. She became a close friend of the Lincolns. She considered the Lincolns good neighbors, good people, honest, sociable, and hospitable.[152]

Hospitality was an important pioneer trait. French traveler Ernest Duvergier de Hauranne captured the essence of pioneer hospitality in his journals.

---

[148] Edward Murr. "Lincoln in Indiana." *Indiana Magazine of History*, page 343.

[149] Louis A. Warren. "Abraham Lincoln's Father." *The Lincoln Kinsman*, page 8.

[150] J. T. Hobson. *Footprints of Abraham Lincoln*, page 24.

[151] Newton Bateman, Paul Selby, and Charles Edward Wilson, Editors. *Historical Encyclopedia of Illinois and History of Coles County*, page 219.

[152] Emanuel Hertz. *The Hidden Lincoln, From the Letters and Papers of William H. Herndon*, page 366.

> *One must go into their homes in order to know how they practice hospitality. It may be that they are unfamiliar with the refinements of our good manners; but on the other hand, they do have an honest, affectionate and cordial simplicity which is at least as attractive as our false solicitousness. We know how to make warm offers and proclamations of devotion, but everyone understands that all this goes no deeper than mere words. The American, on the other, does not like to have his kindness refused; he does not even expect to be thanked. He holds out his hand to you, invites you, and won't take no for an answer. His house, his time, even his money, are yours. Such is the law of hospitality.*[153]

Thomas practiced this hospitality and as the road past his farm became more traveled, more strangers learned of the open-hearted generosity of pioneer hospitality. It was a normal thing for pioneers to get together in the evenings to eat and talk. Strangers were welcomed into these times. It was at such that Abraham became noted for butting in on his elders' conversations, breaking behavioral protocols. But it was also during these times that the young Abraham would become quiet and listen, absorbing the talk as he absorbed Sunday sermons. When a reporter, John C. Gulliver, later asked Abraham about his education, the President told him about listening to the adults talking to Thomas at his Indiana home. Afterwards he would ply Thomas with questions to gain a full understanding of what he had heard.[154] He would take that understanding into his loft bedroom where he would walk up and down the floor to plant what he had heard and learned deep into his memory until he could explain it easily to others.[155]

This story gives light on two facts. One is that the cabin loft was sizeable enough for Abraham, a tall youth, to walk about

---

[153] Ernest Duvergier de Hauranne. *A Frenchman in Lincoln's America*, volume 1, page 26.

[154] Douglas L. Wilson and Rodney O. Davis. *Herndon's Informants*, page 107. From a Herndon interview of Sarah Bush Lincoln on September 8, 1865.

[155] John H. Finley. "The Education of Abraham Lincoln". *Lincoln Centennial Association Papers*, page 83.

easily. Second, Abraham had a respect for his father's wisdom about how things worked in life and asked him to explain things.

October 23, 1824 brought Thomas his third grandchild as Dennis and Betsy Hanks welcomed their third child, a girl they named Nancy Melvina Hanks in honor of Nancy Lincoln.

The close of 1824 brought an event that remains unique in American history. The presidential election of 1824 was anything but normal and the like has not been seen since. With the presidential election, presidential electors were chosen on October 29. There is no historical proof that Thomas voted in that election or who he voted for but it is known that he had strong opinions politically, opinions and party affiliations he passed on to his son Abraham. With the family's strong attachment to Henry Clay, it is very likely Thomas cast his vote for Clay.

In the election of 1824, after winning six consecutive presidential elections, the Democratic-Republican party splintered. The toll on the party from the War of 1812 and the Panic of 1819 with the following and ongoing economic depression broke the party apart. When the party could not come to agreement on a candidate, individuals stepped up on their own. William H. Crawford of Georgia, who had served as Secretary of the Treasury ran, receiving 11% of the popular vote and 40 electoral votes. Henry Clay of Kentucky, Speaker of the House, received 13% of the popular vote and 38 electoral votes. Andrew Jackson of Tennessee, United States Senator, received 41% of the popular vote and 99 electoral votes. John Quincy Adams of Massachusetts, Secretary of State, received 31% of the popular vote and 84 electoral votes. No one had a majority of the popular vote and no one had the 131 electoral votes necessary to win.

On December 1, 1824, when the electoral college could not get to 131 votes for any of the candidates, the election was thrown into the House of Representatives.

1825 - 1826

The House of Representatives took up the election issue in February 1825. Based on the twelfth amendment of the

Constitution[156], three candidates were considered for president. Henry Clay, who had received the least number of electoral votes was not included. Only William Crawford, Andrew Jackson, and John Quincy Adams' names were entered in the contest. Ironically, Henry Clay, as Speaker of the House, presided over the vote in which he was no longer a participating candidate.

On Abraham's 16th birthday, February 9, 1825, on the first and only ballot, John Quincy Adams was elected president of the United States. He received 87 votes to Jackson's 71 and Crawford's 54. Adams received the votes of 13 states to Jackson's 7 to Crawford's 4.

Thomas witnessed history that has never been repeated. The United States has had several presidents who did not receive a majority of the popular vote and a few presidents who received fewer popular votes than their opponent but still won the presidency in the electoral college but only John Quincy Adams has been elected by the House of Representatives, a president who was second in the popular vote and second in the electoral college but the winner in the House. Without Clay in the running, the Clay votes went to Adams and that put Adams in the White House.

Following the raucous and highly discussed presidential election, Andrew Jackson's faction of the Democrat-Republican party went on to become the Democrat party. The Adams and Clay faction of the Democrat-Republican party became the National Republican party and then the Whig party. Most of the Whig party would later merge into the Republican party.

Thomas, as a Clay supporter, found himself in a minority among his friends and neighbors. The majority of Indiana votes and support went to Andrew Jackson. During that election and until it was finally settled in early 1825, there would have been

---

[156] As it stood in 1824, the pertinent portion of the 12th Amendment is: "The person having the greatest Number of votes for President, shall be the President, if such number be a majority of the whole number of Electors appointed; and if no person have such majority, then from the persons having the highest numbers not exceeding three on the list of those voted for as President, the House of Representatives shall choose immediately, by ballot, the President. But in choosing the President, the votes shall be taken by states, the representation from each state having one vote; a quorum for this purpose shall consist of a member or members from two-thirds of the states, and a majority of all the states shall be necessary to a choice."

many very interesting evenings spent sitting around the fireplace discussing national politics and having Abraham read the latest Washington news from the newspapers.

There have been some historians who have speculated that Thomas and Abraham early on supported Andrew Jackson. Considering their later very staunch support for Clay and the Whig party, that is doubtful. The speculation is based on some relatives becoming strong in the Democrat party and having supported Jackson. It is also based on a later statement by Dennis Hanks that he supported Jackson. "We were there in the year 1825, when Jackson and Adams ran for President. I was then but nineteen years of age, yet I acted as Clerk of Election and actually voted for Jackson, therefore I have voted for him three times."[157] Dennis, known for exaggeration and stretching the truth to gain position and attention, at nineteen years of age would not have been legal or allowed to vote and was likely making claims to align himself with Jackson who remained a popular figure in history.

In early 1825, the Pigeon Creek community welcomed Josiah Crawford and family to Spencer County. Crawford's home was built about two miles from Thomas' farm. Crawford learned that Thomas was the man he needed to work on his new home, and he hired Thomas to finish out the cabin. One of the pieces of work Thomas did for Crawford was to whip-saw boards and put in a floor for the cabin. [158]

Thomas was keeping his farm running and he was also doing a lot of carpentry and cabinetmaking. He took other jobs as they were available. There is record of both Thomas and Abraham working in Shadrack Hall's tannery.[159]

In June 1825, Thomas was one of three trustees appointed by Little Pigeon Church to do repairs on the church building. Along with William Barker and Reuben Grigsby, Thomas oversaw the repairs which were done by subscription. Thomas did some of the work himself.[160]

---

[157] Chapman Brothers. *Portrait and Biographical Album of Coles County, Illinois*, page 555.

[158] Douglas L. Wilson and Rodney O. Davis. *Herndon's Informants*, page 660. From a letter of J. W. Wartmann to Weik dated July 20, 1888.

[159] Bess V. Ehrmann. *Lincoln and His Neighbors*, page 22.

[160] Louis A. Warren. "Abraham Lincoln's Father." *The Lincoln Kinsman*, page 8.

In all this work, Abraham, and probably John, helped. In a pioneer subsistence economy, particularly in one just coming out of an economic depression, all members of the family were expected to contribute. Everyone had to carry their share of the work. It was common for fathers to rent out their children in return for future help or needed goods and supplies. Cash was still rare in southern Indiana but by 1825 that was beginning to change. With more families moving in and trade picking up, Thomas was able to trade furniture, cabinets, barrels, and farm surplus. He was able to hire lout Abraham and John for wages as well as barter.

Some of the work took Thomas and Abraham as far as the Ohio River, where they became known amongst the businessmen and traders. As the economic depression ended towns and cities developed and new businesses started. There was opportunity to earn a living in ways other than the pioneer subsistence economy. Thomas saw these changes coming but he was content with his life. He had lived most of his life as a pioneer, living and working on the frontier where families were self-sufficient. Thomas had no ambition to change his way of life.

It was different for Abraham. As Abraham worked for growing businesses, as he talked to businessmen and traders, as he saw the cities growing, as he read about the opportunities for a different kind of life, his ambition grew strong. He wanted to earn his living with his mind, not his hands. Father and son were walking different roads and the gap between them grew.

Southern Indiana was moving to an economy based on urban trade.[161] New career opportunities opened for the young and anyone else that wanted to give them a try. Abraham was ready to try them. Thomas was not. Thomas was comfortable and doing well in the subsistence pioneer way of life and in his businesses of carpentry and craftsmanship. With his eyesight trouble and his comfort with his life, the economic shift to an urban way of life based on trade wealth rather than land wealth, Thomas was left with neither training nor disposition to change with it. He was being left behind.

---

[161] Kenneth J. Winkle does a great job in *The Young Eagle* describing the pioneer subsistence economy and the change to an urban based economy. Anyone wanting a better, more detailed understanding of that change should reference *The Young Eagle*.

Thomas' world demanded that a man do manual labor and hunting. Thomas tried to teach Abraham that world and Thomas taught Abraham to work in that world, but Abraham did not want that world. Abraham saw the changing world and grabbed hold of it. Thomas did not. Abraham was moving into a world where children were not a part of the family's labor to survive and he began to resent having to give much of what he earned into the family treasury instead of being able to begin building a life for himself. From this time, Thomas and Abraham lived in two different worlds with two different worldviews. For Thomas there was one way to live, one way to survive. Abraham did not accept that view of life. Abraham's more liberal views of religion and questioning a literal interpretation of the Bible did not help the situation.[162] Thomas made do with a minimum of reading and math. Abraham valued education and wanted more than the minimum necessary.

During Abraham's teen years, when Thomas' loss of sight caused loss of ability to perform up to previous standard, Abraham was tired and lazy. The tired would have been a natural result of his quick growth. He was 6'2" and only 160 pounds in weight by the time he was sixteen. Tall, skinny, and tired. Plus, Abraham wanted to learn, not work. The neighbors he did work for considered him "awful lazy" and "no hand to pitch in at work".[163] This added to the friction at home.

These factors may have led to a change for Thomas' family. Up to this time, Abraham had worked mainly on the farm, in Thomas' carpentry shop, or with Thomas on other jobs outside the home. In 1825, at age 16, Abraham went to the Ohio River where he lived with and worked for James Taylor. It was during this time that Abraham had opportunity to observe the courts and legal proceedings that would eventually lead him to law and politics. Abraham did farm and ferry work for the Taylor's. They provided him room and board and pay.[164] Some of that pay Abraham sent home to Thomas to help the family. Thomas was legally the owner of wages his children earned and could require

---

[162] See my book, *Not A Technical Christian*, for more detail on Abraham Lincoln's religion and beliefs.

[163] David Herbert Donald. *Lincoln*, page 33.

[164] William E. Bartelt. *There I Grew Up*, page 171.

it all to be handed over. Thomas did not require all of Abraham's earnings. We don't know what the split was between Abraham keeping pocket money and supporting the family. We know Abraham kept some money because he tells of having money and buying books with it..[165]

With the winter of 1825-1826, Abraham was back on Thomas' farm. He had probably returned from working for James Taylor in time to help the Pigeon Creek community bring in the harvest and to join in the gatherings and festivity of a pioneer harvest. Neighbors gathered to help each other, feast, and turn the work into contests. The winter brought another season of schooling.

Thomas sent his children to Azel W. Dorsey's school, about a mile and a half south of the Lincoln home in an evergreen grove in Jonesboro.[166] Dorsey was likely the most able of schoolmasters to which Thomas sent his family. Dorsey was a landowner, merchant, election clerk, Spencer County treasurer, and Spencer County coroner at various points in his life.[167] Where Dorsey lived, he was a leader of the community. He had also been the one to take in, raise, and educate the orphaned James Swaney who had earlier taught the Lincoln family.

Thomas helped construct the school building as all freeholders over age 21 were required to do by law. In 1824, the Indiana Legislature passed new laws regulating the establishment and governance of schools. Under that law every able-bodied freeholder or householder 21 years of age and older had to do one day's worth of work per week on the school building until it was completed. Failure to provide that labor incurred a fine of 37.5¢ per day for each day missed.[168]

The schools Thomas had sent to his children to in earlier years were subscription schools for which Thomas paid. With the new law, Thomas no longer had to pay. Dorsey's salary was undertaken

---

[165] William E. Bartelt. *There I Grew Up*, page 178.

[166] Louis A. Warren. *Abraham Lincoln Association Papers*. "The Environs of Lincoln's Youth", page 135.

[167] Louis A. Warren. "Lincoln's Indiana Schoolmasters." *Indiana Magazine of History*, page 115.

[168] Otho Lionel Newman. "Development or The Common Schools of Indiana To 1851." *Indiana Magazine of History*, page 241.

by the State through taxes[169] and the school was overseen by school trustees.

An old tradition in Indiana schools in the early 1800's may have been one Abraham participated in. Christmas day was not a holiday in pioneer times and was not celebrated as it is now. If Christmas fell on a weekday, work proceeded as normal and schools were in session. However, on Christmas the older boys would get to the schoolhouse early and "bar out" the teacher. Every entrance was blocked so the teacher could not enter to conduct lessons. The teacher would be allowed to continue schooling when he reached an agreement to provide some kind of holiday treat for his students. This is precisely the kind of pioneer prank that would have been popular with the Lincolns.

Much has been made of Abraham's limited education and Thomas has been frequently portrayed as opposing education. In William Herndon's Lincoln biography, Herndon portrays Sarah Lincoln as saying, "I induced my husband to permit Abe to read and study at home as well as at school. At first, he was not easily reconciled to it, but finally he too seemed willing to encourage him to a certain extent. Abe was a dutiful son to me always, and we took particular care when he was reading not to disturb him, would let him read on and on till he quit of his own accord."[170] This statement has guided Lincoln biography over the years to paint Thomas in a negative light regarding educating his children. Unfortunately for that thinking, the quote in Herndon's book does not match up with his notes of the interview with Sarah. What Sarah actually told Herndon was, "When Abe was reading my husband took particular care not to disturb him – would let him read on and on till Abe quit of his own accord." She went on to say, "As a usual thing Mr. Lincoln never made Abe quit reading to do anything if he could avoid it. He would do it himself first." Sarah said that Thomas was not highly educated, so he "wanted, as he himself felt the uses and necessities of education, his boy

---

[169] Louis A. Warren. "Lincoln's Indiana Schoolmasters." *Indiana Magazine of History*, page 113.
[170] William H. Herndon & Jesse W. Weik. *Herndon's Life of Lincoln*, page 33.

Abraham to learn and he encouraged him to it in all ways he could."[171]

Abraham Lincoln later confirmed Thomas favored his education. He told Leonard Swett, "My father had suffered greatly for the want of an education, and he determined at an early day that I should be well educated. And what do you think he said his ideas of a good education were? We had an old dog-eared arithmetic in our house, and Father determined that somehow, or somehow else, I should cipher clear through that book."[172] Thomas ensured that Abraham had paper to do math on. Someone, possibly Abraham himself, stitched pages together to make a sum book in which Abraham copied rules and definitions and worked through problems.[173] Thomas' idea of a good education was far different from what Abraham would come to see as a good education, but that does not diminish the fact that Thomas wanted and encouraged Abraham to be educated.

It is unlikely Thomas' daughter Sarah attended Dorsey's school with the other children. Just as Abraham had spent some of 1825 living with and working for James Taylor, Sarah spent much of 1825 and early 1826 living with and working for Elizabeth Crawford. When speaking of Sarah working for her, Elizabeth noted that there "were enough at home" in the Lincoln house.[174] Thomas' home was a busy place with his step-children, possibly Sophie Hanks, and Dennis Hanks' family often at the farm.

While Sarah was working for the Crawford's, she accepted the marriage proposal of Aaron Grigsby. In line with common custom of the time, Sarah joined Little Pigeon Church on April 4.[175] Sarah was said to be intelligent and a devoted Christian. One friend of the family described her as "just as pretty as Abe was homely."[176]

Sarah's wedding to Aaron Grigsby was on August 2, 1826.[177] History does not record the festivity or any details for it, but a

---

171 Douglas L. Wilson and Rodney O. Davis. *Herndon's Informants*, page 107. From Herndon's interview with Sarah Bush Lincoln on September 8, 1865.
172 Allen Thorndike Rice. *Reminiscences of Abraham Lincoln by Distinguished Men of His Time*, page 457. From a statement by Leonard Swett in 1886.
173 Library of Congress. *Abraham Lincoln: An Exhibition*, page 9.
174 William E. Bartelt. *There I Grew Up*, page 186.
175 Louis A. Warren. "Abraham Lincoln's Father." *The Lincoln Kinsman*, page 8.
176 Michael Burlingame. *Abraham Lincoln: A Life*, volume 1, page 26.
177 Louis A. Warren. "Abraham Lincoln's Father." *The Lincoln Kinsman*, page 8.

pioneer wedding was always a festive occasion with fun and feasting. Thomas would have done his best for his daughter's marriage. Sarah Bush Lincoln would also have done her best by young Sarah, filling in the place left by Nancy's early death.

As part of the festivities, Elizabeth Crawford later provided William Herndon with information regarding a song sung at the wedding which she credited to 17-year-old Abraham.

Adam and Eve's Wedding Song[178]

When Adam was created
He dwelt in Eden's shade,
As Moses has recorded,
And soon a bride was made.

Ten thousand times ten thousand
Of creatures swarmed around
Before a bride was formed,
And yet no mate was found.

The Lord then was not willing
That man should be alone,
But caused a sleep upon him,
And from him took a bone.

And closed the flesh instead thereof,
And then he took the same
And of it made a woman,
And brought her to the man.

Then Adam he rejoiced
To see his loving bride
A part of his own body,
The product of his side.

The woman was not taken
From Adam's feet we see,
So he must not abuse her,
The meaning seems to be.

---

[178] Luther Emerson Robinson. *Abraham Lincoln As A Man of Letters*, pages 322-323.

The woman was not taken
From Adam's head, we know,
To show she must not rule him –
'Tis evidently so.

The woman she was taken
From under Adam's arm,
So she must be protected
From injuries and harm.

The song has long been accredited to young Abraham, but later review showed Abraham borrowed the verse from William H. Bozarth who wrote the poem in Kentucky in 1818 under the title of *The Song of Creation*. Abraham took Bozarth's verse, probably from one of the newspapers he frequently read, and modified it for the wedding.[179] Locals, and many today, still credit the work to Abraham.

Just two days after the wedding, on August 4, Thomas took up his responsibility to the church and served on a committee to interview members and attendees who had in some way violated church discipline and lost their good standing.[180] The purpose of the interviews was to bring the persons to repentance and return them to good standing.

September found the Lincolns once more celebrating. On September 14, Matilda Johnston, Thomas' stepdaughter, married Squire Hall. Squire was half-brother to Dennis Hanks.[181] Squire and Matilda made their home close to Thomas' farm. Thomas' family was growing. The nucleus of the extended family that would move to Illinois was forming.

Along with the celebration of two marriages in the Lincoln family, 1826 also saw sorrow. Dennis Hanks failed in being able to make his farm successful and he assigned his land to James Gentry to get out from under the debt. With that failure, Dennis and his family returned to Thomas' farm. Dennis' family added six

---

[179] Luther Emerson Robinson. *Abraham Lincoln As A Man of Letters*, pages 325-326.
[180] Louis A. Warren. "Abraham Lincoln's Father." *The Lincoln Kinsman*, page 8.
[181] Louis A. Warren. "Abraham Lincoln's Father." *The Lincoln Kinsman*, page 8.

people to the Lincoln home with the birth of Harriet Ann Hanks in 1826.

Abraham remained at Thomas', living at home most of 1826. He worked some in a pork house owned by Bill Jones and he clerked in Gentryville for James Gentry at Gentry's store.[182]

While Thomas was not prospering as he had in Kentucky, he was still doing well. He had a successful farm and was a sought-after woodcraftsman. His family was growing and happy. His children were embarking into life on their own, starting their own families and learning their own skills.

The Pigeon Creek community was getting bigger and the economy was moving into the industrial age. A post office opened at Gentry's store in Gentryville.[183] As one looks at the early adult years of Abraham Lincoln in Illinois, it becomes clear that these early years in Indiana set the path for him. He clerked at a store and that store became the area's first post office. Thomas ensured that Abraham's education was pursued and allowed Abraham to live and work away from home where he met the people and experienced the courts that would spark his interest in law. Everything seen in the Indiana years and in Thomas' raising of Abraham was leading toward destiny.

1827 - 1828

1827 began with a festive celebration. On January 13, Sophie Hanks married Dillings Lynch. The Lynchs would live for a short time in Indiana but then find their way to Arkansas where their connection to the Lincoln family would be lost for many years and questioned when it came to light again.

Thomas' support for his church continued strong in early 1827. Members, who did not frequently have cash to cover expenses or the pastor's salary, would often contribute produce. On March 9, the records of the Little Pigeon Church indicate that Thomas donated twenty-four pounds of manufactured corn to the church.[184]

---

[182] William E. Bartelt. *There I Grew Up*, page 151.
[183] Postal History. www.postalhistory.com/postoffices.
[184] Louis A. Warren. "Abraham Lincoln's Father." *The Lincoln Kinsman*, page 8.

Thomas gained another grandchild on April 12, 1827. Squire and Matilda Hall had their first child, a boy, John Johnston Hall. Throughout the remainder of his life Thomas would be surrounded by children, grandchildren, and great-grandchildren.

1827 was a good year for Thomas. He had long sought a farm with a clear title. Kentucky could not provide that. The Panic of 1819 and the ensuing depression set him back on his plans in Indiana to obtain clear title to land. But where many could not endure the Panic and downturn, Thomas weathered it. He continued to work and plan. The Relief Act had provided him much needed time and prevented him joining hundreds of others in defaulting on their land but he was still unable to gain the cash to make the payments required. Thomas was not alone. Hundreds of landowners were unable to meet their obligations. Once again, the government stepped in. Another relief act was passed on May 4, 1826.[185] Thomas gained benefit from the act of 1826. With this law, Thomas was not only able to keep his land, he was able to get a clear and fully paid title to it.

Following the relief act of 1821, Thomas owed $240 on his 160-acre claim. Under the original Indiana land deals, a settler had to purchase a minimum of 160 acres. By 1827, the minimum was 80 acres. What Thomas did was a complicated deal, but it shows his shrewdness in business affairs though there is some mystery to it.

In 1818, in Posey County (west of Spencer County), Charles Whiting bought a slightly oversized section of land, 160.34 acres (NWV4 of Section 3, T5S, R12W). He had only paid a fourth of the purchase price ($80.17) when on February 2, 1820, Whiting assigned his land to Memorial Forrest. Forrest died, and the guardian for his heirs applied under the Relief Act of 1821 for a longer term of credit, the same process Thomas had followed with the exception that the Forrest heirs also relinquished 80 acres to further reduce their debt.

On April 2, 1827, a special Posey County Probate court ordered the disposal of the property to settle the estate. On April 5, James McCreary, guardian of the heirs, assigned the remaining

---

[185] William E. Bartelt. "The Land Dealings of Spencer County, Indiana, Pioneer Thomas Lincoln." *Indiana Magazine of History*, page 218.

80 acres to Thomas. In exchange for the land, Thomas assumed the remaining debt of $80.17. He paid the other $80.17 of price for the land with what the records call "valuable consideration".[186] This is the mystery. There is no indication in the records of how Thomas knew the Forrests or how he found out about the land offering. There is no explanation of what the "valuable consideration" was that Thomas bartered in trade for the land. Regardless, Thomas gained claim to 80.17 acres in Posey County valued at $160.34 for which he owed $80.17.

With the Posey County deal in play, Thomas went to the Vincennes land office on April 30, 1827. Thomas relinquished the eastern 80 acres of his 160-acre claim, receiving a $160 credit, leaving him owing $80 for his farm. At that point he relinquished his newly acquired Posey County land, receiving an additional credit of $80.17 which he applied to his $80 debt. On June 6, 1827, Thomas received a land patent signed by President John Quincy Adams showing his land paid for and Thomas having clear title.[187] After his struggle in Kentucky with land titles, having clear title to his Pigeon Creek farm must have been a great relief for Thomas and cause for celebration.

There has been some speculation that Thomas purchased another 20 acres of land along the western edge of his farm, but the only strong documentation for his ever owning the land is a deed conveying the land from James Gentry to Joseph Gentry in 1834 that shows Thomas' name.[188] Records show Thomas selling 80 acres of land, not 100, before his move to Illinois.

Sometime in Spring of 1827, Abraham returned to working along the Ohio River. In addition to odd jobs, he ran a ferry business, hauling passengers out onto the river to board ships. It is said that Abraham, using the carpentry skills Thomas taught him, built the rowboat he used to ferry passengers.[189]

---

[186] William E. Bartelt. "The Land Dealings of Spencer County, Indiana, Pioneer Thomas Lincoln." *Indiana Magazine of History*, page 220.

[187] William E. Bartelt. "The Land Dealings of Spencer County, Indiana, Pioneer Thomas Lincoln." *Indiana Magazine of History*, page 220.

[188] Lincoln Log. *A Daily Chronology of the Life of Abraham* Lincoln. www.thelincolnlog.org/. Records for February 20, 1830.

[189] Fred Kaplan. *Lincoln*, page 44.

Stepbrother John Johnston joined Abraham for a least one venture to do some work in Louisville for which they were paid in silver dollars. This was reported as being the first silver dollar Abraham ever owned as his own.[190]

Custom and law of the time made any money earned by children the property of their father. It was customary for the fathers to return a portion of the money to their children for their own use as they saw fit. The fact that Abraham had money, such as the silver dollar, which he considered his own shows that Thomas followed the custom and allowed Abraham to keep most of his earnings as he approached adulthood. Living near the Ohio, Abraham continued his reputation for reading and much of the money he earned went toward obtaining books.[191] Abraham may have grown resentful of Thomas keeping some of the money he earned, but Thomas did not keep it all as the law allowed. With the fairness Abraham is later noted for, it is doubtful he blamed his father for doing what was legal and done by the majority of American fathers. Abraham's resentment was more focused on the unfairness of the law.

Illustrating the social nature of pioneers and how they helped each and made life pleasant, several churches joined together in 1827 for a house raising.

The raising of the Linn house was quite a social affair in 1827 and invitations were sent out to the congregations of Bakers Creek (now Eureka), Pigeon Church, and the church near Maxville and other churches within this territory. At the appointed day there was a large gathering and a big dinner. The Lincolns were present, and Thomas Lincoln carried up the corner. The bottom logs were set on stone pillars and the lower logs and floor were laid the first day and at night there was a big dance, at which Abe danced with Betsy Ray and perhaps other girls, as Jean Murphy, Laura Lahue, etc. Light was furnished by three big brush heaps and "Uncle" Johnnie

---

[190] Douglas L. Wilson and Rodney O. Davis. *Herndon's Informants*, page 100. Statement by A. H. Chapman dated September 8, 1865.
[191] William E. Bartelt. *There I Grew Up*, page 178.

Thomas is credited with carrying up the corner for the house raising. Carrying up the corner means the gathering turned to Thomas to set the first corner of the house, laying out the angles and ensuring the cabin was built sturdy. This was similar to laying a cornerstone for a building. Everything in the construction followed how the corner was carried.

In late 1827 and early 1828, Thomas was looking forward to his first grandchild from his daughter Sarah but it was not to be. On January 20, 1828, Sarah Lincoln Grigsby died in childbirth along with her child.

A neighbor of the Grigsbys remembered the night Sarah died. "I remember old Tommy Lincoln. I sat on his lap many times. I was at Sally Lincoln's infare dinner. I remember the night she died. My mother was there at the time. She had a very strong voice, and I heard her calling father. He awoke the boys and said, 'Something is the matter.' He went after a doctor, but it was too late. They let her lay too long. My old aunt was the midwife."[193]

The Lincolns took Sarah's death hard. Abraham blamed the Grigsbys for not going after the doctor sooner. Relations with the Grigsby family were polite but tense from Sarah's death until Thomas moved his family to Illinois. The Grigsbys had been close friends of the Lincolns and that friendship was greatly strained by Sarah's death. Various of the Grigsbys would later offer memories of Thomas' Indiana years to historians. One of those, from Redmond Grigsby, was of Sarah looking after Abraham and of the banter that passed between the siblings. Redmond was the younger brother of Sarah's husband Aaron. He spoke of frequently hearing Sarah telling Abraham to be good when he was heading off with the other boys. His common rejoinder to her

---

[192] Richard E. Hart. *Thomas Lincoln Reconsidered*, manuscript page 161. Hart credits the quote to an article published in the Monitor, March 5, 1931. Sandy Creek Landing Greets the Lincolns An Historical Sketch of Pioneer Days in This Community and County, 1931, C. T. Baker, Chapter IX, p. 23.

[193] J. T. Hobson. *Footprints of Abraham Lincoln*, pages 21-22. From the reminiscences of Mrs. Lamar, the wife of Captain Lamar, who resided at Buffaloville, a short distance east of Lincoln City. Dated from her home, September 8, 1903.

admonition was, "Oh, you be good yourself, Sally, and Abe will take care of himself."[194] It was Sarah who stepped in for over a year to be surrogate mother and caregiver for Abraham after Nancy Lincoln's death. Even after Sarah Bush Johnston became the second Mrs. Thomas Lincoln, Abraham and his sister remained close, bonded from their shared grief.

History tells much of Abraham Lincoln's life being haunted by death. A little brother, his mother, his sister, a possible first love, two sons – Abraham Lincoln did experience his share of sorrow. It can also be said of Thomas that his life was haunted by death. Some of those deaths, he and Abraham shared. Thomas lost his father, an infant son, Nancy, and his daughter and future grandchild. Thomas was deeply touched with sorrow. Death was common among all ages in the 1800s and Thomas was kept busy building coffins,[195] but frequency of death is poor rationalization to assume there is less sorrow. Frequency of experiencing death does little to negate the pain and loss.

As Thomas dealt with this difficult time in his life, he also experienced another weather anomaly. The winter of 1827-1828 was exceptionally mild and has been referred to as a year with no winter. A strong El Niño effect kept the winter temperatures above average. A false Spring brought trees leafing out and fruit trees blossoming in mid-winter. Grass remained green. Many planted crops early in the Spring of 1828. The weather anomaly ended with a killer frost in April of 1828. Farmers had to replant crops. That warm winter is now considered to have been an outstanding event in the meteorological history. [196]

During his lifetime, Thomas made several trips to New Orleans for himself and others. In 1828, nineteen-year-old Abraham followed in his father's footsteps and made his first trip by flatboat to New Orleans. He earned eight dollars a month for two months plus a steamboat ticket for his return trip. The trip left a lasting impression. He found New Orleans an exciting and burgeoning city, but it was forever tainted in his memory by the filth of slavery.

---

[194] J. T. Hobson. *Footprints of Abraham Lincoln.*, page 21.
[195] Michael Burkhimer. *Lincoln's Christianity*, page 4.
[196] Mock, C.J., J. Mojzisek., and M. McWaters, et al. Climatic Change.

One incident, of unknown date, tells us much about Thomas' home life. Dennis Hanks recalled a prank Abraham pulled on his stepmother. Sarah and Thomas were out but the children were in and around the house. There was a mud puddle near the horse trough. Abraham had the children walk through the puddle and then turned them upside-down and had them "walk" across the cabin ceiling. There must have been much mirth and expectation from Abraham and the children when Sarah returned to the cabin and they waited for her to look up. It is hard to imagine any housekeeper being happy and laughing at muddy footprints tracking across her ceiling, but Sarah is said to have laughed heartily at the prank.

Such was pioneer life. Pranks and jokes were a major part of life and the pioneers enjoyed them, even when the joke was at their expense. While Dennis does not mention Thomas, Thomas' love of pranks and jokes no doubt let his laughter join in loudly along with his son. It would have been a story told frequently over the next days for all the neighbors to enjoy. Abraham cleaned up after his prank by washing the ceiling down and re-whitewashing it.[197]

This story speaks to the love and laughter that filled Thomas' home. It adds to the description of the farm speaking of a horse trough to water Thomas' horses and other livestock. It also adds to the description of the house where there was a ceiling that was kept clean and whitewashed.

In September of 1828, Thomas resigned as a trustee from the Little Pigeon Church. No reason is given in the church record for the resignation.[198] Thomas continued to attend and support the church. He did not remove his membership. He was still sought out to help resolve church issues and discipline concerns. It is possible that his resignation was due to some of the ongoing stress with the Grigsbys who were members in good standing at the church.

The close of 1828 brought the culmination of another raucous presidential election. It rematched incumbent president John Quincy Adams against Andrew Jackson. In 1824 Jackson had won

---

[197] William E. Bartelt. *There I Grew Up*, page 183.
[198] Louis A. Warren. "Abraham Lincoln's Father." *The Lincoln Kinsman*, page 8.

the largest portion of the popular vote and a bigger share of the electoral but without clear majority in either leaving the election to the House of Representatives which elected Adams. 1828 had no such issues. Jackson won a clear majority and was elected to replace Adams in the White House.

Again, there is no record of how Thomas voted, but Thomas was a strong Whig, a party which formed from Adam's National Republican party, and he had a strong aversion to the Democrat party. He later referred to the Democrat party by the derogatory term "locofoco" (locofocos were a splinter group of liberal New York Democrats which disrupted the party in the late 1830s and early 1840s) and expressed the desire that locofoco principals would "crumble to dust".[199] That being Thomas' political reality, it is a near certainty he supported and voted for Adams. Doing so, Thomas again found himself at odds politically with many of his neighbors as Jackson carried Indiana by a 56% to 43% margin.

In tracking Thomas' work as a cabinetmaker, craft experts state that Thomas' work was deteriorating in quality and complexity as his time in Indiana grew short. His health was going down and his eyesight continuing to decline. Though he worked by feel and is said to have had a remarkable sense of touch, there is only so much delicate inlay work that can be done that way. Thomas was still in demand for his woodworking, but it was for simpler pieces and more standard work.[200]

The troubles and economic hardship that came to Thomas in Illinois were beginning to be seen in the decline of what he was able to do in his workshop and carpentry business. He maintained farming and woodworking and was in no danger of losing his farm for which he had clear title. He was doing work as a mechanic,[201] a skill he had not made much use of earlier in life. It was something that had come down to him through the family tradition of

---

[199] David Herbert Donald. *Lincoln*, page 109.

[200] Kathy Tretter. "Lincoln Family Corner Cabinet Hidden for Years in Southern Indiana." *Ferdinand News.*

[201] Douglas L. Wilson and Rodney O. Davis. *Herndon's Informants*, page 27. From an Erastus Wright interview of Dennis Hanks, sent by letter to Herndon from Chicago, Illinois on June 8, 1865.

blacksmithing. He built a mill,[202] something his mechanic work supported. It was a simple horse mill for grinding corn, probably very similar to the mill where Abraham had been kicked in the head. The mill provided a steady income and a steady stream of neighbors to socialize with. As one line of work declined for Thomas, he found other ways to make a living. This speaks well of his industry and determination.

As the Indiana years came close to an end, Abraham was spending more and more time working away from home. He was feeling the draw of the new industrial economy and yearning toward a career where he could use mind instead of muscle. Judge Thomas Pitcher, in Rockport, Indiana, said Abraham had wanted to read law with him. (Reading law was the standard way in Indiana that a person would learn law and prepare to pass the bar to become a lawyer.) Unfortunately for Abraham, he was not of legal age and Thomas still needed his help and work and income to support the family.[203] Thomas could not spare his ambitious son to have the time to read law with the Judge. This no doubt pulled at Abraham and increased the tension between him and Thomas.

1829 - 1830

The year 1829 was a turning point for both Thomas and for Abraham.

Though the story is often placed earlier in his life, it was in 1829 that Abraham borrowed Parson Mason Locke Weems' *The Life of George Washington: With Curious Anecdotes Equally Honourable to Himself, and Exemplary to His Young Countrymen*. It was this book which contained for the first time the story of George Washington and the cherry tree. Weems' work drove the twenty-year-old Lincoln's ambition. He borrowed the book from neighbor and friend Josiah Crawford and it is his wife Elizabeth that puts the

---

[202] Douglas L. Wilson and Rodney O. Davis. *Herndon's Informants.*, pages 662-663] From an Oliver C. Terry letter to Jesse Weik dated July 1888 from Mt. Vernon, Indiana.
[203] Douglas L. Wilson and Rodney O. Davis. *Herndon's Informants.*, pages 662-663] From an Oliver C. Terry letter to Jesse Weik dated July 1888 from Mt. Vernon, Indiana.

date in 1829 for the borrowing.[204] This was the book Abraham carelessly placed in a loft cubbyhole for the night and which was ruined by moisture seeping through the cabin roof into the book. Abraham worked off the price of the book for Crawford and kept the book.

In the Fall of 1829, Thomas began work on a new, bigger, and better cabin for his family. The extended family was growing but at the same time fewer people were living in Thomas' cabin. Dennis and Betsy Hanks had their own home though they frequented Thomas' farm and may have lived with him sometimes. Squire and Matilda Hall were living in their own home. Sophie Hanks, for whatever time she had spent living with Thomas, had moved to Arkansas. In 1829, the cabin housed Thomas and Sarah, his stepson John, sometimes Dennis and Betsy with their children, and sometimes Abraham. Instead of the eight people living full-time in the Lincoln cabin following Thomas' marriage to Sarah, the number varied from three to ten.

The cabin Thomas began to build would have been a fine home for Sarah and him as they aged but it was never to be completed. Dennis Hanks lost four cows to the milk sick in 1829. There is no report of an epidemic or of anyone in the family becoming ill, but the milk sick sent a shiver of fear through the family and woke sad memories of those lost to earlier epidemic. Dennis determined he would find a new place to live where there was no milk sick.

Cousin John Hanks had moved to Illinois and communicated back that the land was good, the soil rich. Dennis was all for moving even though Illinois was known to have the milk sick, a fact John might not have shared with Dennis.

With Dennis and Betsy planning to move, Sarah Bush Lincoln was heartsick. She was close to her daughter, close to all her family. She was unwilling to part ways with her grandchildren. Work on the new cabin ceased. Thomas' family wanted to move, and Thomas took up the cause though perhaps not with great eagerness. He had a good home, a good farm, a good business.

---

[204] Douglas L. Wilson and Rodney O. Davis. *Herndon's Informants*, page 125. From Herndon's interview with Elizabeth Crawford at her Spencer County, Indiana home on September 16, 1865.

His health and eyesight were deteriorating. It was not a good time for him to start fresh in another state.

Abraham and some friends had worked to whipsaw planks for the new house's flooring and framing. When those planks were no longer needed, Abraham sold them to Josiah Crawford.[205]

In December of 1829, Thomas and Sarah requested and received letters of dismission from the Little Pigeon Church. A letter of dismission was an important document for Thomas. It was a document showing they were members in good standing, ready to be accepted into another church.

On January 10, 1830, Nancy Grigsby made a complaint that she was not satisfied with the Lincolns and their membership standing in the church. The church took back the letter of dismission and investigated the complaint.[206] It proved baseless and the letter of dismission was returned to Thomas and Sarah.

In an odd twist of fate, on February 13, Thomas was appointed by the church to a committee to investigate and decide a quarrel between Nancy Grigsby and Elizabeth Crawford. On the same date, Thomas was appointed moderator for an all church meeting.[207] Even though he was leaving, the church still honored him. It shows the church saw Thomas to be fair and honest and forgiving. To sit on a disciplinary committee investigating the woman who had complained about him and tried to have him rejected for a letter of dismission displayed high respect for Thomas' integrity and faith.

The decision to move to Illinois was quick. Thomas had little time to settle his affairs, finish out any obligations, and settle any open tabs at stores in Gentryville. With the limited time, he was unable to seek out a good deal for selling his farm. He ended up selling the farm for $125 to Charles Grigsby, a loss on the cost of the land without even considering the additional value of the buildings and improvements. Thomas and his extended family were ready to move.

---

[205] Douglas L. Wilson and Rodney O. Davis. *Herndon's Informants.*, page 124. From William Wood's interview with Herndon in Spencer County, Indiana on September 15, 1865.

[206] Louis A. Warren. "Abraham Lincoln's Father." *The Lincoln Kinsman*, page 8.

[207] Louis A. Warren. "Abraham Lincoln's Father." *The Lincoln Kinsman*, page 8..

While most historians accept that Thomas sold his Indiana farm at a loss, Wayne Temple proffers a different view. He reports that Grigsby made a down payment of an undisclosed amount on November 26, 1829 and then paid $125 on February 20, 1830 at which time Thomas and Sarah signed over the deed. The undisclosed amount could have allowed Thomas to break even on his land or possibly gain a profit.[208]

Looking back at Abraham's Indiana years, he had experienced a gift from Thomas's way of life, from the pioneer way of life. In Indiana, Thomas raised Abraham from a child into a man and that man gained wisdom that would follow him and serve him throughout his life.

> *It was a life of democratic equality, wherein no man was much richer or wiser than his fellow; a life of open air, neighborly helpfulness and no shams, in which each individual stood or fell on his own merits. In the White House Lincoln continued to measure people and things by these unsophisticated standards of personal worth and usefulness.*[209]

On a visit to Indiana in 1844, Abraham stopped to see his old home and visit with friends and neighbors. He paid honor to his mother at her grave. The visit moved him to become sentimental for the good times of his childhood. He wrote two poems as a result of the visit: *My Childhood Home* and *The Bear Hunt*.[210] The poems speak to life in Indiana, giving more description to life in Thomas Lincoln's home.

---

[208] Wayne C. Temple. *Thomas and Abraham As Farmers*, page 21.
[209] Helen Nicolay. *Personal Traits of Abraham Lincoln*, page 63.
[210] *The Bear Hunt* can be found in the appendices.

My Childhood Home I See Again[211]

My childhood-home I see again,
And gladden with the view;
And still as mem'ries crowd my brain,
There's sadness in it too.

O memory! thou mid-way world
'Twixt Earth and Paradise,
Where things decayed, and loved ones lost
In dreamy shadows rise.

And freed from all that's gross or vile,
Seem hallowed, pure, and bright,
Like scenes in some enchanted isle,
All bathed in liquid light.

As distant mountains please the eye,
When twilight chases day –
As bugle-tones, that, passing by,
In distance die away –

As leaving some grand waterfall
We ling'ring, list its roar,
So memory will hallow all
We've known, but know no more.

Now twenty years have passed away,
Since here I bid farewell
To woods, and fields, and scenes of play
And schoolmates loved so well.

Where many were, how few remain
Of old familiar things!
But seeing these to mind again
The lost and absent brings.

---

211 Roy P. Basler. *The Collected Works of Abraham Lincoln*, volume 1, pages 367-370. The poem is dated to February 25, 1846 but the exact date of Abraham Lincoln writing it is uncertain.

The friends I left that parting day –
How changed, as time has sped!
Young childhood grown, strong manhood grey,
And half of all are dead.

I hear the lone survivors tell
How naught from death could save,
Till every sound appears a knell,
And every spot a grave.

I range the fields with pensive tread,
And pace the hollow rooms;
And feel (companions of the dead)
I'm living in the tombs.

And here's an object more of dread,
Than ought the grave contains---
A human-form, with reason fled,
While wretched life remains.

Poor Matthew! Once of genius bright, –
A fortune-favored child –
Now locked for aye, in mental night,
A haggard madman wild.

Poor Matthew! I have ne'er forgot
When first with maddened will,
Yourself you maimed, your father fought,
And mother strove to kill;

And terror spread, and neighbors ran,
Your dang'rous strength to bind;
And soon a howling crazy man,
Your limbs were fast confined.

How then you writhed and shrieked aloud,
Your bones and sinews bared;
And fiendish on the gaping crowd,
With burning eyeballs glared.

And begged, and swore, and wept, and prayed,
With maniac laughter joined –
How fearful are the signs displayed,
By pangs that kill the mind!

And when at length, tho' drear and long,
Time soothed your fiercer woes –
How plaintively your mournful song,
Upon the still night rose.

I've heard it oft, as if I dreamed,
Far-distant, sweet, and lone;
The funeral dirge it ever seemed
Of reason dead and gone.

To drink its strains, I've stole away,
All silently and still,
Ere yet the rising god of day
Had streaked the Eastern hill.

Air held his breath; the trees all still
Seemed sorr'wing angels round.
Their swelling tears in dewdrops fell
Upon the list'ning ground.

But this is past, and naught remains
That raised you o'er the brute.
Your mad'ning shrieks and soothing strains
Are like forever mute.

Now fare thee well: more thou the cause
Than subject now of woe.
All mental pangs, but time's kind laws,
Hast lost the power to know.

And now away to seek some scene
Less painful than the last –
With less of horror mingled in
The present and the past.

The very spot where grew the bread
That formed my bones, I see.
How strange, old field, on thee to tread,
And feel I'm part of thee!

Moving to Illinois

The traditional interpretation of Thomas' life by historians portrayed the move to Illinois in a negative light. "Shortly after his [Abraham's] return from his first excursion into the out world [his flat boat journey to New Orleans in 1828], his father, tired of failure in Indiana, packed his family and all his worldly goods into a single wagon drawn by two yoke of oxen, and after a fourteen days' tramp through the wilderness, pitched his camp once more in Illinois."[212] That view of the move is not accurate. The true history of the move to Illinois gives a different picture.

Where Thomas was behind every previous move in his adult life, the move to Illinois was pushed on him. He was building a new cabin and continuing to expand his farm. He had built a mill on his land to expand his business ventures. He was settled and content. The impetus for this move began with the Hanks.

When the milk sick broke out again, Dennis Hanks was not making a go of his own farm and livestock. What land he had gotten, he lost. Somewhere along the line, Dennis learned to make shoes but that was not earning a living for his growing family in the Pigeon Creek community. Dennis credited his want to move on the milk sick[213] but it is more likely he was looking for a fresh start somewhere else to try and get a solid footing in life.

Illinois was the new frontier. The soil was rich, and settlers were following the road past Thomas' farm toward Illinois. John Hanks was in Illinois and encouraging Dennis to come. Dennis saw the travelers and heard their hopes and dreams for Illinois. With his failure in Indiana, those hopes spoke to Dennis. As Dennis and Betsy considered the move so did Squire and Matilda. Sarah was about to be separated from her daughters and her grandchildren. She was not happy. Thomas' new cabin was not

---

[212] Joseph H. Choate. *Abraham Lincoln*, page 9.
[213] Douglas L. Wilson and Rodney O. Davis. *Herndon's Informants*, page 226. From a letter of Dennis Hanks to Herndon dated March 7, 1866.

enough if there would not be family to fill it with laughter and love. Thomas, no longer an ambitious man, was caught. His family was set on moving to Illinois. He had little choice but to go along. "If you make a bad bargain, hug it the tighter."[214] That was Thomas' philosophy to take what was bad and try to make it work. Illinois was not a good bargain for Thomas, but he would hug it tight.

The Pigeon Creek farm had 40 acres of land under cultivation in 1830. Thomas had planted an orchard[215] with apple trees. He had a workshop, a smokehouse, and other outbuildings. He had livestock, pastures for livestock, livestock sheds, a chicken coup, and a stable. He had a mill. Thomas was settled and content. His life in Indiana was far being a failure. Still, he put it behind him and prepared to go with his family to Illinois and start again.

There is no record of all the things Thomas sold as he prepared to head to Illinois or what livestock he took with him. He kept his horses but most of the livestock was sold. Goats, lambs, chickens, cows, and hogs were sold. David Turnham reported that he bought 100 hogs from Thomas, a fact that indicates Thomas had a large farm operation. Turnham also bought 400 or 500 bushels of corn. Thomas had a good surplus from his farm.[216] There is no report on who bought the other farm surplus or how much of it there was.

As they prepared to go to Illinois, Thomas and Sarah returned to Elizabethtown, Kentucky. Sarah still owned a lot there and they sold it for $123.[217] It is fairly certain that Thomas stopped to visit his mother, Bathsheba, while in Kentucky.

Another task Thomas undertook was the building of a wagon. The wagon he built for Sarah and his family has been referred to as a kind of chuck wagon and that it was "ironed off", a feature that was rare in southern Indiana.[218] Ironing off a wagon made the

---

[214] Roy P. Basler. *The Collected Works of Abraham Lincoln*, volume 1, page 280. Taken from a letter from Abraham Lincoln to Joshua Speed dated February 25, 1842.

[215] William E. Bartelt. *There I Grew Up*, page 144.

[216] Douglas L. Wilson and Rodney O. Davis. *Herndon's Informants*, page 121. From an interview of David Turnham by Herndon on September 15, 1865.

[217] Charles H. Coleman. *Abraham Lincoln and Coles County, Illinois*, page 7.

[218] Murr, Edward. "Lincoln in Indiana (Concluded)." *Indiana Magazine of History*, pages 165-166.

wagon sturdier and stronger by better securing the axles and other parts that took greater stress during use. Thomas was able to do this kind of blacksmithing and woodwork.

The wagon Thomas built was best handled by oxen. Thomas did not have suitable teams of oxen, so he sent Abraham along with Dennis Hanks to barter and dicker with neighbors. Allen Brooner provided one pair and the other came from the Hall family, delivered to Thomas by Wesley Hall.[219] With the Brooners, Thomas sent a young horse in trade for the yoke of oxen.[220] Evidently Thomas was still keeping horses at the time and the horses were good quality to trade one young horse for a yoke of oxen.

When the extended Lincoln family moved to Illinois, it was a caravan. There were three families: the Lincolns, the Hanks, and the Halls. In early 1830, Thomas was 52 and Sarah was 41. Abraham, less than a month before leaving for Illinois, had turned 21 and could legally choose his own course in life. He chose to travel with the family and relocate. John was 19.

There has been speculation that Thomas' caravan may have had three others in it. Squire Hall's parents were Levi and Nancy (Hanks) Hall. Nancy was Nancy Hanks Lincoln's aunt and the mother of Dennis Hanks, making her children with Levi to be Dennis' half-siblings. Levi died on June 21, 1829[221] and Nancy died on October 5, 1829. They were buried near Nancy Hanks Lincoln. Later, on September 29, 1831, Squire became the legal guardian of three of his siblings: Joseph, Mahala, and Letitia.[222] It is possible that the three siblings traveled with Squire and Matilda to Illinois or that they remained with other siblings until joining Squire in Illinois at a later date. Abraham Lincoln made no mention of Squire's siblings in his references to the party that went to Illinois with Thomas.

---

[219] Murr, Edward. "Lincoln in Indiana (Concluded)." *Indiana Magazine of History*, pages 165-166.
[220] J. T. Hobson. *Footprints of Abraham Lincoln*, page 30.
[221] Find A Grave. www.findagrave.com/cgi-bin/fg.cgi?page=grAGRid=26594272.
[222] Douglas L. Wilson and Rodney O. Davis. *Herndon's Informants*, page 782. From Verduin's genealogical information in the Appendices.

Thomas packed his family's belongings into the wagon he built for the trip. It is possible he built the two other wagons for the journey. Both Dennis and Squire had their own wagons loaded with their family belongings. With Dennis (age 31) and Betsy (22) were their children Sarah Jane (8), John Talbot (7), Nancy (6), and Harriet (4). With Squire (25) and Matilda (20) was their son John (11 months).

In addition to everything in the wagon, Thomas had at least two horses and there was a small number of livestock they kept from which to begin their new farm.[223] Most likely it was a cow or two with a few sheep or goats. Tradition has Abraham driving the wagon much of the way. Thomas scouted ahead on his horse, looking at where the wagons would need to cross roads, streams, and rivers. The Lincoln wagon was pulled by two yokes of oxen. The Hanks and Hall wagons were similar to Thomas', one being pulled by two yoke of oxen and the other by two pairs of horses.[224]

Thomas' wagon was loaded to the maximum. He had three beds and bedding, a bureau, a table, a clothes closet, a set of chairs, farming tools, cooking utensils, axes, rifles, books, seed for his first Illinois planting, clothing, spinning wheels, and whatever else of their personal items they thought might be useful or that they wanted.[225]

Thomas had the monies received from the sale of his livestock and farm surplus, the sale of Sarah's lot in Elizabethtown, the sale of items they did not take with them, and the sale of the farm. The full amount is not known but it would have been a tidy sum with which to begin anew.

With all the preparations complete, Thomas and his caravan left the Pigeon Creek farm and headed for Illinois on March 1, 1830. Moving in March was a slightly different pattern than most settlers followed. The norm was to move in the Fall of the year after bringing in the harvests. Moving in the Fall or early Winter, allowed time to build a cabin and clear land for crops. Thomas had not planned on moving. He was caught up in his children's

---

[223] Douglas L. Wilson and Rodney O. Davis. *Herndon's Informants*, page 103. Statement by A. H. Chapman to Herndon dated September 8, 1865.

[224] The Lincoln Log. www.thelincolnlog.org. Historical documentation recorded for March 1, 1830.

[225] Charles H. Coleman. *Abraham Lincoln and Coles County, Illinois*, page 7.

families wanting to move and Sarah Bush Lincoln refusing to be separated from them. By the time the decision to move had been made and preparations to move were made, which took some time, Thomas' caravan could not leave during the normal traveling time for settlers. They moved in early Spring. This did not give them much time to settle in and be ready to plant crops when they arrived in Illinois.

There is considerable controversy on the route taken from Indiana to Illinois. After Abraham became famous and was elected President, many places and people claimed a stop from the Lincoln family at their town or home during the Illinois move. It is hard to sort out the fiction from the fact.

As the Lincolns started out, friends and neighbors gathered to say farewell. The community was deeply saddened to see them go. Young neighbor Redmond Grigsby, age 12 at the time, says he helped hitch the two yokes of oxen to the wagon and then went with them for half a mile before turning back toward his home. [226]

The first night on the trail, the Lincolns traveled only as far as Gentryville where they spent the night with James Gentry. Friends and neighbors gathered for a heartfelt last evening with the Lincolns. When the morning came, more people gathered. It was quite a crowd and turned into a festive, yet sad, occasion. Many of these friends accompanied the Lincolns down the road for some distance before saying a final goodbye and turning back. [227] With that farewell, Thomas began a 225-mile journey to find a new home.

Abraham took advantage of the stop in Gentryville to dicker for goods. Some report he bargained with Gentry, for whom he had worked on many occasions, and others report he bargained with the Jones store, for which he had also worked. Perhaps he dickered with both. Regardless of with whom, Abraham had $30 in his pocket, a good amount of money for a young man who had just turned 21 less than two months previous. [228] (Some sources report the funds were as much as $36.) He had needed to save for quite a while to have that much money available to him. (Another

---

[226] J. T. Hobson. *Footprints of Abraham Lincoln*, page 33.

[227] Edward Murr. "Lincoln in Indiana (Concluded), page 166.

[228] This is more supporting evidence that Thomas did not demand all of Abraham's money as was his legal right prior to age 21.

indication that Thomas allowed Abraham to keep the money he earned.) With the money, he purchased "notions": buttons, needles, thread, pins, knives, forks, spoons, and other small domestic items. It was Abraham's intent to peddle these goods along the way to Illinois. And peddle them he did. By the time he had sold out, Abraham doubled his money.[229]

Thomas guided his family first to Vincennes, where the land office was located and where he had done business to gain title to his Pigeon Creek farm. The caravan did not dawdle along their way, but it was still a time period when people stopped while traveling to visit and share hospitality. As Thomas had done for many travelers going past his farms, others now did for him. Farms and towns along the way provided places to fix meals or share meals with others in their homes. More homes and families claim to have hosted the Lincolns than is possible along their way.

In Vincennes, there was time to refresh and rest. Abraham, and probably several others in the family, did a little sightseeing. Abraham went to the offices of the Vincennes Western Sun where he saw his first printing press.[230] He no doubt also got the paper to read to the family as they traveled.

The ground in March of 1830 was not thawed completely, which, despite the later start the Lincolns made in moving, still proved to be helpful as the oxen and horses and wagons were able to move along the roads without sinking in. Even a little later in the season, the thawed ground would have been muddy enough to cause major delays in their travel. As it was, the surface would thaw some during the day and then freeze back during the night. Streams, starting to swell with rain and melting snow, were still covered with ice every morning. Traveling to the north helped Thomas' way as their destination was over 100 miles to the north of the slightly warmer weather in southern Indiana. Years later, Abraham would state it simply to his partner, William Herndon, saying that the ground had not yet yielded up the frosts of winter.[231]

---

[229] Kenneth J. Winkle. *The Young Eagle*, page 138.
[230] Ida M. Tarbell. *The Early Life of Abraham Lincoln.*
[231] Charles H. Coleman. *Abraham Lincoln and Coles County, Illinois*, page 6.

It was in Vincennes that they boarded a ferry and crossed the Wabash River into Illinois. From there the road the caravan followed was through low lying prairie that the Spring rains had turned into a swamp. The low region was traveled along a very long stretch of road that was more a slightly elevated bridge made of corduroy log. [232] Such a bridge road was made by laying logs one next to the other across the road. It allowed people to travel but the way was not smooth. Wagons would bump over the logs and animals had to be handled carefully so they could keep their footing. On the corduroy road traveled by the Lincolns, markers were placed short distances apart to mark the road due to it being covered with flood water which in the cold of March nights in 1830 froze over with a thin layer of ice.

It was on this road that Abraham almost lost his favorite dog.

I crossed the Wabash at Vincennes and the river being high the road on the low prairie was covered with water a half mile at a stretch and the water covered with ice. The only means by which I could keep the road was by observing the stakes on each side placed as guides when the water is over the road. When I came to the water, I put a favorite dog I had along into the wagon and got in myself and whipped up my oxen and started into the water to pick my way across as well as I could. After breaking the ice and wading about ¼ of a mile my little dog jumped out of the wagon and the ice being thin he broke through and was struggling for life. I could not bear to lose my dog and I jumped out of the wagon and waded waist deep in the ice and water got hold of him and helped him out and saved him.[233]

Knowing that Abraham related his childhood and youth as being impoverished compared to his adult years, Peter Smith – to whom Abraham told the story of the dog – asked if Abraham had

---

[232] Douglas L. Wilson and Rodney O. Davis. *Herndon's Informants*, page 718. From a Herndon interview with Jess K. Dubois on December 1, 1888.

[233] R. Gerald McMurtry. *Lincoln Highlights in Indiana History*. The story was told to Peter Smith by Abraham Lincoln during the 1860 presidential campaign. Smith told it in a letter to J. Warren Keifer of Springfield, Ohio, dated July 17, 1860.

been barefoot at the time. Abraham replied, "I was afoot but not barefoot. In my young days I frequently went barefooted but, on that occasion, I had on a substantial pair of shoes. It was a cold day in March and I never went barefooted in cold weather."[234]

The route Thomas' caravan took has been reported in several ways over the years but the most accurate is probably reported by Colonel Augustus H. Chapman who became the husband of Thomas' granddaughter Harriet Hanks. Abraham Lincoln, in January 1861, visited Coles County to see his stepmother and his family before leaving for Washington to be sworn in as president. During that visit, he talked about family history and described the route Thomas followed to Illinois.

> *At the time of his last visit to Coles County, in January 1861, Abraham Lincoln is reported by Augustus H. Chapman (husband of Harriet Hanks, Dennis' daughter) to have described the route. Thirty-five years later Chapman wrote to Jesse W. Weik that Lincoln told him that the party crossed the Wabash at Vincennes. They passed through Lawrenceville, Palestine, and Darwin. Here they struck out in a northwesterly direction, passing through Richwoods (about three miles east of the present village of Westfield) and continuing to a point about six miles west of Charleston, called Dead Man's Grove; thence north through Nelsonville (or Nelson, no longer in existence. It was about three miles southeast of Sullivan) and on to Decatur.[235]*

The journey is tracked in the Lincoln Log.[236] Thomas' family left the Pigeon Creek Farm on March 1, 1830. They traveled to Vincennes, Indiana where they crossed the Wabash River by ferry. From the ferry crossing, Thomas traveled through low lying prairie, much of it slightly flooded but bridged by corduroy

---

234 R. Gerald McMurtry. *Lincoln Highlights in Indiana History.*

235 Charles H. Coleman. *Abraham Lincoln and Coles County, Illinois*, page 9. From the Augustus Chapman letter to Jesse Weik dated January 3, 1896 from Charleston.

236 The Lincoln Log. *A Daily Chronology of the Life of Abraham* Lincoln. www.thelincolnlog.org/.

roadwork. By March 6, they were in Lawrenceburg, where they spent the night. It was when they left Lawrenceburg heading for Palestine that Abraham rescued his dog from the flood waters.

From Monday, March 8 through Thursday, March 11, they traveled north along a Native American trail/road to Hutsonville and then on to Paradise where they spent Thursday night with the Sawyers and the Radleys, relatives of Sarah Bush Lincoln.

All along this way, Thomas visited with settlers where they stopped and entertained the townspeople where they stayed overnight with the wealth of his stories and jokes. Thomas and Abraham kept the company happy and laughing through their journey to Illinois. It was hard traveling with the cold and the high water, but Thomas and family took it in stride and met it with laughter.

On Friday, March 12, Thomas led his family north toward Nelson and crossed the Kaskaskia River at Willow Ford. They pressed on through Chipps and Lovington, coming to Decatur on Sunday, March 14. They camped in the village square that night. The town of Decatur had just gained a post office and had fewer than a dozen log houses when Thomas first saw it. It was a pretty setting as the town was nestled in an oak grove.

Thomas' new home was land claimed for him by John Hanks. The land was about ten miles from Decatur, located on the north bank of the Sangamon River where the forest met the prairie. It was in the southeast quarter of the southwest quarter of Section 28, T 16 N, R 1 E of P.M. Thomas arrived at his new home on Monday, March 15, 1830. The 225-mile journey from Pigeon Creek took the caravan two weeks.

Thomas and Abraham

Lincoln history often focuses on the distance that came between Abraham and his father. There were also many similarities.

- Both were very strong physically.
- Both were able to defeat their opponents in wrestling and, when necessary, in fights.

- Both were gifted storytellers and speakers, keeping friends, family, and groups spellbound as they told the many stories and tales they kept in memory.
- Both kept listeners roaring with laughter at their jokes and anecdotes.
- Both were hospitable, welcoming and caring for those who came to them, doing their best to help people and make them feel happy if they could.
- Both were known for their honesty and integrity, going out of their way to do the right thing.
- Both were looked to by others to mitigate quarrels, referee games and events, and make fair decisions when different opinions called for a determination.
- Both suffered from depression or melancholy.

Abraham learned much from Thomas and kept many of those lessons throughout his life but early on their differences were there and those differences would push them apart as Abraham grew older.

Thomas was an intelligent man. He had multiple skills (carpenter, furniture maker, cabinetmaker, wheelwright, cooper, farmer, mechanic) and a natural ability to remember what he needed. This intelligence faired him well in his woodworking and farming. It put him in positions of responsibility, frequently being called on for jury duty and public positions early in his life. But Abraham outshone him on this. Abraham's genius was clearly apparent to everyone. He learned slowly but well, keeping what he learned firmly in his memory. Abraham was always looking to understand. It has been noted how he asked Thomas for explanations and then went over them again and again until he fully understood them and could repeat them in such a way that others could easily grasp them. This ability put him in place as a leading lawyer and a repeatedly elected public servant.

Leonard Swett, a good friend and colleague of Abraham Lincoln, spoke of Abraham telling stories of his childhood. He does not remember those stories as times of pain or bleak poverty. Swett said that Abraham spoke of his childhood "…as the story of a happy childhood. There was nothing of want, and no allusions to want, in any part of it. His own description of his youth was that of a joyous, happy boyhood. It was told with mirth and glee, and illustrated by pointed anecdote, often interrupted by his jocund laugh which echoed over the prairies."[237]

As Abraham grew wealthier, he recognized that his childhood was poor in comparison but the kind of being poor that made up his childhood did not mean he had been wanting in the basics of life. Thomas had provided well for his family. They had food and clothing and shelter. It was simple and old-fashioned and rough in the pioneer way, but it was not abject poverty and need. That kind of poverty, Abraham never experienced.

A few Lincoln historians have tried to portray Thomas' early relationship with Abraham, during Abraham's childhood, as being a time when Abraham doted on Thomas. It would not be unusual for a child to hold his/her father in high esteem. It is possible and even probable that a very young Abraham did dote on his father and see him bigger than life, but there were natural differences in disposition between the two that soon ended the boyish devotion. A distance grew between Thomas and Abraham that no correction in history's understanding of Thomas can change. Thomas is not the worthless, lazy, piece of white trash that Herndon gave to history, but neither is he the lifelong success of whom Abraham was proud.

As Abraham grew and learned, he saw and understood the opportunities a changing world put in front of him. Thomas held to the pioneer way of life, to an agrarian economy where each family produced all that it needed. Thomas wanted nothing more than that. Maybe in his younger days, he did. Had the land titles in Kentucky not worked against him, had the Panic of 1819 not led to a long depression, had he not gone blind in one eye with the other eye weak – maybe then Thomas might have grasped the world in a different way. But those are maybes and they are not the reality of Thomas' life.

Life gave Thomas some bad deals and Thomas hugged those deals the tighter. He hugged them so tight that he became comfortable in a way of life that was passing away. As the industrial revolution lifted the American culture into a new place,

---

[237] Allen Thorndike Rice. *Reminiscences of Abraham Lincoln by Distinguished Men of His Time*, page 80. From the remembrances of Leonard Swett.

Thomas remained following a subsistence economy. As frame houses replaced log cabins, Thomas was content in his old-fashioned home with cramped space. As the world moved on, Thomas did not. It was not long before the world around him saw him not as a pioneer content with his lifestyle, but as a man too lazy, too shiftless, too lacking in intelligence to move beyond the old way of life as those around him were doing, as his own son did.

Despite his falling behind the world, Thomas' kindness and hospitality never faltered. The world may have started to look down on Thomas but those who personally knew him knew he was a man of good temper, ready humor, strong faith in God, and one welcoming of any who came to his door. He greeted all with welcoming hospitality, an offer of food and rest, and always a smile and a laugh and a well-told story.

Thomas' way of life was not enough for Abraham. Abraham had a strong ambition to go farther in life. Abraham had an ambition to earn his money with his mind and his wit rather than his muscles and sweat. Abraham learned to live in the new world and make it his. He could not have done that staying on with Thomas and living in Thomas' world.

A story is told from the time Abraham was working near the Ohio River of his wanting to get a job on a boat. The story is told by William Wood. "Abe came to my house one day and stood around about timid and shy. I knew he wanted something. I said to him, 'Abe what is your case.' Abe replied, 'Uncle I want you to go to the River [Ohio River] and give me some recommendation to some boat.' I remarked, 'Abe, your age is against you. You are not 21 yet.' 'I know that, but I want a start,' said Abe. I concluded not to go for the boy's good, did not go."[238] Some historians have interpreted this to say that Abraham was reluctant to follow Wood's advice but there is nothing in Herndon's records to indicate that reaction. When Abraham turned 21, he had every chance to go back to the Ohio River and find work. He did not. He went to Illinois with his family. There may have been

---

[238] Douglas L. Wilson and Rodney O. Davis. *Herndon's Informants*, page 124. From a Herndon interview with William Wood on September 15, 1865.

differences and distance growing between father and son but there was not the complete break so many write of.

The estrangement between Thomas and Abraham began in Indiana. The story of Nancy's death is almost always told from Abraham's viewpoint and not that of Thomas. Nancy's death hit the whole family hard. Young Abraham grieved his angel mother and held her memory sacred, but Thomas also grieved. It was hard to watch his beloved wife take sick and die. It was harder to build her casket and lay her in it. Undertakers were not a part of frontier life. Thomas was the one who made the caskets and assisted in laying the dead in them and then nailing the casket shut. These things he did for Nancy. No doubt neighbors were there to support him, but the work Thomas did for others he did also for himself and for his dearly deceased wife. It is hard for us to imagine such a world and to put ourselves in the place of Thomas as he grieved, built a casket, laid his wife in it, sealed it shut, and buried his love and the mother of his children.

It is often said that Thomas did little to console Abraham and Sarah in their grief but the truth of this is not known. There is no record of Thomas consoling his children or not consoling them. As was the custom of the times, daughter Sarah picked up the duties of the woman of the house. She was young, she was grieving, but she was raised on the frontiers of Indiana and she knew what was expected. Abraham also grieved and he too carried on with the chores and life of the pioneer. Thomas, somewhat strangely to our customs, went to Kentucky to find another wife. A woman was needed in the home and his children needed a mother. This action was not unusual. It was common to the times for a widower to seek out a widow or unmarried woman to once again make the family whole.

Still this time changed Thomas' relation with his son and the distance between them began to grow. Two families were joined, and other children took Thomas' time. Abraham was one of five instead of one of two. Abraham was one of two boys instead of Thomas' only son. And this other son was much more like Thomas than was Abraham.

Thomas and Abraham continued to work side-by-side but there was another added. John Johnston, a young boy who had lost his father and needed another, stepped into the picture. Where

Abraham was not fond of hunting, John shared Thomas' love of the hunt. Where Abraham spent almost every spare moment – and some that should not have been spared – on reading and study, John was out with others engaged in sport and talk and laughter. John was content to live the life Thomas lived. Education was not the way out for John, he learned from Thomas the old way of gaining wealth and followed it even though that way was quickly falling by the wayside. In many ways, John replaced Abraham as the son closest to Thomas.

With Abraham's forgiving nature and his willingness to give people multiple chances, history does not record a grudge against Thomas or John. Abraham, though 21 and of legal age just before Thomas moved the family to Illinois, still went with Thomas to help the family settle and he stayed with them through the first year in Illinois before setting out on his own. After setting out, Abraham kept close contact with Thomas and the family. He knew what they were doing and how they were doing, and he had an open hand to help Thomas through the difficulties of his Illinois years.

Historians note that in his published writings Abraham said little about his father and what he said and wrote was either neutral or negative. Abraham had moved with the nation into more modern times and away from pioneer ways. As he aged, he remembered his childhood and youth with fondness and laughter, but he also saw it as poor and backward compared to his success and more civilized way of life. He remembered Thomas as he was with weakened eyesight. He likely never saw Thomas' early writing and signatures that showed good penmanship. He saw the scrawl of a signature that limited eyesight gave Thomas. As Abraham's education grew and expanded, he saw Thomas' limited education and knowledge as Thomas being without education.

Thomas wanted to keep his family near him in the way of old pioneers. An extended family working together was the way of survival in the sparsely populated farms and villages of early settlement. Dennis and Betsy Hanks, Squire and Matilda Hall, John and Mary Johnston all stayed near Thomas and Sarah. They were family that understood Thomas' ways and accepted them. No doubt Thomas pushed for Abraham to marry and do the same.

Thomas was the patriarch of the family and Abraham was the son who said his father's ways were not good enough for him.

That is not a condemnation of Abraham. Our nation is thankful that he took the path he did. But for his relationship with his father, it brought tension and sadness and parting.

Grandson-in-law Augustus Chapman took a similar view to Thomas' refusal to give up his pioneer ways and usually spoke negatively of Thomas even though he was close with Thomas and loved him. Chapmam's situation was similar to Abraham's. He loved the man but argued with him about changing the way he lived. Thomas, being the man he was and the personality he was, it was difficult not to like and love him. But Thomas was set in his ways and he did not want a more modern life. It is easy to picture the tension that stubbornness caused with Abraham and Augustus who both wanted to move forward and bring Thomas with them. His refusal to do so was a source of contention.

Chapman tells about that struggle and tension in a letter to William Herndon. "In answer to your enquiries I beg leave to state that Thomas Lincoln never showed by his actions that he thought much of his son Abraham when a boy. He treated him rather unkind than otherwise. Always appeared to think much more of his stepson John D. Johnston than he did of his own son Abraham but after Abe was grown up and had made his mark in the world the old man appeared to be very proud of him."[239]

When Dennis Hanks was asked about Abraham's relationship to Thomas, he put more of the blame for the distance between father and son on Abraham. Dennis was asked if Abraham "loved his father very well or not" and he replied, "He loved him. I never could tell whether Abe loved his father very well or not. I don't think he did for Abe was one of those forward boys." Dennis went on to say of Thomas, "The old man loved his children."[240]

Dennis Hanks was known for exaggeration and stretching stories but he was proud of and devoted to Abraham. He wanted Abraham's legacy to be something great. To protect Abraham's and the family image, Dennis went so far as to claim that Nancy

---

239 Douglas L. Wilson and Rodney O. Davis. *Herndon's Informants*, page 134. From an A. H. Chapman letter to Herndon dated September 28, 1865.
240 Douglas L. Wilson and Rodney O. Davis. *Herndon's Informants*, page 176. From a Dennis Hanks letter to Herndon dated January 26, 1866.

Hanks Lincoln was really a Sparrow and not illegitimately born. He claimed they only called her Hanks because she was so like the Hanks family.[241] Despite all that, here Dennis plainly states he did not believe Abraham had much love for Thomas. Coming as it did, it is a statement that carries weight when discussing Thomas' and Abraham's relationship.

Did Abraham really not love his father very much? The two did grow apart but never is there authentic record of rejection by either one of the other. Much of history has viewed their estrangement as antagonistic but there is little to support such. Throughout their differences and parting of ways, they never stopped being family, somewhat dysfunctional, but still family.

Louis Warren sets Thomas up as a father held in close esteem by Abraham. "Thomas was the type of man to invite a boy's admiration. He was noted in the community for his unusual physical power, which must have brought pride to his son."[242] This is based on child psychology, that it is normal for a child to put his/her father in a position of hero worship for a time. Nothing refutes or confirms this for Thomas and Abraham. There is little in Abraham's writings or reputed sayings where he speaks of such admiration for his father. Abraham's patterns show filial responsibility toward a parent and respect in performing that duty but there is little to indicate a close father-son relationship.

A letter written by Abraham Lincoln to his brother, John Johnston, not long before Thomas' death is often debated as to whether it is scorn and disrespect toward Thomas. The letter dated from Springfield on January 12, 1851.

Dear Brother:

On the day before yesterday I received a letter from Harriett, written at Greenup. She says she has just returned from your house; and that Father is very low and will hardly recover. She also says you have written me two letters; and that although you do not expect me to come

---

[241] Douglas L. Wilson and Rodney O. Davis. *Herndon's Informants*, pages 198-199. From a letter of Dennis Hanks to William Herndon dated February 10, 1866 from Charleston, Illinois.
[242] Louis A. Warren. *Lincoln's Youth Indiana Years Seven to Twenty-one 1816-1830*, page 85.

now, you wonder that I do not write. I received both your letters, and although I have not answered them, it is not because I have forgotten them, or been uninterested about them---but because it appeared to me, I could write nothing which could do any good. You already know I desire that neither Father or Mother shall be in want of any comfort either in health or sickness while they live; and I feel sure you have not failed to use my name, if necessary, to procure a doctor, or anything else for Father in his present sickness. My business is such that I could hardly leave home now, if it were not, as it is, that my own wife is sick-abed. (It is a case of baby-sickness, and I suppose is not dangerous.) I sincerely hope Father may yet recover his health; but at all events tell him to remember to call upon, and confide in, our great, and good, and merciful Maker; who will not turn away from him in any extremity. He notes the fall of a sparrow, and numbers the hairs of our heads; and He will not forget the dying man, who puts his trust in Him. Say to him that if we could meet now, it is doubtful whether it would not be more painful than pleasant; but that if it be his lot to go now, he will soon have a joyous meeting with many loved ones gone before; and where the rest of us, through the help of God, hope ere-long to join them.

Write me again when you receive this. Affectionately

A. LINCOLN[243]

Those who declare that Abraham was expressing loathing for his father and spurning him as he lay dying point to the fact that Abraham did not go to his father and then did not attend the funeral. But to hold this view is to neglect the core characteristics of Abraham's personality. He had waded through icy waters to save a dog. He took great pains to defend the rights of animals from cruelty. He searched long and hard to find any reason to spare the lives of those whom military law would condemn and execute. He preferred that the traitors running the Confederacy be

---

[243] Roy P. Basler. *The Collected Works of Abraham Lincoln*, volume 2, pages 96-97.

allowed to escape the country than to hang them. Abraham's life was not one that expressed loathing and it is an anomaly to see Thomas as the sole exception to Abraham's compassion. The letter expresses his love and care for his parents. It explains that Mary is sick abed leaving Abraham to tend the children, one of whom, Willie, was born the previous month on December 21, just over three weeks before the letter was written. There was little respect and no love from Mary to Thomas. Imagine Abraham's spot as he debated leaving Mary sick abed with a three-week-old baby so he could visit his father.

The letter is not scorn or loathing or disrespect. Nothing in Abraham's nature or personality would have him write such a letter and then sign it "affectionately". Seeing the letter as simply a letter, sorrowful and hard pressed, but still simply a letter is bolstered by knowing that when Mary's father had died in 1849, neither Abraham or Mary went to him as he was dying and neither attended his funeral. That action is not interpreted as disdain and scorn toward Robert Todd. It was a fact of the times. Burials were usually the same day as death or the next day. There was no time for more distant family to be summoned and get there.

Putting the letter in a truer light, however, does not change the fact that Thomas and Abraham had grown apart. Abraham still visited his father. Abraham still did what he could to care for him and help him. Thomas loved Abraham and was proud of him. But nothing brought them close. They were different. They went different paths. They held different ways. Doing so makes neither one into a bad person. Being so makes neither completely wrong nor completely right. Life is not that simple. The father-son relationship of Thomas and Abraham is not that simple either. Unless something more comes to light than the facts now known, it is doubtful their relationship can ever be fully explained or easily understood.

Illinois

As Ernest Duvergier de Hauranne traveled America and wrote home about it, he had a somewhat less than flattering view of the people living in Illinois. "If you wish to live in Illinois, first prune away from your mind all those superfluous branches nurtured by a European education, tender shoots which cannot flourish in the cold wind of American positivism. Confine yourself to facts and arithmetic but learn more arithmetic than facts because your life will be divided between the counting-house, the tavern and the mass-meeting. Happy, perhaps, are those who can reduce their lives to these extremely simple terms."[1]

While Thomas did not fit de Hauranne's description, he had come to accept life in simple terms and it was in Illinois that he lived out the final 20 years of his life. It is in Illinois that the fewest details of his life are known. When Abraham left Thomas' home to make his own way in life, the spotlight of history turned away from Thomas. While Thomas lived in Kentucky and Indiana, the light of history held Thomas in the periphery because Abraham was nearby. After Abraham left home, the light of history moved with him. Still, there are many facts that are known for Thomas' final two decades.

Macon County

Thomas arrived in Macon County, Illinois on March 14, 1830. He met up with John Hanks in Decatur. A new courthouse was being built and John worked chinking and daubing the two-story log building.[2] John led the family to the land he had selected for them. Thomas' new home was ten miles from Decatur and six miles past where John Hanks had settled. Thomas' claim was along the Sangamon River with wooded land that melted away into the Illinois prairie.

The Sangamon was a small river that was part of the Illinois River valley. The river wound its way through buffalo grass prairie and hills covered with oak trees. The land around it was fertile

---

[1] Ernest Duvergier de Hauranne. *A Frenchman in Lincoln's America*, volume 1, pages 498-499.
[2] Kenneth J. Winkle. *The Young Eagle*, page 27.

with rich, good soil. Native Americans had lived along the Sangamon and the word Sangamon was from the Pottawattamie language meaning "where there is plenty to eat."[3] The soil was some of the best in the world. The land was filled with wildlife. Deer roamed the woods and prairies. Wild turkey was plentiful and prairie chickens came in the hundreds. Along the Sangamon, pioneers found large mounds, built by Native Americans to bury their dead with honor.[4]

The prairie Thomas planned to farm was a meadow of buffalo grass embellished with purple mint, lilies, and yellow daisies.[5] It was a field that could be plowed and opened without clearing trees.

Charles Dickens visited the Illinois prairie in 1842 and used his mastery of words to describe it.

> *Looking towards the setting sun there lay, stretched out before my view, a vast expanse of level ground; unbroken save by one thin line of trees, which scarcely amounted to a scratch upon the great blank, until it met the glowing sky, wherein it seemed to dip, mingling with its rich colors, and mellowing in its distant blue. There it lay, a tranquil sea or lake without water, if such a simile be admissible, with the day going down upon it: a few birds wheeling here and there, and solitude and silence reigning paramount around. But the grass was not yet high; there were bare black patches on the ground; and the few wild flowers that the eye could see were poor and scanty. Great as the picture was, its very flatness and extent, which left nothing to the imagination, tamed it down and cramped its interest. I felt little of that sense of freedom and exhilaration which a Scottish heath inspires, or even our English downs awaken. It was lonely and wild, but oppressive in its barren monotony. I felt that in traversing the prairies I could never abandon myself to the scene, forgetful of all else; as I should do instinctively were the*

---

[3] Edward Lee Masters. *The Sangamon*, page 4.
[4] Edward Lee Masters. *The Sangamon*, page 21.
[5] Edward Lee Masters. *The Sangamon*, page 15.

*heather under my feet, or an iron bound coast beyond;
but should often glance towards the distant and
frequently receding line of the horizon and wish it gained
and past. It is a scene not to be forgotten, but it is scarcely
one, I think, at all events as I saw it, to remember with
much pleasure, or to covet the looking on again in after
life.[6]*

Thomas followed standard pioneer practice. He worked the
land for the first year, making improvements, and gathering the
money to purchase the claim. Until the cabin was ready for
Thomas and Sarah, Abraham and John, the family camped in tents
made of wagon sheets.[7] John Hanks had logs ready and waiting
for constructing a cabin. Abraham used the oxen teams to drag
the logs on a dry sled to the building site. Dennis Hanks hewed
them and notched them.[8] John Johnston and Thomas joined the
work along with Squire Hall. As the logs were prepared, word
went out and the neighbors gathered to raise the buildings.
Thomas' cabin stood on ground high above the Sangamon. He
built not only a cabin but also a smokehouse and a barn.[9]

They split rails to fence in livestock and ten acres of prairie
for planting. The cabin and buildings and livestock were in the
woods or at the edge of the woods. Pioneers usually did not
venture onto the prairie in the early years of settlement for their
houses. The fields were on the prairie. As they built their cabin,
barn, outbuildings, and animal pens, they also put the plow to
work and planted their crops. They planted ten acres of corn along
with a garden that held a variety of plants.[10]

John Hanks and his brothers, Charles and William, had farms
nearby. Dennis and Squire settled their families close to Thomas.
The Lincoln-Hanks clan was large, and they were close enough to

---

[6] Edward Lee Masters. *The Sangamon*, pages 17 and 20.
[7] Douglas L. Wilson and Rodney O. Davis. *Herndon's Informants*, page100.
Statement by A. H. Chapman dated September 8, 1865.
[8] Douglas L. Wilson and Rodney O. Davis. *Herndon's Informants*, page 100.
Statement by A. H. Chapman dated September 8, 1865.
[9] The Lincoln Log. www.thelincolnlog.org. March 15, 1830.
[10] Kenneth J. Winkle. *The Young Eagle*, page 27.

help each other as much as needed and to entertain each other after a long day's work.

As the crops grew and the farm buildings were completed, Thomas expanded his ground. By Fall of 1830 he had fifteen acres of ground broken and fenced to use for crops. Abraham took this time to hire himself out to new friends and neighbors and family, often staying the nights with the family he was working for, living only part time with Thomas. He was getting a feel for the land and area and beginning to plan his next step in life, the step that would get him out of farming and into a new career.

Abraham, 21-years-old, was no longer bound to Thomas by law. He could take any path he chose. He chose to stay with Thomas as he settled in and to take time to think through what he wanted to do. Abraham stayed and helped the family make their home and settle on the property. The path Abraham wanted in life led away from cabinetmaking, carpentry, and farming. Thomas had encouraged his son to learn and study. Some say Abraham was anxious to leave home because of the estrangement with his father but it will always be an open question as to whether it was the lack of closeness with his father or the fact that his chosen path could not be attained without leaving that most led Abraham to go to New Salem. Regardless, it would be over a year before Abraham took out on his own. If Abraham was anxious to leave his father's home, it was not a strong anxiousness.

Many biographies of Abraham have him begin his law studies in New Salem, but it was in Macon County while living with Thomas that Abraham began his study of law. Abraham connected with Sheriff William Warnick during the year he lived with Thomas after coming to Illinois and it was at Warnick's home that Abraham found and read law books.[11]

The detail around that start is an interesting story. It was the winter of the deep snow. In February Abraham was going to Sheriff Warnick's home. While crossing the Sangamon River, he fell through the ice. The river was shallow where he fell through so he did not face drowning under the ice but the wet and cold badly frostbit his feet in walking from the river to Warnick's, a distance of two miles trudging in the snow. The Warnick's insisted

---

[11] Michael Burlingame. *Abraham Lincoln: A Life*, page 87.

he remain while recovering and he was there for three weeks. During that time, Abraham found an Illinois statue book in the sheriff's possession which he read and studied. That happenstance incident became the beginning of Abraham's journey into the study of law as a potential career.[12]

Abraham's law career began while he lived in his father's home.

One store record survives that tells of Abraham making a purchase for Thomas in Decatur at James Renshaw's store.[13] Life for Thomas was settling into a routine pattern similar to what he had known in Indiana.

The Fall of 1830 was not an easy time. The family suffered from chills and fever. What pioneers called the ague plagued everyone. The ague was malaria or a malaria-like fever that left a person shivering one moment and sweating and baking in fever the next.

Thomas had built a farm and harvested a plentiful crop from the rich soil, but his luck turned when the ague struck. 1830 was not a good year to have started a new life in Illinois. The ague was quickly followed by one of the worst winters on record. It was the Winter of the Deep Snow.

Snow began falling in November and continued at frequent intervals until late in January, a large part of the time being from two to three feet deep and drifted in many places to a depth of six feet. Besides, the winter was cold and those first settlers, poorly provided with houses and other things that make for comfort, suffered intensely. The melting of the snow in February caused a flood of water, and a sudden reversal of temperature covered the earth with a glare of ice. Horses and oxen both had to be shod to be able to travel, and few had the facilities to shoe them at home. Food supplies ran low and stock suffered for both food and water. People ventured out only for absolute necessities such as food and fuel. It

---

[12] David S. Reynolds, *Abe*, page 94.
[13] Ida M. Tarbell. *In the Footsteps of the Lincolns*, page 161.

> *was a bad time for the pioneers, but as all things have an end, spring came at last to their relief.*[14]

1831

The Winter of the Deep Snow is remembered as one of the most devastating on record. The Christmas blizzard was particularly harsh, lasting until New Year's Day of 1831, it blanketed the land with three feet of snow. The blizzard was followed by freezing rain that put a layer of ice on top of the snow. The ice was strong but not quite strong enough to hold a person.[15] To travel, one had to break through ice while wading in snow. Wild animals, wolves and wild dogs, were desperate for food and preyed on livestock.

Thomas had never seen anything like it. This land had been described to him as a paradise, a land of plenty with fields of rich soil that did not even have to be cleared of timber before they could be plowed and planted. Thomas had been settled and comfortable in Indiana. His farm and business well established. But his family was determined to move, and the family moved. Thomas took hold of the bargain and held it tight. Sometimes a person makes the right decision and sometimes a person is required to make their decision right. The second was what Thomas was attempting. He had a bargain that turned out to be a poor decision and he was hugging it tight, trying to make it right.

Where the Spring and Summer of 1830 had been good, the Fall brought the ague and the Winter brought misery and cold like he had never seen. Topping it off, his brother Mordecai came to Illinois to visit with his sons James, Abraham, and Mordecai Jr., who had moved to Illinois. Mordecai was caught out on horseback when one of the winter storms hit. He contracted pneumonia from cold and exposure and died.[16]

The ague and malaria were common afflictions to newcomers on the prairie. Whatever the cause, a new settler had to endure the ague and build up immunity. Folklore said the remedy for the ague

---

[14] Newton Bateman, Paul Selby, and Charles Edward Wilson, Editors. *Historical Encyclopedia of Illinois and History of Coles County*, page 668.
[15] Kenneth J. Winkle. *The Young Eagle*, page 28.
[16] Ian Hunt. "Winter of the Deep Snows.". *Four Score and Seven*, page 12.

was possum fat and corn but in truth that did nothing to relieve the symptoms. The Lincolns purchased medicines and found they did no better than the folk remedy.[17] Thomas was deeply affected by the ague. It took much of his strength and damaged his health. He was never up to full health again.[18] This along with his blind eye and poor sight hampered Thomas for the remainder of his life. He could do farm work but most of his other skills were limited. He came to depend heavily upon his family, on John Johnston, Dennis Hanks, and Squire Hall.

The Spring came as a relief from the cold and snow, but that relief was accompanied by flooding. The vast snow melted, overflowing streams and rivers, covering the prairie and lowlands with water. During the Winter, Abraham, John Johnston, and John Hanks had met with Denton Offutt and he hired them to take a flatboat of goods to New Orleans. They were to meet Offutt in Springfield, Illinois around the first of March 1831. The flooding was still high, making land travel difficult. The three purchased a large canoe and traveled to Springfield via the Sangamon.

As Abraham, John, and John prepared the flatboat for their trip to New Orleans, Thomas waited out the flooding and made plans with the Hanks and Halls to return to Indiana. They had had enough. Illinois was not where they wanted to live.

As the flooding subsided and travel by land became possible, Thomas and Dennis and Squire loaded their wagons and headed back toward Indiana. The Illinois claims where they lived along with the improvements they had made were left as unclaimed government land for the next settler to lay claim to. That next settler found 15 acres of fenced fields, a cabin, a barn, a smokehouse, and other improvements ready and available to them on the land Thomas abandoned.

As Abraham, John, and John were readying their flatboat, the Lincoln caravan began moving toward Indiana. The fact that Thomas was returning to Indiana in the early Spring when it was time to be working on the fields in preparation for planting shows the depths of their determination to be rid of Illinois. His old farm

---

[17] Kenneth J. Winkle. *The Young Eagle*, page 42.
[18] Ida M. Tarbell. *In the Footsteps of the Lincolns*, page 163.

was sold. It belonged to someone else. Dennis and Squire were in the same position. Perhaps Thomas thought his friends and neighbors would sell the land and stock back to him and he could pick up where he left off. There is no way of knowing what was in his mind as he drove his wagon along the road, tracing in reverse the way he had come.

Once again, the caravan stopped at the homes of friends and family. Two counties to the southeast of Macon County, the Lincolns stopped at the Sawyer's farm in Coles County. The Sawyers were relatives of Sarah. The conversation that occurred there was not noted for history. Whatever it was, it was very persuasive. The Lincoln caravan went no farther. The Lincolns, Hanks, and Halls were persuaded to give Illinois another try. There was land available. The soil was still rich. It was planting season, not traveling season.

Thomas selected another forty-acre tract and as Abraham floated down the Ohio toward the Mississippi, Thomas settled into a new farm and planted crops, praying that this bargain he was hugging could be made better, that the ague which had hit him so hard would not return in the Fall and that the snow would not come with such fury the next Winter. He settled in the Buck Grove neighborhood in Pleasant Grove Township of Coles County, Illinois.[19]

Coles County

Coles County was split out of the larger Clark County in 1830, the year Thomas moved to Illinois. It was described as a beautiful plateau. Largely prairie, the land held rich soil just waiting for settlement and the breaking of the plow to make it home to settlers. On the higher ground, the prairie grass grew as tall as a man. Along the rivers and streams, timber of oak, walnut, cottonwood, maple, hackberry, and elm grew tall and strong.[20] It was here Thomas made his home for the final years of his life. In 1832, about the same time Thomas was settling on the Illinois prairie, poet William Cullen Bryant visited his brother who lived

---

[19] D. M. Coleman. *Thomas Lincoln, The Father of Abraham Lincoln*, page 29.
[20] William Le Baron Jr. *The History of Coles County Illinois*, pages 224-226.

in Illinois. Bryant penned a beautiful poem reflecting his impression of the prairie.

The Prairies

These are the gardens of the Desert, these
The unshorn fields, boundless and beautiful,
For which the speech of England has no name –
The Prairies. I behold them for the first,
And my heart swells, while the dilated sight
Takes in the encircling vastness. Lo! they stretch,
In airy undulations, far away,
As if the ocean, in his gentlest swell,
Stood still, with all his rounded billows fixed,
And motionless forever. – Motionless? –
No – they are all unchained again. The clouds
Sweep over with their shadows, and, beneath,
The surface rolls and fluctuates to the eye;
Dark hollows seem to glide along and chase
The sunny ridges. Breezes of the South!
Who toss the golden and the flame-like flowers,
And pass the prairie-hawk that, poised on high,
Flaps his broad wings, yet moves not – ye have played
Among the palms of Mexico and vines
Of Texas, and have crisped the limpid brooks
That from the fountains of Sonora glide
Into the calm Pacific – have ye fanned
A nobler or a lovelier scene than this?
Man hath no power in all this glorious work:
The hand that built the firmament hath heaved
And smoothed these verdant swells, and sown their slopes
With herbage, planted them with island groves,
And hedged them round with forests. Fitting floor
For this magnificent temple of the sky –
With flowers whose glory and whose multitude
Rival the constellations! The great heavens
Seem to stoop down upon the scene in love, -
A nearer vault, and of a tenderer blue,
Than that which bends above our eastern hills.

As o'er the verdant waste I guide my steed,
Among the high rank grass that sweeps his sides
The hollow beating of his footsteps seems
A sacrilegious sound. I think of those
Upon whose rest he tramples. Are they here —
The dead of other days? — and did the dust
Of these fair solitudes once stir with life
And burn with passion? Let the mighty mounds
That overlook the rivers, or that rise
In the dim forest crowded with old oaks,
Answer. A race, that long has passed away,
Built them; —a disciplined and populous race
Heaped, with long toil, the earth, while yet the Greek
Was hewing the Pentelicus to forms
Of symmetry, and rearing on its rock
The glittering Parthenon. These ample fields
Nourished their harvest, here their herds were fed,
When haply by their stalls the bison lowed,
And bowed his maned shoulder to the yoke.
All day this desert murmured with their toils,
Till twilight blushed, and lovers walked, and wooed
In a forgotten language, and old tunes,
From instruments of unremembered form,
Gave the soft winds a voice. The red man came —
The roaming hunter tribes, warlike and fierce,
And the mound-builders vanished from the earth.
The solitude of centuries untold
Has settled where they dwelt. The prairie-wolf
Hunts in their meadows, and his fresh-dug den
Yawns by my path. The gopher mines the ground
Where stood their swarming cities. All is gone;
All — save the piles of earth that hold their bones,
The platforms where they worshipped unknown gods,
The barriers which they builded from the soil
To keep the foe at bay — till o'er the walls
The wild beleaguerers broke, and, one by one,
The strongholds of the plain were forced, and heaped
With corpses. The brown vultures of the wood
Flocked to those vast uncovered sepulchres,

And sat unscared and silent at their feast.
Haply some solitary fugitive,
Lurking in marsh and forest, till the sense
Of desolation and of fear became
Bitterer than death, yielded himself to die.
Man's better nature triumphed then. Kind words
Welcomed and soothed him; the rude conquerors
Seated the captive with their chiefs; he chose
A bride among their maidens, and at length
Seemed to forget – yet ne'er forgot – the wife
Of his first love, and her sweet little ones,
Butchered, amid their shrieks, with all his race.

Thus change the forms of being. Thus arise
Races of living things, glorious in strength,
And perish, as the quickening breath of God
Fills them or is withdrawn. The red man, too,
Has left the blooming wilds he ranged so long,
And, nearer to the Rocky Mountains, sought
A wilder hunting-ground. The beaver builds
No longer by these streams, but far away,
On waters whose blue surface ne'er gave back
The white man's face – among Missouri's springs,
And pools whose issues swell the Oregon –
He rears his little Venice. In these plains
The bison feeds no more. Twice twenty leagues
Beyond remotest smoke of hunter's camp,
Roams the majestic brute, in herds that shake
The earth with thundering steps – yet here I meet
His ancient footprints stamped beside the pool.

 Still this great solitude is quick with life.
Myriads of insects, gaudy as the flowers
They flutter over, gentle quadrupeds,
And birds, that scarce have learned the fear of man,
Are here, and sliding reptiles of the ground,
Startlingly beautiful. The graceful deer
Bounds to the wood at my approach. The bee,
A more adventurous colonist than man,
With whom he came across the eastern deep,

Fills the savannas with his murmurings,
And hides his sweets, as in the golden age,
Within the hollow oak. I listen long
To his domestic hum, and think I hear
The sound of that advancing multitude
Which soon shall fill these deserts. From the ground
Comes up the laugh of children, the soft voice
Of maidens, and the sweet and solemn hymn
Of Sabbath worshippers. The low of herds
Blends with the rustling of the heavy grain
Over the dark brown furrows. All at once
A fresher wind sweeps by, and breaks my dream,
And I am in the wilderness alone.[21]

Buck Grove Farm

From this point, the story of Thomas Lincoln becomes less clear. The history of his farms is reported differently by different historians and the story told differently by one family member than another.

April of 1831 found Abraham with John Hanks and John Johnston on a flatboat going to New Orleans with a load of cargo for Denton Offutt. One result of that trip was Abraham being offered and accepting a job with Offutt to clerk his store. It was the break Abraham had been looking for, his move away from farming into the industrial revolution where he could begin to earn his living with his mind rather than his muscle. The trip took three to four weeks to go south and another two weeks for the return.[22]

During that five-to-six-week time period while Abraham went to New Orleans, Thomas ended the effort to return to Indiana, built a new home, and planted fields at his Buck Grove Farm. The Buck Grove cabin was raised by Thomas and his family. He was helped by his new neighbors, Sarah's relatives, John Sawyer and Charles Sawyer along with Elisha Linder. Linder had known Thomas in Kentucky and was one of Thomas' best friends.[23] His presence in Coles County was no doubt a strong incentive for

---

[21] Poetry Foundation. http://www.poetryfoundation.org/poems-and-poets/poems/detail/55341.

[22] David S. Reynolds, *Abe*, page 88.

[23] Charles H. Coleman. *Abraham Lincoln and Coles County, Illinois*, page 22.

Thomas to reject returning to Indiana and give Illinois another try. Thomas, Squire Hall, and Dennis Hanks are listed as some of the earliest settlers in Coles County.[24]

The naming of Buck Grove is colorful. John Hall, Thomas' grandson, tells that the men found the remains of two large bucks who had fought, locked horns, and died unable to separate from each other.[25] The Buck Grove farm was public land, open for settling. Thomas lived at Buck Grove from 1831 to 1834. He never made a claim for the land, never purchased it. It remained public land. Most pioneers improved their land before making claim and that is what Thomas usually did. Here, for unknown reasons, Thomas did not make an official claim. Squatting long term was not unusual among pioneers but it was unusual for Thomas. After spending some time on the land, trying it out, Thomas determined he did not want to own the land. He used the time to test Illinois and be sure he wanted to stay. While Thomas would not claim Buck Grove, he did decide to stay in Illinois and in Pleasant Grove Township of Coles County. It is in Pleasant Grove Township that Thomas spent his remaining years.

In April of 1831, as Thomas farmed Buck Grove, the county seat, Charleston, was beginning to build up. It was a small village more than being a town and was surveyed for the first time on April 23. The town Plat was officially filed on June 4.[26] The first county courthouse was built soon after.[27]

Near the end of Spring, Abraham and John returned from New Orleans and came to find the family in their new location. To the best that is known, when Abraham and John started down river to New Orleans, they believed their family was returning to Indiana.[28] It is speculation as to how they knew where to find them. Thomas could have sent word to someone he knew

---

[24] Newton Bateman, Paul Selby, and Charles Edward Wilson, Editors. *Historical Encyclopedia of Illinois and History of Coles County*, page 640.
[25] Eleanor Gridley. *The Story of Abraham Lincoln or The Journey from the Long Cabin to the White House*, page 107.
[26] Newton Bateman, Paul Selby, and Charles Edward Wilson, Editors. *Historical Encyclopedia of Illinois and History of Coles County*, page 680.
[27] Newton Bateman, Paul Selby, and Charles Edward Wilson, Editors. *Historical Encyclopedia of Illinois and History of Coles County*, page 671.
[28] Douglas L. Wilson and Rodney O. Davis. *Herndon's Informants*, page 103. Statement by A. H. Chapman dated September 8, 1865.

Abraham would see on returning from New Orleans, perhaps Denton Offutt. Regardless, Abraham and John found where they needed to go, and Abraham went home to collect his possessions before setting out to New Salem.

Coles County provided abundant game for hunting and wild animals to be defended against. Beasts of prey were the panther, black timber wolf, coyote, large gray wolf, wildcats, badgers, and prairie wolf. The prairie wolf and coyote were found in large numbers. Bears were present but rarer. Of the more peaceable animals, deer were found in abundance along with rabbit, squirrels of many kinds (gray, red, flying, ground), raccoon, gopher, weasel, groundhog, muskrat, possum, and mink.[29]

Though the early population was sparse, Thomas soon connected with the church and ensured meetings were taking place. He arranged with Stanley Walker, a Baptist preacher who had come to Illinois from Kentucky, to come every two or three weeks to hold service at the Lincoln cabin.[30]

How long Abraham stayed with Thomas before heading to New Salem is not clearly defined in history. It was not a long period, but it was long enough to get involved in a lesser-known wrestling match. In a few months, Abraham would find himself pitted against Jack Armstrong of Clary's Grove, a well-known match. But at Buck Grove, Daniel Needham was the local champion. He challenged Abraham to a test of strength in a wrestling match. Abraham was not readily willing to take on Needham, but Needham and others taunted him into matching skills. Abraham defeated Needham in two tries. As normal on the prairie, after proving themselves against one another, the two became great friends.[31]

---

[29] Newton Bateman, Paul Selby, and Charles Edward Wilson, Editors. *Historical Encyclopedia of Illinois and History of Coles County*, page 621.
[30] H. B. Glasco. "Thomas Lincoln. His Tomb – The Old Cabin in Which He Died – His Religion – Some Stories of His Life." *The Independent*, page 136.
[31] Henry L. Williams. *The Lincoln Story Book*. New York: G. W. Dillingham Company, 1907, pages 20-21.

Thomas Lincoln: Abraham's Father

In 1832, Thomas' got his first Illinois grandchild with the birth of Nancy Hall, born to Squire and Matilda Hall. More would follow. The family would grow large on Illinois soil.

As Thomas plowed land and started Spring planting, war came to Illinois. Black Hawk led his warriors into Illinois to attempt to resettle Native American lands lost through earlier wars and treaties. The United States government along with State and Territorial governors sent troops to push Black Hawk back to his treaty lands.

Abraham joined the Sangamon County militia and took a company from New Salem to the war. As Thomas served in the Kentucky militia, it was now Abraham's turn to protect frontier settlers. As it turned out, Abraham saw no action in the war, arriving too late to join any battles.

Along with Abraham serving in the Black Hawk War, John Johnston also served, but he did not serve in a Coles County unit.[32] John is listed as a private in a company from outside Coles County. A later report, after the New Salem company over which Abraham was Captain was disbanded and Abraham had re-enlisted as a private in Captain Elijah Iles' company, tells of John and Abraham being in the same "mess" (a group of five soldiers sharing the same tent).[33] Details are not preserved on how John and Abraham came to serve together but it is possible John went to New Salem and joined the Sangamon militia and then re-enlisted with Abraham.

At the close of their service, Abraham and John were honorably discharged. John returned to Coles County. Abraham also went to Coles County to visit with the family before returning to New Salem.[34] The nights Abraham spent in his father's Buck Grove cabin must have been filled with stories and laughter. Thomas' tales, repeated but still loved, would have covered sorrow

---

[32] Newton Bateman, Paul Selby, and Charles Edward Wilson, Editors. *Historical Encyclopedia of Illinois and History of Coles County*, page 672.

[33] Douglas L. Wilson and Rodney O. Davis. *Herndon's Informants*, page 327. From a letter to Herndon from George M. Harrison tentatively dated in late Summer 1866.

[34] Douglas L. Wilson and Rodney O. Davis. *Herndon's Informants*, page 103. Statement by A. H. Chapman dated September 8, 1865.

and battle and family history. Abraham, who saw no action in his service, may have entertained the family with an early version of a speech he would make in Congress to the delight of all who heard it.

> *By the way, Mr. Speaker, did you know I am a military hero? Yes sir; in the days of the Black Hawk war, I fought, bled, and came away. Speaking of Gen. Cass' career, reminds me of my own. I was not at Stillman's defeat, but I was about as near it, as Cass was to Hulls' surrender; and, like him, I saw the place very soon afterwards. It is quite certain I did not break my sword, for I had none to break; but I bent a musket pretty badly on one occasion. If Cass broke his sword, the idea is, he broke it in desperation; I bent the musket by accident. If Gen. Cass went in advance of me in picking huckleberries [whortleberries], I guess I surpassed him in charges upon the wild onions. If he saw any live, fighting Indians, it was more than I did; but I had a good many bloody struggles with the mosquitoes; and, although I never fainted from loss of blood, I can truly say I was often very hungry. Mr. Speaker, if I should ever conclude to doff whatever our Democratic friends may suppose there is of black cockade federalism about me, and thereupon, they shall take me up as their candidate for the Presidency, I protest they shall not make fun of me, as they have of Gen. Cass, by attempting to write me into a military hero.*[35]

In 1832, Thomas' older sister Mary Lincoln Crumes, died in Breckinridge County, Kentucky.[36] She was 57.

In the Fall, Thomas found himself, for the first time in a long number of years, in a county that was predominately Whig. In Indiana, Spencer County had given a majority of votes and support to the Democrats and Andrew Jackson. In Coles County, when Jackson ran again and won the Presidency, instead of being in a minority who had voted against Jackson, Thomas was in the

---

[35] Roy P. Basler. *The Collected Works of Abraham Lincoln*, volume 1, pages 509-510.
[36] Find A Grave. www.findagrave.com.

majority. Most of Coles County voted for and supported Henry Clay in his run against Jackson. The Whigs lost the election, but it must have been something of a relief to Thomas to be in a County with a Whig majority.

Mrs. Samuel Chowning is quoted in Gridley's Lincoln biography. The story, though having some historical issues around the date[37], gives us insight into Thomas.

In the spring of 1833 when I wus then a girl of only sixteen years Grandpap Lincoln as usual 'sugared off,' and John D. Johnston invited the young folks to come over some evening, when Abe Lincoln wus up to the old home. John D. Johnston sent us word that Brother Abe had come and we made up a little party. Well, John D. and Abe Lincoln took me across the river in a canoe. John had promised us young folks some taffy and purty soon he said to Grandpap Lincoln, "I want some taffy for the girls." You know John D. Johnston was mighty good lookin' and awful takin' and we knowed he'd get some taffy for us. We girls didn't care much about Abraham Lincoln, though, for he wus so quiet and awkward and so awful homely, and he never made up to the girls anyhow, so none of 'em cared about asking any favors of him. Grandpap Lincoln wus terrible savin' and said, "No, John, I can't have the 'lasses wasted that I have worked so hard to get." But Abe Lincoln talked to John D. in a low voice, and purty soon when grandpap had scooped out all but a little in the bottom of the kettle, John D. caught up a bucket of cold water and throwed it into the kettle. When the sugar rose to the top he stuck his hands in and pulled it all out in a lump and divided it among us. Of course we all laughed and shouted but grandpap only stuck his lips out and

---

[37] Mrs. Chowning claims to have been 16 in 1833 but Coles County records from both Le Baron's and Bateman's histories of Coles County report the only Samuel Chowning, an early settler in Coles County, as married to Mary Ann (Polly) Gordon who was born in 1824 by genealogical records. She would only have been 9 in 1833. In this and other instances, the Coles County histories show that Mrs. Chowning's memory for dates is not completely accurate.

From what is known of Thomas, he was always giving, and his sense of hospitality was strong. Granddaughter Sarah Jane (Hanks) Dowling tells of often hearing Sarah Lincoln speak of Thomas saying, "…he was kind and loving, and kept his word, and always paid his way, and never turned a dog from his door."[39] It seems out of character for anyone to say Thomas was "terrible saving". Of course, for a young girl wanting taffy and with what looks like a crush on the young man trying to get it for her, negative reaction to the adult trying to turn the youth aside would not be unusual. What Thomas said of John Johnston wasting things is accurate from what history knows. John was not known for handling money or property well and his wasting things had a devastating impact on Thomas in Illinois.

Regardless of the circumstances of the story, it does show Thomas was in the habit of "sugaring off." Sugaring off usually refers to boiling down maple sap into syrup and here refers to making molasses. Syrup and molasses were treats for the pioneers and Thomas worked to provide these to his family as a usual thing. On May 3, 1833, Abraham was appointed postmaster at New Salem, Illinois. Some take the party story of Mrs. Chowning to have been when Abraham went home to tell his family of his good fortune and success.

On May 23, John Johnston entered a claim for 40 acres of land at a cost of $50.[40] Thomas did not move there nor is it likely John did. Still, John had made a purchase that would prove eventful for Thomas' life come the next Spring.

No other important family event is known to have occurred in 1833. Granddaughter Amanda Hanks was born to Dennis and Betsy Hanks at an unknown date and later in the year came the event known as *Falling Stars*.

On November 13, the Leonid meteor storm came. One astronomy writer described it. "On the night of November 12-13,

---

[38] Eleanor Gridley. *The Story of Abraham Lincoln or The Journey from the Long Cabin to the White House*, pages 166-167.

[39] Eleanor Atkinson. *The Boyhood of Lincoln*, page 45.

[40] Charles H. Coleman. *Abraham Lincoln and Coles County, Illinois*, page 28.

1833, a tempest of falling stars broke over the Earth. The sky was scored in every direction with shining tracks and illuminated with majestic fireballs. At Boston, the frequency of meteors was estimated to be about half that of flakes of snow in an average snowstorm. Their numbers were quite beyond counting; but as it waned, a reckoning was attempted, from which it was computed, on the basis of that much-diminished rate, that 240,000 must have been visible during the nine hours they continued to fall."[41]

In Coles County, the event was startling to the pioneers and vividly recalled. Early settler and County leader Hiram Tremble told of it.

> *The air was full of falling drops of fire that immediately expired as they neared the ground. Sometimes they would alight on a leaf of a bush of a tree and go out with a peculiar noise difficult to describe. It sounded something like 'tchuck,' given with the shortest possible sound of the vowel.' Early in the morning before daybreak, Mr. Tremble was out with his ox-team the air was cool, with a light frost. "At the start," said he, "I had nearly a mile of timber to pass through. The meteors were falling about me as thick as hail or as rain-drops in an ordinary shower. Some were so large as to cast shadows on the trees. Many of them came in contact with trees in falling, and burst, throwing off a myriad of sparks, illuminating the forest all about me. Emerging into the prairie, the sight was even more grand. All about and above me the air was full of the falling sparks, none of which touched me or my oxen. They did not seem to reach the ground but expired as they neared it." [42]*

Thomas' response to this astounding meteor storm is not recorded but for many, and possibly Thomas who was very religious and very fundamentalist in his beliefs, this space storm breaking over the earth was seen as a sign of the end. As eyes

---

[41] Report of Victorian Astronomy Writer Agnes Clerke, leonid.arc.nasa.gov/history.html.

[42] Newton Bateman, Paul Selby, and Charles Edward Wilson, Editors. *Historical Encyclopedia of Illinois and History of Coles County*, page 668.

turned to the sky, many thoughts would have gone to a well-known prophecy for the time just before the return of Jesus. "Immediately after the tribulation of those days shall the sun be darkened, and the moon shall not give her light, and the stars shall fall from heaven, and the powers of the heavens shall be shaken."[43]   In Coles County, history records that it was a long while before the fear of that night calmed down and settlers resumed their routine day-to-day living.[44]

1834

On March 14, 1834, Thomas purchased his first land in Illinois. He bought the 40 acres John Johnston claimed in 1833. Thomas provided John a profit of $25, purchasing the land John paid $50 for at a price of $75.[45] This land would become the Muddy Point farm where Thomas lived until 1837. Thomas relocated his family to Muddy Point in time for Spring planting.

Muddy Point

At an early but unknown point in Thomas' Coles County history, Dennis Hanks separated from the rest of the extended family to live in the growing town of Charleston. Being the county seat and not far distant from any of the farms where Thomas lived, the Hanks stayed in close contact with the family but Dennis and Betsy would be city dwellers while Thomas' family and the Halls continued to dwell on farms out in the country.

In town, Dennis worked as a cobbler and shoemaker. While he never gained wealth, he did well enough for himself and his family. His business provided for his family's needs in Charleston. He did prospered enough that he and Betsy also ran a tavern/inn for a time called the Illinois House.[46]

The Halls staked out land not far from Thomas. They remained his neighbors for the remainder of his life. John Johnston continued living with Thomas and Sarah.

---

[43] Matthew 24:29. King James Version.
[44] Newton Bateman, Paul Selby, and Charles Edward Wilson, Editors. *Historical Encyclopedia of Illinois and History of Coles County*, page 668.
[45] Charles H. Coleman. *Abraham Lincoln and Coles County, Illinois*, page 28.
[46] Find A Grave. https://www.findagrave.com

On the Muddy Point farm, Thomas and John built a cabin and other farm buildings. Thomas continued woodworking but his eyesight limited him and his craftsmanship continued to decline.

Some say Thomas had a double cabin, a two-room cabin, at Muddy Point. That is possible but more likely he continued to live in a standard one room cabin, though of hewn logs rather than rounded logs. The thinking that Thomas had a two room cabin at Muddy Point comes from Gridley's biography of Abraham Lincoln where she reports a two room cabin for Thomas in 1831.[47] Her main source, John J. Hall, son of Squire and Matilda Hall, was not overly reliable[48] and he described the Goosenest Prairie home as the first home Thomas built on arrival in Coles County in 1831. The story has been applied to Buck Grove and Muddy Point when it was only accurate for Goosenest Prairie.

As Thomas settled in on the Muddy Point farm, Abraham was working to become the representative from his district to the Illinois House of Representatives. On August 4 of 1834, Abraham succeeded in being elected. He would be re-elected every two years until 1842 when he decided to not seek re-election. Nothing in history speaks to Thomas' reaction to his son's success, but with Thomas' pride in Abraham there can be little doubt that he was pleased.

October 1834 was a momentous occasion in the Lincoln household. John Johnston married Mary Barker on October 16. There is a slight discrepancy in the date as the Lincoln family Bible says the date was the 13th of October, but the Coles County record book states the marriage occurred on the 16th.[49] Regardless of exact date, the festivity of another wedding in the Lincoln family would have been great. John and Mary stayed with Thomas and Sarah after the wedding.

Thomas owned the 40-acre Muddy Point farm outright when he moved there in 1834. He expanded his land holdings late that same year. On November 25, 1834, Thomas entered a mortgage arrangement to purchase what would be known as the Plummer Place. It was an 80-acre tract he purchased and farmed but did not

---

[47] Eleanor Gridley. *The Story of Abraham Lincoln or The Journey from the Long Cabin to the White House*, page 108.

[48] Charles H. Coleman. *Abraham Lincoln and Coles County, Illinois*, pages 40 and 41.

[49] Charles H. Coleman. *Abraham Lincoln and Coles County, Illinois*, page 29.

live on. The purchase price was $100 but the mortgage to Charles S. Morgan, the School Commissioner, was for $102. The Plummer Place land was school land being sold to support the schools. Thomas' mortgage obligated him to pay $34 a year for three years.[50]

Thomas never fared well in Kentucky with gaining title and his land dealings did not work to his favor. In Indiana he struggled and worked to obtain clear title to his Pigeon Creek farm but sold it cheap when the family decided to move to Illinois. In Coles County, Thomas did well in his land dealings. His purchases of both Muddy Point and the Plummer Place proved profitable. He purchased the two farms for a total of $177. He would sell them three years later for $362.50, over doubling his money.

1835 – 1836

The first courthouse built in Charleston was abandoned in 1835 and a new courthouse built, a brick building.[51] For a frontier town, moving to a brick structure was a matter of great civic pride. There is no record of Thomas helping with the construction of the new courthouse, but it is well within reason to think he did in some capacity. The new courthouse in the County seat drew almost everyone living in the county to come and see it while it was being built and to tour it once it opened. It was a major event for Coles County.

Thomas settled into farming in Coles County and he continued to work as he was able in construction and other jobs. Joseph Allison opened a blacksmith shop in the county and Thomas assisted him with blacksmithing when the work came in faster than Joseph could handle it on his own.[52]

On March 4, 1835 Thomas signed a lease to operate a saw and grist mill. It was known as Slow Mill and was located along Embarrass River.[53] Thomas shared the lease with Dennis Hanks, John Johnston, Squire Hall, and William Moffett. The mill lease

---

[50] Charles H. Coleman. *Abraham Lincoln and Coles County, Illinois*, page 28.

[51] Newton Bateman, Paul Selby, and Charles Edward Wilson, Editors. *Historical Encyclopedia of Illinois and History of Coles County*, page 671.

[52] Etta Mae Allison. *Pioneers of Coles County Illinois*, page 3.

[53] Douglas L. Wilson and Rodney O. Davis. *Herndon's Informants*, page 102. Statement by A. H. Chapman dated September 8, 1865.

was for one year, leasing the property from Noel Jones and Benjamin Norton. At the close of the lease, $220.125 was due.[54] The mill itself had been the property of James Shaw, deceased, with Jones and Norton acting as guardians of Shaw's children Lucinda and Millis.

$50 of the lease was credited for repairs done on the mill structure and works. Thomas' carpentry skills, mechanic skills, and blacksmithing skills were key to the repairs done. An additional $35.25 was earlier paid toward the lease[55], making an $85.25 credit toward fulfillment.

During the year when Thomas ran the mill, Abraham came home and stayed on a ten-day visit. It is likely that Abraham helped at the mill while he was home. Augustus Chapman reported that Thomas lived at the mill during the lease.[56] That is unlikely. William Greene also visited while Thomas was tending the water mill and stayed for several days with Thomas and Sarah. He makes no mention of Thomas living at the mill though he does mention that the profits from the mill were nearly supporting Thomas and Sarah.[57]

Somewhere in this time period, granddaughter Mary Hanks was born to Dennis and Betsy. The actual date of birth is uncertain. While Thomas' family grew in size, his childhood family continued to shrink. On September 19, 1835 his brother Josiah died in Harrison County, Indiana.[58] He was 62.

At some point in the Fall of 1835, Abraham visited his father.[59] The visit is recorded by Linder Usher, an Illinois attorney who was a friend of the Lincoln family in Kentucky. Whether the visit coincided with Josiah's death is unknown.

November of 1835 brought legal drama. John Johnston and Squire Hall were accused of gaming and arrested on November 5. They were also charged with assault against the officer who

---

[54] Charles H. Coleman. *Abraham Lincoln and Coles County, Illinois*, pages 30-31.

[55] Charles H. Coleman. *Abraham Lincoln and Coles County, Illinois*, pages 30-31.

[56] Douglas L. Wilson and Rodney O. Davis. *Herndon's Informants*, page 102. Statement by A. H. Chapman dated September 8, 1865.

[57] Douglas L. Wilson and Rodney O. Davis. *Herndon's Informants*, page 12. From a letter to Herndon from William G. Greene dated from Tallula, Illinois on May 29th, 1865.

[58] Find A Grave. www.findagrave.com.

[59] F. Linder Usher. *Reminiscences*, page 37.

arrested them.[60] According to the Criminal Code of the State of Illinois, gaming was gambling. Section 127 of the code was very specific.

> *If any person or persons shall play for money, or other valuable thing, at any game with cards, dice, checks, or at billiards, or with any other article or instrument, thing or things whatsoever, which may be used for the purpose of playing or betting, upon, or winning or losing money, or any other thing or things, article or articles of value, or shall bet on any game others may be playing, every person so offending shall be fined not exceeding one hundred dollars, and not less than ten dollars.[61]*

Bail was set at $100 on the gaming charge, which covered the maximum fine if imposed, and $50 on the assault charge. Thomas must have posted bail for them because they were released and did not stand trial until the April 1836 court session.

On April 6, 1836, John and Squire stood trial before a jury. On the assault charge, John was found not guilty and Squire was convicted. No verdict was given on the gaming charges. Sentencing for Squire's assault conviction was postponed until the October term when the gaming charge was to be determined. On October 8, both John and Squire were acquitted on the gaming charges. Squire was sentenced to 24 hours in jail and a $5 fine for assaulting the arresting officer.[62]

Around the same time in early 1836, the results of the Slow Mill lease caught up with Thomas. He had done repairs and managed the mill, making some money but not enough. Had each of the five participants simply put up less than $50 each, the lease would have been covered. Even less would have sufficed considering that $50 in repairs were credited. But that was not the case. When the one-year lease expired in March of 1836, the only amount paid toward it was the $50 credit and the $35.25 in cash. How the profits from the mill were divvied up and why they had

---

[60] Charles H. Coleman. *Abraham Lincoln and Coles County, Illinois*, pages 30-31.
[61] Illinois General Assembly. *The Public and General Statute Laws of the State of Illinois*, page 222.
[62] Charles H. Coleman. *Abraham Lincoln and Coles County, Illinois*, page 30.

not been put back to cover the lease is an open and unanswered question.

John Johnston was known to be poor with money and always looking for ways to make easy money without having to work at it. He wanted what Abraham had wanted but he did not have the gumption to work for it as Abraham did. Dennis Hanks may have been living in Charleston by this time and trying to make a start for himself and his family. He was not noted for thinking toward the long term at this stage in his life. Neither John or Dennis had the means to furnish their part of the venture. Squire's finances are uncertain. William Moffett had abandoned the venture and left the area for parts unknown. The mill venture was a failure despite Thomas' best efforts.[63]

On June 6, 1836, Jones and Norton brought suit against Thomas and his partners. They sued for the full amount of the lease, ignoring the partial payment and work credit. Thomas did not contest the lawsuit. He knew he owed the money. The suit was settled by confession of rightful judgment with $138.67 paid to cover the remainder of the lease period.[64] The division of how the settlement monies were obtained is uncertain but, considering Johnson's and Hanks' financial condition, the likelihood is that Thomas paid the majority of the money with some help from Squire Hall.

Regarding this time period, Etta Mae Allison, a neighbor of the Lincolns, told a story of her childhood that illustrates Thomas' generosity and shows why he was loved by those who knew him. Etta was the daughter of the James Allison in whose blacksmith shop Thomas sometimes worked. The Allison's lived close to the Lincolns.

> *I remember well one year we lived there. Abe's father had a watermelon patch and every evening my younger brother and sister carried water from their well. One evening they were coming slowly along the edge of the melon patch. First my brother would thump a melon and say, "I'll bet this'n ripe," then my sister would say, "I'll bet*

---

63 Charles H. Coleman. *Abraham Lincoln and Coles County, Illinois*, page 54. Also: D. M. Coleman. *Thomas Lincoln, The Father of Abraham Lincoln*, page 29.

64 Charles H. Coleman. *Abraham Lincoln and Coles County, Illinois*, pages 30-31.

*this'n ripe," and just as she pulled it Tommy Lincoln came
out. They were very much frightened at first but when he
told them to take all they wanted they were so tickled
they ran all the way home and always held Tommy Lincoln
in high esteem.[65]*

From this remembrance it is known Thomas had a good well
on his Muddy Point land and he let the neighbors use it. He also
kept a garden where he grew watermelons and even when he
caught children filching his melons, he offered them to take
whatever they wanted. There was nothing stingy about Thomas
Lincoln.

Thomas would be involved in six lawsuits during his years in
Coles County. It was this generosity and giving nature, often
without fully discerning the consequences, that led him into his
own financial struggles. John Johnston, irresponsible and
impulsive, was included in four of them. Thomas was always ready
to co-sign for a friend or family member and he was always ready
to lend a hand if someone asked for help. As the Johnston family
grew and stayed living with Thomas and Sarah, Thomas' finances
were taxed to the extreme to support the family.

A controversy in Thomas' history arose with the visit of
William Greene to Thomas and Sarah's. Greene's visit occurred
because Greene knew Abraham. Greene was a clerk in Denton
Offutt's store, working with Abraham. When Greene decided to
take a trip to Kentucky to visit family, Abraham asked him to
deliver a letter to Thomas as he passed that way. The report of
that visit, as Greene supposedly told it to William Whitney, has
put a lie into history that has long been believed about Thomas.

Whitney has Greene saying Thomas told him, "I suppose that
Abe is still fooling hisself with eddication. I tried to stop it, but he
has got that fool idea in his head, and it can't be got out. Now I
hain't got no eddication, but I get along far better than ef I had.
Take bookkeepin' – why, I'm the best bookkeeper in the world!
Look up at that rafter thar. Thar's three straight lines made with a
firebrand; ef I sell a peck of meal I draw a black line across, and

---

[65] Etta Mae Allison. *Pioneers of Coles County Illinois*, page 2.

when they pay, I take the dishcloth and jest rub it out; and that thar's a heap better'n yer eddication."[66]

This story has been repeated many, many times, portraying Thomas as backward, uneducated, and opposed to Abraham and his educational dreams. In point of fact, documentation presented has already clearly shown that Thomas was proud of Abraham's education and supported it in any way he could. Whitney also has Greene considering Thomas to have been a garrulous host, something nothing on record supports as being Thomas' nature. Whitney, in his book, simply followed the bias found in both Herndon's Lincoln biography and Lamon's biography. This story from the time period when Thomas was working hard to tend Slow Mill is simply a fiction without solid foundation in history.

In addition, Whitney has Greene giving the opinion that Thomas was intellectually great but unpolished and uncultivated. It is in this that the world does catch a fair glimpse of Thomas. He was a highly intelligent man and he was content to remain unpolished and, to developing society, uncultivated.

Somewhere in 1836, Thomas again felt the sting of death. His mother, Bathsheba Lincoln, died. Bathsheba had continued to live with William and Nancy (Thomas' sister) Brumfield in Kentucky. At the time of her death, she had lost her husband and three of her children who entered the next life before her. Though the families had kept in touch, the miles between them were too great for Thomas to be at his mother's funeral. Bathsheba was buried in the First Mill Creek Baptist Cemetery (now named the Lincoln Memorial Cemetery). The cemetery is on land Fort Knox acquired for a base. A fieldstone marker, some three feet tall, was engraved with her initials, "B. L.", and set to mark her final resting place. In 1960, Governor William Stratton of Illinois provided a granite marker to place at the gravesite. In front of the gravestone is embedded a stone from President Lincoln's tomb in Springfield.[67]

On December 20, 1836, Thomas experienced another memorable event at his home in Illinois. He had lived through the Winter of the Deep Snow and the night of the Falling Stars. In 1836 he experienced the Sudden Freeze. December 19 was a

---

[66] Henry C. Whitney. *Lincoln the Citizen: Volume One of A Life of Lincoln*, page 75.
[67] Hardin County Historical Society. www.hardinkyhistory.org.

snowy day, covering the ground with eight inches of snow. The weather turned warmer and the snow turned to rain making a slushy mess of the ground. The afternoon of December 20 brought a cold front like none the pioneers on the Illinois prairie had ever seen. The temperature dropped from forty degrees Fahrenheit to near zero within a few minutes time.[68]

It had been rather warm, and a slight rain had fallen in the forenoon upon a few inches of snow that lay upon the ground, turning it into slush. About the middle of the afternoon, a heavy cloud was noticed coming rapidly from the northwest. It came with a wind blowing at the rate of sixty or seventy miles an hour and was accompanied by a terrific roaring noise. As it passed over the country everything was frozen instantly. Water in little streams and gullies was thrown into waves by the wind and then frozen before it could subside. Chickens running through the slush and mud for shelter were caught, held fast and frozen to death.

Animals, both domestic and wild, that were out in exposed positions, were chilled through and many were frozen standing in their tracks. Men attending to work out of doors and wading about in the water and slush walked upon ice before they could reach a house for shelter, even though it were nearby. Many human lives were lost. In this county, three men were said to have perished near the Seven Hickories. The wave passed over Central Illinois, a strip of country in the southern half of Indiana and was last heard from just below Cincinnati.[69]

Knowing that Sarah and Thomas were both very religious and somewhat superstitious, a trait they would pass on to Abraham, this event could have been seen as a sign of judgment, a time calling for prayer and soul searching. As the date stretched into

---

68 National Weather Service.   https://www.weather.gov/abr/This_Day_in_Weather_History_Dec_20
69 Newton Bateman, Paul Selby, and Charles Edward Wilson, Editors. *Historical Encyclopedia of Illinois and History of Coles County*, pages 668-669.

the past, it became another great story for a great storyteller to repeat in the coming winters.

1837

Despite all the troubles John Johnston brought Thomas, the two remained close. They were kindred souls traveling life together. On January 10, 1837, John and Mary named their firstborn son after Thomas, Thomas Lincoln Davis Johnston.

Four days later, Thomas entered a purchase of 80 acres of government land for $100 in Goosenest Prairie. These 80 acres were just to the north of land he later purchased and made into his final farm. Thomas never lived on this land. He did develop and farm it beginning in the Spring of 1837. The distance, a little over five miles from Muddy Point, was not a deterrent to farming the land.

That Spring, Thomas planted crops on the Goosenest Prairie land and at Plummer Place. However, he may not have planted crops at Muddy Point. His intention was to sell the land and, for once, he did not need to follow the usual pioneer saga of moving in late Fall or during Winter in order to settle in time to plant Spring crops. Thomas was settled and he had plenty of land for plenty of crops.

Abraham moved to Springfield on April 15 and three weeks later Thomas sold the Muddy Point farm to Alexander Montgomery for $140, almost twice what he paid for it.[70] Eleanor Gridley mentions a story from early 1837 as told by John Hall. "Ag'in, one time when I was goin' by, I seed Grandaddy Lincoln out grubbin' up some hazelnut bushes, and so I said to him: 'Why, Grandpap, I thought you wanted to sell your farm?' 'And so I do,' says he, 'but I haint goin' to let my farm know it.'"[71] Thomas was a hard worker, he kept that habit throughout his life even in circumstances where he could have relaxed. There is nothing in John Hall's remembrance to indicate Thomas was anything but industrious.

---

[70] Charles H. Coleman. *Abraham Lincoln and Coles County, Illinois*, page 31.
[71] Eleanor Gridley. *The Story of Abraham Lincoln or The Journey from the Long Cabin to the White House*, pages 168-169.

As Thomas' land holdings grew, so did his family. Another granddaughter was born, Elizabeth Jane Hall to Squire and Matilda.

With the sale of Muddy Point in May, Thomas' timeline has a little confusion. It is known he will be at Goosenest by August but it is unknown if he stayed at Muddy Point very long after selling the land, something that is not likely to have happened, or whether he moved to Goosenest or possibly stayed at Plummer Place for a few months while in transition. History has told the story in all those ways.

Plummer Place

The naming of Plummer Place is misleading to some extent. The name comes from the name of one of the people who later owned the land. The Plummer Place was never closely associated with Thomas, so it came to be called by the name of another owner, an owner who made it his place of residence. This very fact is taken by some historians to indicate Thomas never lived on Plummer Place.

Thomas purchased the 80-acre Plummer Place in late 1834. It was land belonging to the School Commission, and he bought it on installments over three years. By the time he sold the Muddy Point farm in 1837, Plummer Place was close to fully paid.

Despite his ill fortunes and the drag put on his finances by John Johnston, Thomas stayed current on his payments for Plummer Place. In this, he may have had help from Abraham. Etta Mae Allison reports that possibility. "He [David Dryden] was an elder in the Presbyterian church at Indian Creek for many years and served as justice of the peace. He was school treasurer at the time Thomas Lincoln bought his farm near Farmington [referring to the Plummer Place] which was a part of the school land and was paid for in installments. When the payments came due and Thomas Lincoln could not meet them, often Abe Lincoln would call on David Dryden and make arrangements for paying the amounts."[72]

This story is not widely told. At this time in his life, Abraham had barely begun his legal career and was not wealthy. He was

---

[72] Etta Mae Allison. *Pioneers of Coles County Illinois*, page 3.

beginning to prosper, a politician who could pay his way in life after early struggles, but he was still paying the debts from his failed merchant ventures. That circumstance does not negate the story that he helped Thomas with payments on Plummer Place, but it does make the story questionable. Still, it would have been like Abraham to do such on for his family.

Regardless of whether Thomas made payment or Abraham made payment or a combination of both, the mortgage on Plummer Place was kept current and is recorded as satisfied in early 1838.

With the sale of Muddy Point in May of 1837, one tradition says Thomas moved directly to Goosenest Prairie. Thomas' first home at Goosenest Prairie was on land John Johnston purchased in August of 1837. The fact that Thomas sold Muddy Point in May and John did not buy the Goosenest land until August does not mean the family did not move there in May. It was government land and it was still common practice on the frontier for a settler to live on land prior to making claim and purchasing. Thomas could easily have moved to Goosenest with his family.

Another tradition is Thomas moved to Plummer Place between May and August. Having purchased 80 acres at Goosenest Prairie in January and knowing John was looking at land there, it is unlikely Thomas would have moved his family to Plummer Place for just a few months while knowing he had land where the family was intending to settle. Moving to the Plummer Place makes little sense. The most likely scenario is that Thomas moved directly to Goosenest from Muddy Point.

On December 27, 1837, Thomas sold Plummer Place to Daniel Needham for $222.50.[73] Having paid a mortgage of $102, Thomas profited by over double of what he paid for the property. Needham took over the mortgage and made the final payment to settle the mortgage and gain title on February 23, 1838.

Goosenest Prairie

In August of 1837, Thomas moved to his last farm. He would change the location of the cabin on the farm, but Goosenest Prairie was the final stop in his lifetime. The traditional Thomas

---

[73] Charles H. Coleman. *Abraham Lincoln and Coles County, Illinois*, page 37.

has been pictured as nomadic, never really settling in any place, always ready to move. There is even a reported quote from Sarah Bush Lincoln telling she was the one who put a stop to Thomas moving away from Goosenest Prairie.

John J. Hall, Thomas and Sarah's son-in-law, is paraphrased as telling one of his nephews that Thomas wanted to move again, and that Sarah was not happy about it. She is reported to have said something to the effect "that they had moved so often that it reminded her of the children of Israel trying to find the Promised Land."[74] While a poignant quip, the likelihood of this being accurate is slim. It was Sarah and John J. Hall and the Hanks who had persuaded Thomas to move to Illinois after Sarah had lived in the same Indiana location with Thomas for over a decade, where Thomas had lived the entire time he had been in Indiana. There had been some quick moves in Illinois as the family searched for a home spot, moving four times in seven years, but those moves (with the exception of going from Macon County to Coles County) were all from one spot to another spot close by. There is no indication outside this paraphrased memory about Sarah of Thomas wanting to make another move. The very fact that Abraham bought the land to offer security to Thomas as he aged speaks against such.

From his birth in Virginia, a long path had taken Thomas to Illinois and the place he called home for the final years of his earthly journey. Goosenest Prairie provided a good home for Thomas.

The impetus for Thomas's move to Goosenest was twofold. He had purchased 80 acres of the Gooosenest ground he was farming, and he may have intended moving there but when John Johnston purchased 40 acres bordering Thomas' land to the south on August 4,[75] the decision was settled. The cabin Thomas and John built with help of family and neighbors was the standard one room cabin and it was set on Johnston's land. The cabin was home to Thomas and Sarah, John and Mary and their young son. Mary was pregnant with her second child.

---

74 Michael Burlingame. *Abraham Lincoln: A Life*, volume one, page 50-51.
75 Michael Burlingame. *Abraham Lincoln: A Life*, volume one, page 33.

Thomas' life at Goosenest Prairie followed his usual pattern. He farmed and did other jobs to supplement the earnings from his farm. David Dryden, who lived a mile north of Goosenest, ran a blacksmith shop where Thomas helped with blacksmithing during the winter months. Thomas also did carpentry and cabinet work in Dryden's shop.[76]

Despite his hard work, Thomas' financial fortunes continued to decline at Goosenest Prairie. One of the main reasons was his stepson John Johnston. Over the coming years, John pulled Thomas into projects that lost Thomas' investment, projects that failed because they were poorly thought out or because John lost interest and did not carry his part.[77] Thomas loved his stepson and stood by him, but it cost Thomas. He was left paying for John's mistakes.

As the years passed, Thomas became more and more dependent on John and Squire. Dennis Hanks helped out but he lived farther away, in Charleston, whereas John lived with Thomas and Squire's land bordered Thomas'. The family grew and Thomas became a much-loved patriarch of a large extended family. He was well thought of as a person, but he was not moving forward with the changing times. He remained content to live an agrarian self-sustaining lifestyle just as he had known as a child fresh out of Virginia in the wilderness of Kentucky. He never went hungry, but his home was poor and backward, his life simple and primitive. He allowed the changing world to move on without him.

In that lifestyle, John and Squire stayed with him and were content to remain as Thomas did. Dennis Hanks did not gain a lot of success in life but he did change his ways and try to make it in the industrial, city economy. Dennis became a part of the same world Abraham knew. Thomas and John and Squire did not. This contentment with the old ways bonded them together and separated them from both Abraham and Dennis.

Panic of 1837

The Panic of 1837 was the direct result of Andrew Jackson's failed economic policies regarding dissolving the national bank.

---

[76] Michael Burlingame. *Abraham Lincoln: A Life*, volume one, page 53.
[77] Michael Burlingame. *Abraham Lincoln: A Life*, volume one, page 54.

The panic became a major depression lasting until the mid-1840s. Business slowed and profits lowered. Prices and wages dropped. Unemployment rose. Expansion stalled. The country was mired by a negative impression of the economy.

The impact to Illinois from the Panic was the collapse of a massive internal improvements program that Abraham had pushed and supported in the state legislature. Illinois was driven to the brink of bankruptcy.

Whereas the Panic of 1819 had an impact on Thomas, there is little to show that he was impacted by this 1937 downturn. Thomas was buying and swapping and selling land in Illinois that led to his final farm at Goosenest Prairie. Those deals were successful. Thomas continued to hunt and farm and maintain his family. No doubt money and trade were impacted for Thomas to some extent but the overall impact of the Panic of 1837 on Thomas appears minimal.

1838 -1840

The Johnston's second child, a boy, was born on March 27, 1838 at Goosenest Prairie. John and Mary named him after his uncle, Abraham Lincoln Barker Johnston. Uncle Abraham was living in Springfield and practicing law with John T. Stuart. Having a nephew named after him became a matter of pride for Abraham and he took an interest in the boy's life. Later, Abraham offered to bring his nephew to Springfield, giving him room and board and paying for his education, but when Mary learned of the offer, she quickly ended it, wanting nothing to do with Abraham's backward family.[78]

Somewhere in the early years at Goosenest Prairie, John C. Gulliver told of an interesting story regarding Abraham Lincoln's early efforts at learning law and that story in turn tells us something about Thomas and Abraham. Dr. Gulliver, a former President of Knox College in Galesburg, Illinois, interviewed Abraham as part of an article he wrote for the New York *Independent*.

---

[78] Douglas L. Wilson and Rodney O. Davis. *Herndon's Informants*, pages 532-533. From a Herndon interview of Thomas L. D. Johnston in 1866.

Gulliver question to Lincoln: "Did you not have a law education? How did you prepare for your profession?"

Lincoln answer: "O, yes. I read law, as the phrase is; that is, I became lawyer's clerk in Springfield, and copied tedious documents, and picked up what I could of law in the intervals of other work. But your question reminds me of a bit of education I had, which I am bound in honesty to mention. I thought, at first, that I understood its meaning, but soon became satisfied that I did not. I said to myself, 'What do I do when I demonstrate, more than when I reason and prove? How does demonstration differ from any other proof?' I consulted Webster's Dictionary. That told of certain proof, 'proof beyond possibility of doubt'; but I could form no idea of what sort of proof that was. I thought a great many things were proved beyond a possibility of doubt, without recourse to any such extraordinary process of reasoning as I understood 'demonstration' to be. I consulted all the dictionaries and books of reference I could find, but with no better results. You might as well have defined 'blue' to a blind man. At last I said: 'Lincoln, you can never make a lawyer if you do not understand what demonstrate means.' And I left my situation in Springfield, went home to my father's house, and stayed there until I could give any propositions in the six books of Euclid at sight. I then found out what 'demonstrate' means and went back to my law studies.'" [79]

While the timing of this event can vary, the interesting point found here in relation to Thomas is that when Abraham had something to work out, something he needed to do before he could even continue in his chosen career, he went home to his father's house. Abraham had many friends he could have turned to. He had other family he could have turned to. Yet when he needed this time to study and ponder, he went to Thomas. With

---

[79]John H. Finley. "The Education of Abraham Lincoln". *Lincoln Centennial Association Papers*, pages 84-85.

all the separation spoken of between Thomas and Abraham due to their difference in life approach, there was still a bond and a trust. They may not have been as close as many fathers and sons, but in his time of need, Abraham's eyes turned home to his father's house. That home, rejected lifestyle though it was, was still a haven.

Within that home, religion continued to be a strong part of life. That religion was mixed with some superstition, but family tradition gives Thomas and Sarah a righteous power that was respected by family and neighbors. John Hall told one story illustrating that power and presence.

"Both Grandpap and Grandmarm Lincoln prayed so much," said he, "that they hed a wonderful power about 'em to cure folks. Why, grandmarm could draw out fire and grandpap could cure a felon. Folks would come for ten miles around to get grandpap to cure 'em, and all he'd do wus jest to hold the sore finger in his hands a few minutes and say somethin' in a whisper, and every time he'd cure 'em shore nuff. Grandmarm, she would jest lay her hand on the burn and shet up her eyes and say two or three words and it would never hurt you no more. She hes drawed the fire out of my hands lots of times, and onct she told me that if she told arry a woman she'd never hev the power to cure no more, but that if she told a man it wouldn't make no difference, and she did tell me afore she died what she said when she cured 'em, but I can't tell nobody." [80]

Harriet Hanks (Chapman) remembered how religious Thomas was and how he expected his family to respect his beliefs. When she was twelve or thirteen (1838 or 1839), she was visiting her grandparents' home. Thomas was in the barn milking the cows and goats and feeding the livestock. The barnyard was crowded with sheep, geese, ducks, turkeys, chickens, and guinea fowl. Thomas kept a large number of such. Harriet tells of an old wether (a castrated male ram or sheep) being among the sheep. He was a

---

[80] [80] Eleanor Gridley. *The Story of Abraham Lincoln or The Journey from the Long Cabin to the White House*, page 173.

contentious creature and she was wearing a brightly colored dress. The wether made a rush at her and, in avoiding his charge, Harriet fell in the barnyard, dirtying her dress. She managed to get up and run to the fence. Climbing the fence to safety, still frightened, she shouted out "O Holy Ghost." Thomas, having heard the commotion, looked into the barnyard and heard her. He went to a nearby tree and broke off a small limb to use as a switch. As he stood in front of her at the fence, he waved the switch menacingly and solemnly warned her that if she ever used such language again, he would "whip her good."[81]

The year 1839 brought two more celebrations for Thomas. Another grandson was born. Squire and Matilda had their fourth child and second son, Alfred Hall. The second celebration was a trip for the family to Charleston to attend the marriage of granddaughter Sarah Jane Hanks to Thomas Scott Dowling. Sarah was the first grandchild to be married.

With one granddaughter married and out into her own life in Charleston, another granddaughter was born to live in Thomas' cabin. Marietta Sarah Jane Johnston was born to John and Mary January 21, 1840. The small cabin was getting crowded.

January of 1840 presented more of the struggles in Thomas' life related to John Johnston and Thomas signing notes to support him. Isaac Sears won two judgments against Johnston which Johnston was unable to pay. Johnston managed to avoid greater fines and trouble by getting Thomas to co-sign a new note with Sears for $26.825 on April 18, 1839. The note bore 12% interest with a due date of December 25, 1839. Sears sued Thomas and John for payment and won another judgment on January 11, 1840, Thomas and John were ordered to pay a total of $30.77 plus costs. In this instance Thomas was fortunate. Following the verdict by Justice of the Peace Stephen Shelley, Thomas went through his papers at the farm and found a receipt signed by Sears showing payment had been made on the earlier judgments. Thomas filed an appeal on March 21, 1840 and won at the Fall court sessions,

---

[81] H. B. Glasco. "Thomas Lincoln. His Tomb – The Old Cabin in Which He Died – His Religion – Some Stories of His Life." *The Independent*, page 136.

getting the earlier decision reversed and being awarded costs and charges on September 30, 1840.[82]

One of Thomas' best land deals was done in March of 1840. From 1837 to 1840, Thomas and Sarah lived in a cabin on land owned by John Johnston. To the north of Johnston's land lay the 80 acres of Goosenest Prairie land Thomas had purchased in 1837. To the west of Johnston's land was an 80-acre tract owned by Reuben Moore. Thomas preferred that land to his own.

On March 5, 1840, Thomas worked an even swap with Moore, trading his 80 acres for Moore's. On the land deal, they each listed their land as worth $400, a very high price. While no money changed hands, on paper this was a 400% increase in land value for Thomas. No one has ever found a reason why the two men set such a high value on land that was not worth nearly that amount.

As history looked back on this deal and evaluated the condition of the two tracts, this was seen as a poor deal by Thomas. The land Thomas ended up with was not nearly as valuable in later years as the land he traded away. Charles Coleman brought in an expert (Dr. Byron K. Barton, head of Eastern Illinois State College's Department of Geography) to review the land as it was and as it turned out to try and understand Thomas' deal with Moore. Barton determined that Thomas made a good deal, for his time period.

> *A comparison of the land in these two tracts indicates that Thomas Lincoln not only was ambitious to obtain an estate but also desired a farm which would produce an adequate living for himself and his family. The 80 acres which he had obtained by public land entry was largely upland prairie land. Numerous swales are found which even with modern methods of land drainage are difficult to farm in "rainy" years. Thomas Lincoln undoubtedly found farming this wet prairie land a very trying task.*

> *Immediately to the south and west Reuben Moore owned 80 acres of land which was a well-drained forest soil and contained only three small areas of wet prairie. It is not*

---

[82] Charles H. Coleman. *Abraham Lincoln and Coles County, Illinois*, page 38.

inconceivable that Thomas Lincoln viewed this more rolling, well-drained and more easily worked land with an envious eye and when the opportunity presented itself traded with Moore for a farm which Lincoln considered more desirable.

Developments of the past one hundred years on this farm land have altered the picture. The prairie soils through adequate farm management have been improved and their productive capacity increased while the rolling forest soil shows the ravages of erosion, but Thomas Lincoln, as many farmers of today, was considering the present and the immediate future and like his contemporaries could not see that agricultural techniques would someday make his decision appear erroneous.[83]

Following his land deal, Thomas decided the current cabin home was not suitable to the family's needs. He and John built a new cabin on Thomas' land not too far from where the Johnston cabin stood. When the new cabin was built, they dismantled and moved the old cabin to be next to the new one, joining the two together to form a double cabin. This double cabin was Thomas' final home.

Eleanor Gridley records a colorful story of the new cabin as told by John Hall. John, Thomas' grandson, purchased the home and farm after Sarah's death, adding it to his own land holdings.

The trees wus so thick when we cum here we couldn't see nowhare. Grandpap and Uncle Abe and Uncle John D. Johnston jest cleared away a little spot right over there, [pointing to the cornfield a few rods to the east of us] and purty soon they hed up a right smart house which is the east room of this yere cabin. It stood over there alone for a while, then grandpap and the boys built the west room and moved the other house over here and jined it onto the new part. Why, ye ought to hev been around here in those

---

[83] Charles H. Coleman. *Abraham Lincoln and Coles County, Illinois*, page 40.

days; the wild-cats, wolves, panthers, and other varmint wus as thick as bees around a molasses pot.[84]

It is doubtful, considering the time of the move in the Spring of 1840, that Abraham helped in the construction of the new cabin. Records show he was busy in and around Springfield during that time. There has been some discrepancy in Lincoln history for the time of this move to the double cabin. Lincoln historian William Barton tells that the double cabin was completed approximately a year and a half before Thomas' death but Thomas was moved into it only a few days prior to his death and he lived in it for no more than two days.[85] While Barton has provided a wealth of documentation valuable to Lincoln history, he is in error regarding the cabin. The story of the double cabin is remembered with variances but family tradition and local history in Coles County shows Thomas moved to his new cabin around 1840.[86]

Thomas planned the new cabin for some time before constructing it. He made wood shingles for the roof with his drawing knife. He used his two yoke of oxen and a wagon to bring in the white oak logs he cut. These logs he hewed and set aside for the cabin. He prepared the items he needed to finish the windows and door. Thomas intended a nice home, by his pioneer standards, for his family. He applied the knowledge and experience he had gained over the years building barns and houses for his neighbors.[87]

The two rooms of the cabin were different due to being built at two different times. The space where they were joined made a small extra area where things were stored. A huge brick fireplace with a mantle crafted by Thomas adorned the interior and made the home cozy in the winter. The floors were hackberry boards Thomas whipsawed and installed with tongue and groove. A loft stretched over the two joined cabins where the old roofs were

---

[84] Eleanor Gridley. *The Story of Abraham Lincoln or The Journey from the Long Cabin to the White House*, page 29.

[85] William E. Barton. *The Lineage of Lincoln*, page 85.

[86] See Charles Coleman's work, *Abraham Lincoln and Coles County, Illinois*, pages 42-43 for an excellent summary of why Barton misses the mark on the building of the double cabin.

[87] H. B. Glasco, "Thomas Lincoln. His Tomb – The Old Cabin in Which He Died – His Religion – Some Stories of His Life." *The Independent*, page 136.

replaced with the new roof composed of Thomas' wood shingles.[88] The cabin was whitewashed and painted. Sarah and Mary tended the house to make it comfortable and efficient. Thomas' new home was enlarged for his growing family and built sturdy to last for years.

An interesting side note for 1840 is the census. Thomas is listed as the head of family for himself and Sarah. His main employment at this time had become agriculture. In a question regarding the number of people in the household over twenty years of age who could not read, the answer is one. It is known that Sarah could neither read nor write. The census confirms that Thomas did read and write though it does not provide his competency level in those skills.[89]

As 1840 drew to a close, Thomas purchased John Johnston's 40 acres on December 31. The circumstances of the purchase are unknown but evidently Johnston needed the money and Thomas was willing to make the deal. Thomas paid Johnston $50 for the land, the same price Johnston paid when he bought it.[90] Considering that Thomas had covered John financially and was supporting his family by his labor and income, Thomas must have been unwilling to give Johnston any profit from the sale as he had when he bought the Muddy Point land from Johnston.

John was considered a handsome man. He was lively and social in nature though less inclined to apply that liveliness to a consistent work habit. He was known as the "Beau Brummell"[91] of Goosenest Prairie. He bought and wore the best clothes, even though he did not have the means to pay for them on his own. He had a drinking problem on top of his poor handling of finances. Records show he purchased fourteen gallons of whiskey in just

---

[88] H. B. Glasco, "Thomas Lincoln. His Tomb – The Old Cabin in Which He Died – His Religion – Some Stories of His Life." *The Independent*, page 137.
[89] Illinois Genealogy Trails. genealogytrails.com/ill/coles/censusindex.html. Coles County 1840 census.
[90] Charles H. Coleman. *Abraham Lincoln and Coles County, Illinois*, page 41.
[91] "Beau Brummell" was the nickname by which George Bryan Brummell was called. Brummell was a close friend of Prince George (later King George IV) of England. He was known for his flair and style. In the early 19th century, he was the leader of fashion, the one after whom those who wanted to be considered fashionable styled their wardrobe.

four months.[92] It is possible John drank all this on his own, but it is more likely, while drinking heavily himself, that he hosted for his friends. This behavior must have stretched Thomas' tolerance to its limits as Thomas abided closely to the standards of his church and rarely touched any liquor for himself.

Thomas' love for John showed patience, a patience and care that kept John for the sake of that love and because of his wife and children. This is another strong representation of Thomas following his favorite saying, "If you make a bad bargain, hold it the tighter."

It is possible that much of the belittling Herndon and history would place on Thomas came from John's character and practice being applied to Thomas. William Herndon recorded John as an indolent and shiftless man who was born tired.[93] Even with that analysis, Herndon considered Johnston a very clever, generous, and hospitable person. Neighbors remembered John as profligate and dissipated.[94] This characteristic of John was applied to Thomas in Lincoln biographies without any historical foundation to support it.

1841 – 1843

1841 gave Thomas three new grandchildren. Charles Friend M. Hanks was born to Dennis and Betsy, Sarah Louisa Hall to Squire and Matilda, and on December 15, Squire H. Johnston to John and Mary. Squire Johnston would serve in the Civil War, fighting for the Union.

1841 also brought more financial troubles for Thomas. Everything going on was not recorded but the issues were serious. Abraham worried his father would lose his farm and the family have nowhere to go. He stepped in to ensure Thomas and Sarah's future. On October 25, he bought the 40 acres Thomas purchased from John. This land is known as the Abraham 40. Abraham paid the same rate for the land Thomas had claimed as the land value for the 80 acres he traded with Reuben Moore. He paid $200 for 40 acres. It was a high price. It was a gift more than a purchase.

---

92 Michael Burlingame. *Abraham Lincoln: A Life. Volume one*, page 129.
93 John Y. Simon. *House Divided: Lincoln and His Father*, page 11.
94 John Y. Simon. *House Divided: Lincoln and His Father*, page 11.

Abraham wrote the legal documents to reserve the land for Thomas and Sarah's use for as long as they lived. Thomas' cabin was not on the Abraham 40 but if Thomas had sold his remaining 80 acres, the cabin could have been moved. Thomas never used that option.

Abraham's actions gave Thomas security in his old age. The indenture Abraham wrote for the land was very clear.

"This Indenture made this twenty-fifth day of October in the year of our Lord one thousand eight hundred and forty-one by and between Thomas Lincoln and Sarah his wife, of the county of Coles and State of Illinois, party of the first part, and Abraham Lincoln of the county of Sangamon and State aforesaid, party of the second part, Witnesseth:

That the said party of the first part, for, and in consideration of the sum of two hundred dollars to them in hand paid by the said party of the second part, the receipt whereof is hereby acknowledged, have granted, bargained, and sold; and by these presents do grant, bargain and sell unto the said party of the second part, his heirs and assigns forever, all their right, title, interest, and estate in and to the North East fourth of the South East quarter of Section Twenty one, in Township Eleven North, Range Nine East containing forty acres, more or less; reserving, however the occupation, use, and entire control of said tract of land, and the appurtenances thereunto belonging, to the said party of the first part, and to the survivor of them, during both and each of their natural-lives.

To have and to hold to the said party of the second part, his heirs and assigns forever, subject to the reservation aforesaid, the above described tract or parcel of land, aforesaid together with all and singular the privileges and appurtenances thereunto belonging."[95]

Abraham topped off the land deal by writing into the legal documents an agreement to sale the Abraham 40 back to John Johnston after both Thomas and Sarah were deceased. The sale price was set at $200. Abraham did not give his stepbrother any leeway. He knew what John was costing Thomas and the turmoil his lifestyle was making for him. He set a high price knowing John would have to change his ways to meet it.

"Whereas I have purchased of Thomas Lincoln and his wife, the North East fourth of the South East quarter of Section Twenty-one in Township Eleven North of Range Nine East, for which I have paid them the sum of two hundred dollars, and have taken their deed of conveyance for the same, with a reservation of a life estate therein to them and the survivor of them. Now I bind myself, my heirs and assigns, to convey said tract of land to John D. Johnston, or his heirs, at any time after the death of the survivor of the said Thomas Lincoln & wife, provided he shall pay me, my heirs or assigns, the said sum of two hundred dollars, at any time within one year after the death of the survivor of the said Thomas Lincoln & wife, and the same may be paid without interest except after the death of the survivor as aforesaid."[96]

Samuel Haycraft, who confused several facts of both Thomas' and Abraham's lives, told of the Goosenest Prairie farm being purchased for Thomas by Abraham. He stated that "as soon as Abraham began to prosper in the world, he remembered his father and stepmother, bought and presented to them the farm on which

---

[95] Roy P. Basler. *The Collected Works of Abraham Lincoln*, volume 1, page 262. The handwriting on the document is Abraham Lincoln's. Thomas Lincoln signed the document. Sarah Bush Lincoln made her mark. The document is dated October 25, 1841.

[96] Roy P. Basler. *The Collected Works of Abraham Lincoln*, volume 1, page 263. This bond is dated October 25, 1841 and is in Abraham Lincoln's hand, bearing his signature. The land was never sold. A cousin of the Lincoln's, John J. Hall, claimed the land by undisputed possession of over twenty years.

Thomas Lincoln died."[97] Haycraft is wrong on the details but he gets the reason behind Abraham's purchase correctly. Despite the differences between Thomas and Abraham, Abraham cared for his father and stepmother and he did good by them.

Goosenest Prairie farm had 120 acres. The title was clear and the land debt free. The farm had a new double cabin housing Thomas and Sarah along with the Johnston family. The fields were in good shape and all of them were fenced with rails made mainly by Thomas. He had a barn, animal pens, and other outbuildings. He was raising field crops and a large garden along with keeping livestock. He hunted and fished. The Lincoln family, though without substantial cash flow, never went hungry. Thomas, because of his lifestyle choices, was considered poor and backward. His food and clothing were simple, but he had family and friends to share his sturdy hewn-log cabin and with them he celebrated and enjoyed life. Thomas was content.

Abraham kept close contact with his father. He knew what was going on and he did what he could to help. Abraham went on the circuit twice a year. During those travels, when the court circuit brought him close to Coles County, he went to visit his father. When he did so, he loaded his buggy with provisions and gifts.[98] The gifts usually included $10 or $15 dollars in cash for Thomas to use as needed.[99]

On these twice a year visits, the provisions and gifts Abraham brought were well remembered and welcomed. John Hall told that every time Abraham came there was something in the buggy for Thomas and Sarah and John and "the balance of the family."[100] Later, sometime after Thomas' death, as Abraham became busier with politics and stopped regularly riding the circuit, the visits became less frequent. Sarah told Herndon that she only saw

---

[97] Douglas L. Wilson and Rodney O. Davis. *Herndon's Informants*, page 67. Letter of Samuel Haycraft to Herndon from Elizabethtown, Kentucky dated June 1865.
[98] William L. Baron Jr. *The History of Coles County Illinois*, page 422.
[99] Charles H. Coleman. *Abraham Lincoln and Coles County, Illinois*, page 67. The information on the cash gifting was given to Coleman by Amanda Hanks (Poorman) who would frequently travel to the Goosenest Prairie farm with Abraham so she could visit her grandparents.
[100] Eleanor Gridley. *The Story of Abraham Lincoln or The Journey from the Long Cabin to the White House*, page 174.

Abraham every year or two.[101] But regardless of the frequency of his visits, Abraham ensured that his father and stepmother were cared for and had what they needed.

Despite Thomas' hard work and Abraham's help, Thomas struggled financially in 1842. In January, Thomas and John were sued in another instance where Thomas had signed for John and John failed to meet his obligations. The judgment in the lawsuit went against them and they were ordered to pay $19.47.

On March 31, Thomas mortgaged the eastern 40 acres of the 80 to which he held title. The mortgage was with the School Trustees. It called for repayment of $12.50 every six months plus interest for two years. Abraham paid the interest and then cleared the mortgage, paying the $50 dollars.[102] His love for John never waned but his patience with him would wear thin as evidenced in a letter he wrote to John after Thomas' death.

Dear Brother,

When I came into Charleston day-before yesterday I learned that you are anxious to sell the land where you live and move to Missouri. I have been thinking of this ever since; and cannot but think such a notion is utterly foolish. What can you do in Missouri, better than here? Is the land any richer? Can you there, any more than here, raise corn, & wheat & oats, without work? Will any body there, any more than here, do your work for you? If you intend to go to work, there is no better place than right where you are; if you do not intend to go to work, you cannot get along anywhere. Squirming & crawling about from place to place can do no good. You have raised no crop this year, and what you really want is to sell the land, get the money and spend it − part with the land you have, and my life upon it, you will never after, own a spot big enough to bury you in. Half you will get for the land, you spend in moving to Missouri, and the other half you will eat and drink, and wear out, & no foot of land will be bought. Now

---

[101] Douglas L. Wilson and Rodney O. Davis. *Herndon's Informants*, page 108. From the statement of Sarah Bush Lincoln to Herndon dated September 8, 1865.
[102] Charles H. Coleman. *Abraham Lincoln and Coles County, Illinois*, page 63.

I feel it is my duty to have no hand in such a piece of foolery. I feel that it is so even on your own account; and particularly on Mother's account. The Eastern forty acres I intend to keep for Mother while she lives – if you will not cultivate it; it will rent for enough to support her – at least it will rent for something. Her Dower in the other two forties, she can let you have, and no thanks to [me].

Now do not misunderstand this letter. I do not write it in any unkindness. I write it in order, if possible, to get you to face the truth – which truth is, you are destitute because you have idled away all your time. Your thousand pretenses for not getting along better, are all nonsense – they deceive no body but yourself. Go to work is the only cure for your case.[103]

Another momentous event occurred in Thomas' life in November of 1842. Thomas, and the rest of the country, did not realize how momentous it would turn out to be. On November 4, Abraham Lincoln married Mary Todd. History was moving Abraham into position to move forward with his career and connecting him with the people he needed to meet to get there. Thomas and Sarah did not even know Abraham was getting married. He had been engaged but the engagement fell apart. As far as history knows, Thomas was neither informed nor invited to his son's wedding.

Historians have made much of this in portraying the distance between father and son, but the simple fact is that Abraham's wedding was a small event, hurriedly arranged. No more than thirty people were in attendance and those were notified the morning of the wedding. The wedding party was selected that morning with both Abraham and Mary notifying the best man and maid of honor they needed to come to the wedding that evening. Mary did not tell her father. For all practical purposes, it was an impromptu wedding.

Abraham did not disrespect his father by not inviting him to the wedding. If that were reality, Abraham – and Mary –

---

[103] Roy P. Basler. *The Collected Works of Abraham Lincoln*, volume 2, page 111. The letter is dated November 4, 1851.

disrespected a lot of friends and family. The harsh reality of Abraham's marriage is that Mary refused to have anything to do with his family. She held the Lincolns in contempt. She was from southern aristocracy and intended Abraham to move forward in society and politics. She saw his family as an obstacle to her designs. Abraham could not be seen as coming from someone such as her version of what Thomas Lincoln was like.

After the marriage, Thomas and Sarah were never invited to Springfield to visit Abraham's family. Mary never considered visiting Goosenest Prairie. Abraham was caught in the middle. He visited Thomas and he spent money and time to support Thomas. That could not have been a friendly discussion between Abraham and Mary, but Mary could not stop Abraham from caring for his family.

How and when Abraham told Thomas and Sarah and the rest of the family about his wedding is unknown. No doubt there were some hard feelings as those who had known Abraham his entire life were left out and no reception was held for them to meet Mary and welcome her to the family. But life at Goosenest Prairie went on. Thomas took it in stride as just another item God had placed on the table.

Grandson Joseph Hall was born in 1843 to Squire and Matilda. On October 26 John and Mary welcomed another son, Richard Johnston. Richard would grow up to serve in the 8th Illinois Infantry in the Civil War. In Springfield, Abraham's first son, Robert Todd Lincoln, was born on August 1.

In the Fall of 1843, Thomas received word his sister Nancy Lincoln Brumfield died on October 9 in Hardin County, Kentucky. She was 63. Thomas had brought Nancy, her husband William, and his mother Bathsheba to live on his first farm near Elizabethtown. William had helped Thomas move. Thomas had been closer with this sister than with others in his immediate family. Her loss was felt deeply. Nancy was buried in the Lincoln Memorial Cemetery near her mother.[104]

With Nancy Brumfield's death, Thomas had lost his parents and most of his childhood family. Only his youngest sister Abigail

---

[104] Find A Grave. www.findagrave.com.

was left with him and that is an assumption. The death date for Abigail Lincoln Morse is unknown.

December 1843 brought some joy to Thomas. The family went to Charleston to celebrate the wedding of granddaughter Nancy Melvina Hanks to James Shoaff.

1844 – 1847

Relations between Mary Todd Lincoln and at least a part of Thomas' family thawed a little in 1844. For about a year and a half during 1844 and 1845, Harriet Hanks (Chapman) was permitted to stay with the Lincolns while she attended schools in Springfield. Why Mary changed her mind about allowing some of Thomas' grandchildren to stay with them in Springfield while schooling is unknown. Perhaps Harriet had shown more of the expected etiquette, having been raised in Charleston and not in a log cabin on the prairie. Perhaps Abraham wore Mary down and won consent by persistence. Regardless of the why, Harriet lived with the Lincolns until her relationship with Mary became so strained, she considered it a great relief to return to her life in Charleston.[105]

For the years 1844 to 1846, history does not provide a lot of information about Thomas. He farmed Goosenest Prairie and worked carpentry, cabinet making, and blacksmithing as he found the work available. He put food on the table and took life as it came.

One of Thomas' crops was tobacco. Though Thomas did not smoke, he did occasionally chew. In Kentucky, he purchased tobacco for chewing. In Illinois, he chewed what he grew. Tobacco was a cash crop. He advertised his tobacco with a sign on the gateposts by the road charging ten cents a pound or exchanging tobacco for other produce. Thomas enjoyed a good business in tobacco with his neighbors, furnishing much of the area's supply.[106]

Thomas stored his seed sweet potatoes in the space between the cabin rooms. John Hall told of sneaking in there and worrying Thomas. Thomas kept the seed potatoes packed in sand. John

---

[105] Jesse W. Weik. *The Real Lincoln: A Portrait*, page 54.
[106] H. B. Glasco, "Thomas Lincoln. His Tomb – The Old Cabin in Which He Died – His Religion – Some Stories of His Life." *The Independent*, pages 136-137.

loved sweet potatoes and he would unpack the seed potatoes from the sand and eat them raw, as many as he could stuff in. John never talked of Thomas punishing him for eating the seed potatoes, but he did say Thomas feared the boy would eat all of them and he would have none to plant.[107] Thomas may not have looked far into the future with his planning, but he did look to provide for the next year's crops.

Over 1845 and 1846, Thomas gained more grandchildren. Squire and Matilda welcomed daughter Amanda Hall in 1845. On November 18, 1845 another person was added to Thomas' cabin. John and Mary had another son, Dennis Friend Johnston. Dennis became another of Thomas' grandsons to serve in the Civil War, fighting in the Illinois 135th Infantry. He earned the Distinguished Service Award. On March 10, 1846, Abraham's second son was born to him and Mary, Edward Baker Lincoln. These two years also brought Thomas his first great-grandchildren. Missouri Shoaff was born to James and Nancy Shoaff in 1845 and Thomas Benton Shoaff was born in 1846. Elizabeth Jane Dowling was born in 1846 to Thomas and Sarah Dowling.

With added mouths to feed and clothe and care for, Thomas' finances did not improve. Abraham found another way to support his father. He began assigning Thomas legal fees from his cases. Thomas was to collect the fees and keep the money for his own use. One such instance was in May of 1845 when Thomas received a $35 legal fee assignment from Abraham.[108]

One event later in Thomas' life was a conversion of sorts. All his life, Thomas had been associated with one form or other of a Baptist church. At some point in Coles County that changed. Thomas and Sarah frequently visited with Dennis and Betsy Hanks in Charleston. On one of these visits, the Christian Church (Restoration Movement) was hosting a revival meeting at the old Coles County courthouse. Thomas went. He was captivated by the teaching and the services. The result was that both Thomas and Sarah joined the movement and became what was being called Campbellites.

---

[107] Eleanor Gridley. *The Story of Abraham Lincoln or The Journey from the Log Cabin to the White House*, page 172.
[108] Charles H. Coleman. *Abraham Lincoln and Coles County, Illinois*, page 66.

The Restoration Movement was a back-to-basics theology. Alexander Campbell was distressed by divisions within the Church and wanted to bring unity, a unity around his movement as the only true church. He was from a Puritan tradition and, based on his beliefs, saw unity for the Church in recovering the primitive Christianity shown in Scripture. He forsook all creeds and traditions that he felt divided the Church rather than bringing it together.[109]

Campbell's records show he was traveling through Indiana, Illinois, and Missouri holding revival meetings in 1845.[110] It is possible Thomas and Sarah attended one of these meetings where Campbell himself was preaching. Campbell offered structure, order, and certainty in his teaching. This appealed to Thomas. He was a member of the Christian Church (Restoration Movement) for the remainder of his life. From the time he joined the Christian Church, Thomas traveled to Charleston on Saturday, attended both Sunday services, and returned home on Monday.[111]

The war between the United States and Mexico began in 1846. Coles County sent a company of troops into battle at Vera Cruz but there is no record of any of Thomas' children or grandchildren serving in the war. Cousin John Hanks did serve in the war.[112] Neither Abraham nor John Johnston volunteered their services. Abraham was preparing for a run for Congress. Abraham won his election on August 4, 1846 to represent the Illinois Seventh Congressional District. He would not take office until the end of the following year.

Squire and Matilda Hall gave Thomas another grandchild in 1847, Harriet Hall, and the family celebrated yet another Charleston wedding on September 8 as Harriet Ann Hanks wed Colonel Augustus H. Chapman.

A landmark trial occurred in Coles County in the Fall court session on October 16, 1847. It involved Abraham. Robert

---

[109] Restoration Movement. www.therestorationmovement.com.

[110] Restoration Movement. www.therestorationmovement.com.
www.therestorationmovement.com/_states/wv/cmblachronology.htm.

[111] Eleanor Gridley. *The Story of Abraham Lincoln or The Journey from the Long Cabin to the White House*, page 169.

[112] Newton Bateman, Paul Selby, and Charles Edward Wilson, Editors. *Historical Encyclopedia of Illinois and History of Coles County*, page 219.

Matson, a Kentucky slaveholder, purchased a farm in Coles County in addition to his Kentucky holdings. He brought a freed slave, Anthony Bryant, to act as his foreman for the Illinois farm. Matson also brought slaves back and forth from Kentucky for short periods of time to work the Illinois land and, because the slaves were only on the land for short time periods, he skirted Illinois anti-slavery laws by saying the slaves were in transit.

The issue came when Matson brought Anthony Bryant's wife Jane and their children to Illinois. Jane and the children were still slaves to Matson. Mrs. Bryant fell afoul of Matson's housekeeper and mistress who threatened to have the children returned to Kentucky and sold. The Bryants enlisted the help of local abolitionists. Jane and the children left Maston's farm but were arrested as runaway slaves and held in custody. When Matson demanded their release to him, a suit was filed on their behalf claiming they were free under Illinois law because they had been in the state for longer than could be considered in transit.

Matson retained attorneys to defend his rights as a slaveowner. One of those attorneys was Abraham Lincoln. The trial attracted a lot of attention, so much that two justices on the Illinois Supreme Court – including the Chief Justice – came to Coles County to hear the case. Abraham argued for Matson on the grounds that the slaves were in transit and therefore could not be freed. The court ruled against Abraham and Matson lost. The slaves were freed.[113]

At the time of the trial, both of the attorneys Matson hired were antislavery and yet both took the case. The fact that Abraham came to Coles County, Thomas's home county, to defend a slaveowner in court after Thomas had brought his family out of Kentucky partially because of opposition to slavery must have been hard for Thomas to bear. Thomas had affiliated with anti-slavery churches all of Abraham's life and Abraham had sat under that teaching. Much has been made in history of Abraham taking this case and defending a slaveowner. Little has been noted of the angst and embarrassment this must have caused Thomas. If Abraham followed his normal pattern, he visited his father and the

---

[113] Newton Bateman, Paul Selby, and Charles Edward Wilson, Editors. *Historical Encyclopedia of Illinois and History of Coles County*, pages 663-664.

family following the trial. Thomas and some of the family probably went to Charleston for the trial. It was highly publicized, drew a large crowd, and was just the kind of event Thomas would not have missed. Nothing is recorded of Abraham visiting with Thomas – either in Charleston or at Goosenest Prairie – during the trial, but it could have been nothing less than very awkward for Abraham to explain to his father and his relatives why he took the case and argued in favor of the slaveholder.

Before Abraham left to take his seat in the 30th Congress on December 6, 1847, he gave Thomas four notes for legal fees for cases in Coles County.[114]

On December 13, 1847, Daniel W. Johnston was born to John and Mary, another mouth for Thomas to help feed and clothe and care for.

As the year waned, Charleston newspapers carried the text of a speech Abraham made in Congress on December 22. Following the chagrin of Abraham defending a slaveowner in Charleston, Thomas now listened as Abraham was ridiculed for his "Spot Resolutions" speech which was taken as opposition to the troops fighting in the war. John Hanks was in the war from Coles County. As the year closed, Abraham's family was torn between pride and love on the one hand and chagrin and angst on the other. Abraham's ill-timed and poorly received speech cost the Whigs the 7th District seat in Congress in the 1848 election.

1848 – 1850

Thomas gained another great-grandchild in 1848 with the birth of Zachariah T. Dowling to Thomas and Sarah Dowling.

The year turned out to be tumultuous. The Dred Scott case was decided by the Supreme Court, ending with a disgraceful decision by highly pro-slavery Chief Justice Taney, tearing the country apart and strengthening the traitorous hands of those who would lead the push for Southern victory.

The Fall of the year brought presidential elections with Zachary Taylor winning for the Whigs. Coles County went with the Whigs as it did in every national election during the time Thomas lived there. The close of the year saw Abraham back in

---

[114] Charles H. Coleman. *Abraham Lincoln and Coles County, Illinois*, page 66.

Washington to finish out his term in Congress. Thomas wrote to Abraham on December 7.

Dear Son.

I will inform you I and the old woman is in the best health at this time and so is all of the relations at present. I believe I enjoy as good health at this time as I have for many years past and I hope these few lines will find you enjoying the same state of health, I was greatly in hopes that you would have come a past here on your way to Washington as I wished to see you, but as you failed to come a past, I am compelled to make a request by letter to you for the loan of twenty dollars, which sum I am compelled to raise, or my land will be sold. I have begged time till I could write to you to send me that amount of money by letter. Send it to me if you can, for neither I nor Johnston can raise it for we have nothing that will bring money. I do expect you will think strange at this request, for that much money & it was equally as strange to me & John when I was called on for it not long since for it was an old transcript of about eight years standing, that we thought was paid long ago & still think so, but we have lost the receipt if we ever had one, & all, the Plaintiff & officers denies it ever being paid so we have to pay again and I know you can't appreciate the reluctance that I have made this request of you for money but I am compelled to do so & I hope you will grant it, & excuse me for so doing and I am in hopes I will be able to make you recompense for all of your favors. I suppose it would be of satisfaction to you to know how I have disposed of them notes you gave me, the one on James Gill I got the money for & the one Robert Mattison I tried to sell it for $15 in cash and couldn't do it. So James M. Miller offered John twenty dollars in goods at his trade prices & Monroe advised him to take it, so he sold it to him without recourse on any body & the two small notes we are likely not to do much with, but I am glad that I have lived to see another Whig President elected & hope live to see monarcha or Locofoco *principals crumble to dust. Be of good cheer for you are on a good cause and I think old Zak will make all things right. We have raised this summer as much as fifty bushels of corn to the acre & our wheat was very good. Your father in haste.*

Thomas Lincoln[115]

Thomas does not fully explain how the $20 debt came about. His finances were in such a place he could not get $20 together to pay. Abraham replied on December 24. Abraham lightly chastised Thomas but does not use harsh criticism. He gladly sent the money.

My dear father:

Your letter of the 7th was received night before last. I very cheerfully send you the twenty dollars, which sum you say is necessary to save your land from sale. It is singular that you should have forgotten a judgment against you; and it is more singular that the plaintiff should have let you forget it so long, particularly as I suppose you have always had property enough to satisfy a judgment of that amount. Before you pay it, it would be well to be sure you have not paid it; or, at least, that you cannot prove you have paid it. Give my love to Mother, and all the connections. Affectionately your son.

A. Lincoln[116]

John Johnston had included a letter from himself to Abraham with the letter he penned for Thomas. Abraham responded to John when he responded with money to his father. It is easy to tell from the context of Abraham's response to John as to where Abraham believed the problem with Thomas' finances lay.

---

[115] Charles H. Coleman. *Abraham Lincoln and Coles County, Illinois*, page p73. Thomas' letter to Abraham is dated from Coles County on December 7, 1848. John Johnston penned the letter for Thomas. Some spelling was corrected for ease of reading.

[116] Roy P. Basler. *The Collected Works of Abraham Lincoln*, volume 2, page 15. The letter was from Abraham Lincoln to his father, Thomas Lincoln, dated from Washington, D.C. December 24, 1848.

Dear Brother Lincoln:

I owe seventy or eighty dollars and I cannot pay, as I have neither cash nor property. I am dunned and dodged to death by creditors. So I am most tired of living, and I would almost swap my place in Heaven for that much money.

Now you think little of this, for you never had the trial, but Abe, I would rather live on bread and water than to have men always dunning me. I will pay you interest on money you send me. I could raise the money to repay you in three years. I could raise a calf and a pig of my own, for now my sons can do nearly as much work in a crop as a man.

I candidly would rather never own a foot of land than to not pay my debts, nor leave any debts to my children. Indeed, I would rather give possession now than to live here and have men a watching me to see if I had something the law would take.

Your brother,

John D. Johnston[117]

Abraham's response:

Dear Johnston:

Your request for eighty dollars, I do not think it best, to comply with now. At the various times when I have helped you a little, you have said to me ``We can get along very well now'' but in a very short time I find you in the same difficulty again. Now this can only happen by some defect in your conduct. What that defect is I think I know. You are not lazy, and still you are an idler. I doubt whether since I saw you, you have done a good whole day's work in any one day. You do not very much dislike to work; and

---

[117] Lincoln Log Cabin. www.lincolnlogcabin.org/education-kits/Abraham-Lincoln_Lesson-Plans/Lesson-1.pdf. The letter from John Johnston to Abraham Lincoln is dated from Coles County on December 7, 1848.

still you do not work much, merely because it does not seem to you that you could get much for it. This habit of uselessly wasting time, is the whole difficulty; and it is vastly important to you, and still more so to your children that you should break this habit. It is more important to them, because they have longer to live, and can keep out of an idle habit before they are in it; easier than they can get out after they are in.

You are now in need of some ready money; and what I propose is, that you shall go to work, "tooth and nails" for somebody who will give you money for it. Let father and your boys take charge of things at home - prepare for a crop, and make the crop; and you go to work for the best money wages, or in discharge of any debt you owe, that you can get. And to secure you a fair reward for your labor, I now promise you, that for every dollar you will, between this and the first of next May, get for your own labor, either in money, or in your own indebtedness, I will then give you one other dollar. By this, if you hire yourself at ten dollars a month, from me you will get ten more, making twenty dollars a month for your work. In this, I do not mean you shall go off to St. Louis, or the lead mines, or the gold mines, in California, but I mean for you to go at it for the best wages you can get close to home in Coles county. Now if you will do this, you will soon be out of debt, and what is better, you will have a habit that will keep you from getting in debt again. But if I should now clear you out, next year you will be just as deep in as ever. You say you would almost give your place in Heaven for $70 or $80. Then you value your place in Heaven very cheaply for I am sure you can with the offer I make you get the seventy or eighty dollars for four or five months work. You say if I furnish you the money you will deed me the land, and, if you don't pay the money back, you will deliver possession. Nonsense! If you can't now live with the land, how will you then live without it? You have always been [kind] to me, and I do not now mean to *be unkind to you. On the contrary, if you will but follow my advice, you will find it worth more than eight times eighty dollars to you. Affectionately Your brother,*

A. Lincoln[118]

These letters are very clear and to the point. Abraham viewed John as the problem underlying the financial issues. Interesting is John's note on land being offered as surety. Abraham does not dispute John's statement but there is no record of John owning any land. He was living on Thomas' land, in Thomas' cabin. He did not have his own place. Perhaps John was speaking of his share of the inheritance on Thomas' land. The question remains open.

During the final two years of Thomas' life, his family grew and also experienced death. In 1849 a grandson was added to the family with the birth of Theophilus Hanks to Dennis and Betsy. A grandson was lost on July 5, 1849 with the death of Daniel Johnston. A great-grandson was added to the family as Harriet and Augustus Chapman had their first child, Robert Newton Chapman, and a great-granddaughter was added with Alice Shoaff born to James and Nancy Shoaff, their second child.

Thomas had wealth in a large family that loved him dearly. When he turned 72 in January of 1850, he was the patriarch of the third largest household in Coles County. He was in the 98th percentile for age, one of the oldest people in the county.[119] At that age, that he could maintain such a large household speaks well of his effort, but it does not mean he was a success. The many years he spent successfully in Kentucky and Indiana are overshadowed by his final years in Illinois.

John Johnston lived with Thomas with his five sons, sons on whom he bragged to Abraham about their ability to work the fields. Yet the family was tilling and planting only 40 of the 120 acres available to them. Some report the number of tilled acres even lower. The 1850 census lists Thomas' farm as valued at $100

---

[118] Roy P. Basler. *The Collected Works of Abraham Lincoln*, volume 2, pages 15-16. Letter from Abraham Lincoln to John Johnston, dated from Washington, D.C. on December 24, 1848 and included with his letter to his father on the same date.
[119] Kenneth J. Winkle. *The Young Eagle*, page 144.

for the 80 acres in his name. He had dropped a long way from Kentucky and Indiana where he was doing better than most of his neighbors. In Illinois in 1850, 79% of his neighbors were doing better than Thomas.[120] Even at that low level, all is not dreary in the 1850 census. Thomas is listed as having two horses, two milk cows, sixteen sheep, and twenty pigs. His farm had produced four hundred bushels of Indian corn, one hundred bushels of oats, twenty-five pounds of wool, twenty bushels of Irish potatoes, one hundred and fifty pounds of butter, and four tons of hay.[121]

Thomas maintained a habit of rising early, building up the fire in the fireplace, and going out to grub the fields until breakfast. He was stooped with age and had a stepson and grandsons in the house, but he could not gain on life as he did when he was younger, when he was not burdened with a family living off his efforts and contributing little. With his declining health, there was little more he could do.

February 1850 brought news of the death of Edward Baker Lincoln in Springfield on the first of the month. In September, as Thomas' health failed and death became more apparent for him, Mary Barker Johnston died a half hour before sundown on the 21st.

The year closed with the celebration of another grandson. William Wallace Lincoln was born to Abraham and Mary on December 21.

Death & Burial

When Thomas' health began the final decline, he reached out to Abraham and Mary. He sensed he was facing his finish in this world and preparing for the next. He wanted to see and talk with Abraham. Thomas loved all his family, but Abraham was his only living child by blood. There had been some false alarms sent to Abraham regarding his father's condition.

In May of 1849, John Johnston sent word that Thomas was nearing death.

---

[120] Michael Burlingame. *Abraham Lincoln: A Life. Volume one*, page 8.
[121] Wayne C. Temple. *Thomas and Abraham Lincoln As Farmers*, page 28.

Dear Brother,

I haste to inform you that father is yet alive and that is all and he craves to see you all the time and he wonts you to come if you are able to git here, for you are his only child that is of his own flesh and blood and it is nothing more than nature for him to crave to see you. He says he has almost despaired of seeing you, and he wants you to prepare to meet him in the unknown world, or in heaven, for he thinks that our Savior has a crown of glory, prepared for him. I write this with a bursting heart. I came to town for the doctor, and I want you to make an effort [to] come, if you are able to get here, and he wants me to tell your wife that he Loves her and wants her to prepare to meet him at our Savior's feet. We are all well. Your brother in haste,

J. D. Johnston[122]

Thomas, as one of the oldest people in Coles Ccounty did not know how soon death would take him. With the evangelistic emphasis of the Restoration Movement, conveying the gospel message to Abraham was in front of his mind. He was not so much concerned with his own death as with his son's future. That sentiment, expressed in John's letter to Abraham, speaks of Thomas' love for Abraham.

John, knowing his own word with Abraham was doubted because of the ways he had tried to manipulate money out of Abraham in the past, went to Augustus Chapman and persuaded him to also write Abraham and reinforce the message that Abraham should come.

Mr. Lincoln,

Sir, at the special request of J. D. Johnston I write you to inform you of the very severe illness of your Father. He was atacken [sic] with a lesion of the heart some time

---

[122] David C. Mearns. *The Lincoln Papers, Volume 1*, page 179. Letter from John Johnston to Abraham Lincoln dated from Charleston on May 25, 1849. Spelling corrected for ease of reading.

since and for the last four days has been getting much worse and at this time he is very low indeed. He is very anxious to see you before he dies and I am told that his cries for you for the last few days are truly heart-rendering. He wished you to come and see him instantly if you possibly can. If you are fearful of leaving your family on account of the children and can bring them with you, we would be very glad for you to bring them with you. The health of our place is excellent and Harriett and I would be very glad to have [you] bring them with you as we are very comfortably fixed and will do all we can to render your stay agreeable. Yours in great Haste,

A. H. Chapman[123]

Augustus Chapman, Dennis Hanks son-in-law, was very familiar with the circumstances of the Lincoln household in Springfield, his wife having stayed with them earlier in life. He understood Mary's objections to Thomas. In his letter, he does his best to assure Abraham that the Chapman home is suitable to entertain Abraham's children and bring them to meet their grandfather before he died. That effort failed. Mary did not go to Charleston. The Lincoln children did not leave Springfield.

What becomes apparent in Chapman's next letter is John Johnston was not held in high regard. Chapman felt used and that he in turn had used Abraham. Chapman found out Thomas' condition was not so dire or dramatic as John had led him to believe.

Mr. Lincoln,

Sir on Friday last I wrote you at the request of J. D. Johnson which I suppose has given you considerable unnecessary trouble on account of your father. I was fearful at the time I wrote to you that I was giving you considerable unnecessary uneasiness and so told Johnston, but he said that it was not so. I wished him to

---

[123] David C. Mearns. *The Lincoln Papers, Volume 1*, pages 178-179. Letter from Augustus Chapman to Abraham Lincoln dated May 24, 1849 from Charleston.

wait until Allison returned from your father's but he would not consent on the grounds that if he did not send you a letter then that he would not have the opportunity of writing until the present mail. So I wrote you at his earnest solicitation and he had the letter mailed instantly. I now have the pleasure of informing you that your father is not only out of all danger but that he is not afflicted with a disease of the heart as Dr. Allison had supposed all along but that his illness arose from an unusual amount of matter being confined in his Lungs which occasioned the oppression of the heart and led Allison to suppose this disease was one of the heart. Yesterday and today he has raised a large amount of matter or flehm from lungs and is almost entirely relieved and will doubtless be well in a short time. I hope you will receive this before you get off for this place if you are intending to come here as I would be very sorry indeed for my last letter to cause you to leave any important business that you might have on hand and that required your immediate attention. I hope you will forgive me for writing you as I did without knowing what I was about and promise for the future to be more careful. Harriett sends Her love to you all.

Respectfully yours

A. H. Chapman[124]

Chapman's second letter did not reach Abraham before he had left for Goosenest Prairie. Abraham was indeed in the midst of important business. Not only was he busy in his law practice, he was pursuing an appointment from President Taylor to the General Land Office. It was not a convenient time for him to be away from business. Still, the word he received was his father was dying and family trumped business. He set things in order, planned as best he could, and left Springfield for Goosenest Prairie. He arrived at his father's home on May 29 and stayed three days to visit and help out.

---

[124] David C. Mearns. *The Lincoln Papers, Volume 1*, page 180. Letter from Augustus Chapman to Abraham Lincoln dated May 28, 1849 from Charleston.

Thomas' health improved for a time but in 1850, it took another turn for the worse. This time there was no recovery. Friends and family came to the home to pay their respect and visit with Thomas before he died. A neighbor, Jane Fury, made a habit of going frequently and reading the Bible to Thomas. Thomas loved to read his Bible, but his sickness combined with his poor eyesight made that difficult, if not impossible. Mrs. Fury did Thomas and the family a great kindness.[125]

With Abraham's normal routine, he would have visited the family when the Fall sessions of circuit court brought him near Thomas' home. It is possible, though the letter exchanges of 1849 have confused the issue, that Abraham visited as Thomas' health worsened. Augustus Chapman indicated Abraham was with Thomas a short time before Thomas died.[126] John Hall gave a similar statement to Eleanor Gridley.

> *Grandpap Lincoln was taken with smotherin' spells and we sent for Uncle Abe. He come up and stayed a few days and then his father got better. Uncle Abe went back, but he'd hardly got home before Grandpap Lincoln went off mighty sudden like. He died of heart disease, and we sent for Uncle Abe, but he was so busy with important business he couldn't come up to the funeral. Shortly afterwards he come up to straighten out the property.[127]*

The time between that final visit and Thomas's death was probably longer than John Hall makes it appear. John Johnston wrote at least two letters to Abraham following that visit, letters that Abraham ignored until he received a letter from Harriet Chapman.

Dear Brother,

On the day before yesterday I received a letter from Harriett, written at Greenup. She says she has just

---

125 Charles H. Coleman. *Abraham Lincoln and Coles County, Illinois*, page 132.
126 Douglas L. Wilson and Rodney O. Davis. *Herndon's Informants*, page 103. Statement by A. H. Chapman dated September 8, 1865.
127 Eleanor Gridley. *The Story of Abraham Lincoln or The Journey from the Long Cabin to the White House*, page 174.

returned from your house; and that Father is very low and will hardly recover. She also says you have written me two letters; and that [although] you do not expect me to come now, you wonder that I do not write. I received both your letters, and although I have not answered them, it is not because I have forgotten them, or been uninterested about them---but because it appeared to me I could write nothing which could do any good. You already know I desire that neither Father or Mother shall be in want of any comfort either in health or sickness while they live; and I feel sure you have not failed to use my name, if necessary, to procure a doctor, or anything else for Father in his present sickness. My business is such that I could hardly leave home now, if it were not, as it is, that my own wife is sick-abed. (It is a case of baby-sickness, and I suppose is not dangerous.) I sincerely hope Father may yet recover his health; but at all events tell him to remember to call upon, and confide in, our great, and good, and merciful Maker; who will not turn away from him in any extremity. He notes the fall of a sparrow, and numbers the hairs of our heads; and He will not forget the dying man, who puts his trust in Him. Say to him that if we could meet now, it is doubtful whether it would not be more painful than pleasant; but that if it be his lot to go now, he will soon have a joyous [meeting] with many loved ones gone before; and where the rest of us, through the help of God, hope ere-long to join them.

Write me again when you receive this. Affectionately

A. Lincoln[128]

This letter has been used over time to portray Abraham with harbored disdain for Thomas. Taken in context of history, it is just the letter of a son who has already taken final leave of his father. In January of 1851, Mary was between six and seven months

---

[128] Roy P. Basler. *The Collected Works of Abraham Lincoln*, volume 2, pages 96-97. Taken from a letter from Abraham Lincoln to his stepbrother John D. Johnston dated from Springfield on January 12, 1851.

pregnant. Abraham leaving home, again, to visit Goosenest Prairie was not feasible in that day and time or for the relationship with his sometimes-fiery bride.

What was said between Thomas and Abraham on Abraham's final visit in 1850 is not recorded. In his letter, Abraham has John assure Thomas that he is ready to meet him in Heaven. Those words would have been a great comfort to Thomas.

Thomas died on January 17, 1851 at age 73 years and 11 days. Cause of death was disease of the kidneys.[129]

Thomas' funeral was conducted at the Lincoln cabin. Thomas Goodman, the Disciples of Christ church pastor from Charleston, preached the service. Thomas attended Goodman's church in Charleston. (The Disciples of Christ was one of the denominations formed from the Restoration Movement.) Pastor Goodman stood in the door of the cabin. The women and children sat inside. The men stood outside. Goodman had only good things to say. He noted Thomas as always truthful, conscientious, and religious.[130]

Thomas was buried in the Gordon Graveyard, now often referred to as the Thomas Lincoln Cemetery. The graveyard was the burial ground at a small country church. The grave was marked with a small boulder and a mound of earth until 1876.

Thomas "Tad" Lincoln was born to Abraham and Mary on April 4, 1851. Abraham named his new son after his recently lost father.[131] With Mary no longer pregnant, Abraham followed the court circuit in May and stopped to visit with his family. While visiting, Abraham picked up Thomas' family Bible and entered Thomas' date of death.[132]

There is a story that when Abraham visited his father's grave before going to Washington to assume the office of President, that he carved the initials "T. L." into an oak board and pushed the

---

[129] Douglas L. Wilson and Rodney O. Davis. *Herndon's Informants*, page 103. Statement by A. H. Chapman dated September 8, 1865.

[130] Charles H. Coleman. *Abraham Lincoln and Coles County, Illinois*, page 133.

[131] Mary would confirm Tad being named after Thomas in a letter to Sarah Bush Lincoln. "Perhaps you know that our youngest boy, is named for your husband, Thomas Lincoln, this child, the idol of his father." Lincoln Financial Foundation Collection. "Mary Todd Lincoln's Letter to Her Mother-in-Law.

[132] Charles H. Coleman. *Abraham Lincoln and Coles County, Illinois*, page 133.

board into the ground at the head of the grave.[133] That tale appears more legend than fact. What did happen was that Abraham asked Augustus Chapman to find out the cost of a gravestone and to let him know. Abraham said he would send the inscription he wanted on the stone. With the coming of the war, the stone was never purchased, and the inscription Abraham wanted is unknown. Chapman reported that Abraham did not carve anything into any board. A board with the initials "T. E." was at the foot of a grave and the story grew from that.[134]

There has been pushback from some scholars saying that Abraham had never really talked about a headstone for his father's grave, that the story arose as a kind of cover to mask the poor relationship between father and son. That misconception about the truth was put to rest in a letter from Mary Lincoln to Sarah Bush Lincoln.

Mary wrote to Sarah, "My husband a few weeks before his death mentioned to me, that he intended that summer, paying proper respect to his father's grave, by a head & foot stone, with his name, age && and I propose very soon carrying out his intentions. It was not from want of affection for his father, as you are well aware, that it was not done, but his time was so greatly occupied always."[135] For whatever reason, Mary did not get around to having the headstone and footstone put up to fulfill Abraham's intention. Mary also noted there was no lack of affection for Thomas by Abraham and that Sarah already knew that as fact.

In 1876, a local Illinois poet, George Balch, began to fear that the grave, marked only with the boulder and mound of earth, would be lost to history. He penned a poem that gathered wide appeal and resulted in markers being placed at Thomas' grave.

---

[133] Douglas L. Wilson and Rodney O. Davis. *Herndon's Informants*, page 596. From a Jesse W. Weik interview with George B. Balch thought to have occurred in 1885.

[134] William Le Baron Jr. *The History of Coles County Illinois*, pages 223-224.

[135] Lincoln Financial Foundation Colletion. *Mary Todd Lincoln's Letter to Her Mother-in-Law*. December 19, 1867.

THE GRAVE OF THE FATHER OF ABRAHAM LINCOLN

In a low, sweet vale, by a murmuring rill,
The pioneer's ashes are sleeping;
Where the white marble slabs so lonely and still,
In silence their vigils are keeping.

On their sad, lonely faces, are words of fame,
But none of them speak of his glory;
When the pioneer died, his age and his name,
No monument whispers the story.

No myrtle, nor ivy, nor hyacinth blows
O'er the lonely grave where they laid him;
No cedar, nor holly, nor almond tree grows
Near the plebeian's grave to shade him.

Bright evergreens wave o'er many a grave,
O'er some bow the sad weeping willow;
But no willow trees bow, nor evergreens wave
Where the pioneer sleeps on his pillow.

While some are inhumed with honors of State,
And laid beneath temples to molder,
The grave of the father of Lincoln, the great,
Is known by a hillock and boulder.

Let him take his lone sleep, and quietly rest,
With naught to disturb or awake him,
When the angels shall come to gather the blest,
"To Abraham's bosom, they'll take him." [136]

The Goosenest Cabin

Thomas' two-room Goosenest Prairie cabin was lost to history. It was allowed to become rundown over the years and was then picked up as an oddity item, disassembled, and shipped to Chicago for display at the 1893 World's Columbian Exposition. What happened to the cabin following the Exposition is unknown.

---

[136] George B. Balch. *Poems*, pages 111-112.

Thomas Lincoln's Legacy

In his annual message to Congress in December 1862, President Lincoln said, "Fellow-citizens, we cannot escape history…No personal significance, or insignificance, can spare one or another of us. The fiery trial through which we pass, will light us down, in honor or dishonor, to the latest generation."[1] His words apply to all of us. History cannot be escaped.

The traditional story of Thomas Lincoln was built on making him less in order for Abraham to be seen as overcoming great odds to become the United States' greatest president. It was a common literary device in biography and fiction in the late 1800's and early 1900's. Thomas failing to advance and change with the times fed the image of him being backward and ignorant, shiftless and lazy. His last years were spent in a cabin that suited pioneers but such a cabin appeared poor and uncouth in populated areas that were developing and growing with the times.

Thomas loved living on the frontier. He loved making his own way with the help of neighbors, family, and friends. He loved helping others. Thomas' life preference was simple. He needed little and he was content with little. He took what life threw at him, accepted it, and was satisfied.

Thomas approached life in a way most people find strange. He believed strongly in a fatalistic predestination. Fate was set. What would come would come. For Thomas, God set the course of the world and of each person in his creation. No one could thwart the will of God. Thomas knew his Bible well. He read where Apostle Paul talked of having plenty and being in need. He took to heart the words Paul wrote to the Philippians. "Not that I speak in respect of want: for I have learned, in whatsoever state I am, therewith to be content. I know both how to be abased, and I know how to abound: every where and in all things I am instructed both to be full and to be hungry, both to abound and to suffer need. I can do all things through Christ which strengtheneth me."[2]

---

[1] Roy P. Basler. Editor. *The Collected Works of Abraham Lincoln*, volume 5, page 537.

[2] Philippians 4:11-13. King James Version (KJV).

The traditional Thomas of early Lincoln biography (and even of some newer biography) is not the Thomas Lincoln of history. Thomas' life is much more complex than portrayed, with success and failure, love and loss, accomplishment and disappointment. Lincoln history no longer needs to debase the father to honor the son. Abraham Lincoln would be appalled and angered if he knew what traditional history said about his father and mother.

> *History has not treated Thomas Lincoln fairly. He is normally presented as a lowly, ignorant rube who was lazy, unambitious, and resistant to the young Abe's penchant for reading. Several biographies of Lincoln use his father as the bogeyman against whom Lincoln vigorously rebelled. The facts, however, say otherwise. Tom Lincoln was known as a solid, upstanding, honest man who provided for his family even in hard time.*[3]

The real Thomas Lincoln of history is an intelligent man. Carpenter, cabinetmaker, furniture maker, wheelwright, cooper, mechanic, blacksmith, farmer, hunter – Thomas had all these skills. He was meticulously honest, very religious, generous to a fault, and kind. He loved laughter, humor, discussion, storytelling, jokes, and pranks. He was a peacemaker and arbitrator. He was physically strong and capable of winning a fight when needed.

An early history of Spencer County sums up Thomas in Indiana. "Thomas Lincoln is remembered as an industrious carpenter and farmer, as a man of good brain and no culture, a quiet, unassuming man."[4] Thomas worked hard and had a good mind, but he never cared for fashion or manners or culture beyond what was standard for a pioneer. His family did not have stylish clothes, but they never lacked clothing. His table lacked fancy fare, but it was never empty.

Thomas was a church member and a respected citizen of his community. He served on juries, as constable, and as jailer. He took up arms for his state and country. He was an officer in the militia.

---

[3] Sara Gabbard. *Interview with Daid S. Reynolds*, page 5.
[4] Selwyn A. Brant and Weston A. Goodspeed. *History of Warrick, Spencer, and Perry Counties, Indiana*, page 274.

He bartered, traded, and conducted business. He was a businessman, a family man, and a friend. Thomas' life was a life very similar to the life of any other pioneer.

In early life, Thomas found success and was ahead of many, even most, in his communities, but his ambition was not strong. He had no thirst for power and fame. When life turned and times in Illinois became hard, his family was still fed and clothed. He stood by his friends and kept his word. He may have struggled to meet debt that came to him from his decisions to co-sign with John Johnston on ventures that were not thought out, but he always found a way to meet his obligations. At the end of his life, there were no known outstanding debts or encumberments.

Was Thomas Lincoln successful in life? In Kentucky and Indiana, the answer would be yes. Was he highly successful at achieving wealth? No. He was content with simple things and had no need or desire for a life in city society and culture. He was a pioneer and he never stopped being a pioneer, never stopped living like a pioneer. In Illinois, as the frontier became populated and was no longer the frontier, Thomas remained a pioneer. He fell behind the times and was content in doing so.

Is that success? No, not in the eyes of society. Thomas went from being among the best off in his county to being one of the poorest. He would not let go of his pioneer ways. Dennis Hanks moved to the city and learned the way of life in a changing world. Others in the family did the same. Thomas Lincoln and John Johnston lived in a world that was no longer reality for those around them and those around them looked down on them for that choice.

It is the state of these last years, the poor years, for which Thomas is remembered. History most often ignored the skills that sustained him and made him successful in his youth and middle adult years. History remembered the poverty and the backward, outdated lifestyle, not seeing the full tapestry that was Thomas Lincoln. It is now time to see Thomas for all he was and to understand he was a good man, a loved man, a happy man.

Thomas' legacy? The legacy for which he will have fame is his son. Abraham Lincoln was a storyteller, a gift and inheritance from his father. Abraham Lincoln knew how to bargain to get what he needed, a skill he learned from his father. Abraham

Lincoln was devoted to his family, just as his father before him. Abraham Lincoln was honest and just and fair, something else he learned from his father. There were many differences between father and son but the foundation on which Abraham Lincoln built his life was the foundation he received from Thomas.

Granddaughter Sarah Jane (Hanks) Dowling knew her grandfather and her Uncle Abraham. She saw what was happening in early Lincoln biography. She told one of those early biographers:

> *I don't want you to go away thinking so bad of Grandfather Lincoln. That's what us younger ones called Uncle Abe's father; and we called him Uncle Abe, though he was only father's second cousin. I reckon kinfolks counted for more in early days. I'm just tired of hearing Grandfather Lincoln abused. Everybody runs him down. Father never gave him credit for what he was. He made a good living, and I reckon he would have got something ahead if he hadn't been so generous. He had the old Virginia notion of hospitality – liked to see people sit up to the table and eat hearty, and there were always plenty of his relations and grandmother's willing to live on him. Uncle Abe got his honesty, and his clean notions of living and his kind heart from his father. Maybe the Hanks family was smarter, but some of them couldn't hold a candle to Grandfather Lincoln, when it came to morals. I've heard Grandmother Lincoln say, many a time, that he was kind and loving, and kept his word, and always paid his way, and never turned a dog from his door. You couldn't say that of every man....[5]*

No. You cannot say that for every man, but you can for Thomas Lincoln. Thomas was a warm-hearted man who loved well and was well loved. His name and reputation have suffered greatly over the years, but the truth of the man is that he left a powerful legacy for the world. His successes and failures guided

---

[5] Eleanor Atkinson. *The Boyhood of Lincoln*, pages 44-45. As told to Atkinson by Sarah Jane (Hanks) Lincoln.

the growing years of his son Abraham and Abraham guided the path of a nation torn in two by treason and slavery.

In 1934, a dedication service was held at Thomas' gravesite for the new ornamental fence surrounding it. John T. Thomas spoke briefly and simply at the service.

"Thomas Lincoln, we are gathered today to honor your memory as a worthy sire of a noble son."[6] "Your free spirit has gone forth to a fairer land and a fuller life. But you will ever walk among us and be an inspiration to us."[7]

---

[6] John T. Thomas. *Thomas Lincoln, Father of Abraham Lincoln*, page 1.
[7] John T. Thomas. *Thomas Lincoln, Father of Abraham Lincoln*, page 3.

Appendices

Abraham Lincoln's Ancestry Letters

In Abraham Lincoln's collected works are several letters from Lincoln to relatives telling what he knew about the family history. Unfortunately, we do not have a good record of the letters to which he is responding.

The letter show that Lincoln had a scanty knowledge of his family history. Thomas, through the early death of his father, was raised apart from the family and clearly had heard little of family history to pass on to his son.

> *"I was born Feb: 12th. 1809 in Hardin County, Kentucky. My father's name is Thomas; my grandfather's was Abraham, - the same of [sic] my own. My grandfather went from Rockingham County in Virginia, to Kentucky, about the year 1782; and, two years afterwards, was killed by the Indians. We have a vague tradition, that my great-grand father went from Pennsylvania to Virginia; and that he was a Quaker. Further back than this, I have never heard anything. It may do no harm to say that 'Abraham' and 'Mordecai' are common names in our family; while the name 'Levi' so common among the Lincolns of New England, I have not known in any instance among us."[1]*

> *"I have mentioned that my grandfather's name was Abraham. He had, as I think I have heard, four brothers, Isaac, Jacob, Thomas, and John. He had three sons, Mordecai, Josiah, and Thomas, the last, my father. My uncle Mordecai had three sons, Abraham, James, and Mordecai. Uncle Josiah had several daughters, and an only son, Thomas. My father has an only child, myself, of course. This is all I know certainly on the subject of names; it is, however, my father's understanding that, Abraham. Mordecai, and Thomas are old family names of ours. The*

---

[1] Roy P. Basler. *The Collected Works of Abraham Lincoln*, volume 1, page 456. Taken from a letter from Abraham Lincoln to Solomon Lincoln dated March 6, 1848.

reason I did not mention Thomas as a family name in my other letter was because it is so very common a name, as to prove but little, if anything, in the way of identification. Since I wrote you, it occurred to me to enquire of Gov. McDowell, who represents the district in Virginia, including Rockingham, whether he knew persons of our name there. He informs he does; though none very intimately except one, an old man by the Christian name of David. That he is of our family I have no doubt."[2]

"Last evening, I was much gratified by receiving and reading your letter of the 30th of March. There is no longer any doubt that your uncle Abraham, and my grandfather was the same man. His family did reside in Washington County, Kentucky, just as you say you found them in 1801 or 2. The oldest son, uncle Mordecai, near twenty years ago, removed from Kentucky to Hancock County, Illinois, where within a year or two afterwards, he died, and where his surviving children now live. His two sons there now are Abraham & Mordecai; and their Post-office is 'La Harpe.' Uncle Josiah, farther back than my recollection, went from Kentucky to Blue River in Indiana. I have not heard from him in a great many years, and whether he is still living I cannot say. My recollection of what I have heard is, that he has several daughters & only one son, Thomas. Their Post-office is 'Corydon, Harrison County, Indiana.' My father, Thomas, is still living, in Coles county Illinois, being in the 71st. year of his age. His Post-office is Charleston, Coles co. Ill. I am his only child. I am now in my 40th. year; and I live in Springfield, Sangamon county, Illinois. This is the outline of my grandfather's family in the West. I think my father has told me that grandfather had four brothers, Isaac, Jacob, John and Thomas. Is that correct? And which of them was your father? Are any of them alive? I am quite sure that Isaac resided on

---

[2] Roy P. Basler. *The Collected Works of Abraham Lincoln*, volume 1, page 459. Taken from a letter from Abraham Lincoln to Solomon Lincoln dated March 24, 1848.

Watauga, near a point where Virginia and Tennessee join; and that he has been dead more than twenty, perhaps thirty, years. Also, that Thomas removed to Kentucky, near Lexington, where he died a good while ago. What was your grandfather's Christian name? Was he or not, a Quaker? About what time did he emigrate from Berks County, Pa. to Virginia? Do you know anything of your family (or rather I may now say, our family) farther back than your grandfather? If it be not too much trouble to you, I shall be much pleased to hear from you again. Be assured I will call on you, should anything ever bring me near you."[3]

"On yesterday I had the pleasure of receiving your letter of the 16th of March. From what you say there can be no doubt that you and I are of the same family. The history of your family, as you give it, is precisely what I have always heard, and partly know, of my own. As you have supposed, I am the grandson of your uncle Abraham; and the story of his death by the Indians, and of Uncle Mordecai, then fourteen years old, killing one of the Indians, is the legend more strongly than all others imprinted upon my mind and memory. I am the son of grandfather's youngest son, Thomas. I have often heard my father speak of his uncle Isaac residing at Watauga (I think), near where the then States of Virginia, North Carolina, and Tennessee join, - you seem now to be some hundred miles or so west of that. I often saw Uncle Mordecai, and Uncle Josiah but once in my life; but I never resided near either of them. Uncle Mordecai died in 1831 or 2, in Hancock County, Illinois, where he had then recently removed from Kentucky, and where his children had also removed, and still reside, as I understand. Whether Uncle Josiah is dead or living, I cannot tell, not having heard from him for more than twenty years. When

---

[3] Roy P. Basler. *The Collected Works of Abraham Lincoln*, volume 1, pages 461-462. Taken from a letter from Abraham Lincoln to David Lincoln dated April 2, 1848.

I last heard of him, he was living on Big Blue River, in Indiana (Harrison Co., I think), and where he had resided ever since before the beginning of my recollection. My father (Thomas) died the 17th of January 1851, in Coles County, Illinois, where he had resided twenty years. I am his only child. I have resided here, and here-abouts, twenty-three years. I am forty-five years of age, and have a wife and three children, the oldest eleven years. My wife was born and raised at Lexington, Kentucky; and my connection with her has sometimes taken me there, where I have heard the older people of her relations speak of your uncle Thomas and his family. He is dead long ago, and his descendants have gone to some part of Missouri, as I recollect what I was told. When I was at Washington in 1848, I got up a correspondence with David Lincoln, residing at Sparta, Rockingham County, Virginia, who, like yourself, was a first cousin of my father; but I forget, if he informed me, which of my grandfather's brothers was his father. With Col. Crozier, of whom you speak, I formed quite an intimate acquaintance, for a short one, while at Washington; and when you meet him again, I will thank you to present him my respects. Your present governor, Andrew Johnson, was also at Washington while I was; and he told me of there being people of the name of Lincoln in Carter County, I think. I can no longer claim to be a young man myself; but I infer that, as you are of the same generation as my father, you are some older. I shall be very glad to hear from you again."[4]

"You are a little mistaken. My grand-father did not go from Berks Co. Pa; but, as I learn, his ancestors did, some time before his birth. He was born in Rockingham Co Va; went from there to Kentucky, and there was killed by Indians about 1784. That the family originally came from Berks, I learned a dozen years ago, by letter, from one of

---

[4] Roy P. Basler. *The Collected Works of Abraham Lincoln*, volume 2, pages 217-218. Taken from a letter from Abraham Lincoln to Jesse Lincoln dated April 1, 1854.

them, then residing at Sparta, Rockingham Co. Va. His name was David Lincoln. I remember, long ago, seeing Austin Lincoln, & Davis Lincoln, said to be sons of Hannaniah, or Annaniah Lincoln, who was said to have been a cousin of my grand-father. I have no doubt you and I are distantly related. I should think from what you say, that you and my father were second cousins. ¶ I shall be glad to hear from you at any time."[5]

"Your letter informs me that your maiden name was Crume, and that you were raised in Washington County, Kentucky, by which I infer that an uncle of mine by marriage was a relative of yours. Nearly, or quite sixty years ago, Ralph Crume married Mary Lincoln, a sister of my father, in Washington county, Kentucky."[6]

---

[5] Roy P. Basler. *The Collected Works of Abraham Lincoln*, volume 4, page 37. Taken from a letter from Abraham Lincoln to Richard V. B. Lincoln dated April 6, 1860.

[6] Roy P. Basler. *The Collected Works of Abraham Lincoln*, volume 5, page 57. Taken from a letter from Abraham Lincoln to Susannah Weathers dated December 4, 1861.

Autobiography of Abraham Lincoln

Lincoln's autobiography was written in June 1860 for John Locke Scripps and used for campaign purposes.

"Abraham Lincoln was born Feb. 12, 1809, then in Hardin, now in the more recently formed county of Larue, Kentucky. His father, Thomas, & grandfather, Abraham, were born in Rockingham county Virginia, whither their ancestors had come from Berks county Pennsylvania. His lineage has been traced no farther back than this. The family were originally Quakers, though in later times they have fallen away from the peculiar habits of that people. The grandfather Abraham had four brothers – Isaac Jacob, John & Thomas. So far as known, the descendants of Jacob and John are still in Virginia. Isaac went to a place near where Virginia, North Carolina, and Tennessee, join; and his descendants are in that region. Thomas came to Kentucky, and after many years, died there, whence his descendants went to Missouri. Abraham, grandfather of the subject of this sketch, came to Kentucky, and was killed by Indians about the year 1784. He left a widow, three sons and two daughters. The eldest son, Mordecai, remained in Kentucky till late in life, when he removed to Hancock County, Illinois, where soon after he died, and where several of his descendants still reside. The second son, Josiah, removed at an early day to a place on Blue River, now within Harrison [Hancock] county, Indiana; but no recent information of him, or his family, has been obtained. The eldest sister, Mary, married Ralph Crume and some of her descendants are now known to be in Breckenridge county Kentucky. The second sister, Nancy, married William Brumfield, and her family are not known to have left Kentucky, but there is no recent information from them. Thomas, the youngest son, and father of the present subject, by the early death of his father, and very narrow circumstances of his mother, even in childhood was a wandering laboring boy, and grew up literally without education. He never did more in the way of writing than to bunglingly sign his own name. Before he was grown, he passed one year as a hired hand with his uncle Isaac on Watauga, a branch of the Holsteen [Holston] River. Getting back into Kentucky, and having reached his 28th year, he married Nancy Hanks – mother of the present subject – in the year 1806. She also was born in Virginia; and relatives of hers of the name of Hanks, and of other names, now reside in Coles, in Macon, and in Adams counties, Illinois, and also in Iowa. The present subject has no brother or sister of the whole or half blood. He had a sister, older than himself, who was grown and married, but died many years ago, leaving no child. Also, a brother, younger than himself, who died in infancy. Before leaving Kentucky he and his sister were sent for short periods, to A.B.C. schools, the first kept by Zachariah Riney, and the second by Caleb Hazel.

"At this time his father resided on Knob-creek, on the road from Bardstown Ky. to Nashville Tenn. at a point three, or three and a half miles South or South-West of Atherton's ferry on the Rolling Fork. From this place he removed to what is now Spencer county Indiana, in the autumn of 1816, A. then being in his eighth year. This removal was partly on account of slavery; but chiefly on account of the difficulty in land titles in Ky. He settled in an unbroken forest; and the clearing away of surplus wood was the great task ahead. A. though very young, was large of his age, and had an axe put into his hands at once; and from that till within his twenty-third year, he was almost constantly handling that most useful instrument---less, of course, in plowing and harvesting seasons. At this place A. took an early start as a hunter, which was never much improved afterwards. (A few days before the completion of his eighth year, in the absence of his father, a flock of wild turkeys approached the new log-cabin, and A. with a rifle gun, standing inside, shot through a crack, and killed one of them. He has never since pulled a trigger on any larger game.) In the autumn of 1818, his mother died; and a year afterwards his father married Mrs. Sally Johnston, at Elizabeth-Town, Ky---a widow, with three children of her first marriage. She proved a good and kind mother to A. and is still living in Coles Co. Illinois. There were no children of this second marriage. His father's residence continued at the same place in Indiana, till 1830. While here A. went to A.B.C. schools by littles, kept successively by Andrew Crawford, Sweeney, and Azel W. Dorsey. He does not remember any other. The family of Mr. Dorsey now resides in Schuyler Co. Illinois. A. now thinks that the aggregate of all his schooling did not amount to one year. He was never in a college or Academy as a student; and never inside of a college or academy building till since he had a law-license. What he has in the way of education, he has picked up. After he was twenty-three, and had separated from his father, he studied English grammar, imperfectly of course, but so as to speak and write as well as he now does. He studied and nearly mastered the Six-books of Euclid, since he was a member of Congress. He regrets his want of education and does what he can to supply the want. In his tenth year he was kicked by a horse, and apparently killed for a time. When he was nineteen, still residing in Indiana, he made his first trip upon a flat-boat to New-Orleans. He was a hired hand merely; and he and a son of the owner, without other assistance, made the trip. The nature of part of the cargo-load, as it was called – made it necessary for them to linger and trade along the Sugar coast---and one night they were attacked by seven Negroes with intent to kill and rob them. They were hurt some in the melee, but succeeded in driving the Negroes from the boat, and then 'cut cable' 'weighed anchor' and left.

"March 1st. 1830 – A. having just completed his 21st. year, his father and family, with the families of the two daughters and sons-in-law, of his step-mother, left the old homestead in Indiana, and came to Illinois. Their mode of conveyance was wagons drawn by ox-teams, or A. drove one of the teams. They reached the county of Macon and stopped there sometime within the same month of March. His father and family settled a new place on the North side of the Sangamon River, at the junction of the timberland and prairie, about ten miles Westerly from Decatur. Here they built a log-cabin, into which they removed, and made sufficient of rails to fence ten acres of ground, fenced and broke the ground, and raised a crop of sown corn upon it the same year. These are, or are supposed to be, the rails about which so much is being said just now, though they are far from being the first, or only rails ever made by A.

"The sons-in-law were temporarily settled at other places in the county. In the autumn all hands were greatly afflicted with ague and fever, to which they had not been used, and by which they were greatly discouraged---so much so that they determined on leaving the county. They remained however, through the succeeding winter, which was the winter of the very celebrated ``deep snow'' of Illinois. During that winter, A. together with his step-mother's son, John D. Johnston, and John Hanks, yet residing in Macon county, hired themselves to one Denton Offutt, to take a flat boat from Beardstown Illinois to New-Orleans; and for that purpose, were to join him – Offutt – at Springfield, Ills so soon as the snow should go off. When it did go off which was about the 1st. of March 1831 – the county was so flooded, as to make traveling by land impracticable; to obviate which difficulty the[y] purchased a large canoe and came down the Sangamon river in it. This is the time and the manner of A's first entrance into Sangamon County. They found Offutt at Springfield but learned from him that he had failed in getting a boat at Beardstown. This led to their hiring themselves to him at $12 per month, each; and getting the timber out of the trees and building a boat at old Sangamon Town on the Sangamon river, seven miles N.W. of Springfield, which boat they took to New-Orleans, substantially upon the old contract. It was in connection with this boat that occurred the ludicrous incident of sewing up the hog's eyes. Offutt bought thirty odd large fat live hogs but found difficulty in driving them from where [he] purchased them to the boat, and thereupon conceived the whim that he could sew up their eyes and drive them where he pleased. No sooner thought of than decided, he put his hands, including A. at the job, which they completed---all but the driving. In their blind condition they could not be driven out of the lot or field they were in. This expedient failing, they were tied and hauled on carts to the boat. It was near the Sangamon River, within what is now Menard County.

"During this boat enterprise acquaintance with Offutt, who was previously an entire stranger, he conceived a liking for A. and believing he could turn him to account, he contracted with him to act as clerk for him, on his return from New-Orleans, in charge of a store and Mill at New-Salem, then in Sangamon, now in Menard County. Hanks had not gone to New-Orleans, but having a family, and being likely to be detained from home longer than at first expected, had turned back from St. Louis. He is the same John Hanks who now engineers the ``rail enterprise'' at Decatur; and is a first cousin to A's mother. A's father, with his own family & others mentioned, had, in pursuance of their intention, removed from Macon to Coles county. John D. Johnston, the step-mother's son, went to them; and A. stopped indefinitely, and, for the first time, as it were, by himself at New-Salem, before mentioned. This was in July 1831. Here he rapidly made acquaintances and friends. In less than a year Offutt's business was failing – had almost failed – when the Black-Hawk war of 1832 – broke out. A joined a volunteer company, and to his own surprise, was elected captain of it. He says he has not since had any success in life which gave him so much satisfaction. He went the campaign, served near three months, met the ordinary hardships of such an expedition, but was in no battle. He now owns in Iowa, the land upon which his own warrants for this service, were located. Returning from the campaign and encouraged by his great popularity among his immediate neighbors, he, the same year, ran for the Legislature and was beaten---his own precinct, however, casting its votes 277 for and 7, against him. And this too while he was an avowed Clay man, and the precinct the autumn afterwards, giving a majority of 115 to Genl. Jackson over Mr. Clay. This was the only time A was ever beaten on a direct vote of the people. He was now without means and out of business but was anxious to remain with his friends who had treated him with so much generosity, especially as he had nothing elsewhere to go to. He studied what he should do – thought of learning the black-smith trade – thought of trying to study law – rather thought he could not succeed at that without a better education. Before long, strangely enough, a man offered to sell and did sell, to A. and another as poor as himself, an old stock of goods, upon credit. They opened as merchants; and he says that was the store. Of course, they did nothing but get deeper and deeper in debt. He was appointed Post-master at New-Salem – the office being too insignificant, to make his politics an objection. The store winked out. The Surveyor of Sangamon offered to depute to A that portion of his work which was within his part of the county. He accepted, procured a compass and chain, studied Flint, and Gibson a little, and went at it. This procured bread and kept soul and body together. The election of 1834 came, and he was then elected to the Legislature by the highest vote cast for any candidate. Major John T. Stuart, then in full practice of the law, was also elected. During the canvass, in a private conversation he encouraged A. to study law. After the election he borrowed books of Stuart, took them home with him, and went at it in good earnest. He studied with nobody. He still mixed in the surveying to pay board and clothing bills. When the Legislature met, the law books were dropped, but were taken up again at the end of the session. He was re-elected in 1836, 1838, and 1840. In the autumn of 1836, he obtained a law license, and on April 15, 1837 removed to Springfield, and commenced the practice, his old friend, Stuart taking him into partnership. March 3rd. 1837, by a protest entered upon the Ills. House Journal of that date, at pages 817, 818, A. with Dan Stone, another representative of Sangamon, briefly defined his position on the slavery question; and so far, as it goes, it was then the same that it is now. The protest is as follows (here insert it). In 1838, & 1840 Mr. L's party in the Legislature voted for him as Speaker; but being in the minority, he was not elected. After 1840 he declined a re-election to the Legislature. He was on the Harrison electoral ticket in 1840, and on that of Clay in 1844, and spent much time and labor in both those canvasses. In Nov. 1842 he was married to Mary, daughter of Robert S. Todd, of Lexington, Kentucky. They have three living children, all sons---one born in 1843, one in 1850, and one in 1853. They lost one, who was born in 1846. In 1846, he was elected to the lower House of Congress, and served one term only, commencing in Dec. 1847 and ending with the inauguration of Gen. Taylor, in March 1849. All the battles of the Mexican war had been fought before Mr. L. took his seat in congress, but the American army was still in Mexico, and the treaty of peace was not fully and formally ratified till the June afterwards. Much has been said of his course in Congress in regard to this war. A careful examination of the Journals and Congressional Globe shows, that he voted for all the supply measures which came up, and for all the measures in any way favorable to the officers, soldiers, and their families, who conducted the war through; with this exception that some of these measures passed without years and nays, leaving no record as to how particular men voted. The Journals and Globe also show him voting that the war was unnecessarily and unconstitutionally begun by the President of the United States. This is the language of Mr. Ashmun's amendment, for which Mr. L. and nearly or quite all, other Whigs of the H. R. voted.

"Mr. L's reasons for the opinion expressed by this vote were briefly that the President had sent Genl. Taylor into an inhabited part of the country belonging to Mexico, and not to the U.S. and thereby had provoked the first act of hostility---in fact the commencement of the war; that the place, being the country bordering on the East bank of the Rio Grande, was inhabited by native Mexicans, born there under the Mexican government; and had never submitted to, nor been conquered by Texas, or the U.S. nor transferred to either by treaty---that although Texas claimed the Rio Grande as her boundary, Mexico had never recognized it, the people on the ground had never recognized it, and neither Texas nor the U.S. had ever enforced it---that there was a broad desert between that, and the country over which Texas had actual control---that the country where hostilities commenced, having once belonged to Mexico, must remain so, until it was somehow legally transferred, which had never been done.

"Mr. L. thought the act of sending an armed force among the Mexicans, was unnecessary, inasmuch as Mexico was in no way molesting, or menacing the U.S. or the people thereof; and that it was unconstitutional, because the power of levying war is vested in Congress, and not in the President. He thought the principal motive for the act, was to divert public attention from the surrender of ``Fifty-four, forty, or fight'' to Great Britain, on the Oregon boundary question.

"Mr. L. was not a candidate for re-election. This was determined upon, and declared before he went to Washington, in accordance with an understanding among Whig friends, by which Col. Hardin, and Col. Baker had each previously served a single term in the same District.

"In 1848, during his term in congress, he advocated Gen. Taylor's nomination for the Presidency, in opposition to all others, and also took an active part for his election, after his nomination – speaking a few times in Maryland, near Washington, several times in Massachusetts, and canvassing quite fully his own district in Illinois, which was followed by a majority in the district of over 1500 for Gen. Taylor.

"Upon his return from Congress he went to the practice of the law with greater earnestness than ever before. In 1852 he was upon the Scott electoral ticket, and did something in the way of canvassing, but owning to the hopelessness of the cause in Illinois, he did less than in previous presidential canvasses.

"In 1854, his profession had almost superseded the thought of politics in his mind, when the repeal of the Missouri compromise aroused him as he had never been before.

"In the autumn of that year he took the stump with no broader practical aim or object that [than?] to secure, if possible, the re-election of Hon Richard Yates to congress. His speeches at once attracted a more marked attention than they had ever before done. As the canvass proceeded, he was drawn to different parts of the state, outside of Mr. Yates' district. He did not abandon the law, but gave his attention, by turns, to that and politics. The State agricultural fair was at Springfield that year, and Douglas was announced to speak there.

"In the canvass of 1856, Mr. L. made over fifty speeches, no one of which, so far as he remembers, was put in print. One of them was made at Galena, but Mr. L. has no recollection of any part of it being printed; nor does he remember whether in that speech he said anything about a Supreme Court decision. He may have spoken upon that subject; and some of the newspapers may have reported him as saying what is now ascribed to him; but he thinks he could not have expressed himself as represented."[1]

---

[1] Roy P. Basler. *The Collected Works of Abraham Lincoln*, volume 4, pages 60-67. Lincoln's autobiography was written in June 1860 for John Locke Scripps and used for campaign purposes.

Memorial Highway Commission Report

REPORT OF THE LINCOLN MEMORIAL HIGHWAY COMMISSION OF KENTUCKY

Hon. Ruby Laffoon,

Governor of Kentucky,

Frankfort, Kentucky.

Your commission realizes that after a lapse of more than a century it is impossible to locate with absolute certainty the route traveled by Thomas Lincoln with his family in 1816 from their home in Hardin (now LaRue) County, Kentucky, to their future home in what is now Spencer County, Indiana. We have not hoped to satisfy the public at large. Not even the commission is a unit on all the Report as submitted. Among the hundreds of traditional affidavits submitted to the commission, it is rather easy to select those that should be considered evidence when studied and compared with other facts. We believe the great majority of these affidavits were submitted in good faith and we want to express our thanks to all who earnestly and honestly expressed their claims.

Even the court records which are complete and abundant in regard to the opening and upkeep of roads in the early days are confusing. Like the calls in early land surveys, their land marks were of a temporary nature. The identity of the farms and plantations they passed has been lost. The "black jack groves," the "maple swamps," the meadows and the barrens that constituted the field notes have long since disappeared. In some cases, even the names of the smaller streams have been changed. Yet the salient features of the traditions and road records, taken into consideration with other facts, make the location rather satisfactory when associated with the scant recorded history. In the following report, references will be indicated to the material so that interested students may have easy access to the documentary facts upon which this report is based.

Your commission was impressed with the importance of its task and entered upon its labors with an ambition to find if possible, the actual route over which Thomas Lincoln and his family traveled in their migration. It has tried to avoid being influenced by the selfishness and ambitions of individuals and communities, and has based its findings on the following considerations:

First—The reasonableness of the route as determined by distances, directions available roads, and natural attractions, such as friends and kindred to be visited before undertaking such a journey.

Second—Traditions existing in various communities traversed as shown by sworn affidavits of responsible citizens.

Third—Certified court records as to the opening and upkeep of the roads.

Fourth—Recorded history.

Upon this basis the Lincolns' journey as finally determined naturally divides itself into six sections.

First—From the birthplace of Abraham on the South Fork of Nolin River to the Knob Creek home.

Second—From the Knob Creek home to Elizabethtown.

Third—From Elizabethtown to the Mill Creek home of the mother of Thomas, Bersheba Lincoln, and his sister, Mrs. William Brumfield.

Fourth—From Mill Creek to Big Spring.

Fifth—From Big Spring to Hardinsburg.

Sixth—From Hardinsburg to the Ohio River.

Section I

FROM THE BIRTHPLACE WHERE THE NATIONAL MEMORIAL NOW STANDS TO KNOB CREEK.

Thomas Lincoln moved in the year 1811 from the farm on the South Fork of Nolin River where Abraham was born February 12, 1809, to the Knob Creek farm. While there is no evidence filed with the commission to prove any particular route on this section, it is a well-established fact that the Nolin-Bardstown road (now U. S. 31 E) was then in existence. He would naturally follow that road through what is now Hodgenville to their new home, the place that remained their home until the fall of 1816 when they moved to what is now Spencer County, Indiana. It was from this home that the future President attended his first school, taught by Zachariah Riney and Caleb Hazel and where the foundations of his character were laid, amid the rugged hills and babbling brooks of primitive nature.

Section II

FROM THE KNOB CREEK HOME TO ELIZABETHTOWN

This section meets all the requirements as the Elizabethtown-Springfield road was the most direct road between the Knob Creek home and Elizabethtown. Certified road records in the Hardin County Court House show that it was opened and kept in repair from 1793 until the time of the migration in the year 1816. Local tradition has it that this was the road traveled by Thomas Lincoln when he went to Springfield to be married and over which he returned to Elizabethtown in the year 1806 with his bride, Nancy Hanks. It was, and is yet, a ridge road with no streams to cross, being located on the divide between Nolin River on the south and the Rolling Fork of Salt River on the north. This route is amply supported by traditional affidavits made by reliable people whose families have lived in this (Elizabethtown) territory from the earliest days. Historically, according to Dr. Louis A. Warren, it is "probably the road followed by the Lincolns."

Section III

FROM ELIZABETHTOWN TO MILL CREEK

This section is the only one on the entire route on which Thomas Lincoln turned from the direct course to his destination. This route over what is now the Shepherdsville road, at that time was called Bullitt's Salt Lick road. This road ran by the farm of Thomas Lincoln, now called the Mill Creek farm.

The Shepherdsville road was selected by the commission as being the most available road to reach the home of his mother, Bersheba Lincoln, widow of the pioneer Abraham Lincoln, the grandfather of the President. This section carries us not only to the site of the home of his mother, but also to the old Mill Creek cemetery, the final resting place of Bersheba Lincoln and her youngest daughter, Mrs. William Brumfield, as well as many other descendants of this worthy pioneer mother.

This place should be made a national shrine to the memory of this pioneer mother who, from the time her husband fell a victim to a savage bullet in 1786 until 1803 held her orphan family of three sons and two daughters together amid the vicissitudes and hardships of pioneer life.

This particular section of country is rich in early social, commercial, political and religious history. The location of this road is established by court records, traditional affidavits, the substance of which was secured forty years ago, before the subject of a memorial highway was under consideration.

Section IV

FROM MILL CREEK TO BIG SPRING

After his visit with his mother and sister at the Brumfield home Thomas Lincoln traveled directly west on the road leading through "Viney Grove" (now the town of Vine Grove) and on through Flaherty to Big Spring.

It is a peculiar fact that of the four routes suggested to the commissioners leading out of Elizabethtown all terminated at Big Spring. It seems that at that early date Big Spring was one of the important towns in the county. Tradition shows that all the emigrants on their trek to the then rapidly developing west, passed through and usually camped at Big Spring.

The road selected for this section meets the necessary requirements laid down in our schedule of premises. It was the most direct route as it avoided deep streams, and was under constant upkeep, and is amply supported by traditional affidavits.

Section V

FROM BIG SPRING TO HARDINSBURG

The county officials and other interested citizens of Breckinridge County furnished certified court records showing that there were different roads leading from Big Spring to Hardinsburg. The commission selected what, in their opinion, is the best and most direct route. It follows what is known locally as the "Lost Run" road to Harned Station on Federal Highway No. 60 and then along that Highway to and through Hardinsburg.

Section VI

FROM HARDSINSBURG TO THE OHIO RIVER

The Yellow Banks road, later called the Owensboro road, leads from Hardinsburg in almost a direct line towards the Lincolns' destination. It is a ridge road avoiding deep fords, and the Ohio River crossing put the party beyond any deep streams and on an established road in Indiana.

This route is supported by scores of affidavits as to the traditional passage of this party, that bear all the earmarks of truth and much of it was developed before a memorial road was under consideration.

Many certified court records from Breckinridge County show that this road had been established and was kept in repair from 1801 up to the time of the migration. All the records show that the road was kept in repair fifteen feet wide continuously.

As to recorded history:

L. P. Brockett, Life and Times of Abraham Lincoln" 38. The crossing is placed "at or near the mouth of Anderson Creek."

Joseph H. Barrett, The Life of Abraham Lincoln, 22. The writer makes the same location.

John G. Nicolay and John Hay make the same location.

Louis A. Warren, Parentage and Childhood of Lincoln, 294. The same location is quoted.

W. M. Thayer, in The Pioneer Boy, puts them across the river on Thompson's Ferry at the mouth of Anderson Creek.

So also, other biographers place the crossing at Thompson's Ferry. These include Holland, Lamon, Herndon, Tarbell, and Barton.

Were this commission to ignore all this historical background it would succeed only in laying itself open to ridicule by competent Lincoln biographers.

While it is not practical at this time to carry this memorial highway to the actual point of crossing of the Ohio, on account of the unfavorable terrain, and physical characteristics of the river, we believe the best and most reasonable thing to do is to locate the route over the old Yellow Banks road from Hardinsburg through Breckinridge and Hancock Counties to Pellville, and there to turn to the Ohio River at Hawesville and connect with the terminus of the Indiana division as located by that State's commission. This is the most practical bridge site, and this location is in near proximity to the site of the actual crossing. *

Signed

J. R. Miller, Commissioner from Meade County

Porter H. Hodges, Commissioner from Hancock County

Frank Dean, Commissioner from Breckinridge County

D. E. McClure, Commissioner from Hardin County

R. Gerald McMurtry, Commissioner from Hardin Co.

"Accepted and Approved"

Ruby Laffoon, Governor

Thomas Lincoln: Abraham's Father

December 5, 1935 [1]

---

[1] R. Gerald McMurtry. "The Lincoln Migration from Kentucky to Indiana. 1816. *Indiana Magazine of History*, pages 39-44. Reprint edition.

Marker to note militia service of Lincoln's father

The Associated Press
Posted Aug 08, 2013 @ 06:23 AM

LERNA – A marker recognizing the military service of Abraham Lincoln's father will be placed on his grave during a ceremony in east-central Illinois later this month.

The president's father, Thomas Lincoln, was a military officer on the Kentucky frontier.

The marker will be put into place Aug. 31. Descendants of the Hall and Hanks families, cousins to Abraham Lincoln, will lay a memorial wreath. Historian James Siberell plans to speak about Thomas Lincoln's experiences in the militia.

The event is set for 11 a.m. at the Thomas Lincoln Cemetery in Lerna, near the Lincoln Log Cabin State Historic Site.

The marker is being presented by the Sangamon River Chapter of the National Society United States Daughters of 1812, the Illinois Historic Preservation Agency and the Lincoln Log Cabin site.

The Bear Hunt

It is possible that Abraham Lincoln intended this poem to be a section in his other poem about Indiana, *My Childhood Home*. *The Bear Hunt* is dated September 6, 1846 but the actual date of writing is uncertain.

The Bear Hunt

A wild-bear chase, didst never see?
Then hast thou lived in vain.
Thy richest bump of glorious glee,
Lies desert in thy brain.

When first my father settled here,
'Twas then the frontier line:
The panther's scream, filled night with fear
And bears preyed on the swine.

But woe for Bruin's short lived fun,
When rose the squealing cry;
Now man and horse, with dog and gun,
For vengeance, at him fly.

A sound of danger strikes his ear;
He gives the breeze a snuff:
Away he bounds, with little fear,
And seeks the tangled *rough*.

On press his foes, and reach the ground,
Where's left his half munched meal;
The dogs, in circles, scent around,
And find his fresh made trail.

With instant cry, away they dash,
And men as fast pursue;
O'er logs they leap, through water splash,
And shout the brisk halloo.

Now to elude the eager pack,
Bear shuns the open ground;
Through matted vines, he shapes his track
And runs it, round and round.

The tall fleet cur, with deep-mouthed voice,
Now speeds him, as the wind;
While half-grown pup, and short-legged fice,
Are yelping far behind.

And fresh recruits are dropping in
To join the merry *corps*:
With yelp and yell, – a mingled din –
The woods are in a roar.

And round, and round the chase now goes,
The world's alive with fun;
Nick Carter's horse, his rider throws,
And more, Hill drops his gun.

Now sorely pressed, bear glances back,
And lolls his tired tongue;
When as, to force him from his track,
An ambush on him sprung.

Across the glade he sweeps for flight,
And fully is in view.
The dogs, new-fired, by the sight,
Their cry, and speed, renew.

The foremost ones, now reach his rear,
He turns, they dash away;
And circling now, the wrathful bear,
They have him full at bay.

At top of speed, the horse-men come,
All screaming in a row.
"Whoop! Take him Tiger. Seize him Drum."
Bang, – bang – the rifles go.

And furious now, the dogs he tears,
And crushes in his ire.
Wheels right and left, and upward rears,
With eyes of burning fire.

But leaden death is at his heart,
Vain all the strength he plies.
And, spouting blood from every part,

Thomas Lincoln: Abraham's Father

He reels, and sinks, and dies.

And now a dinsome clamor rose,
'Bout who should have his skin;
Who first draws blood, each hunter knows,
This prize must always win.

But who did this, and how to trace
What's true from what's a lie,
Like lawyers, in a murder case
They stoutly *argufy*.

Aforesaid fice, of blustering mood,
Behind, and quite forgot,
Just now emerging from the wood,
Arrives upon the spot.

With grinning teeth, and upturned hair –
Brim full of spunk and wrath,
He growls, and seizes on dead bear,
And shakes for life and death.

And swells as if his skin would tear,
And growls and shakes again;
And swears, as plain as dog can swear,
That he has won the skin.

Conceited whelp! we laugh at thee---
Nor mind, that not a few
Of pompous, two-legged dogs there be,
Conceited quite as you. [1]

---

[1] Roy P. Basler. *The Collected Works of Abraham Lincoln*, volume 1, pages 386-389.

Illustrations / Accreditations

At front of book – Picture of Abraham Lincoln by Nicholas H. Shepherd in 1846 or 1847. Age 37. Library of Congress Prints and Photographs Division. Washington, D.C. Reproduction Number: LC-USZCR-2439. In the public domain.

At front of book – Picture of Thomas. Library of Congress, 2008680251. In the public domain.

Bibliography

Books

Abbott, John S. C. and Russell H. Conwell. *Lives of the Presidents of the United States of America, From Washington to the Present Time.* Portland, Maine: H. Hallett & Company, 1893.

Alger, Horatio Jr. *Abraham Lincoln, The Backwoods Boy; or, How a Young Rail-Splitter Became President.* New York: American Publishers Corporation, 1883.

Arnold, Isaac N. *The Life of Abraham Lincoln.* Chicago: Jansen, McClurg, & Company, 1885.

Atkinson, Eleanor. *The Boyhood of Lincoln.* New York: Doubleday, Page & Company, 1908.

Balch, George B. *Poems.* Boston: Sherman, French & Company, 1912.

Bartelt, William E. & Joshua A. Claybourn. *Abe's Youth: Shaping the Future President.* Bloomington, Indiana: Indiana University Press, 2019.

Bartelt, William E. *There I Grew Up.* Indianapolis: Indiana Historical Society Press, 2008.

Barton, William E. *The Life of Abraham Lincoln, Volumes I & II.* London: The Bobbs-Merrill Company, 1925.

Barton, William E. *The Parents of Abraham Lincoln.* Charleston, Illinois: The Charleston Daily Courier, 1922.

Barton, William E. *The Paternity of Abraham Lincoln.* New York: George H. Doran Company, 1920.

Barton, William E. *The Lineage of Lincoln.* Indianapolis: Bobbs-Merrill Company, 1929.

Barton, William E. *The Soul of Abraham Lincoln.* Chicago: University of Illinois Press, 2005. Originally published in 1920.

Barton, William E. *The Women Lincoln Loved.* Indianapolis: The Bobbs-Merrill Company, 1927.

Basler, Roy P. Editor. *The Collected Works of Abraham Lincoln*. Rutgers University Press: New Brunswick, New Jersey; 1953.

Bateman, Newton, Paul Selby, and Charles Edward Wilson, Editors. *Historical Encyclopedia of Illinois and History of Coles County*. Munsell Publishing Company: Chicago, 1906.

Bearss, Edwin Coles. *Lincoln Boyhood – As a Living Historical Farm*. Springfield, Virginia: National Park Service, 1967.

Beveridge, Albert J. *Abraham Lincoln, Volume 1*. Boston: Houghton Mifflin Company, 1928.

Brant, Selwyn A. and Weston A. Goodspeed. *History of Warrick, Spencer, and Perry Counties, Indiana*. Chicago: Goodspeed, Bros. & Co., Publishers, 1885.

Briggs, Harold E. & Ernestine B. Briggs. *Nancy Hanks Lincoln: A Frontier Portrait*. New York: Bookman Associates, 1952.

Brookhiser, Richard. *Founder's Son: A Life of Abraham Lincoln*. New York: Basic Books, 2014.

Brooks, Noah. *Abraham Lincoln*. Washington, DC: National Tribune, 1888.

Brown, Kent Masterson. *Report on the Title of Thomas Lincoln to, and the History of, the Lincoln Boyhood Home along Knob Creek in LaRue County, Kentucky*. Danville, Kentucky: Locally published.

Burkhimer, Michael. *100 Essential Lincoln Books*. Nashville, Tennessee: Cumberland House, 2003.

Burkhimer, Michael. *Lincoln's Christianity*. Yardley, Pennsylvania: Westholme Publishing, 2007.

Burlingame, Michael. *Abraham Lincoln: A Life. Volumes One & Two*. Baltimore: The John Hopkins University Press, 2008.

Butterworth, Hezekiah. *In the Boyhood of Lincoln*. New York: D. Appleton and Company, 1907.

Carwardine, Richard. *Lincoln*. New York: Alfred A. Knopf, 2006.

Chapman Brothers. *Portrait and Biographical Album of Coles County, Illinois.* Chicago: Chapman Brothers, 1887.

Charnwood, Lord. *Abraham Lincoln.* New York: Garden City Publishing Co., Inc., 1938.

Choate, Joseph H. *Abraham Lincoln.* New York: Thomas Y. Crowell & Company, 1901.

Chrisman, Herring. *Memoirs of Lincoln.* Mapleton, Iowa: William Herring Chrisman, 1930.

Coleman, Charles H. *Abraham Lincoln and Coles County, Illinois.* New LaBrunswick, New Jersey: Scarecrow Press, 1955.

Coleman, Charles H. and Mary Coleman. *Thomas Lincoln.* Bloomington, Indiana: iUniverse, 2015.

Davenport, Don. *In Lincoln's Footsteps.* Black Earth, Wisconsin: Trails Books, Revised Edition, 2002.

De La Hunt, Thomas James. *Perry County, A History.* Indianapolis: The W. K. Stewart Company, 1916.

Donald, David Herbert. *Lincoln.* London: Jonathan Cape, 1995.

Duvergier de Hauranne, Ernest. *A Frenchman in Lincoln's America.* Chicago: R. R. Donnelley & Sons Company, 1974.

Ehrmann, Bess V. *Lincoln and His Neighbors.* Rockport, IN: Democrat Publishing Co., 1948.

Faragher, John Mack. *Daniel Boone, The Life and Legend of an American Pioneer.* New York: Henry Holt and Company, 1992.

Fehrenbacher, Don E. and Virginia Fehrenbacher. *Recollected Words of Abraham Lincoln.* Stanford, CA: Stanford University Press, 1996.

Gary, Ralph. *Following in Lincoln's Footsteps.* New York: Carroll & Graf Publishers, 2001.

Goodwin, Doris Kearns. *Team of Rivals.* New York: Simon & Schuster, 2005.

Gridley, Eleanor. *The Story of Abraham Lincoln or The Journey from the Long Cabin to the White House*. Chicago: Wabash Publishing House, 1900.

Griffing, B. N. *An Illustrated Historical Atlas of Spencer County, Indiana*. Philadelphia, Pennsylvania: D. J. Lake & Company, 1879.

Guelzo, Allen C. *Lincoln*. New York: Sterling, 2009.

Hart, Richard E. *The Collected Works of Thomas Lincoln: Carpenter and Cabinetmaker*. Springfield, Illinois: Richard E Hart, 2019.

Hart, Richard E. *Thomas Lincoln Reconsidered*. Unpublished work. 2018.

Herndon, William H. & Jesse W. Weik. *Herndon's Life of Lincoln*. Cleveland: The World Publishing Company, 1943.

Herndon, William H. Douglas L. Wilson & Rodney O. Davis, Editors. *Herndon on Lincoln, Letters*. Chicago: Knox College Lincoln Studies Center and University of Illinois Press, 2016.

Hertz, Emanuel. *The Hidden Lincoln, From the Letters and Papers of William H. Herndon*. Garden City, NY: Blue Ribbon Books, 1940.

Hitchcock, Caroline Hanks. *Nancy Hanks*. New York: Doubleday & McClure Co., 1899.

Hobson, J. T. *Footprints of Abraham Lincoln*. Dayton, Ohio: The Otterbein Press, 1909.

Holland, J. G. *Holland's Life of Abraham Lincoln*. Lincoln, NE: University of Nebraska Press, 1998.

Holzer, Harold. *Lincoln As I Knew Him*. Chapel Hill, NC: Algonquin Books of Chapel Hill, 1999.

Illinois General Assembly. *The Public and General Statute Laws of the State of Illinois*. Containing the Revised Statues of 1833 along with Acts of the Ninth General Assembly and Tenth General Assembly. Chicago: Stephen F. Gale, 1839.

Kaplan. Fred. *Lincoln: The Biography of a Writer*. New York: Harper Collins Publishers, 2008.

Lamon, Ward Hill. *The Life of Abraham Lincoln*. Boston: James R. Osgood and Company, 1872.

Le Baron, William Jr. *The History of Coles County Illinois*. Chicago: Wm. Le Baron Jr. & Co., 1879.

Lea, J. Henry & J. R. Hutchinson. *The Ancestry of Abraham Lincoln*. Boston: Houghton Mifflin Company, 1909.

Learned, Marion Dexter. *Abraham Lincoln, An American Migration, Family English Not German*. Philadelphia: William J. Campbell, 1909.

Leidner, Gordon. *Abraham Lincoln: The Complete Book of Facts, Quizzes, & Trivia*. Shippensburg, Pennsylvania: Burd Street Press, 2001.

Library of Congress. *Abraham Lincoln: An Exhibition at the Library of Congress in Honor of the 150th Anniversary of His Birth*. Washington, D.C.: Library of Congress, 1959.

Masters, Edward Lee. *The Sangamon*. New York: Farrar & Rinehart, 1942.

McCallister, J. T. *Virginia Militia in the Revolutionary War*. Hot Springs, Virginia: McAllister Publishing Co., 1913.

McCord, Shirley S. *Travel Accounts of Indiana 1679-1961*. Indianapolis: Indiana Historical Bureau, 1970.

McMurtry, R. Gerald. *A Series of Monographs Concerning the Lincolns and Hardin County, Kentucky*. Elizabethtown, Kentucky: The Enterprise Press, 1938.

Mearns, David C. *The Lincoln Papers, Volume 1*. Garden City, New York: Doubleday & Company, Inc., 1948.

Miller, Richard Lawrence. *Lincoln and His World, Volume 1*. Mechanicsburg, Pennsylvania: Stackpole Books, 2006.

Morgan, Robert. *Boone*. Chapel Hill, North Carolina: Algonquin Books, 2007.

Nation, Richard F. *At Home in the Hoosier Hills: Agriculture, Politics, and Religion in Southern Indiana, 1810 – 1870*. Indianapolis: Indiana University Press, 2005.

Nichols, Clifton M. *Abraham Lincoln*. New York: Mast, Crowell & Kirkpatrick, 1896.

Nicolay, Helen. *Personal Traits of Abraham Lincoln*. New York: The Century Company, 1912.

Nicolay, John G. *A Short Life of Abraham Lincoln*. New York: The Century Company, 1903.

Nicolay, John G. and John Hay. *Abraham Lincoln, A History*. New York: The Century Company, 1917. 10 volumes.

Peterson, Kurt W. *Lincoln's Land: The History of Abraham Lincoln's Coles County Farm*. Inverness, Illinois: Friends of the Abraham Lincoln Historical Farm.

Phillips, Donald T. *Lincoln on Leadership*. New York: Warner Books, 1992.

Reynolds, David S. *Abe: Abraham Lincoln in His Times*. New York: Penguin Press, 2020.

Rice, Allen Thorndike. *Reminiscences of Abraham Lincoln by Distinguished Men of His Time*.

Robinson, Luther Emerson. *Abraham Lincoln As A Man of Letters*. Chicago: The Reilly & Britton Co., 1918.

Sandburg, Carl. *Abe Lincoln Grows Up*. New York: Harcourt, Bruce, and Company, Inc., 1926.

Sandburg, Carl. *The Prairie Years*. New York: Harcourt, Brace & World, Inc., 1926.

Schwartz, Thomas F. and Thomas Cussans. *Abraham Lincoln: An Illustrated Life and Legacy*. San Diego: Thunder Bay Press, 2013.

Scripps, John Locke. *The First Published Life of Abraham Lincoln*. Detroit: Cranbrook Press, 1900. (Written in the year 1860 and published originally by the Chicago Press & Tribune Co. in 1860.)

Shammas, Carole. Marylynn Salmon. Michel Dahlin. *Inheritance in America: from Colonial Times to the Present*. New Brunswick, New Jersey: Rutgers University Press, 1987.

Simpson-Poffenbarger, Livia Nye. *The Battle of Point Pleasant: A Battle of the Revolution*. Point Pleasant, West Virginia: The State Gazette Publisher, 1909.

Speed, Thomas. *The Wilderness Road*. Louisville, Kentucky: John P. Morton & Co., 1886.

Steers, Edward Jr. *Lincoln Legends: Myths, Hoaxes, and Confabulations Associated with Our Greatest President*. Lexington, KY: The University Press of Kentucky, 2007.

Stephenson, Nathaniel W. *Lincoln*. Indianapolis: The Bobbs-Merrill Company Publishers, 1924.

Stevens, Walter B. *A Reporter's Lincoln*. Lincoln, Nebraska: University of Nebraska Press, 1998.

Tarbell, Ida. *Boy Scouts Life of Lincoln*. New York: The MacMillan Company, 1943.

Tarbell, Ida M. *In the Footsteps of the Lincolns*. New York: Harper & Brothers, 1924.

Tarbell, Ida M. *The Early Life of Abraham Lincoln*. New York: S. S. McClure, Limited, 1896.

Tarbell, Ida M. *The Life of Abraham Lincoln*. New York: Lincoln History Society, 1900.

Taylor, Daniel Cravens. *Not a Technical Christian*. Anderson, IN: Kindle Direct, 2013.

Thayer, William M. *The Pioneer Boy and How He Became President*. Boston: Walker, Wise, and Company, 1864.

Thornbrough, Gayle and Dorothy Riker, Compilers. *Readings in Indiana History*. Indianapolis: Indiana Historical Bureau, 1956.

Usher, F. Linder. *Reminiscences of the Early Bench and Bar of Illinois, Second Edition*. Chicago: The Chicago Legal news Company, 1879.

Walters, Betty Lawson. *Furniture Makers of Indiana 1793 – 1850*. Indianapolis: Indiana Historical Society, 1972.

Warren, Louis A. *Abraham Lincoln Association Papers*. "The Environs of Lincoln's Youth". Springfield, Illinois: Abraham Lincoln Association, 1933.

Warren, Louis A. *Lincoln's Parentage & Childhood*. New York: The Century Company, 1926.

Warren, Louis A. *Lincoln's Youth Indiana Years Seven to Twenty-one 1816-1830*. New York: Appleton, 1959.

Warren, Raymond. *The Prairie President Living Through the Years with Lincoln 1809-1861*. Chicago: The Reilly & Lee Co., 1930.

Wayland, John W. *The Lincolns in Virginia*. Staunton, Virginia: The McClure Printing Company, 1946.

Weik, Jesse W. *The Real Lincoln: A Portrait*. Boston: Houghton Mifflin Company, 1922.

Wheeler, Joe. *Abraham Lincoln: A Man of Faith and Courage*. New York: Howard Books, 2008.

White, Ronald C. Jr. *A. Lincoln*. New York: Random House. 2009.

White, Ronald C. *Lincoln in Private*. New York: Random House, 2021.

Whitney, Henry C. *Lincoln the Citizen: Volume One of A Life of Lincoln*. New York: The Baker & Taylor Company, 1908.

Williams, Henry L. *The Lincoln Story Book*. New York: G. W. Dillingham Company, 1907.

Wilson, Douglas L. and Rodney O. Davis. *Herndon's Informants*. Chicago: University of Illinois Press, 1998.

Winkle, Kenneth J. *The Young Eagle*. Dallas: Taylor Trade Publishing. 2001.

Zane, John Maxcy. *Abraham Lincoln Association Papers*. "Lincoln, the Constitutional Lawyer". Springfield, Illinois: Abraham Lincoln Association, 1933.

Pamphlets

Allison, Etta Mae. *Pioneers of Coles County Illinois*. Illinois, 1942.

Blair, Francis G., Superindendent of Public Instruction. *The one Hundredth Anniversary of the Birth of Abraham Lincoln. For the Schools of Illinois*. Springfield, Illinois: Illinois State Journal Co., State Printers: 1908.

Breckinridge-Perry County Lincoln Highway Association. *At the End of the Trail*. Cloverport, Kentucky: The Breckenridge News, February 1938.

Coleman, D. M. *Thomas Lincoln, The Father of Abraham Lincoln*. D. M. Coleman, 1956.

Couch, James Fitton. *Trembles (or Milk Sickness)*. Washington, D.C.: United States Department of Agriculture, Circular Number 306, November 1933.

Evans, Lewis. *An Analysis of a General Map of the Middle British Colonies in America*. Philadelphia: B. Franklin and D. Hall, 1755.

Finley, John H. "The Education of Abraham Lincoln". *Lincoln Centennial Association Papers*. Springfield, Illinois: Lincoln Centennial Association, 1925.

Historical Folk Toys. *Children's Manners and Morals*. Charlotte, North Carolina: Historical Folk Toys, 2006.

Historical Folk Toys. *Toys & Games from the Past*. Charlotte, North Carolina: Historical Folk Toys, 2004.

McMurtry, R. Gerald. *Lincoln Highlights in Indiana History*. Fort Wayne, Indiana: The Lincoln National Life Insurance Company, date unknown.

McMurtry, R. Gerald. *The Lincolns in Elizabethtown, Kentucky*. Fort Wayne, Indiana: Lincolniana Publishers, 1932.

McMurtry, R. Gerald. *The Thomas Lincoln Mill Creek Farm*. Fort Wayne, Indiana: Lincoln National Life Foundation, no date given.

Simon, John Y. *House Divided: Lincoln and His Father.* Fort Wayne, Indiana: The Louis A. Warren Lincoln Library and Museum, 1987.

Stover, Carl W. and Jerry L. Coffman. *Seismicity of the United States, 1568 – 1989 (Revised).* U.S. Geological Survey Professional Paper 1527. Washington, D.C.: United States Government Printing Office, 1993.

Temple, Wayne C. *Thomas and Abraham Lincoln As Farmers.* Racine, Wisconsin: The Lincoln Fellowship of Wisconsin, Historical Bulletin Numer 53, 1995.

Thomas, John T. *Thomas Lincoln, Father of Abraham Lincoln.* Address at dedication of new fencing for Thomas Lincoln gravesite. Springfield, Illinois: December 2, 1934.

Periodicals, Magazines, Newspapers, Reports

Abraham Lincoln Association. *Thomas Lincoln: Carpenter and Cabinetmaker 2016 Calendar.* Springfield, Illinois: The Abraham Lincoln Association, 2016.

Alston, Lee J. & Morton Owen Schapiro. "Inheritance Laws Across Colonies: Causes and Consequences." *The Journal of Economic History.* New York: Cambridge University Press, Volume 44, Number 2, June 1984, Pages 277-287.

Banta, D. D. "The Early Schools of Indiana." *Indiana Magazine of History.* Bloomington, Indiana: Indiana Historical Society, Volume 2, Issue 4, December 1906, pages 191-194.

Bartelt, William E. "The Land Dealings of Spencer County, Indiana, Pioneer Thomas Lincoln." *Indiana Magazine of History.* Bloomington, Indiana: Indiana Historical Society, Volume 87, Number 3, September 1991, pages 211-223.

Barton, William E. "Where the Mother of Lincoln Was Born." *The Dearborn Independent.* Dearborn, Michigan: The Dearborn Independent, June 25, 1927, pages 12-13, 21.

Blythe, Robert W., Maureen Carroll, Steven Moffson. Revised and updated by Brian F. Coffey. *Abraham Lincoln Birthplace*

National Historic Site, Historic Resource Study. Atlanta: National Park Service, 2001.

Bodine, Marcy G. "Story of the Lincolns of Hancock County." *Macomb Daily Journal*. Macomb, Illinois: Daily Journal, February 12, 1955. From the files of Lincoln Financial Foundation: *Thomas Lincoln Family – Uncles and Aunts*.

Brown, Kent Masterson. "The Lincoln's in Kentucky". Lexington, Kentucky: Lexington Convention Center. June 13, 2018.

Cady, John F. "The Religious Environment of Lincoln's Youth." *Indiana Magazine of History*. Bloomington, Indiana: Indiana Historical Society, Volume 37, Issue 1, pages 16-30.

Caldwell, Sandy. "The Life and Family of Lt. Gov. John Caldwell." *Kentucky Ancestors*. Frankfort, Kentucky: Kentucky Historical Society, Volume 40, Number 3, Spring 2005, pages 118-123.

Coleman, Charles H. "The Half-Faced Camp in Indiana – Fact or Myth?" *The Abraham Lincoln Quarterly*. Springfield, Illinois: The Abraham Lincoln Association, Volume VII, Number 3, September 1952, pages138-146.

Davis, Rich. "Teacher Quickly Becoming a Lincoln Furniture Expert". *Evansville Courier-Press*. Evansville, Indiana: Evansville Courier-Press. April 18, 2009.

Fratcher, Major William F. "Notes on the History of the Judge Advocate General's Department, 1775-1941." *The Judge Advocate Journal*.Washington, D.C.: Judge Advocates Association, Volume 1, Number 1, June 15, 1944. Pages 5-11.

Gabbard, Sara. "Interview with David S. Reynolds Regarding His New Book *Abe: Abraham Lincoln in His Time*." *Lincoln Lore*. Fort Wayne, Indiana: Friends of the Lincoln Collection, Number 1927, Fall 2020, pages 3-10.

Gabbard, Sara. "Lincoln through the Lens of History: An Interview with Brian Dirck.". *Lincoln Lore*. Fort Wayne, Indiana: The Friends of the Lincoln Collection of Indiana. Number 1915, Summer 2017, pages 12 - 15.

Gabbard, Sara. "Lincoln through the Lens of History: An Interview with Richard Brookhiser.". *Lincoln Lore*. Fort Wayne, Indiana: The Friends of the Lincoln Collection of Indiana. Number 1915, Summer 2017, pages 8 – 11.

Gerbner, Katharine. *Frendsjournal.org*. "Slavery in the Quaker World." September 1, 2019.

Gibson, Kevn. "Louisville Unearthed: Abraham Lincoln's grandfather lived and was murdered in Middletown." *Hello Louisville*, April 17, 2020, pages 1-6.

Glasco, H. B. "Thomas Lincoln. His Tomb – The Old Cabin in Which He Died – His Religion – Some Stories of His Life." *The Independent*. New York: The Independent, Volume LIII, No. 2720, January 17, 1901, pages 135-138.

Greer, Thomas H. "Economic and Social Effects of the Depression of 1819 in the Old Northwest". *Indiana Magazine of History*. Bloomington, Indiana: Indiana Historical Society, Volume 44, Issue 3, September 1948, pages 227-243.

Guelzo, Allen C. "Abraham Lincoln and the Doctrine of Necessity." *Journal of the Abraham Lincoln Association*. Springfield, Illinois: The Abraham Lincoln Association, Winter 1997, Volume 18, Issue 1, pages 57-81.

Hamilton, J. G. De Roulhac. "The Many-Sired Lincoln." *The American Mercury*. New York: Alfred A. Knopf, Inc. June 1925, volume V, number 18. Pages 129-135.

Hart, Richard E. "Slavery in Lincoln's Hardin County, Kentucky." *For the People*. Springfield, Illinois: The Abraham Lincoln Association, Winter 2020, Volume 22, Number 4, page 6.

Hart, Richard E. "Thomas Lincoln Reconsidered." *For the People*. Springfield, Illinois: The Abraham Lincoln Association, Spring 2017, Volume 19, Number 1, pages 9-10.

Hays, Roy. "Is the Lincoln Birthplace Cabin Authentic?" *Abraham Lincoln Quarterly*. Springfield, Illinois: Abraham Lincoln Association, Volume 5, Number 3, September 1948, pages 127-163.

Hunt, Ian. "Winter of the Deep Snows.". *Four Score and Seven.* Springfield, Illinois: The Abraham Lincoln Presidential Library Foundation, 2015-2016 Issue Three.

Kemper, Charles E. "Valley of Virginia Notes." *The Virginia Magazine of History and Biography*. Richmond, Virginia: The Virginia Historical Society, Volume XXX, 1922, pages 398-402.

Kent, William L. "Tommy Lincoln's Grave Marked," *Lincoln Herald.* Harrogate, Tennessee: Lincoln Memorial University, Summer, 1960, pp. 51-53.

Leonard, Adam A. "Personal Politics in Indiana: 1816 to 1840." *Indiana Magazine of History*. Bloomington, Indiana: Indiana Historical Society, Volume 19, Number 1, March 1923, pages 1-56.

Leonard, Adam A. "Personal Politics in Indiana: 1816 to 1840 (Continued)." *Indiana Magazine of History*. Bloomington, Indiana: Indiana Historical Society, Volume 19, Number 2, June 1923, pages 132-168.

Leonard, Adam A. "Personal Politics in Indiana: 1816 to 1840. (Concluded)" *Indiana Magazine of History*. Bloomington, Indiana: Indiana Historical Society, Volume 19, Number 3, September 1923, pages 241-281.

Lincoln Financial Foundation Collection. *Lincolncollection.org.* "Mary Todd Lincoln's Letter to Her Mother-in-Law", December 19, 1867.

McMurtry, R. Gerald, Editor. "Furniture Made By Thomas Lincoln". *Lincoln Lore*. Fort Wayne, Indiana: Lincoln National Life Foundation, Number 1512, February 1964, pages 1-4.

McMurtry, R. Gerald, Editor. "Re-Discovering the Supposed Grave of Lincoln's Brother". *Lincoln Lore*. Fort Wayne, Indiana: Lincoln National Life Foundation, Number 1619, January 1973, pages 1-3.

McMurtry, R. Gerald. "The Lincoln Migration from Kentucky to Indiana. 1816." *Indiana Magazine of History*. Bloomington,

Indiana: Indiana Historical Society, Volume 33, Number 4, December 1937, pages 385-421.

McMurtry, R. Gerald, Editor. "Thomas Lincoln's Corner Cupboards". *Lincoln Lore*. Fort Wayne, Indiana: Lincoln National Life Foundation, Number 1476, February 1961, pages 1-4.

Morgan, Arthur E. "New Light on Lincoln's Boyhood." *The Atlantic Monthly*. Washington, D.C.: February 1920, Volume 125, Number 2, pages 208-218.

Morris, Robert B. "Primogeniture and Entailed Estates in America," *Columbia Law Review*, volume 27, January 1927, pages 24-51.

Murr, Edward. "Lincoln in Indiana." *Indiana Magazine of History*. Bloomington, Indiana: Indiana Historical Society, Volume 13, Issue 4, December 1917, pages 307-348.

Murr, Edward. "Lincoln in Indiana (Concluded)." *Indiana Magazine of History*. Bloomington, Indiana: Indiana Historical Society, Volume 14, Issue 2, June 1918, pages 148-182.

Newman, Otho Lionel. "Development or The Common Schools of Indiana to 1851." *Indiana Magazine of History*. Bloomington, Indiana: Indiana Historical Society, Volume 22, Issue 3, September 1926, pages 229-276.

Nolan, Alan T. "Abraham Lincoln and Indiana." *Traces of Indiana and Midwestern History*. Indianapolis, IN: Indiana Historical Society. Volume 20, Number One. Winter 2008.

Quisenberry, A. C. "Kentucky Troops in the War of 1812." *The Register of the Kentucky Historical Society*. Frankfort, Kentucky: The State Journal Company, Volume 10, Number 30, September 1912, pages 47-66.

Price, Andrew. "The Riddle of the Run." *The Piedmont Herald*. Piedmont, West Virginia: The Piedmont Herald, August 1, 1929.

Ray C. Keim, "Primogeniture and Entail in Colonial Virginia," *The William and Mary Quarterly*, volume 25, October 1968, pages 545-586.

Rose, Gregory S. "Upland Southerners: The County Origins of Southern Migrants to Indiana by 1850." *Indiana Magazine of History.* Bloomington, Indiana: Indiana Historical Society, Volume 82, Issue 3, September 1986, pages 242-263.

Siberell, Jim. *The Lincoln Herald.* Harrogate, Tennessee: Lincoln Memorial University Press, Winter 2010, Volume 112, Number 4, pages 234-245.

Star-Times. "Rumors Regarding Lincoln Family's Origin Disproved." *St. Louis Star-Times.* St. Louis: Star-Times. February 12, 1934.

Strozier, Charles B. and Wayne Soini. "Lincoln's 'Angel Mother' and His Surrogate Fathers." *Journal of the Abraham Lincoln Association.* Springfield, Illinois: The Abraham Lincoln Association, Spring 2024, Volume 45, Issue Number 1, pages 1-16.

Tarbell, Ida M. "Abraham Lincoln." *McClure's Magazine.* New York: S. S. McClure, November 1895, Volume V, Number 6, pages 483-512.

Taylor, Daniel Cravens. "An Assessment of Thomas Lincoln." *Lincoln Lore.* Fort Wayne, Indiana: Lincoln Financial Life Foundation, Number 1925. Spring 2020, pages 3-6.

Temple, Wayne C. *Thomas and Abraham Lincoln As Farmers.* Racine, Wisconsin: The Lincoln Fellowship of Wisconsin, Historical Bulletin Number 53, 1995.

Tretter, Kathy. "Lincoln Family Corner Cabinet Hidden for Years in Southern Indiana." *Ferdinand News.* Ferdinand, Indiana: Ferdinand News. June 26, 2013.

Warren, Louis A. "A June Bride." *Lincoln Lore.* Fort Wayne, Indiana: Lincoln Financial Life Foundation, Number 112. June 1, 1931. Page 1.

Warren, Louis A. "A June Bridegroom." *Lincoln Lore*. Fort Wayne, Indiana: Lincoln Financial Life Foundation, Number 165. June 6, 1932. Page 1.

Warren, Louis A. "A. Lincoln and J. D. Johnston – Step-Brothers". *Lincoln Lore*. Fort Wayne, Indiana: Lincoln Financial Life Foundation, Number 964. September 29, 1947. Page 1.

Warren, Louis A. "Abraham Lincoln, Senior, Grandfather of the President". *The Filson Club History Quarterly*. Louisville, Kentucky: The Filson Club, Volume 5, Number 3, July 1931, pages 136-152.

Warren, Louis A., Editor. "Abraham Lincoln's Father." *The Lincoln Kinsman*. Fort Wayne, Indiana: Lincolniana Publishers. Number 9. March 1939.

Warren, Louis A. "Hananiah Lincoln in Revolutionary and Pioneer History". *Indiana Magazine of History*. Bloomington, Indiana: Indiana Historical Society, Volume 25, Issue 1, pages 28-39.

Warren, Louis A. "Lincoln's Honored Stepmother." *Lincoln Lore*. Fort Wayne, Indiana: Lincoln Financial Life Foundation, Number 213. May 8, 1933. Page 1.

Warren, Louis A. "Kentucky's Most Important Wedding." *Lincoln Lore*. Fort Wayne, Indiana: Lincoln Financial Life Foundation, Number 688. June 15, 1942. Page 1.

Warren, Louis A. "Legendary Lincolniana." *Lincoln Lore*. Fort Wayne, Indiana: Lincoln Financial Life Foundation, Number 570. March 11, 1940. Page 1.

Warren, Louis A. "Lincoln's Indiana Schoolmasters." *Indiana Magazine of History*. Bloomington, Indiana: Indiana Historical Society, Volume 27, Issue 2, pages 104-118.

Warren, Louis A. "Lincoln's Respect for His Father." *Lincoln Lore*. Fort Wayne, Indiana: Lincoln Financial Life Foundation, Number 197. January 16, 1933. Page 1.

Warren, Louis A. "Mr. and Mrs. T. Lincoln's Second Child." *Lincoln Lore*. Fort Wayne, Indiana: Lincoln Financial Life Foundation, Number 148. February 8, 1932. Page 1.

Warren, Louis A. "Nancy Hanks' Birthplace." *Lincoln Lore*. Fort Wayne, Indiana: Lincoln Financial Life Foundation, Number 28. October 21, 1929. Page 1.

Warren, Louis A. "Nancy Hanks' Birthplace, Continued." *Lincoln Lore*. Fort Wayne, Indiana: Lincoln Financial Life Foundation, Number 29. October 28, 1929. Page 1.

Warren, Louis A., Editor. "Pigeon Creek Church." *Bulletin of the Lincoln National Life Foundation*. Fort Wayne, Indiana: Lincoln National Life Foundation, Number 661, December 8, 1941.

Warren, Louis A. "The Elizabethtown Carpenter." *Lincoln Lore*. Fort Wayne, Indiana: Lincoln Financial Life Foundation, Number 513. February 6, 1939. Page 1.

Warren, Louis A. "The Knob Creek Farm – Playground of Lincoln." *Lincoln Lore*. Fort Wayne, Indiana: Lincoln Financial Life Foundation, Number 411. February 22, 1937. Page 1.

Warren, Louis A. "The Lincolns, Hoosier Pioneers." *Indiana Magazine of History*. Bloomington, Indiana: Indiana Historical Society, Volume 38, Issue 3, pages 251-264.

Warren, Louis A. "The Romance of Thomas Lincoln and Nancy Hanks." *Indiana Magazine of History*. Bloomington, Indiana: Indiana Historical Society, Volume 25, Issue 1, pages 213-222.

Warren, Louis A. Editor. "The Shiftless Father Myth." *The Lincoln Kinsman*. Fort Wayne, Indiana: Lincolniana Publishers. Number 32. February 1941.

Warren, Louis A. Editor. "The President's Uncle Josiah." *The Lincoln Kinsman*. Fort Wayne, Indiana: Lincolniana Publishers. Number 39. September 1941.

Warren, Louis A. Editor. "The Richard Berry Family." *The Lincoln Kinsman*. Fort Wayne, Indiana: Lincolniana Publishers. Number 16. October 1939.

Warren, Louis A. "Thomas Lincoln Chronology". *Lincoln Lore*. Fort Wayne, Indiana: Lincoln Financial Life Foundation, Number 44. February 10, 1930. Page 1.

Warren, Louis A. "Thomas Lincoln Testimonials". *Lincoln Lore*. Fort Wayne, Indiana: Lincoln Financial Life Foundation, Number 44. February 17, 1930. Page 1.

Warren, Louis A. "Thomas Lincoln's Cabin Homes". *Lincoln Lore*. Fort Wayne, Indiana: Lincoln Financial Life Foundation, Number 24. September 23, 1929. Page 1.

Warren, Louis A. Editor. "Uncle Mordecai Lincoln." *The Lincoln Kinsman*. Fort Wayne, Indiana: Lincolniana Publishers. Number 12. June 1939.

Warren, Louis A. "Untenable Theories About Lincoln's Early Environment". *Lincoln Lore*. Fort Wayne, Indiana: Lincoln Financial Life Foundation, Number 43. February 3, 1930. Page 1.

Warren, Louis A. "Widower Lincoln Marries Widow Johnston". *Lincoln Lore*. Fort Wayne, Indiana: Lincoln Financial Life Foundation, Number 765. December 6, 1943. Page 1.

Websites

Abraham Lincoln Association. www.abrahamlincolnassociation.org.

Abraham Lincoln Association. *The Collected Works of Abraham Lincoln*. quod.lib.umich.edu/l/lincoln/.

Allegheny College. *Documents of Ida M. Tarbell. The Ida M. Tarbell Collection of Lincolniana*. dspace.allegheny.edu/handle/10456/13708. dspace.allegheny.edu/handle/10456/13717.

Mock, C.J., J. Mojzisek., and M. McWaters, et al. Climatic Change (2007) 83: 87. https://doi.org/10.1007/s10584-006-9126-2.

Connor Prairie. www.connerprairie.org/education-research/indiana-history-1800-1860/native-americans-in-indiana.

Cornelius, James. "Episode 22, Abraham Lincoln's Relationship with His Father, Thomas." www.alplm.org/blog/tag/thomas-lincoln/. July 25, 2011.

Cowan, Troy. "Abraham Lincoln and Jefferson Davis were Brothers." www.angelfire.com/ planet/check/davis.html. 2013.

Daniel Boone Wilderness Trail Association. www.danielboonetrail.com.

Find A Grave. www.findagrave.com.

Greer, Warren. "Jesse Head Homesite." explorekyhistory.ky.gov.

Hallstrom, Suzanne. "Nancy Hanks Lincoln mtDNA Study." *Family Tree DNA.* www.familytreedna.com/public/HanksDNAProject/default.aspx?section=news. October 2015.

Indiana Public Media. www.indianapublicmedia.org/momentof indianahistory/.

Jenson, Hal B., M.D. and Charles T. Leach, M.D. www.pediatricweb.com/webpost/iframe/MedicalConditions_465.asp?tArticleId=173.

Kentucky Historical Society. "Nancy Hanks Lincoln (1784-1818)." *Kentucky's Abraham Lincoln.* www.history.ky.gov. 2010.

Illinois Genealogy Trails. http://genealogytrails.com/ill/coles/censusindex.html

Indiana State Government. www.in.gov/history/markers/.

Leonid MAC. leonid.arc.nasa.gov/history/html.

Library of Congress. www.loc.gov/picture/

Lincoln Financial Foundation Collection. www.lincolncollection.org/.

Lincoln Log. *A Daily Chronology of the Life of Abraham* Lincoln. www.thelincolnlog.org/.

Lincoln Log Cabin. www.lincolnlogcabin.org.

McNamara, Robert. *Mount Tambora Was the Largest Volcanic Eruption of 19th Century.* www.history1800s.com.

McNamara, Robert. *The Year Without a Summer Was a Bizarre Weather Disaster in 1816.* www.history1800s.com.

National Park Service. *Boyhood Home at Knob Creek.* www.nps.gov/ abli/planyourvisit/boyhood-home.htm.

National Park Service. *Lincoln Boyhood: Historic Resource Study.* www.nps.gov/parkhistory/online_books/libo/hrs/hrs5a.htm .

National Park Service. *Lincoln Home National Historic Site.* www.nps.gov/liho/index.htm.

National Park Service. *Lincoln Home National Historic Site.* "Lincoln on Slavery." www.nps.gov/liho/learn/historyculture/slavery.htm.

National Weather Service. www.weather.gov.

Norton, Roger. rogernorton.com.

Oregon State University. *Volcano World.* volcano.oregonstate.edu/laki-iceland-1783.

Poetry Foundation. http://www.poetryfoundation.org/poems-and-poets/poems/detail/55341.

Pokorski, Doug. *The Sad Tale of Thomas Lincoln.* Springfield, Illinois: The State Journal Register Online. www.abrahamlincolnonline.org/ lincoln/news/thomas.htm.

Postal History. www.postalhistory.com.

Restoration Movement. www.therestorationmovement.com.

Rice, Doyle. "200 Years Ago, We Endured a 'Year Without a Summer'". *USA Today.* www.usatoday.com: June 9, 2016.

Roberts, Warren E. Thomas Lincoln: Cabinetmaker. www.indiana.edu/ ~wer/about/documents/ Roberts-Lincoln.pdf.

The Lehrman Institute. www.mrlincolnandfreedom.org/pre-civil-war/experiences-with-slavery-2/.

The Lincoln Log. www.thelincolnlog.org. Compiled by the Lincoln Sesquicentennial Commission.

Ultimate History Project. *The Eruption of Laki.* ultimatehistoryproject.com/the-eruption-oflaki.html.

U. S. Geological Survey. *Summary of 1811-1812 New Madrid Earthquakes Sequence.* earthquake.usgs.gov/earthquakes/events/1811-1812newmadrid/summary.php.

ushistory.org. *U. S. History Online Textbook.* "Economic Growth and the Early Industrial Revolution". www.ushistory.org/us/22a.asp.

Wood, Gillen D'Arcy. *1816, The Year Without a Summer.* www.branchcollective.org.